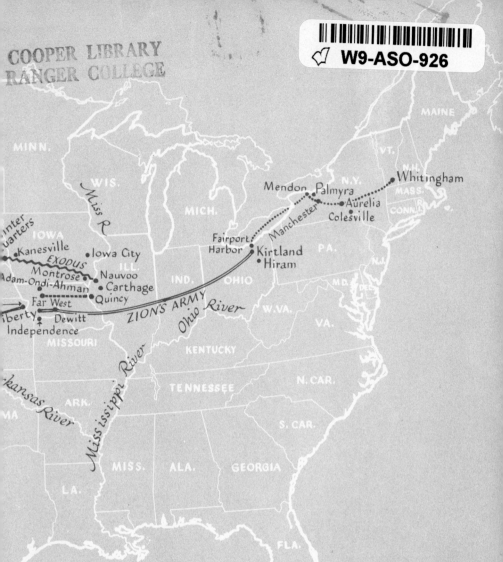

W9-ASO-926

MAINE

MINN.

WIS.

Miss R

MICH.

N.Y.

VT.

N.H.

Whitingham

MASS.

Mendon Palmyra

Aurelia

CONN.

Manchester

Colesville

inter
Quarters

IOWA

Kanesville

Iowa City

EXODUS

Montrose

Nauvoo

Fairport
Harbor

Kirtland
Hiram

PA.

N.J.

Adam-Ondi-Ahman

Carthage

IND.

OHIO

MD.

DEL.

Far West

Quincy

ZION'S ARMY

Ohio River

W.VA.

iberty

Dewitt

Independence

MISSOURI

VA.

Mississippi River

KENTUCKY

kansas River

ARK.

TENNESSEE

N.CAR.

S.CAR.

MISS.

ALA.

GEORGIA

LA.

FLA.

MORMON TRAILS & LANDMARKS

1	....	Young family migration from Whitingham
2	═══════	Zion's Army route from Kirtland
3	--------------	Mormon migration from Far West
4	∿∿∿∿∿	Mormon exodus from Nauvoo
5	▬ ▬ ▬ ▬	Mormon pioneer trail from Winter Quarters
6	━━━━━━	Mormon Battalion route

KINGDOM
OF THE SAINTS

OTHER BOOKS BY RAY B. WEST, JR.

WRITING IN THE ROCKY MOUNTAINS
THE ART OF MODERN FICTION (WITH R. W. STALLMAN)
THE SHORT STORY IN AMERICA

EDITED BY RAY B. WEST, JR.

ROCKY MOUNTAIN STORIES
ROCKY MOUNTAIN READER
ROCKY MOUNTAIN CITIES
ESSAYS IN MODERN LITERARY CRITICISM

KINGDOM
OF THE SAINTS

*The Story of Brigham Young
and the Mormons*

by RAY B. WEST, Jr.

9009

1957

THE VIKING PRESS
New York

Library of Congress catalog card number: 57-6437

PRINTED IN THE U.S.A. BY THE COLONIAL PRESS INC.

*To the memory of my Mormon forebears,
many of whom experienced the events
portrayed in this book*

The inspiration of religion lies in the history of religion. By this I mean that it is to be found in the primary expressions of the intuitions of the finest types of religious lives.

—ALFRED NORTH WHITEHEAD

CONTENTS

ILLUSTRATIONS

PREFACE

The Mormon story, insofar as it has been told with any degree of sympathy, has usually been seen as a comic episode in American history. Like so many figures of the frontier, the Mormons seemed to the more genteel East to be only a somewhat different version of that legendary world celebrated by our native humorists of the nineteenth century—a world in which the facts of nature and the life in nature could be understood only in terms of fantasy. What were the experiences of the Mormons but the "tall tale" come to life? Claims of visions, rumors of polygamy and of "Destroying Angels," of violent conflict between Mormons and non-Mormons, plus the epic of a mass march into an unsettled wilderness, could be accommodated by the rational mind only by making them the subject of laughter. Joseph Smith could be seen as a harmless fraud, in a tradition which combined two typical figures in American humor—the shrewd rustic, seeing through the affectations of his more elevated compatriots; and the Yankee peddler, whose harmless swindles were a small price to pay for the amusement they afforded. Brigham Young could become the mock-hero of frontier legend, whose incredible exploits rivaled those of the riverman Mike Fink, the Mountain Man Jim Bridger, or the Indian-fighter and frontier politician Davy Crockett; whose marital experiences, in particular, were of a magnitude appropriate to the Great West.

Writers who took the Mormons seriously were generally either pious reformers outraged by the Mormons' peculiar brand of religion, or popular journalists to whom the Mormons were grist for the mill of recently established monthly magazines. Their accounts began, as did the mock-heroic versions, with assumptions of fraud and delusion. Joseph Smith became Peep-Stone Joe, the charlatan, taking advantage of the religious enthusiasms of the credulous Americans of the Western frontier. Brigham Young became a wily autocrat, plotting overthrow of the government and keeping his restive followers in check only by threats of holy murder. Such authors shed bitter tears over the fate of the misguided followers of the Mormon prophets, particularly the defenseless women in the Mormon harems, whom they saw as helpless victims of a barbarous system of marriage.

Of the two methods, the comic is the only valid one, for it parades not as fact but as exaggeration. Comedy is valid, however, only when its intentions are clear. It is a limited form, for the comic method applied to any subject says more about the society that produces it than it does about its subject. According to Henri Bergson's theory of laughter, comedy has no means of accounting for the unique society or the unique individual; it creates types in order to define a species. Insofar as these types are a reflection of the truth, they may represent truth in general; they cannot reveal the singularity of it. Comics such as Mark Twain and Artemus Ward, both of whom wrote amusing accounts of the Mormons, admitted an *unwillingness* to see the Mormons, or indeed any of the West, in any light other than that of the humorous tradition of the frontier. Their method was consciously chosen and, for the most part, skillfully applied; but we continue to read them today more for the examples they provide of a particular attitude toward society than to obtain specific information about that society.

The journalists and reformers, on the other hand, reveal an *inability* to see the Mormons in any other light than that of fraudulence and fanaticism. They make their appeal on the basis of general, established emotional attitudes existing in the society outside their subject. Because of the general nature of these attitudes, the subject can be dealt with fairly only if it fits perfectly, as a type, into the framework of actions which has given rise to the emotions. If the subject is unique, instead of an exposé we have a sentimental appeal to our emotions over and above what the facts warrant, and eventually such sentiment turns into a kind of unintentional social comedy.

Perhaps the best proof of the singularity of the Mormons as subject matter resides in the fact that we read most polemical books on the Mormons today as a kind of accidental humor, not as serious appeals. We respond much as playgoers do who take pleasure in a modern production of such old-time melodramas as *East Lynne* or *Ten Nights in a Barroom*, which tell us more about the society that produced them than they do about their subject. Likewise, when Kimball Young, in 1954, in a book about polygamy titled *Isn't One Wife Enough?* reproduced illustrations from William Jarman's *Uncle Sam's Abscess*, a polemical anti-Mormon book of the 1880s, he betrayed amusement less at the expense of Mormon polygamy than at the attitude of Mr. Jarman and his nineteenth-century reading public.

Of course, the comic treatment and the polemical are not mutually exclusive. In the best-known books on the Mormons, they are mixed. As late as 1901, when William A. Linn published *The Story of the Mormons*, there was a good deal of righteous indignation blended with what was essentially a "comic" view. By 1925, when M. R. Werner published his biography *Brigham Young*, much of the indignation had been replaced by an indulgent admiration, but the method remained the same—a highly ironic style which treated the unique aspects of Mormonism as a typical American joke. The difficulty with such books (and they still represent two of the best books written about the Mormons) resides in their mixture of intentions. Both works pretend to be serious historical and biographical studies, which they are so far as their research on the subject is concerned; but by presenting their material humorously they distort certain facts about the Mormons and generalize their conclusions. Not that their methods are broad comedy, such as that represented by Twain and Ward, whose very personalities as writers were comic masks and presented as such. Linn and Werner were not conscious of masks, but because of their stylistic exaggerations their attitudes (of being serious research scholars) became masks as surely as the poses struck by the native American humorists.

It is interesting to note here that the aim of the serious researcher is often very similar to that suggested by Bergson for the comic: to create types in order to define a species; but the scientific scholar, according to the ideal, should remain neutral before the facts; his hypothetical types should conform to them. If he does not, then the type becomes a distortion and results in comedy. This seems to be what happened in the case of Linn and Werner, but particularly with Linn. Note almost the final picture we get of Brigham Young in *The Story of the Mormons*. It is of "an openly jolly old hypocrite," for whom "one can scarcely resist the feeling that he would like to pass around the hat." This is an amusing summary, but it more nearly resembles Mark Twain's minor comic characters, such as the Duke in *Huckleberry Finn*, than it does the facts of Brigham Young's career, even the highly colored facts as Linn reports them.

Somewhat the same is true, but to a lesser degree and in a more subtle manner, in a more recent work of historical scholarship, Fawn Brodie's biography of Joseph Smith, *No Man Knows My History*, published in 1945. Here, where research is even more penetratingly pursued than in Linn and Werner, a new difficulty arises. It is reflected in the apparent embarrassment of much modern scholarship in dealing with a religious subject. Despite the limitations of Mrs. Brodie's book, which can deal with Mormonism only up to the year 1844, it represents the most thorough treatment of early Mormon history. Her scholarship is praiseworthy, and she lays for once and all the ghosts of those two bugaboos of Mormon scholarship—the origins of polygamy and the Spaulding theory of the authorship of the *Book of Mormon*. She even comes nearest of anyone who has yet written of Joseph Smith to presenting him as a recognizable human being. Yet by utilizing an ironic style in her presentation, Mrs. Brodie shoots beyond the mark. It is Joseph Smith's very humanity—an excess of human characteristics—which distorts the image of her subject, the founder of a modern religion, and converts him into a comic figure. Perhaps the following description of his struggle with his conscience over the matter of polygamy will clarify what I mean.

Joseph could with a certain honesty inveigh against adultery in the same week that he slept with another man's wife, or indeed several men's wives, because he interposed a very special marriage ceremony. And who was to say him nay, since in the gentile world the simple pronouncement of a few time-worn phrases by any justice of the peace was all that was necessary to transform fornication into blessed matrimony? The spoken word stood between him and his own guilt. And with Joseph the word was God.

The implications here, betrayed by the lightness of the style, are not too different in their final intent from those of Linn. Instead of a jolly humbug, we have a kind of jolly fornicator, justifying polygamy in theological terms much as a Restoration comic might justify it in terms of social manners. What Mrs. Brodie leaves out of account in this passage is the important fact that Joseph Smith's "deception" became a religious principle of Mormonism and that in order to apply her interpretation to Mormon society, we should then have to account for many thousands of such deceptions—a tall tale indeed. One might say that Fawn Brodie's regard for irony— or her subjective lack of sympathy which it discloses—has betrayed her into an interpretation unwarranted by her facts.

Perhaps the clue to Mrs. Brodie's difficulty, on a primary level, is revealed in one of her serious passages:

The intellectual appeal of Mormonism, which eventually became its greatest weakness as the historical and "scientific" aspects of Mormon dogma were cruelly disemboweled by twentieth-century scholarship, was in the beginning its greatest strength.

Perhaps this is so. I say "perhaps," because this is a statement that cannot be disproved any more than it can be proved. Mrs. Brodie obviously believes it to be a factual statement; but a Mormon scientist (and as an indication of how many Mormons are scientists, a recent study showed Utah to have produced proportionately more entries for *American Men of Science* than any other state) would dispute it. Mrs. Brodie's assumption is the kind that the "scientific" rationalist dealing with a religious subject has to assume, but the assumption could be justified only if the author had been able to show that this so-called weakness had brought about a decline in the effectiveness of the religion—as a religion. Such an assumption might seem true to a reader of any other religious faith when applied to the Mormons, untrue when applied to his own religion. It represents no more than our modern phase of the old theological dispute between faith and reason, a dispute which most scientists as well as theologians believe incapable of any final resolution.

I do not say that Mrs. Brodie did not have a perfect right to hold such a belief herself, but it is an attitude which is destined to distort any religious figure—to reduce him to the level of comedy or of pathetic self-delusion. If the study is presented as a serious study of the Mormons, it results in bewilderment for anyone who knows anything about Mormon society. Was it no more than humbuggery or comic self-delusion which drove a whole society, numbering between fifteen and twenty-five thousand souls, from territory to territory, and eventually into the wasteland of the Far West? Was it for this that they suffered persecution and death? Was it upon such a foundation that they built a society and a belief capable today of affecting almost a million and a half persons?

Such questioning first stimulated me to consider writing about the Mormons. The question arose: Could one conceivably write about the Mormons in a manner which would make their experience understandable? Understanding of a unique experience (which I believe the life of Brigham Young and the history of Mormonism to be) implies tolerance. The books I have mentioned were, in varying degrees, intolerant. The Mormons themselves had written books, but these were intolerant in another way: Mormon authors could see little or no reason why anyone could not accept and share their beliefs. Would it not be possible, I asked myself, so to present the Mormon experience that it could be understood without either sharing or denying the beliefs which made it possible?

Fortunately there were in existence two books which succeeded almost in accomplishing this aim. The first was Jules Rémy's *A Journey to Great Salt Lake City*, written after a visit to Utah Territory in 1856. The other was Richard Burton's *The City of the Saints*, written after a similar visit in 1859. Both authors were Europeans, and thus lacked the prejudice of most Americans of the last century. Both took their subject seriously. Both had the advantage of writing about the Mormons from direct, first-hand observation. Burton in particular was a learned man, already noted as an explorer, whose interest in world religions had led him to the Mormons. He believed that in them he had discovered the birth of an American religion. While the fashion in America was to treat the Mormons as a passing phase of frontier history, predicting their end, first with the death of Joseph Smith, then with Brigham Young's death, and finally with the passing of polygamy, Burton saw them as a new chapter in a long history of religious societies. He did not prejudge them on the basis of any existing prejudice, but attempted, rather, to see them with his own eyes and to subject them only to the test of comparison with other more traditional forms of religious worship. Such a method allowed him to recognize the eclectic nature of Mormon beliefs and to see it as the recurrence of an essential eclecticism present in all new religions:

The Mormons are like the Pythagorians in their procreation, transmigration, and exaltation of souls; like the followers of Leucippus and Democritus in their atomic materialism; like the Epicureans in their pure atomic theories, their summum bonum, and their sensuous speculations; and like the Platonists and Gnostics in their belief of the Aeon, of ideas, and of moving principles in element. They are fetichists in their ghostly fancies, their *evestra*, which became souls and spirits. They are Jews in their theocracy, their ideas of angels, their hatred of Gentiles, and their utter segregation from their great brotherhood of mankind. They are Christians inasmuch as they base their faith upon the Bible, and hold to the divinity of Christ, the fall of man, the atonement and regeneration. They are Arians inasmuch as they hold Christ to be "the first of God's creatures," a "perfect creature, but still a creature." They are Moslems in their views of the inferior status of womankind, in their polygamy, and in their resurrection of the material body; like the followers of the Arabian prophet, they hardly fear death, because they have elaborated "continuation." They take no leap in the dark; they spring from this sublunary stage into a known, not into an unknown world.

The point is that Burton's attitude of tolerance allowed him to take Mormonism seriously, but without either undue solemnity or sentimentality.

Tolerance implies neither belief nor unbelief in the subject. It suggests, rather, a kind of neutral middle ground. Richard Burton and Jules Rémy admirably illustrate such a position, and their books reflect honest attempts to penetrate the controversy surrounding the subject of Mormonism at the time they were written. They succeed also, in a way that most books do not, in making the Mormon experience understandable as a religious and social phenomenon of American history in the nineteenth century. Almost their only limitation (aside from the time in which they were written) results from the fact that both authors were foreigners. They failed to see the typically American aspects of the Mormon story and of Mormon theology: the struggle against fragmentation and isolation in a society in the process of change; the progressivism, pragmatism, relativism of the frontier, which had, somehow, to be fashioned into a systematic whole; the rationalism and the native superstition which demanded some kind of reconciliation. Neither Burton nor Rémy may be criticized for these shortcomings, for most Americans did not recognize the fermentation that was going on in American society, except as it was visible in constant movement and change, and for most of them, so long as the frontier remained open, the idea which became known as Manifest Destiny seemed a worthy enough belief. The Mormons were part and parcel of this struggle to mold some kind of national character out of the fragmentary stuff that was American life, but they were unique in the days of their violent history by the degree in which they showed themselves aware of their own aims. The ideal of Manifest Destiny, Joseph Smith transformed into an image of the Kingdom of God— an image which, under the direction of Brigham Young, came to contain as much American earth as it did divine spirit, but which represented an attempt somehow to combine the two in terms which would be both modern and American.

My own desire to write a book about the Mormons and their colorful leader came as a result of my recognition of the singular nature of their experience combined with a wish to understand it. Allen Tate has stated recently: "I never knew what I thought about anything until I had written about it." From my own knowledge of Mormonism, which came from being raised in Mormon society as a descendant of pioneer leaders, I had been left dissatisfied by most of the books written upon the subject by Mormons and non-Mormons alike; but I had only the vaguest notions as to what the experience really meant, either to the Mormons themselves or to the country in which it occurred. I felt that the story had epic proportions, both in the movement of the society from east to west and in the character of the person who directed the major portion of that movement, Brigham Young. I did not believe it to be a comic-epic or that Brigham Young could be portrayed as a mock-hero without doing damage to the essential seriousness of it as a significant chapter in American history.

In a sense my researches began, without my knowing it, when I was young and undergoing a typical Mormon boyhood in Utah. They continued when I served for two years as a Mormon missionary in Germany, 1927-29. One of my most remarkable discoveries came when I realized, sometime in the 1930s, that even though I had lost my faith in the Mormon religion I could not somehow dissociate myself from the society that it had constructed, that there was a sense in which I would forever be a Mormon, even though not a communicant in the theological sense. Still later I made a study of the uses of Mormon history in American fiction as a requirement for an advanced degree, and this demanded much reading in the libraries of Salt Lake City—the library of the Mormon Church, the Salt Lake City Public Library, and the library at the University of Utah. Research for the present book was begun when I was granted a fellowship at the Newberry Library in Chicago during the summer of 1954 and allowed to use their excellent collection, not only of Mormon books, but of books on Western American History. It was continued in Salt Lake City, particularly at the library of the Utah State Historical Society and the Salt Lake Public Library; also at the New York Public Library, the Cleveland Public Library, the library of the Ohio State Historical Society in Columbus, and the libraries of the State University of Iowa, the University of Minnesota, and the University of Oregon.

The aim that I have attempted to keep constantly before me both in my reading about the Mormons and in the writing of this book has been to understand as completely as possible why the Mormons believed as they did, in order to understand why they acted as they did. How successfully I have managed to accomplish my aim in the pages of the book is not for me to judge. I have attempted to present the historical facts objectively, but I am aware that there is room for honest differences of opinion about certain events which it was necessary for me to portray. My own attitudes toward such activities as Mormon persecution, the practice of polygamy, and Mormon-gentile opposition were not taken without much thought, so I am prepared to be held fully responsible for them.

I should be ungrateful if I did not acknowledge the kindness of my friends, Thomas Mabry and Hansford Martin, who read the manuscript of this book and offered valuable advice and encouragement. I am indebted to Stanley Pargellis, librarian of the Newberry Library, Chicago, for a fellowship which made much of the research possible; to A. R. Mortensen, secretary of the Utah State Historical Society, for checking an early draft for historical errors; and to Malcolm Cowley for intelligent and devoted editorial assistance. I should also acknowledge the assistance of my friend Jarvis Thurston, who led me to certain materials not previously used, and of Marguerite Young, who first proposed that I write this book.

RAY B. WEST, JR.

KINGDOM
OF THE SAINTS

CHAPTER ONE

THE PROPHET
AND THE SAINTS

I

The village of Kirtland, Ohio, lay at the crossroads of two main immigrant highways into the Western Reserve. The east-west road paralleled a busier thoroughfare which ran along the coast of Lake Erie a few miles north. The north-south highway carried the traffic southward from Fairport Harbor, through Mentor and Kirtland, toward Cincinnati. Kirtland was situated on the banks of the north branch of the Chagrin River at a point where it flowed from the west and made a sweeping turn toward the south. Its houses lay mostly at the bottom of the green valley, near the river and west of the bridge over which the highway entered the village. Before the Mormons came, the few houses had been dominated by the Gilbert and Whitney store, located at the crossroads.

Joseph Smith, the Mormon prophet who had founded the church less than a year before, arrived in Kirtland suddenly, by sleigh, early in January 1831. He had stopped his team before the store, got out from beneath the heavy buffalo robe, and strode into the little establishment. He was then twenty-five years old, more than six feet tall, a handsome and striking young man. He confronted the clerk behind the counter.

"Newell K. Whitney, thou art the man," he said.

"I am sorry, sir," Whitney is reported to have replied. "I don't seem able to place you, although you appear to know me."

3

"I am Joseph the Prophet," Joseph said. "You've prayed me here. Now what do you want of me?"

Newell Whitney and his partner, Sidney Gilbert, had been members of Sidney Rigdon's Campbellite congregation, which early in the fall had been converted in a body to Mormonism by Joseph Smith's missionaries. Rigdon's Campbellites had been practicing a limited form of communism in which their community was known as "the Family," but the system had broken down, and Rigdon seemed powerless to do anything about it.

Sidney Rigdon, formerly a Baptist minister in Pittsburgh, had left the Baptists in 1824 and, with Alexander Campbell and Walter Scott, had been prominent in founding the Disciples of Christ, who soon became known in the West as Campbellites. Still later Rigdon had fallen out with Campbell over community ownership of property, which Rigdon believed to have been the economic order of early Christianity, and the reliance to be placed upon individual miracles and what Rigdon considered to be manifestations of the Spirit of God displayed by his followers. In the fall of 1830, following his conversion to Joseph Smith's infant church, Sidney Rigdon traveled east to central New York, where he met Joseph and convinced him that he should come with his small band of followers to Ohio.

When Joseph Smith arrived in Kirtland, he found that the two aspects of Rigdon's belief that had caused his quarrel with Campbell were to be his first problem. Under Rigdon's plan of "common stock" all members of the community owned everything in common, including the clothes they wore and the houses they lived in; but resentment had arisen over the manner in which the system was administered. Also, Rigdon's congregation engaged in forms of worship which appeared to Joseph unseemly, such as the uncontrollable twitches and jerks of the extreme evangelical sects. After their conversion to Mormonism their practices had become even more extreme. Encouraged by Joseph's claim to visionary power, some of them began to receive their own revelations from heaven and to announce them boldly as the Word of God.

Joseph was not prepared at once to solve the problem of the Family, but within a few days of his arrival he presented his new members with a revelation which promised, ". . . on condition of their assembling with prayer and faith, that a law should be given 'that ye may know how to govern my church, and have all things right before me.'" In regard to their forms of worship, he had already met the problem among his followers in New York. Some of them too had taken his claims of prophecy as license to experiment in mystical exercises of their own. Joseph had told them forthrightly that only he had the prophetic gift, and that if his followers had had visions or heard voices, they were the work of the devil seeking to deceive them. In Kirtland he denounced the excessive fervor of his more extreme converts, and set to work at once to formulate means by which such enthusiasm could be tempered to the work of the church.

The Mormon Church had been founded in April 1830, with six members, at Fayette, Seneca County, New York, in the Finger Lakes region. Within a few months its converts numbered several thousand. Considering its brief existence at the time Joseph Smith moved to Kirtland, the completeness of its organization was astonishing. Adult baptism by immersion was practiced. A priesthood had been organized, open to all male members, consisting of two orders, the Aaronic and the Melkizidek. They included the offices of deacon, teacher, priest, elder, seventy, and high priest, with a bishop to superintend the secular affairs and a council of high priests to administer the sacred offices. It was a lay priesthood, with no payment allowed for services. Communion had been provided in the form of a sacrament service, and a missionary system established which created of each new convert a proselyter of the faith.

Many of the forms had been taken from the Scriptures, but they had been enlarged upon and their functions clarified by passages in the *Book of Mormon*—a holy book which Joseph asserted he had translated from golden plates revealed to him by an angel, a record of the peoples who had been the original settlers of the American continent. When these two sources did not suffice, Joseph supplied additional guidance in the form of revelations, which became commandments to his followers, setting down the specific duties and obligations of individual members.

Nothing in the Mormon religion, excepting Joseph's claim that the plates to the *Book of Mormon* had been delivered to him personally by an angel, was subject to more ridicule by unbelievers than was this pretension of Joseph Smith's that God spoke to him directly in overseeing the affairs of the young church. Much of the advice given in the revelations was mundane and particular, dealing with minor local problems. Some of its language was forthright to the point of crudeness. Yet the book of *Doctrine and Covenants* (as these revelations later became known) played an important part, particularly in the early history of the Mormons, and it contains almost as much doctrine as the better known *Book of Mormon*.

Sidney Rigdon's common-stock society had come into being as the result of the statement in the New Testament that the original disciples had "all things common; and sold their possessions and goods, and parted them to all men as every man had need." It had also followed the example of Robert Owen's New Harmony community, which, although it was even then in trouble and would soon break up, was the admiration of Rigdon.

Soon after Joseph Smith's arrival, he was followed by most of his converts from New York, then by new members from other Eastern states as his missionary system began to operate. Visitors, too, came to view this strange man who called himself a prophet of God. Within a few months the population of Kirtland doubled, then tripled. Common sense told Joseph that so radical a society, which had already broken down, could not be overhauled while both the religion and the community were in such a process of change.

His method of handling the situation was characteristic of him. He received a revelation which did not deny the principle of community ownership, but which was less utopian and more simple in operation than Rigdon's. He called it the Order of Enoch and declared that it was an even more ancient system than that of the early Christians, that it was, in fact, the model for them, and that it represented a foretaste of the divine order of heavenly society. Hadn't Enoch's city become so pure that it had been transported bodily to heaven? The words of the revelation which announced this order said:

And with one heart and one mind, gather up your riches that ye may purchase an inheritance which shall hereafter be appointed to you. And it shall be called the New Jerusalem, a land of peace, a city of refuge, a place of safety for the saints of the most high God. . . . And there shall be gathered unto it out of every nation under heaven; and it shall be the only people that shall not be at war with one another.

What this meant was that the converts, as they arrived, deposited their money and possessions with the bishop, who gave them land in exchange, and this represented their inheritance in the New Jerusalem. Actually, even this limited communism had little opportunity to operate in Kirtland, for in a city already established and growing rapidly there were too many opportunities for private initiative, too little means of apportioning land to the new arrivals. Joseph did not insist that each man share the proceeds of his labor with his fellows, except as special contributions were called for to support the church or assist the poor. Although he established a Bishop's Storehouse and invited contributions, the store remained mostly a repository from which the exceedingly needy could be outfitted and given a start.

Earlier Joseph had conceived of a settlement in the West—on the far reaches of the frontier. Late in the summer of 1830, just a few months after the founding of the church, he had sent a group of missionaries from New York with orders to travel into Indian territory beyond the Missouri River, which then marked the boundary of white settlement. It was they who had stopped in Ohio and converted Sidney Rigdon's congregations in Mentor and Kirtland. They had then gone on to Missouri and preached to the settlers and Indians near Independence in Jackson County. Some of them returned to Ohio early in the spring after Joseph's arrival in Kirtland. They had had no such success in Missouri as they had had in Ohio earlier, but Missouri was sparsely settled, and they reported enthusiastically upon the country and the possibilities of settlement. Caught up by their enthusiasm, Joseph announced one of his boldest schemes—the concept of the Mormon church as the gathering of Israel. He would send colonists to Missouri, where they would settle upon new land. Here they could establish the Order of Enoch, and here would be established the New Jerusalem, the City of Saints. He announced that the true name of the church, which was not new, but merely the reappearance of the true church after generations of apostasy, was the Church of Jesus Christ of Latter-day Saints.

In the summer after his arrival in Kirtland, Joseph led a group of his elders to Independence, Missouri, which he told his followers was to be the future gathering place of the saints. He established the first colony by moving families, and even one whole congregation that had emigrated to Kirtland, on to the land in and about Independence. He also encouraged some of his ablest leaders to settle with them, and here he began his most wholehearted experiment with the pseudo-communistic Order of Enoch. Each member, as he settled in Missouri, consecrated all his goods to the church by depositing his possessions in the Bishop's Storehouse. From this stock the bishop would purchase land and settle the members on it. He would supply them with the necessary tools and equipment, and each member was to draw from the store as his needs demanded.

Joseph himself did not remain in Missouri to supervise the working out of the order. The greatest concentration of members (by now several thousand) was still in Kirtland. He returned to Ohio and spent the winter of 1831-32 in studying the Scriptures with Sidney Rigdon and in working upon a new translation of the Old Testament.

Joseph had not at this time learned Hebrew, but Sidney Rigdon had pondered the question of the correctness of the Biblical text, and Joseph's claims that he had "translated" the *Book of Mormon* had given him a certain status in Rigdon's eyes. Together they studied the original text, and, as Joseph reported in his journal, "It seems as if the Lord opens our minds in a marvelous manner, to understand His word in the original language; and my prayer is that God will speedily endow us with a knowledge of all languages and all tongues." The translation was never completed and never published. What the experience did for Joseph was to endow him with a lasting interest in ancient languages (he would soon set up a school for the study of Hebrew and Greek in Kirtland), as well as to supply him with tutelage in the theological problems of the Old Testament under Rigdon, who possessed much of the formal knowledge which Joseph lacked.

Meanwhile Joseph was as energetic in supplying the Word of God to his followers as he was in all other activities. He made public thirty-seven revelations in 1831 alone, many of them directed at the misdeeds of individual members. In August 1831, soon after his return from Missouri, one revelation announced: "And now behold, verily I say unto you, I, the Lord, am not pleased with my servant Sidney Rigdon; he exalted himself in his heart, and received not counsel, but grieved the Spirit." More often they were directed at members generally: "Call upon the Lord, that His kingdom may go forth upon the earth, that the inhabitants thereof may receive it, and be prepared for the days to come, in which the Son of Man shall come down from heaven, clothed in the brightness of His glory, to meet the kingdom of God which is set up on the earth."

Sidney Rigdon had been disappointed by Joseph's determination to settle so many of the saints in Missouri. Rigdon's displeasure encouraged others, and one influential member, a former Methodist preacher, who had been converted in June 1831 as the result of a miraculous healing he had seen performed by Joseph, left the church and justified his apostasy in a series of letters, some of which he published in the newspaper of a nearby village.

In a letter to one of his associates, he stated his specific objections:

Have you not frequently observed in Joseph, a want of that sobriety, prudence, and stability, which are some of the most prominent traits in a Christian character? Have you not often discovered in him, a spirit of lightness and levity, a temper easily irritated, and an habitual proneness to jesting and joking? . . . Some suppose his weakness, nay his *wickedness*, can form no reasonable objection to his revelation; and "were he to get another man's wife and seek to kill her husband, it could be no reason why he should not believe revelations through him, for David did the same."

Joseph's lack of dignity undoubtedly pained Sidney Rigdon, for he was himself a solemn, almost dour man, making up in intensity of feeling what he lacked in humor. He was also better educated than Joseph, although less genuinely intelligent and quick-witted. Several times during Joseph's second winter in Kirtland he seemed on the point of rebelling against Joseph's leadership of the church. Once, while Joseph was away on a visit to a nearby town, Sidney got up before the Kirtland congregation and announced that the keys to the kingdom of heaven, so recently restored to Joseph Smith, had been taken away again. At this many of his hearers wept, and when someone undertook to dismiss the meeting with prayer Sidney said praying would do them no good. The meeting broke up in confusion.

Recalling the recent apostasies and letters of the newspapers, members immediately began to whisper that Sidney Rigdon was preparing to "expose" Mormonism. Joseph's brother Hyrum, who was one of his stanchest supporters and one of his councilors, had attended the meeting. He sent at once for his brother, telling him to come and right Sidney's wrong. Joseph rushed back to Kirtland, called another meeting, and almost every inhabitant of the community turned out to hear him.

"Joseph arose in our midst," one of the members present reported, "and spoke in mighty power, saying: 'I can contend with wicked men and devils—yes, with angels. No power can pluck those keys from me, except the power that gave them to me: that was Peter, James and John. But for what Sidney has done, the devil shall handle him as one man handles another.'"

Rigdon had not attended the meeting. When confronted by Joseph's words as reported to him by another member, he retracted.

"Is it possible that I have been so deceived?" he asked. "But if Joseph says so, it is so."

During Joseph's second year in Ohio apostasy gradually diminished. Kirtland was still active, thriving with the continuous arrival of new converts from the states in the East. What had seemed at times earlier to resemble chaos appeared now as prosperity and order. Local inhabitants who did not join the Mormons watched events, first with interest, then with wonder and trepidation. Conversions they had seen before, but this rapid gathering of the converted to a single spot confounded them. Mormons on their way to the new settlements in Missouri paused in Kirtland for a sight of their prophet. Claims of miracles all had heard, too, but seldom had they been given the chance to see and speak with the person upon whom a miracle had been performed. Was the phenomenon, as the prophet said, the gathering to Zion in the latter days? The little city was, at times, almost as crowded with the curious as it was with its own citizens.

Joseph was almost always cautious in claiming to have the power to work miracles beyond the claims of his original visions that an angel had appeared to him and revealed to him the golden plates of the *Book of Mormon*, that the apostles had appeared and conferred the rights of the apostolic priesthood, and that a power of translating had been granted him; but he himself had been astonished by the effects which his voice had occasionally had on some afflicted person. After a few words of solemn blessing, a new convert might stand up and walk without the aid of crutches for the first time; another might arise from a sickbed and announce that he was wholly well. When confronted by unbelievers who challenged him to swear that he had this power, Joseph would reply merely that he refused to swear, or he would say softly, "The gift has returned back again, as in former times, to illiterate fishermen."

As one of his leading elders later reported, "I recollect a Campbellite preacher who came to Joseph Smith, I think his name was Hayden. He came in and made himself known to Joseph, and said that he had come a considerable distance to be convinced of the truth. 'Why,' said he, 'Mr. Smith, I want to know the truth, and when I am convinced, I will spend all my talents and time in defending and spreading the doctrine of your religion, and I will give you to understand to convince me is equivalent to convincing all my society, amounting to several hundreds.' Well, Joseph commenced laying before him the coming forth of the work, and the first principles of the gospel, when Mr. Hayden exclaimed, 'O this is not the evidence I want, the evidence that I wish to have is a notable miracle; I want to see some powerful manifestation of the power of God, I want to see a notable miracle performed; and if you perform such a one, then I will believe with all my heart and soul, and will exert all my power and all my extensive influence to convince others; and if you will not perform a miracle of this kind, then I am your worst and bitterest enemy.' 'Well,' said Joseph, 'what will you have done? Will you be struck dumb, or blind? Will you be paralyzed, or will you have one hand withered? Take your choice, choose which you please, and in the name of the Lord Jesus Christ it shall be done.' 'That is not the kind of miracle I want,' said the preacher. 'Then, sir,' replied Joseph, 'I can perform none, I am not going to bring trouble upon any body else sir, to convince you.' "

As the prosperity of the Mormons increased, settlers in the vicinity who had not joined the church began to fear that Joseph's community might come to dominate the whole area—that they were becoming aliens in their own land. The Mormons were buying up so much of the surrounding property that their influence already extended far beyond the limits of the village of Kirtland. Occasionally, too, an overly enthusiastic Mormon might accompany his offer to buy land with the threat that if it was not sold at the prices he offered the Lord would see that he got it anyway. Non-Mormons found themselves labeled "gentiles," and they knew this was no term of respect. Sometimes conversions disrupted families, as when the wife and daughter of a well-known newspaper owner in Painesville joined the church against his wishes. The mere industry displayed by the Mormons, their success in establishing farms and homes and building up a city, aroused the envy of their neighbors; and the Mormons' claim that the power of heaven was guiding their affairs seemed to outsiders preposterous and arrogant.

Joseph had run into a similar condition in New York State, where unsympathetic neighbors had attempted to disrupt his meetings, then, when the police arrived, had charged Joseph and his followers with disturbing the peace. In no instance could a judgment be obtained against him, but the harassment continued, and Joseph had even come to feel that his life was in danger. Now a similar feeling arose in Ohio. The idea gained hold among non-Mormons that, if the prophet could be discouraged, the saints either would move away or could be persuaded to settle down and live the lives of ordinary citizens. The gentiles first attacked with scorn Joseph's claims as a religious leader; then they spread rumors concerning his morality. Because of his handsome figure, Joseph was attractive to women, and this aroused jealousies, perhaps not always without some reason, for Joseph was attracted to them as well. It is said that he once told a friend, "Whenever I see a pretty woman, I have to pray for grace."

In order to free himself of the threats commonly made against him, Joseph moved himself and his family from Kirtland to Hiram in the spring of 1832, where he and Sidney Rigdon continued to confer on religious matters and to push forward with their translation of the Bible. One evening Joseph was sitting up late with a child who was ill with measles, when he was startled by a shriek from his wife, Emma. He had been dozing, and the first thing he knew, he was in the hands of about a dozen men, who attempted to carry him from the room. The task was not easy. Joseph was a powerful man. He freed a foot and kicked one assailant over the doorstep, bloodying the man's nose and causing the others to cry out that they would kill him if he didn't hold still. They carried him about thirty rods from the house, abusing him constantly. Then they stripped him, and one of the men fell upon him and began to rake his naked body with his fingernails. "God damn ye," he cried. "That's the way the Holy Ghost falls on folks." After they had smeared tar over his cuts and bruises they threw him on the ground and left him.

When Joseph had recovered a little of his strength he got up and made his way stiffly back to the house. His friends spent the remainder of the night scraping the tar from his body and washing and bandaging the wounds.

The next day was Sunday, and Joseph was expected to speak in the meeting of the local congregation. Members of the mob arrived, prepared to mock the Mormons when their leader did not appear. But Joseph did appear, covered still with his cuts and bruises, but paying no attention to the visitors. He preached his sermon as though nothing had happened; and that afternoon three persons presented themselves to him for baptism.

2

Joseph Smith was born in Sharon, Windsor County, Vermont, December 23, 1805, the fourth child of Joseph and Lucy Mack Smith. When he was ten years old the family moved to western New York, and Joseph grew up in and around Palmyra in Wayne County, in the vicinity of Rochester. The religious attitude of this portion of the country during Joseph's youth was violent and fanatical. Crossed and recrossed by revival preachers, it had become so wrought up emotionally that it was known as the "burnt-over" district. Within it a multitude of conflicting sects competed for the attention and the loyalty of a roving and rootless population. Established sects, such as the Baptists and the Methodists, splintered into competing factions. Adventism was in the air, and preachers shouted the coming of judgment. New sects sprouted on every hand: the Pilgrims, the Shakers, the Millerites, the Universal Friends, the Disciples of Christ. Converts were made, unmade, then reconverted to competing sects.

Revivalism had begun east of the Appalachians as a more or less sober response to the surge of religious liberalism which followed the Revolutionary War. West of the mountains few preachers had been trained in the seminaries, and even these were less impressed by the niceties of theological dialectics than they were by the uncertainties and the hardships of life on the frontier. Religious dissension gave rise to frightening questions when a man was alone with an ax or a gun in the dark woods and found himself assailed by doubts and fears for his ultimate salvation.

An eminent French visitor to America in 1831 noted the gravity with which ordinary Americans contemplated the problems of theology. "There is no country in the world where the Christian religion retains a greater influence over the souls of men than in America," Alexis de Tocqueville wrote. This fact he accounted for by pointing out that there was no general authority, such as a central church, to define and limit the area of discussion. An unprecedented body of fact and knowledge was at the disposal of the common American, and, unwary and optimistic, he plunged into it, undertaking to solve problems that had confounded professional theologians through the ages.

It was in such an atmosphere that Joseph grew up, and the ideas and the emotions which swept the land were particularly available to him because his family was credulously superstitious. "My mind at times was greatly excited, the cry and tumult were so great and incessant," he reported later. "The Presbyterians were most decided against the Baptists and Methodists, and used all the powers of both reason and sophistry to prove their errors, or, at least, to make the people think they were in error. On the other hand, the Baptists and Methodists in their turn were equally zealous in endeavoring to establish their own tenets and disprove all others."

When Joseph was fifteen his father and mother and two members of his family joined the Presbyterians, but Joseph held off, asking himself, "What is to be done? Who of all these parties are right; or, are they all wrong together? If any one of them be right, which is it, and how shall I know it?"

The problem was not made easier by the peculiarities of his family, whose interest in religion seemed not to be the usual one of mingled hope and fear that the Millennium was approaching (although it must have contained some of this); but rather, a particularly heightened belief in the actual nearness of the spirit world and a faith in the efficacy of certain charms and spells by which that world could be influenced. Also, there was in Joseph's life the memory of a grandfather, Solomon Mack, his mother's father, who had written a pseudo-religious book entitled *A Narrative of the Life of Solomon Mack, containing an account of the many severe accidents he met with during a long series of years, together with the extraordinary manner in which he was converted to the Christian Faith. To which is added a number of hymns, composed on the death of several of his relatives.* This book, which was read to each of the children in turn by Joseph's mother, Lucy Mack, maintained in all of them a belief that they were descended from a better than usual stock and heightened the feeling they all seemed to have that some unusual fate awaited them. Despite the fact that the family was always poor, failing on one farm after another, they felt their mother to be an unusually sharp and intelligent woman, and many of their neighbors concurred in this; so the children, and particularly Joseph, grew up firm in the belief that they had inherited some mysterious and unusual powers from their mother's side of the family.

Such beliefs, combined with their natural superstition, led the Smith family to participate more often than others in those semi-occult activities so common on the frontier—the hunt for buried treasure and hidden water sources, usually with the aid of a forked stick or a seer-stone, the latter being any unusual stone which, gazed at in darkness, was said to call forth spirits to reveal the location of what was being sought. It was said, too, that in such activity Joseph revealed unusual talent, so that his family and some of his neighbors came gradually to look upon him as especially "set apart" in his gift.

If the young Joseph did have a reputation as a medium and money-digger, this alone would not have marked him as extraordinary in the West of his day. A more recognizable figure emerges when we discount these early portraits enough to allow for a natural exaggeration and examine what remains: the image of a somewhat precocious although uneducated boy, only a little more stirred than his fellows by events of his day, yet touched by a sense of personal destiny. One person who knew him as a boy reported:

Joseph had a little ambition, and some very laudable aspirations; the mother's intellect shone out of him feebly, especially when he used to help us solve some portentous questions of moral or political ethics in our juvenile debating club. . . . And subsequently, after catching a spark of Methodism in the camp meeting . . . he was a very passable exhorter in the evening meetings.

Another person, who knew Joseph as late as the time when the *Book of Mormon* had been written, for he was a typesetter in the shop that did the printing, wrote that Joseph had "a jovial, easy, don't-care way about him that made him a lot of warm friends." He added:

He was known among the young men I associated with as a romancer of the first water. I never knew so ignorant a man as Joe was to have so fertile an imagination. He could never tell a common occurrence in his daily life without embellishing the story with his imagination; yet I remember that he was grieved one day when old Parson Reed told Joe that he was going to hell for his lying habits.

These descriptions of the young Joseph Smith suggest both his strength and weakness, the early religious interest, the love of public speaking, and, above all, the fertile imagination. They only hint at the overwhelming ambition which must even then have been stirring within him. What they do not recognize is the mind which could absorb the experiences not only of himself but of the time, and sift and store them in its prodigious memory.

Supernatural events of great importance in his life were said to have occurred beginning on the night of September 21, 1823, when he was eighteen years old. An angel, as Joseph later reported, appeared to him as he was praying in his bedroom and announced that God had work for him to do. The angel told him that his "name should be had for good and evil among all nations, kindreds and tongues." He went on to say, according to Joseph, that "there was a book deposited, written upon gold plates, giving an account of the former inhabitants of this continent, and the sources from which they sprang. He also said that the fullness of the everlasting Gospel was contained in it, as delivered by the Savior to the ancient inhabitants; also that there were two stones in silver bows—and these stones, fastened to a breastplate, constituted what is called the Urim and Thummim—deposited with the plates; and the possession and use of these stones were what constituted 'Seers' in ancient or former times; and that God had prepared them for the purpose of translating the book."

The angel, who was Moroni, said by Joseph to be the last recorded prophet among the people with whom the *Book of Mormon* deals, appeared three times that night to repeat his message.

The next day the angel appeared again, after Joseph had been working in the fields with his father. Moroni repeated what he had told
the boy the night before, but this time told him to relate his experiences to his father. Joseph did so, and his father assured him that
the vision was of God. Joseph went at once to a hill nearby and uncovered the plates, which he said were just as the angel had
described them. When he attempted to remove the plates, the angel
appeared again and said that the time for their revelation had not
yet come. He commanded Joseph to return each year for four years,
and at the end of that time he could obtain the plates.

The so-called translation of the plates occupied Joseph during
the years 1827-30, after which the story they contained was printed
and released to the world as the *Book of Mormon*. The plates, Joseph explained, were engraved in "reformed Egyptian," and he read
them by the power of the Urim and Thummim, which he discovered with them. The narrative purported to account for approximately one thousand years of hitherto unknown American history
—the years 600 B.C to A.D. 421. It recorded the fortunes of two
groups of settlers, the family of one Lehi, which later split into two
factions, the Nephites and the Lamanites, and a less important group
known as the Jaradites. The latter group, the book reports, were
guided to the American continent "from the great tower at the time
the Lord confounded the language of the people," while Lehi was
guided westward at the time of the destruction of Jerusalem during
the reign of Zedekiah.

The account, as given by Nephi in the early books, begins slowly,
relating a series of conflicts within the family of Lehi, and record-
ing a succession of visions in which the past history of the Hebrews
is clarified and the future is foretold, including a prophecy of the
coming of the Messiah and even of the great apostasy to follow—
the growth of "the mother of harlots, which is the great and abomi-
nable church of all the earth." Later, the restoration is predicted.

The body of the book deals with the sailing of the family of Lehi
to the American continent on a vessel constructed according to
divine plans and guided by the "seer-stone." It tells of the division
of the family into good and evil factions, their propagation, wars,

the appearance of Christ, the extinction of the good faction by the evil one, and the cursing of the Lamanites with a dark skin. The final record claims to be an abridgment made by the last survivor of the devout Nephites, Mormon, who concludes with the exhortation of the prophet Moroni, the angel who revealed the plates to Joseph:

And when ye shall receive these things, I would exhort you that ye would ask God the Eternal Father, in the name of Christ, if these things are not true; and if ye shall ask with a sincere heart, with real intent, having faith in Christ, he will manifest the truth of it unto you, by the power of the Holy Ghost.

The *Book of Mormon*, according to an early review of it by Alexander Campbell, the founder of the Disciples of Christ, dealt with "every error and almost every truth discussed in New York for the last ten years." It took a definite stand on all the controversies, enumerated by Campbell as: "infant baptism, ordination, the trinity, regeneration, repentance, justification, the fall of man, the atonement, transubstantiation, fasting, penance, church government, religious experience, the call to the ministry, the general resurrection, eternal punishment, who may baptize, and even the question of free masonry, republican government, and the rights of man."

During the period of composition, Joseph dictated his words from behind a screen, at first to his wife, Emma, whom he had married in 1825; then to a neighbor, Martin Harris, whom he had convinced of the value of the plates and who helped finance his labors; and finally to a local schoolteacher, Oliver Cowdery, whose better than average education must have been of great assistance in preparing the final manuscript. During this time, too, Joseph claimed to have experienced other instances of divine revelation, the first in May 1829, when a puzzling reference in the text of what they were writing led him and Cowdery into the woods to pray for enlightenment. An angel appeared to them, they said, and announced himself as John the Baptist, conferring upon them the keys to the Aaronic Priesthood. A month later the two men were visited by the apostles Peter, James, and John, who conferred upon them the higher, or Melkizidek, priesthood, which provided them with the authority to administer the full ordinances of the apostolic church.

In June, Joseph and Oliver Cowdery moved to Fayette, Seneca County, New York, thirty miles south and east of Joseph's home at Manchester, upon the invitation of Peter Whitmer and his sons, who offered them free board and assistance in continuing the translation. Here, during the final weeks of the work, they came upon another reference which suggested that the golden plates (hitherto kept hidden behind a screen as Joseph worked) were eventually to be displayed before three witnesses who would testify to their existence. Oliver Cowdery, Martin Harris, and David Whitmer requested that this honor be allowed them, and their request was granted by a revelation to Joseph, in which it was said that if they were faithful they were to be granted sight of the plates, as well as of the Urim and Thummim.

A few days later the four knelt in prayer, and, as they related it, an angel appeared, holding in his hands the plates. "He turned over the leaves one by one," Joseph reported, "so that we could see them, and discern the engraving thereon distinctly." They heard a voice say, "These plates have been revealed by the power of God. The translation of them which you have seen is correct, and I command you to bear record of what you now see and hear."

The three men bore witness, and their testimony has ever since appeared as a preface to the *Book of Mormon*. A little later eight additional witnesses, including Joseph's brothers Hyrum and Samuel, his father, four members of the Whitmer family, and their brother-in-law Hiram Page, were given a similar revelation (to supply the Biblical number of eleven persons required to substantiate a miracle), and their testimony was also recorded.

The *Book of Mormon* was published in March 1830 by a country printer who refused to release the printed copies until he was paid in full. Martin Harris sold his farm to settle the bill for the initial printing of five thousand copies, after which Joseph's father and his brothers set out to sell copies from door to door throughout the villages and towns of central New York and northern Pennsylvania.

In April the Mormon Church was officially organized in Fayette with six members. A revelation to Joseph outlined the offices and duties of its membership. He asserted that it was the same organization as that set up by Christ during His ministry; he claimed for it the same authority; and he enjoined all members to "preach, teach, expound, exhort, and baptize." Joseph's religion settled for itself the trinitarian controversy, so vigorously debated on the frontier, by a full acceptance of the threefold nature of God. It affirmed the orthodoxy of the fall of men and his redemption, although it put greater emphasis upon works than upon free grace. It announced itself as adventist by proclaiming itself the Church of Christ in the last dispensation of time. By its claim of the power of receiving direct revelation, it accounted for its own authority; by its charge of a wholesale apostasy following the death of the apostles, it avoided the necessity of competing with other sects in justifying that authority.

None of these claims was unique, but, taken all in all, they provided a unified structure which settled most of the controversies of the "awakening." More unusual was the fact that Joseph reaffirmed and strengthened the ties of Christianity with Judaism. The Puritans had done this implicitly, but Joseph made it explicit, first by combining Christians and Jews in the narrative of the *Book of Mormon*, second by insisting that his book represented "the stick of Joseph" (that puzzle of Biblical scholarship foretold by the prophet Ezekiel and usually interpreted, but not without learned objections, as the New Testament—the twin rod of authority which would eventually match the stick of Judah). Different to the point of boldness, particularly considering the time and place of its origins, was the claim to direct revelation, not only in the composition of the *Book of Mormon*, but in the day-by-day direction of the church.

3

Many attempts have been made to explain Joseph Smith's reports of revelation and his asserted power of prophecy. The earliest explanations were attempted by the Smiths' neighbors in New York, who recalled Joseph's early reputation for having occult powers. In achieving this reputation, they maintained, Joseph was encouraged by his entire family, and with this simple beginning he had conceived a grandiose plan of founding a religion. The golden plates were of a piece with the buried treasure he had earlier dreamed of uncovering, except that now he had introduced angels in place of the mysterious powers which formerly were supposed to have answered the call of his peepstone.

Such an explanation might conceivably account for the visions; it did not explain the existence of the *Book of Mormon*. Could a young man twenty-two years old, with no formal education, produce such a work? At first it was suggested that Oliver Cowdery might have supplied the skill and knowledge, but to those who knew Cowdery, particularly when it was learned how short a time he had collaborated on the book, such a thought became untenable.

What seemed to be an answer to this question was discovered accidentally in 1833 by a disillusioned follower of Joseph, who heard rumors of a manuscript by a certain Solomon Spaulding, dealing with similar materials. Spaulding's manuscript, it was maintained, had been deposited with a printer in Pittsburgh in the hope of obtaining publication. Sidney Rigdon was known to have frequented Pittsburgh, and it was supposed that he had done business with this particular shop. Seeing the manuscript and recognizing its possibilities, Rigdon carried it off, corrected and revised it, and eventually arranged for Joseph Smith, of whose reputation as a medium he had heard, to release it as the translation from plates of gold revealed by an angel. At the opportune moment, after Joseph (whose relationship with Rigdon had been kept secret) had released the printed text, Rigdon stepped forward, bringing his entire Mentor and Kirtland congregations with him as members of the new church.

According to this theory, it had been Rigdon's plan to step into Joseph's place as titular head of the church, but Joseph, having tasted a moment of glory, refused to relinquish his position. Thus the hundreds, and soon thousands, of honest but simple souls who had accepted Mormonism were seen as dupes of one of the most complicated and improbable conspiracies of all time.

The so-called "Spaulding theory" was greatly discredited when, years later, the lost manuscript came to light and was found to have no significant resemblance to Joseph's book. Discovery of the manuscript did not wholly dispose of the theory, because its proponents then came forward with an ingenious second explanation. The manuscript found was not the one which Sidney Rigdon had stolen. A second manuscript had existed, a revision of the first, and this had been used by Smith and then, undoubtedly, destroyed. It remained finally for historians to dispose of the Spaulding theory by pointing out the improbabilities of the intrigue. In the first place, it would have been virtually impossible for Sidney Rigdon and Joseph Smith to have met in New York or elsewhere before the autumn of 1830, when they did meet; secondly, actions upon which the theory rested were contrary to the known characters of both Rigdon and Smith.

With the gradual disappearance of the Spaulding theory, succeeding explanations have been based, for the most part, upon pseudo-scientific postulates, less with the idea of proving Joseph Smith a fraud than in an attempt to explain his self-delusion. In the mid-nineteenth century, during the wave of interest aroused by experiments in mesmerism, an apostate Mormon, who left the church after years of service in some of its highest offices, convinced himself that Joseph had indeed had communication with supernatural beings, but that they were evil spirits who misled him. In the twentieth century a historian proposed the possibility that Joseph had suffered from epilepsy, and that his visions had occurred during the period of the mysterious aura which accompanied that disease. Still later, as was inevitable, a Freudian interpretation was added: "The *Book of Mormon* is a product of an adolescent mind and a mind characterized by the symptoms of the most prevalent of mental diseases of adolescence—dementia praecox."

Such explanations are unsatisfactory if for no other reason than that they could, with equal justification, be applied to claims of all religious mystics—from the Hebrew prophets through St. Paul and Mohammed, and including the whole canon of Christian saints. They assume that any strong religious interest reflects a pathological state. The theory that Joseph suffered from schizophrenia is preposterous in terms of Joseph's later life, and it is based upon a mis-judgment of both Joseph's religion and the *Book of Mormon*, which were the products of his youth. In any case, the facts of Joseph's early life are too beclouded to form a sound basis for psychoanalysis. The theory of epilepsy was based upon the belief that Joseph's grandfather, Solomon Mack, suffered from such a disease, because he was known to be subject to occasional fits, but these were later discovered to have been caused by an early accident.

The chief difficulty with such explanations is that they can be neither proved nor wholly disproved. As speculation concerning a possible explanation they may be weighed and considered, but they neglect the important point that such visionary powers as Joseph claimed were the principal appeal of a religion which, in a short time, numbered its converts in the tens of thousands, and which, after a century, contained more than a million believers. What such attitudes represent in our day is simply a recent version of the old debate between faith and reason.

Most of the explanations concerning Joseph's claim to revelation in the founding of the church have been based upon postulates that their holders considered at the time to be scientific. Since then, more scientific methods have been utilized to disprove them; and later additional speculation was added to replace that which had been discarded. Perhaps it is because of the nature of scientific knowledge that the latest theory, that of Fawn M. Brodie, Joseph Smith's most accomplished biographer, seems the most reasonable. Mrs. Brodie suggests that Joseph was a talented but embryonic au-thor, whose gifts might have led him to a career as a writer of ro-mances, except that the spirit of the "awakening" encouraged him to interpret his "inspiration" as a series of heavenly visitations—to ob-jectify these, to clothe them first in the forms of personages of heavenly origin, then in the shape of an imagined history. Such speculation does account for the *Book of Mormon* by suggesting its value as a promising early work of historical fiction. The "golden plates" may be accounted for by suggesting that Joseph did actually discover an object of some kind, buried in one of the hills of northern New York, and that his fervid imagination, fed on his belief in supernatural beings and his belief in his own ability to communicate with them, allowed him to create an imagined reality more actual to him than the real one.

Despite the attractiveness of so ingenious an explanation, it still has all the aspects of the modernist movement, and it fails to take into consideration any of the modifications of that movement, such as those supplied by Karl Barth and Albert Schweitzer in Europe, and more recently by Reinhold Niebuhr in America. Most important, it fails to take into account the faith of the Mormons themselves, who persist in believing that Joseph Smith was not a promising young author, but that he was a prophet of God. Mrs. Brodie's book may have caused a few Mormons to take a closer and more considered look at their prophet, it may even have caused many of them to re-examine the basis of their faith, but in the end the Mormons responded to her book much as a number of theologians approached by Dr. Duncan Howlett responded to a question about the Dead Sea Scrolls. "The finding of the Dead Sea Scrolls will increase our knowledge of Christian origins," they said. "On this all are agreed. And in the end we find that the discovery does not affect our theology at all."

An intelligent reader will agree that such biographies as Mrs. Brodie's add documentation to many details of Joseph Smith's life that had remained obscure. What the devout Mormon cannot agree with is any assumption that Joseph Smith was not, in any theological sense, a prophet; that he was, in fact, a deluded man. Logically, biographers who take this attitude might equally well have begun with the assumption that Joseph was a religious mystic, for, as William James remarked in *The Varieties of Religious Experience*, "In all sad sincerity I think we must conclude that the attempt to demonstrate by purely intellectual processes the truth of the deliverance of direct religious experience is absolutely hopeless."

Traditional justification for revelation was stated by Thomas Aquinas, who made it the basis for the distinction between faith and reason. "Faith," he declared, "is assent to revelation; knowledge is assent to something proved by reason." He goes on to say that "Supernatural revelation is true and necessary, because it was important for man to have this divine knowledge, and to have it quickly."

A modern religious scholar, Don Cameron Allen, has stated the proposition somewhat differently, and in a way that applies more aptly to Joseph Smith:

[Man] has felt . . . that there is a wide area of knowledge that transcends the plane of ordinary wisdom, that seems to arise from no basic premise, from no data of the senses. The source and validity of this type of knowledge has troubled him even more. He has called it by many names—revelation, instinct, intuition, the lore of the heart—but all that he really knows about it is that it cannot be proved and must be believed.

This is the only point of view that can present the Mormon religion for what it is, the basis of a belief which holds the faith of almost a million and a half today.

The more one studies the evidence, the more Joseph Smith's life seems to fit the pattern established by religious mystics throughout the ages. Philosophy, as distinguished from science (which, when it is honest, frankly admits its inability to deal with the mystical), has granted the religious mystic his role and recognized his experience as a special means of obtaining knowledge.

William James wrote:

Mystics break down the authority of the non-mystical or rationalistic consciousness, based upon the understanding and the senses alone. They show it to be only one kind of consciousness. They open out the possibility of other orders of truth, in which so far as anything in us vitally responds to them, we may freely continue to have faith.

Henri Bergson, the French nineteenth-century philosopher, makes the mystical experience the culminating point in his theory of creative evolution. Of the mystic, he says: "If all men, if any large number of men, could have soared as high as this privileged man, nature would not have stopped at the human species, for such a one is in fact more than a man."

Bergson adds further enlightenment when he says: "Yet there is no denying that ecstasies, visions, raptures, are abnormal states, and that it is difficult to distinguish between the abnormal and the morbid." But he adds:

And such indeed has been the opinion of the great mystics themselves. They have been the first to warn their disciples against visions which were quite likely to be pure hallucinations. And they generally regarded their own visions, when they had any, as of secondary importance, as wayside incidents; they had had to go beyond them, leaving raptures and ecstasies far behind, to reach the goal, which was identification of the human will with the divine will.

In Joseph Smith's case, the identification was achieved through the establishment of what he considered the true church and in his concept of the gathering of the saints. These were actions, not states of mind, and as actions they led him back from the world of vision and contemplation and into society. He felt himself to be doing the will of God as his visions commanded him, with an enlarged understanding and a concentrated certainty; and of one thing he was most certain: that the will of God could be known in the nineteenth century.

Fortunately for the historian, religion is made up of more than visions and miracles. On its most important level it is a guide for conduct; and on this level it is available for examination and evaluation. Some such conclusion as this William James reached after his lengthy study of religious experience:

To the medical mind these ecstasies [of the mystics] signify nothing but suggested and imitated hypnoid states, on an intellectual basis of superstition, and a corporeal one of degeneration and hysteria. Undoubtedly these pathological conditions have existed in many and possibly in all the cases, but that fact tells us nothing about the value for knowledge of the subconsciousness which they induce. To pass a spiritual judgement upon these states, we must not content ourselves with superficial medical talk, but *inquire into their fruits for life*. [Italics mine.]

Joseph Smith himself, in words uttered just a few months before his death expressed bewilderment at his gifts. "You do not know me," he told his followers; "you never knew my heart. No man knows my history. I cannot tell it; I shall never undertake it. I don't blame anyone for not believing my history. If I had not experienced what I have, I could not believe it myself."

Such is an example of the straightforward nature of Joseph's talk about himself, particularly toward the end of his life. The causes remained a mystery to him; the "fruits for life" did not. They were the church which he created—the creed which his followers accepted. Joseph's religion was "mystical" only in a very modern sense, in the sense that it attempted an entirely new synthesis between matter and spirit. In another respect Mormonism is really a return to the rationalism of the Renaissance, combining the faith of the Renaissance man with an admiration for reason as a means of understanding. The dilemma was posed for Joseph Smith, in the America of his day, by the necessity to choose between the deism and atheism of the post-Revolutionary War era and the adventism of the great revival. Robert Boyle wrote in his preface to *The Excellency of Theology Compared with Natural Philosophy*, that "although he devotes himself to natural studies, he does not regard them as having the same merit as theological pursuits. They are not handmaidens to divinity, but ladies of a lower rank."

Such a view would approximate the view of the Mormons. Oswald Spengler, the German social historian and philosopher, once predicted that an American religion, if one ever arose, would be based upon adventism, not upon reason and science. The ordinary Mormon recognized in Joseph Smith's community of saints, gathering in the American West, the answer to many questions which he could not find in the religions of the day. He saw Mormonism, first, as the most rational version of the more extreme adventist beliefs. He discovered in Joseph's creed, in the organization and the ritual which came into being, the fulfillment of certain emotional needs both of the time and of his own nature. Whatever else he found, we may be sure that as a nineteenth-century American on the frontier he found it less difficult to accept the claims of divine guidance put forth by Joseph Smith than do most of us today.

CHAPTER TWO

THE CONVERSION
AND A MEETING

I

The most important single convert ever made to Joseph Smith's religion was a rawboned, somewhat stocky young man named Brigham Young. In 1830 Brigham worked as a carpenter and painter in the frontier community of Mendon, Monroe County, New York. He was twenty-nine and he had not yet heard of the Mormons. In appearance he was less prepossessing than Joseph Smith. His hands bore the calluses of the common workman. His shoulders were broad and muscled, but his legs were short and his body long. His auburn hair, which he wore in the Western style, was parted loosely on the right and hung over his ears. His pale blue, almost gray eyes were his most impressive feature.

Seven years earlier Brigham had married Miriam Works, a frail girl who had since become an invalid. She had borne him two children, named Elizabeth and Vilate. Brigham, in 1830, was a Methodist and a Mason. He had lived in Mendon only a year, having come there to join his father and members of his family, who had moved several years earlier from Aurelia in Cayuga County. In the year Brigham had been at Mendon he had earned the reputation for being a conscientious worker and a good fellow. His dry, somewhat sly humor had won him friends, but he had not made them easily; and—except for one, Heber C. Kimball, a neighbor—he felt nearer to his father, his stepmother, and his brothers and sisters than he did to most of the townspeople.

His father's life had not been a settled one. John Young, like the father of Joseph Smith, had begun life as a farmer and had moved from one farm to another in an attempt to make a living for his family. He had begun in Hopkinton, Massachusetts. Failing as a farmer there, he moved to Vermont, where his ninth child, Brigham, was born at Whitingham, June 1, 1801. Two years later he moved again, this time to Sherburne, New York, about a hundred miles west of Albany. In 1815 Nabby Young, Brigham's mother, died, and again the family moved westward, first into Cayuga County (where Brigham married), then on to Mendon, near Rochester.

Brigham's wife, Miriam, had tuberculosis, and her illness made life difficult for him. By the time they arrived in Mendon, she could not move from bed by herself. Each morning Brigham would dress and feed the two little girls, then carry his wife to a rocking chair before the fire. After serving her breakfast, he would leave for work, promising to look in during the day. Miriam, it must have seemed to him, was too young to die, yet she was too frail to keep pace with his restless energy. Solemnly, but without hope, he prayed for her recovery.

Brigham's father was among those most affected by the revivalism of the frontier and reared his children with strictness and piety. All the Young family joined the Methodists, and three of Brigham's brothers became lay preachers. Brigham himself, although he joined the church at his family's urging, seems to have remained always somewhat critical of it. He did not join until he was twenty-one, and even after the arrival of his two daughters he remained unconvinced of the need for so extreme a piety as he had been forced to show.

"I had not the chance to dance when I was young," he said later, "and I never heard the enchanting tones of the violin until I was eleven years of age; and then I thought I was on the highroad to hell if I suffered myself to linger and listen to it."

At that time Brigham concluded that "the mantle of tradition" was over him to such an extent that he could scarcely contemplate the problem of religion at all. His friend Heber Kimball, a likable and witty young man, was a Baptist. Brigham's elder brother Joseph, whom he greatly admired, was a reformed Methodist. Each had, as Brigham put it, "got a mantle for himself," but which was the right mantle? The two sects differed in many respects, both in their forms and in their beliefs, and he asked himself, if the one was true, could the other be also? He also asked himself, "What is Christianity?" Was it the forms and observations of which the rival preachers made so much? Was it the teaching of Scripture? If so, which Scripture? The sects offered conflicting interpretations of identical texts. Brigham came to the conclusion that in each case it was tradition— "The tradition of the people was all the religion they had." What he hoped to discover was what there was behind, or beyond, the traditions that could truly be called the spirit of religion.

Brigham, with almost no formal schooling, had taught himself to read by studying the words of the Bible. "So far as the letter of the book was concerned I understood it," he told his friends later; "but as for understanding by the Spirit of the Lord I never did. . . . I was well acquainted with many of the priests of the day, and I would frequently think to myself that I would get some knowledge from them. And as I became acquainted with smart, intelligent, literary priests and professors of religion, I thought, 'Now I can obtain some intelligence from this or that man,' and I would begin to ask questions on certain texts of Scripture, but they would always leave me as they found me, in the dark." The preachers, Brigham concluded, were themselves blind, leading the blind.

His regard for family tradition had led him to join the Methodists, but it is likely that Masonry held a stronger grip on his emotions than Methodism. Comradeship he could understand. Masonic ritual intensified his relationship with his fellow workers, heightened the sense of belonging to a group less bounded than either the family or the nation. Religious communion, in the sense that it was advocated by the sects of the day, must have seemed vague and unreal. Mainly the revival sects looked to the future, living less in hope of salvation than in terror of judgment.

The religion of Brigham's father and his brothers was only a milder form of this adventism as practiced by the extreme sects of William Miller and John Humphrey Noyes. Miller was to set a date for the advent of the Millennium in 1843, when his followers would assemble in a body to greet the returned Messiah. Noyes proposed the novel idea that Millennium—the final days of man— had already set in, and at his community in Oneida, New York, practiced a form of communal living that precluded private posses- sions of any kind, including the possession of a single wife. The ex- tent to which Brigham's father went in holding similar beliefs may be indicated by an experience in September 1827, when a phenom- enon known as "the shower of stars" was visible in the vicinity of Mendon. Called from his bed by his son-in-law John P. Green, a lay minister in the Methodist Church, the elder Young observed the spectacular display of lights in the heavens. Vilate Kimball, Heber's wife, who was watching with the Young family, turned to him anx- iously and asked, "Father Young, what does all this mean?"

"Why, it's one of the signs of the coming of the Son of Man," the elder Young replied.

Later the Young family came to believe that the heavenly display had occurred at exactly the time when Joseph Smith, not many miles away in Ontario County, received a set of golden plates from an angel of heaven.

Brigham was not without superstition, and he was not without a grain of his father's belief in adventism. Not to have been supersti- tious in the West in the year 1827 would have been to be the ex- ception, not the rule. Adventism flourished in America for many reasons, but one of them was the strong sense of the pioneer that in the midst of nature he was in the presence of supernatural powers. The Puritans a century before had seen these powers as evil, inhabit- ing the dark corners of the world and waging a continuous war- fare against the saints of God. By the nineteenth century the same powers had become the spirits of God announcing the coming of judgment.

Revival preachers had, for the moment, obscured an important element in the make-up of the American character—optimism. Brigham did not doubt that great events were forthcoming, perhaps even a day of judgment; but wouldn't a wise God, he asked his friends, prepare for such events in a more rational manner than through the agency of such fanaticism as he had witnessed? Besides, to him, the present did not contain an atmosphere of completion so much as it did one of anticipation. There was a sense of impending change, of movement toward completion. He had often asked himself, "What does such movement mean?"

Brigham's restlessness must have driven him to seek an answer to this question, for it was the riddle of the American frontier. Those who pretended to have an answer failed always at the last minute to provide it, preacher and tippler alike. It was, Brigham said, like a series of boxes, one fitted inside the other, each smaller than the last, so that what you had finally was nothing except the smallest box.

Then, in the early summer of 1830, an event occurred—a small event at the time, with none of the portentousness even of his own emotions, but one that was destined to settle the course of his entire future life. A young man by the name of Samuel Smith called at the home of the Reverend John P. Green, the husband of Brigham's sister Rhoda. He was carrying a book which he called the *Book of Mormon*. He described the book to them and told them that it was for sale. The Greens were only mildly interested. The salesman left the book with them, telling them to examine it more closely. He would be coming back that way soon again, he told them, and when he did they could tell him whether or not they wanted to keep it.

The book lay for several days on a table in the Greens' parlor. One day Brigham stopped in to see them, and he saw the book, picked it up, and examined it. He asked his sister what it was. Samuel Smith, she said, had told her that his brother Joseph had translated the record by divine aid, and that anyone who read the book with a genuine desire to know the truth would be given a testimony of its divine origins.

Brigham Young did not read the book at once. He might never have read it if his older brother Phineas had not bought a copy from the same man, read it with interest, and then passed it on to his father for his judgment. The elder Young read it and pronounced it "the greatest work and clearest of error of anything he had ever seen, the Bible not excepted."

With this recommendation, Brigham looked at the book again. He knew of his father's quick enthusiasm for anything of a theological nature, so he did not take the old man's statement at its face value; but he knew too that John Young was no fool and would not be easily duped. Perhaps the book was worthy of his attention.

2

On the surface, the *Book of Mormon* presented a familiar pattern. It contained accounts reminiscent of what was best known to Brigham and his brothers, the Bible. It contained sermons such as might have been delivered anywhere on the frontier, even from their own local pulpits, except for a kind of refreshing boldness with which the old topics were treated. Its events portrayed political controversy such as they knew well and about which they had themselves argued. Social conditions depicted in the book were like mirrors held up to reveal an image of their own lives, heightened and romanticized by its setting in a remote past.

Brigham found the book interesting, but he was not at first as excited about it as were other members of his family. His full response did not come until almost a year after he had first seen it. In the fall of 1831 five men visited Mendon from the village of Columbia, Pennsylvania. They represented themselves as elders of the Church of Christ—followers of the prophet Joseph Smith. They stopped at the home of Phineas Young, and Brigham was invited in to hear them deliver their message. It was that they knew by the power of the Holy Spirit that the *Book of Mormon* was a divine revelation and that Joseph was a true prophet. Brigham listened to their words and compared their utterance with what he had heard from revival preachers to whom he had listened both in Cayuga County and in Mendon. He was impressed by the simple sincerity with which they attempted to answer the questions he put to them.

"If all the talent, tact, wisdom, and refinement of the world," he said a few years later, "had been sent to me with the *Book of Mormon*, and had declared in the most exalted of earthly eloquence the truth of it, undertaking to prove it by learning and worldly wisdom, they would have been to me like the smoke which arises, only to vanish away." His suspicion of "earthly eloquence" and "worldly wisdom" was both the result of his dealings with rival preachers of the awakening and an inheritance of the frontier, where too smooth a manner and too glib a tongue were often looked upon as signs of chicanery and crookedness.

When Brigham heard the testimony of the followers of Joseph Smith, uttered, as he said, "without eloquence or talent for public speaking," he felt "the Holy Ghost proceeding from them illuminating my understanding, and light, glory, and immortality were before me." But he did not, as did many converts at that time, rush immediately to the waters of baptism. First he made a trip with his brother Phineas and his friend Heber to the branch at Columbia, perhaps suspecting that the five elders he had met in Mendon were not representative members of the new church. When he returned he made another trip, this time into Canada to confer with his brother Joseph, who was there preaching Methodism. Joseph returned with him to Mendon to talk with other members of the family. Then another visit was made to the branch in Pennsylvania. Here Brigham's father and his two brothers were converted and baptized. Still Brigham refrained. There was another week of solemn discussion and questioning, after which he finally became convinced. He was baptized by one of the Pennsylvania elders at Mendon on April 14, 1832.

What was there about this doctrine preached by Joseph Smith's missionaries that so attracted Brigham and the whole family of John Young? Brigham's own statement of his conversion only hints at the preparatory explorations made between the first visit of the missionaries in the fall of 1831 and his baptism the following spring.

"When I first undertook to sound the doctrine of 'Mormonism,' " he said, "I supposed I could handle it as I could the Methodist, Presbyterian, and other creeds of Christendom, which I had paid some considerable attention to. . . . I found all religions . . . so defi-

cient in doctrine that when I tried to tie the loose ends and frag-
ments together, they would break in my hands. When I commenced
to examine 'Mormonism,' I found it impossible to take hold of either
end of it; I found it was from eternity, passing through time, and
into eternity again. When I discovered this, I said, 'It is worthy of
the notice of men.' Then I applied my heart to wisdom, and sought
diligently for understanding."

By the time Brigham allowed himself to be led into the water,
twenty persons in Mendon had been baptized. By May the little
congregation numbered thirty people. Among them were Brigham's father and his stepmother, his brothers Phineas and Lorenzo
with their wives, his brother Joseph, his two sisters, Rhoda and
Fanny, along with Rhoda's husband, John P. Green; also, Brigham's
friend Heber C. Kimball and his wife, and Brigham's ailing wife,
Miriam. The Mormon Church was by then barely two years old.

During the summer of 1832 Brigham, his brother Joseph, and
Heber Kimball traveled through the surrounding country, preaching and converting members and organizing branches of the young
church. Brigham had had no previous experience as a public speaker,
and at first the words did not come easily to him. He soon discovered, however, that when he thought least about what he was going
to say and how he was to say it expressions formed most readily in
his mind, and this convinced him that his utterances came not from
himself but from some outside power.

Brigham was not, in the beginning, the leader. Joseph Young,
with his experience, took the commanding role. Joseph was a ro-
tund little man, excessively solemn, and his speech tended toward
the rhetorical elaboration of a revival preacher. Heber Kimball,
who was a potter by trade, was Joseph's opposite. He was slim and
willowy, swift to see humor, even ribaldry, in the most common
remarks, and quick in his movements. Brigham's manner lay some-
where in between. He was not without humor, and his eyes often
glistened with amusement at the turn Heber's speech would take.
His own presence was less sanctimonious than masterful. He won
the attention of his listeners when they had stopped chuckling at

Heber's rude humor or nodding at Joseph's sanctimonious pro-
nouncements.

A New York reporter who heard him speak many years later
described his manner as being cool and deliberate, so that every
word could be heard. "His gesticulations were not elaborate or
constant, but strong and impressive. His style of elocution was not
so winning as commanding, though he by no means lacked suavity.
. . . He uses whatever words come first to express his ideas, so his
language is quite original and his expressions frequently very telling."

The message of the three missionaries was never received impas-
sively. From the first it aroused either intense interest or violent opposition. No sooner had they announced themselves members of
the new church than their neighbors in Mendon who had not joined
became their enemies. In the communities they visited in lower Canada, New York, and upper Pennsylvania they made many converts,
but they also aroused much hatred. Brigham blamed much of this
antagonism on the enmity of the clergy, who could not find words
too strong to abuse them. Even more, he saw such opposition as the
work of Satan, stirred to the height of his powers to prevent the
spread of the gospel.

Joseph Smith's claims to prophecy had been given prominent
space in the rural press of New York State; but the accounts had
either reflected the outrage of the editor or served as an occasion for
ridicule. Joe Smith, as the editors called him, was a fool and a fraud.
Brigham and his companions were confronted by these charges
wherever they went. In reply they would resort to their own reasons for accepting Smith's doctrines, and they would point out that
the opposition of so-called learned men was no new thing in the
history of the Christian church.

"Was Christ himself not attacked by the Pharisees?" Brigham
would ask his hearers. "Didn't the original Christians suffer such
persecution? Did this make Christianity any the less true?" He assumed that he was addressing a Christian congregation. Was it any
more difficult, he asked them, to believe that Joseph Smith had re-

ceived revelations from God than it was to believe that Paul the Apostle had? Those who accepted Paul's testimony, he told them, were saints of God; those who accepted the message of Joseph Smith today were just as surely saints, for it was the same gospel and the same church that Paul had had revealed to him.

The more Brigham talked about Joseph Smith and his message, the more anxious he became to meet the man who had brought so enormous a change into his life. He had seen his sister Rhoda and her husband depart from Mendon with the intention of settling in Kirtland. His father and his brothers were making plans to leave.

Listening to their talk, Brigham was torn by his desire to move with them and his knowledge that Miriam's illness made any such journey impossible. His wife had accepted the church with the same enthusiasm as had other members of the family. Despite her frailty, she had insisted upon baptism in the cold waters of a little stream near Mendon early in May. Brigham had feared that the shock and effort might be too much for her, but he had told himself that the Lord would not punish her for exhibiting such a faith; He might even perform the miracle of her recovery. During the months following the baptism Miriam seemed somewhat better; then as the summer wore on she grew worse. Suddenly, in September, she died. Brigham's account of her death says that "in her expiring moments, she clapped her hands and praised the Lord, and called upon Brother Kimball and all around to also praise the Lord."

When Vilate Kimball offered to take his two children into her own family, Brigham was free to follow his strongest desire. Almost at once, before the weather turned cold, he and his brother Joseph and Heber Kimball set out for Ohio. They traveled in Heber's wagon, taking the slower route overland because it was cheaper than sailing by boat down Lake Erie to Fairport Harbor. The distance was almost three hundred miles, over the lush countryside of western New York and eastern Ohio. Settlements were few and widely scattered, and most of the settlers had but recently moved into the country, but all along the way they came upon newly founded branches of the church or members who were themselves en route to Kirtland.

3

Brigham and his two companions entered the village from the north, driving Heber's team and wagon down the Mentor road until they reached the bridge, then crossing the river as Joseph had done and pausing at the store to ask the way to the house of J. P. Green. By the autumn of 1832 Kirtland was no longer a sleepy village. The preceding two summers had seen the influx of more than two thousand new converts. As one reporter said, "Kirtland presented the appearance of a modern religious Mecca. Like Eastern pilgrims [the converts] came full of zeal for their new religion. They came in rude vehicles, on horseback, on foot. They came almost any way, filling on their arrival every house, shop, and barn to the utmost capacity." Many of them still lived in their wagons, or they had houses under construction or recently constructed. Sawmills had been established to keep up with the demand for lumber. Forges were blown into flame, and their fires glowed day and night. Oxen lowed and horses neighed from the pastures on the hillside or at the river bottom. From the surrounding groves came the ring of axes and the crashing of timber.

When the visitors called at the Smith house, they were told that Joseph and his brothers were in a nearby grove chopping wood, and they were directed to the place. Even if Joseph had not claimed to be a prophet, he and his four brothers and their father would have impressed any visitor to Kirtland. They all stood above six feet and were strong and powerfully built. Despite their differences of temperament, they too were a close-knit family group. Hyrum, the oldest son, was five years older than Joseph. A quiet and even-tempered man, he was intensely loyal to his brother. The others were all younger. There was Samuel, who had brought the first copy of the *Book of Mormon* to Brigham's attention; William, who was a violent-tempered and jealous young man and who was to cause his brother trouble and embarrassment most of his life; and Don Carlos, still scarcely more than a boy and a favorite of his parents as well as of his older brothers.

All the Smith boys except Hyrum were still under thirty. In their working clothes, with their sleeves rolled up, they must have looked even more youthful. Brigham said later of his meeting with Joseph that he knew at once that he was in the presence of a great man, "that he was all that any man could believe him to be as a true prophet."

Joseph put up his ax and accompanied his visitors back to the family homestead, where, in their first talk, he and Brigham must have discovered how much they had in common in the similarity of their backgrounds. Both had been born in Vermont, both had moved at an early age into eastern New York, then farther and farther west. The fathers of both had been unsuccessful farmers.

Joseph suggested that they all meet together for religious discussion and worship that evening at his house, where the visitors would have the opportunity to meet others of their leading brethren. Brigham later described that meeting:

In the evening a few of the brethren came in and we conversed together upon the things of the kingdom. He [Joseph] called upon me to pray; in my prayer I spoke in tongues. As soon as we arose from our knees the brethren flocked around him, and asked his opinion concerning the gift of tongues that was upon me. He told them it was the pure Adamic language. Some said to him they expected he would condemn the gift Brother Brigham had, but he said, "No, it is of God."

Brigham's speaking in tongues would not have amazed one of those present—Martin Harris—for he had testified to seeing an angel of heaven holding the tablets from which Joseph claimed to have translated the *Book of Mormon*. It probably surprised the others, not because Brigham spoke in what seemed to them an incomprehensible babble of sound—such an occurrence was common among the frontier sects; what surprised them was Joseph's approval of it, because he had disapproved of others who had "spoken in tongues." Those who knew Brigham before his conversion would have been surprised because, of the members of his family, he was the least subject to such displays of emotion.

Brigham said of his feelings at Joseph Smith's house that evening, "I wanted to thunder and roar out the gospel to the nations. . . . It burned in my bones like a fire pent up . . . nothing would satisfy me but to cry abroad to the world, what the Lord was doing in the latter-days." Here finally was the fulfillment of the vague hopes that had troubled him. Later, in more sober recollection, Brigham reported his reaction to meeting the prophet: "I never met anyone, until I met Joseph Smith, who could tell me anything about the character, personality and dwelling place of God, or anything satisfactory about angels, or the relationship of man to his Maker. Yet I was as diligent as any man need be to try to find out those things."

This meeting between Joseph and Brigham seems now one of the most significant events in Mormon history. At the time it may have been only one of hundreds of such meetings for Joseph. In Brigham's features he may have detected the quiet humor, the sparkle of the eye that denoted perception and intelligence, for these were the qualities which were later to impress others. He could not have been impressed by the squat body, almost a head shorter than his own, or the rough-hewn features of Brigham's face. He could not have known Brigham's talent for organization and statesmanship, for Brigham himself was as yet unaware of these qualities. He could not have known of the firm will or the stored-up supply of vital energy. Above all, he could not yet know of that one quality which, in combination with the others, Joseph was just then most in need of—the quality of loyalty and devotion to a cause that Brigham was to display.

Joseph was essentially a dreamer, a planner, a mystic; Brigham was to become a man of practical actions, a statesman, decisive, vigorous and determined. What the two men had in common in their early years were poverty and near-illiteracy; what they retained later were curiosity, independence, and an ability to learn from experience.

By the time they met, Joseph had put all but the finishing touches to the doctrine which has become known as Mormonism, and it was to be complete by the time of his early death. Even many of the superficial aspects of Mormon society, which can be seen in the society of Utah today and which are often credited to Brigham Young, were of Joseph's creation. At the time when Joseph's genius, or his inspiration, had created a religion, Brigham was just beginning his apprenticeship as a religious leader. It was he who was destined to make Joseph's dream of a community of saints come true.

Once convinced that Joseph Smith's cause was what he had thought it to be—that Joseph was a prophet of God, as he put it—Brigham never swerved from that belief. The three witnesses, Cowdery, Whitmer, and Harris, did, even though they could never be brought to deny their testimony, and each insisted upon his deathbed that what he had sworn to was the absolute truth. Sidney Rigdon wavered, as did Parley P. Pratt and others of those who were to become Brigham's companions.

Brigham left Kirtland assured of Joseph's mission, more strongly determined to do all he could to further it and to return as soon as possible to settle in Zion. "What I have received from the Lord," he said later to a congregation, "I have received by Joseph Smith; he was the instrument made use of. If I drop him, I must drop those principles; they have not been revealed, declared, or explained by any other man since the days of the apostles. If I lay down the *Book of Mormon*, I shall deny that Joseph is a prophet; and if I lay down the doctrine and cease to preach the gathering of Israel and the building up of Zion, I must lay down the Bible; and, consequently, I might as well go home as undertake to preach without these three items."

CHAPTER THREE

KIRTLAND

I

After Brigham Young's meeting with Joseph Smith he did not remain long in Kirtland. He and his companions returned to Mendon, then spent the winter in missionary work in Canada and New York. They prepared to emigrate to Kirtland in the spring. It was the end of June before all their affairs were in order. Their goods they sent by water, down Lake Erie to Fairport Harbor; then, again utilizing Heber's wagon and team, they repeated the journey overland, this time accompanied by several families of converts from the vicinity of Mendon.

In Kirtland in July, Brigham was struck again by the activity and the progress. The little city had continued to grow beyond all expectation, outdistancing the surrounding towns of Mentor and Painesville, to say nothing of the little village of Cleveland a few miles down the lake.

Joseph had been forced by the influx of converts to enlarge his organization in order to free his own hands of the minor tasks of administration. He had appointed a council of twelve of his leading elders to govern in Kirtland, as well as another council in the Missouri settlements, and these he called High Councils. Each administered what he termed a "stake" of Zion. Within each stake were individual congregations, which came to be known as wards. In May he had revealed plans for the building of a temple in Kirtland—in a communication which gave even the exact dimensions: "It shall be built fifty-five by sixty-five feet in the width thereof and the length thereof, in the inner court." By June he had a plan for the entire city—a city to be built anew from the ground up. Its area was to cover one square mile, divided into squares of ten acres each, with half-acre building lots, the center squares reserved for public buildings, including the Bishop's Storehouse and the central temple, and twelve additional temples. Farms were to have been located outside the city, in the European manner.

Joseph's attempt at city planning was not destined to be fulfilled in Kirtland, but it was clear from the beginning that he did not think of it merely in theoretical terms. He had set out at once to bring his plan to completion. He appointed committees to raise funds for the temple, he established a brick-yard, and he called upon converts with special skills to come and labor on the building.

With money collected from converts, a farm was purchased that included the hilltop overlooking the valley. Joseph's followers set to work laying the foundations of the temple. The ingenuity and industry represented by the project awed the surrounding communities. Local newspapers wrote of the Mormon "cathedral" to rise above the banks of the little Ohio river. Accustomed as they were to laugh at Mormon claims of visions and miracles, they were suddenly sobered by the evidence beginning to appear before their eyes.

Brigham Young, too, was impressed when he returned to Kirtland in July 1833. There were now one thousand Mormons in Kirtland, and Brigham stood among them as the cornerstone of the temple was put in place, fired by Joseph's energy and enthusiasm. A week later he heard of even greater wonders to come. There were by now several hundred more Mormons in Missouri than in Kirtland, and Joseph announced that a temple would be built in Independence as well. Even before the walls had begun to rise on the first building, he called upon his followers to contribute their tithes to construct another, promising that if they did Zion would become "very glorious, very great, and very terrible," with all the nations of the earth paying tribute to her.

Despite the industry and outward prosperity of Kirtland, many
of the new settlers found it difficult to obtain employment. Much of
the land had been bought on credit or in exchange for goods.
Money was scarce. Brigham Young reported that when he began
work on two houses which he was commissioned to build, neither
employer knew whether he would be able to pay when the work
was completed. In order to make a suitable living, many of the saints
went off to Willoughby, Painesville, or Cleveland to work during
the winter. Brigham was determined to remain in Kirtland, as he
said, to "seek the things that pertained to the Kingdom of God."

In February 1834 Brigham married again. He took as his second
wife a woman who, although she had remained unmarried, was
only three years younger than himself. Her name was Mary Ann
Angell, a former free-will Baptist who had emigrated from Providence, Rhode Island, and had become a Mormon in 1831.

Even before Brigham's marriage, soon after his arrival in Kirtland, Oliver Cowdery brought news of an alarming nature from the
Mormon settlements in Missouri, a foretaste of the difficulties the
saints were to face in their push westward.

In Ohio the Mormons were surrounded by folks of their own
kind, mostly emigrants from New England and New York, as they
were themselves. But in Missouri the old settlers were mostly Southerners and slaveholders, and Jackson County was then the last out-
post of the American frontier. These old settlers were frontiersmen
of the most extreme type, accustomed by necessity to violence and
quick to take the administration of order and justice into their own
hands.

The Mormons were of that stock which supplied the abolition
movement with its energetic fanaticism a generation later. The
early Missouri settlers were of the same class, and in some cases
the same families, who were to participate in the bloody raids against
Kansas. Two such different groups were incompatible, and it is not
surprising that the spark which set off the explosion was the question of slavery.

No sooner had the Mormons settled in Missouri than they had
begun sending missionaries into the states to the south. Among their

early converts were a number of free Negroes, whom they invited to join them in Zion. To their embarrassment, they soon discovered that a Missouri statute forbade Negroes to move into the state without a certificate of citizenship from elsewhere. "To prevent misunderstanding," as editor W. W. Phelps of the Mormon newspaper *The Evening and the Morning Star*, of Independence, Missouri, put it, he published a reprint of the law in an early issue of his newspaper. He felt it his obligation to warn any prospective immigrants who were "free people of color" of this condition.

Even the thought that the Mormons would welcome the Negroes as brothers infuriated and disgusted the native Missourians. The real damage was done, however, when editor Phelps added: "So long as we have no special rule in the church as to people of color, let prudence guide, and while they, as well as we, are in the hands of a merciful God. We say, 'Shun every appearance of evil.' . . . As to slaves, we have nothing to say; in connection with the wonderful events of this age, much is doing toward abolishing slavery, and colonizing the blacks in Africa."

To the old settlers this sounded like abolition talk, if not an open invitation for their slaves to rebel. Phelps soon realized his mistake and published an extra edition of the *Star* in order to explain. But the dam of resentment had broken. A flood of anti-Mormon articles appeared in the Missouri press and spread from there into newspapers in the East. From the slavery question the attacks broadened to vilification of Mormon beliefs; and rival clergymen, many of whom had lost followers to Mormon missionaries, entered the fray.

In Missouri some of the most active opposition came from a clergyman by the name of Pixley, who, as one Mormon reported in his journal, "did not content himself with slandering us to the people of Jackson County, but also wrote to Eastern papers, telling horrible lies about us." Inflamed by such articles and resentful of Phelps's statements about slavery, the residents of Independence called a meeting on the twentieth of July—a meeting which was attended, according to the Mormons, "not only by the rabble of the county, but also by men of official standing."

The demands made at this meeting express the degree of feeling that had grown up:

But little more than two years ago, some two or three of this people made their appearance on the Upper Missouri, and now they number twelve hundred souls in this county; and each successive autumn and spring pours forth its swarm among us, with a gradual falling off of the character of those who compose them, until it seems these communities from which they come, were flooding us with the very dregs of their composition. Elevated as they are, but little above the condition of our blacks, either as regard to property or education; they have become a subject of such anxiety on that part, serious and well grounded complaints having been already made of their corrupting influence on our slaves.

We are daily told, and not by the ignorant alone, but by all classes of them, that we (the gentiles) of this county are to be cut off, and our lands appropriated by them for inheritances. Whether this is to be accomplished by the hand of the destroying angel, the judgments of God, or the arm of power, they are not fully agreed among themselves.

It was resolved that "no Mormon shall in the future move and settle in this county; that those now here shall give a definite pledge of this intention to move out of the county within a reasonable time; that the editor of the *Star* be required forthwith to close his office and discontinue the business of printing in this county; that the Mormon leaders here be required to use their influence to prevent any further migration of their distant brethren here to comply with the above requisitions, and that those who fail to do so, be referred to those of their brethren who have the gift of divination and of known tongues to inform them of the lot that awaits them."

When this resolution was presented to the leaders of the Mormon colonies they pleaded for more time to consider. The Missourians, who by now had become an unruly mob, demanded a decision in fifteen minutes. When it was not forthcoming, a mob assembled and attacked the newspaper office, wrecking the press, destroying the home of the editor, and tarring and feathering the bishop and one of his associates.

When Oliver Cowdery reported these events to Joseph Smith in

Kirtland, some of the Kirtland members were all for marching at once to Missouri in defense of their brethren. Joseph's counsel was for milder measures. The Mormons had the law on their side, he told them, and through it they would find redress. He sent messengers back to Missouri with the advice not to dispose of their land, and instructed them to petition the proper authorities.

By September 26 Joseph's emissaries were calling upon Governor Daniel Dunklin in Jefferson City. They had prepared a petition of their own, recounting their side of the controversy, including accounts of violence practiced against them by the old settlers as early as the spring of 1832, when houses of Mormons had been stoned, barns had been burned, and even shots had been fired.

Governor Dunklin advised them that he could do nothing at the moment, since his attorney general was absent from the capital. He promised to write them a reply, which he did on October 19. In it he assured the Mormons that if they would make affidavit to the court that their lives were threatened the offenders would be apprehended and bound to keep the peace. As to damage to their homes, they should seek redress in the courts.

With this communication, Joseph's judgment seemed vindicated. The Mormons began looking for an attorney who could bring their cause to trial and finally hired the firm of Wood, Reese, Doniphan, and Atchison from nearby Clay County, at a fee of one thousand dollars. So high a fee was necessary, the attorney explained, because the case would offend many prospective clients from Jackson County. As it turned out, the fee was a bargain, for the attorneys Doniphan and Atchison were to represent the Mormons for many years and to defend them beyond the obligations of this retainer.

No sooner had the Mormons shown their intention of fighting for their rights, even though by legal means and upon the advice of the governor, than the aroused citizens of Independence showed they had been making no idle threats. The next day a Mormon settlement west of the Blue River was attacked, and ten dwellings were unroofed and partly demolished. The men of the little community were taken into the woods and beaten with ox goads; the women and children were threatened with the same if they did not depart. In Independence the residence of A. S. Gilbert and the Mormon storehouse of which he was in charge were broken into, their furnishings and goods destroyed.

Rights or no rights, the Mormons could no longer remain in Independence in safety. On November 2, under threats of more violence, all the men, women, and children left the city and camped in the near-winter cold on the river bottoms a mile outside the town. That same night a settlement six miles distant was attacked by the mob.

In the meantime at Lexington, about forty miles east down the river, the circuit judge had refused to issue a peace warrant because of fear for his own safety. About the same time Mormon property in Independence was again attacked. Mormons rushed to its defense and captured one of the marauders. When they took him to the justice of the peace, the justice not only refused to arrest him but arrested and jailed the Mormons when their captive charged them with false arrest.

The Mormons had done their best to follow Joseph's advice; now they determined to defend themselves. On November 4 word came that an outlying settlement east of the Blue River was to be attacked. Nineteen Mormon men set out to assist its defense. Later enlarged to about thirty, only half of whom were armed, they engaged a mob of about fifty and a few shots were fired, fatally wounding one Mormon and two members of the mob, one of whom, Hugh Brazeale, is reported to have said, "I will wade to my knees in blood, but that I drive the Mormons from Jackson County." Much Mormon property had been destroyed by the mob before the battle.

News of the encounter spread from community to community —word that the Mormons were collecting and arming, that they intended to march on Independence. At this point the governor ordered out the state militia, which turned out to be little more than the mob more efficiently armed and given official status. The Mormons were told that they must surrender their arms and deliver up certain of their leaders.

For the next two days bands of armed ruffians circulated among the Mormon settlements, threatening and bullying the defenseless people until they were forced to desert their homes. Both banks of the Missouri River near the ferry station were crowded with Mormons and their possessions for several days as the saints fled into Clay County, where the residents had offered them temporary sanctuary.

Because of the sudden flare-up of violence, there had been no time to send information back to Ohio. When the news finally did get to the saints in Kirtland, the enormity of the injustice inflamed the whole community. Where formerly Joseph had advised his brethren to "be wise as serpents, harmless as doves," now he took a stronger stand. "Behold I say unto you," he proclaimed, "that the redemption of Zion must needs come by power, therefore, I will raise up unto my people, a man who shall lead them like Moses led the children of Israel; for ye are the children of Israel and the seed of Abraham, and ye must needs be led out of bondage, by power with a stretched out arm." In February 1834, two months after the Missouri saints had been driven from Jackson County, he announced that an army would be formed to march to the relief of Zion. They would set out as soon as equipment could be gathered and word could be got to the outlying branches. The army would be known as Zion's Camp.

2

It was at the organization of Zion's Camp that Brigham Young came into his first close and official relationship with Joseph Smith. From this time on his name began frequently to appear in the public records of the church. No sooner had the wedding ceremony making Mary Ann Angell his wife been performed than he was called by Joseph to travel east in search of money and enlistments for the army—the first of many missions he was to perform. He visited converts in the eastern branches of Pennsylvania, New York, Connecticut, and Massachusetts and explained what had happened in Missouri. He urged them to supply financial assistance if they were able, or, if they were young men without families, to join their brethren in righting the wrongs perpetrated by the gentiles in the western settlements. Upon his return to Kirtland he was appointed one of the ten captains who were to supervise the march to Missouri.

The main body of the Mormon army, organized in tens and fifties, and accompanied by Joseph Smith, left Kirtland on the fifth of May. They arrived at the Salt River in Missouri on June 7, where they met Lyman Wight and Hyrum Smith with an additional company of recruits from Michigan. By this time the camp totaled 205 men.

Lyman Wight, a colorful convert from Rigdon's congregation in Kirtland, was a veteran of the War of 1812. Joseph appointed him general, and the soldiers remained at the Salt River encampment a week, then continued their march.

There were hardships on the march—and fears. There were rumors of spies in camp, rumors of angels flying overhead. Most of the men knew nothing of army life. They were not adequately supplied with food or clothing. Yet Brigham Young always considered the march one of the great experiences of his life. He was engaged in an activity which brought him in close daily contact with Joseph, and there was an air of excitement about the whole expedition. When settlers in the villages through which they passed asked who they were, they replied that they were just a group of men headed west.

"Who is your leader?" they were asked.

"We're all leaders," would be the reply.

"But isn't there some particular one among you who is leader?"

"Sometimes one leads, sometimes another."

They felt the need to keep Joseph Smith's identity secret. This led them sometimes to take a special pleasure in misleading the curious. On Sunday, June 1, they were encamped one mile from Jacksonville, Illinois. In the morning they held a religious service at which some of the local residents concluded that they were "professors of religion." The whole town flocked to their camp in the afternoon. Joseph got the idea of holding a meeting at which various members of the company would expound certain features of religion as held by different groups. He called upon Joseph Young, who preached upon the principle of free salvation. He then called upon Brigham, who set forth baptism as essential for salvation. Brigham was followed by Orson Hyde, who proved by the Scriptures that baptism was for the remission of sin. Lyman Johnson spoke upon the necessity for upright action and keeping the sabbath holy. Orson Pratt, who was the most philosophically minded, delivered a discourse on "the principles of the final restoration of things."

When the meeting ended, the townspeople guessed what sect each speaker represented. They thought Joseph Young was a Methodist. Brigham Young, they said, might be a close-communion Baptist. Orson Hyde, they supposed, was a Campbellite or a reformed Baptist. Lyman Johnson must be a Presbyterian. When they asked Joseph Smith what the speakers really were, Joseph laughed and replied, "Some are one thing, some another."

On June 3, on the banks of the Illinois River, they came upon a large Indian mound. Joseph and Brigham climbed to the top of it and discovered at its summit a scattered heap of bones. They sent back to camp for a hoe and shovel and began to dig. In a shallow, rock-lined grave, they found the skeleton of an extremely tall man. Between his ribs was embedded the stone head of an arrow. Joseph was asked who this man might have been, and he replied that he had been an officer in the wars recorded in the *Book of Mormon*. His name was Zelph, and he had been mighty in battle. Some of the men carried bones from the skeleton away as souvenirs. Brigham took the arrowhead, which he kept to the end of his life.

But the journey was not merely a pleasant outing. At times tempers flared, and they had not been long on the road when dissension developed. The chief offender was Sylvester Smith. Smith, who was no relation to Joseph, was a high councilman at Kirtland, and that he had been considered one of the most worthy of the company is indicated by the fact that he had been selected to preach the sermon the first Sunday they were on the road. His rebellion, which was primarily against Joseph's leadership, did not occur until after he had been reprimanded one day by Joseph when he refused to share his rations with another brother who had none. Also he attracted partisans who were critical of Joseph for bringing his dog along and who grumbled with him at men like Brigham Young and Heber Kimball, who always stood behind the prophet.

While they were still in Illinois, Joseph indicated the amount of dissatisfaction that existed in the camp by prophesying "that there would come a scourge upon the camp in consequence of the fractious and unruly spirits that appeared among them, and they should die like sheep with the rot."

Apparently this warning was not enough, for after they had crossed the Mississippi, Joseph's dog growled at Sylvester as he was marching his company up to the camp. Sylvester swore, if "that damn dog bit him, he would kill it."

A short time later Joseph, in the company of Brigham and Heber Kimball, said, "I will descend to that spirit that is in the camp, to show you the spirit you are of, for I want to drive it from the camp."

He had begun to collect a crowd about him. In his best imitation of Sylvester, he growled, "The first man that kills my dog, I will whip him."

Just at the moment, Sylvester joined the group. He thrust himself forward. "Yes, and I'll say it again," he shouted. "If that dog bites me, I will kill him."

"If you do, I'll whip you," Joseph replied in the same tone.

"If you do," Sylvester said, "I will defend myself."

"I can, too," Joseph continued. "I can whip you in the name of the Lord."

He then turned to the group of men around him. "Are you not ashamed of such a spirit?" he asked. "I am!"

Sylvester may not have realized that Joseph was acting, and there may have been more than acting in Joseph's angry words. Later, when charges were brought against Sylvester Smith by the High Council in Kirtland, Brigham Young testified for Joseph. When Sylvester asked him if he did not think his character had been injured by Joseph's reproof, Brigham replied emphatically, "I did not!"

As the army proceeded across Missouri, threats against them became common. Rumor had spread from Independence that the Mormons intended to take over the state. In the towns they marched through, settlers would stand beside the road and shout derogatory remarks about their religion and about "ol' Joe Smith." Approaching Richmond, the last large settlement east of Clay County, where their dispossessed fellows had found refuge, the Mormons heard rumors of a force preparing to attack them from Jackson County. They broke camp early and passed through Richmond before daybreak. They were now separated only by the Missouri River from the county from which the Mormons had been driven.

That day four men rode into camp and asked where Joe Smith was. When no one would point him out they became angry and left the camp, threatening that all Mormons would "see hell before morning." Actually a force of one hundred Missourians had been recruited at Independence and were even then assembling on the opposite bank of the river, preparing to cross and meet with other groups from the north bank to attack the Mormons. James Campbell, one of their leaders, is reported to have sworn when he heard of the Mormons' coming, "The Eagles and Turkey Buzzards shall eat my flesh if I do not fix Joe Smith and his army so that their skins will not hold shucks, before two days are passed."

Campbell took off on the first boat to load from the Jackson County shore. While they were crossing, a severe storm came up, and Campbell's boat was swamped. Seven men, including Campbell, were drowned. The storm saved the Mormons from attack, but it also wrecked their camp, blowing down tents and wagon covers. For the next few days the countryside was littered with hailstones as large as eggs, rivers were swollen, and the soil was too watersoaked to allow progress with their teams and wagons. As an aftermath of the storm, three members of Zion's Camp came down with a strange illness.

Joseph saw in the storm the work of the Lord, but the nearer he came to the end of the journey, the less certain he felt that the Mormons' troubles could be solved by force. On June 21 he met the first of a series of envoys who came to meet him in the hope of avoiding more violence—a Colonel Spenser of the State Militia. Before the colonel, Joseph revealed his identity for the first time. He told him that the Mormons were coming not to make war, but only to the defense of their brethren, who had been disarmed and driven from their homes. The colonel recounted the efforts the governor had been making to arrive at a settlement. He said the coming of Joseph's force had disrupted the negotiations. The prophet was skeptical, but he was impressed by Colonel Spenser. To allay the fears of the Missourians, he offered to disperse his men among the various Mormon families in Clay County.

The next day Joseph met with the sheriff of Clay County, Cornelius Gilliam, to whom he gave similar assurances. On June 23 General Atchison, a member of the law firm representing the Mormons, came out from Liberty, the county seat of Clay County, and persuaded Joseph not to take his men into the town. Joseph agreed, and the army turned and camped on Rush Creek, on the newly acquired property of their brother A. S. Gilbert.

Only the day before, Joseph had announced a revelation which stated that the time was not yet ripe for "the redemption of Zion." On June 24 cholera, which had raged through Missouri the year before, struck the camp. Almost half the Mormon army, including Joseph, came down with the disease. Fourteen died, including A. S. Gilbert, one of their most respected leaders.

The Mormons' cause in Independence was clearly lost by the time the army arrived. Governor Dunklin was unsure of his power and insisted at first that matters could be settled by legal means, and, when that seemed hopeless, urged compromise. At the time Joseph Smith arrived the Missouri Mormons were trying to negotiate with their enemies in Independence. Hopeless as these attempts were, Joseph saw that they had to be pursued. To attempt to resettle his followers by force would have been absolute folly.

All that he could do, he did. He consulted with the attorneys, Doniphan and Atchison, who assured him that his people had legal right on their side. He dropped the warlike attitude of Zion's Camp and set about to establish good feelings between the saints and their new neighbors in Clay County. He advised his leaders who had been at the forefront of the trouble to return with him to Ohio. He instructed all members of the army who had no family obligations in Kirtland to settle in Missouri and assist their brethren. He arranged for continued negotiations through the state government.

Joseph's sudden change in attitude has been seen by some historians as evidence of cowardice. Actually he showed suppleness and common sense. Zion's Camp, seen in one light, was a quixotic gesture. In the long run, however, it served several worthy purposes. It re-established the unity of the Missouri and Ohio colonies at a time when the Missouri Mormons had begun to feel neglected by their more prosperous Kirtland brethren. It allowed Joseph to measure the strength and weakness of his leaders, both those who had been with him in Zion's Camp and those who worked for the Mormon cause in Independence. It provided the Mormons, both in Ohio and in Missouri, with their first example of persecution— what they came to think of as Satan's power to thwart the purposes of the Lord.

Joseph did not give up the idea that Zion was to be located in Missouri, and he did not agree to dispose of the Mormon property in Jackson County. This land had been decreed as theirs by heaven, and he told his saints now only that the gathering would be delayed. The cause of the church had been set back by the wickedness of men, not by the insufficiency of God.

3

When Joseph called Zion's Camp together for the last time, money remaining from the original contributions was divided equally among them, and the men were told to find their own way back to Ohio. Brigham Young and his companions received one dollar and sixteen cents apiece to carry them over the almost one thousand miles separating them from their homes. About the first of July, Brigham left with a small company of men and one team. Arriving in Kirtland a month later, he found that, despite the absence of so many young men on the march to Missouri, progress had been made on the temple. More immigrants had arrived to swell the population of the little city.

Yet all was not well in Kirtland. Discontent, which had not been unusual before the expedition, was increased by the return of Sylvester Smith and his friends from the West; they immediately began to spread charges that Joseph had been overbearing and dictatorial, that the trek had been a mistake. Joseph, who had arrived home about the same time as Brigham, wrote bitterly to some of the saints in the East about his experience: "I was met in the face and eyes, as soon as I got home, with a catalogue as black as the author himself. And the cry was Tyrant! Pope!! Usurper!!! King!!!! Abuser of men!!!!! Angel!!!!!! False Prophet!!!!!!! Prophesying lies in the name of the Lord!!!!!!!! Taking consecrated money!!!!!!!!! and every other lie to fill up and complete the catalogue."

With the accusations of Sylvester Smith, Joseph's authority was being challenged seriously for the first time by someone within the church. If he was a fallen prophet, as Smith maintained, Joseph could do little to defend himself. Others must come to his defense.

Brigham Young was among the first. He testified before the High Council to the impropriety of Sylvester Smith's behavior during the march of Zion's Camp and denied that Joseph had exercised more than his warranted authority in reprimanding him. He called Joseph a man who could "unite heaven and earth." Such petty charges as Sylvester brought, he maintained, even if true, could not cancel all that Joseph had accomplished in his less than five years of ministry. In the end Sylvester Smith was reprimanded by the council, and he reluctantly admitted his error.

After the trial someone asked Brigham Young what he had gained by the journey into Missouri. Brigham replied, "Just what we went for. I would not exchange the knowledge I received this season for the whole of Geauga County; for property and mines of wealth are not to be compared to the worth of knowledge."

More serious charges against Joseph were soon to be made. A recent convert, Dr. Philastus Hurlbut, had been cut off from the church shortly before the march of Zion's Camp. The first accusation against him had been of "unchristianlike conduct with the female sex." Dr. Hurlbut confessed and repented and was taken back into fellowship. Later he was heard to say that he had "deceived Joseph Smith's God, or the spirit by which he was activated, &c." and was again excommunicated. Thereupon Hurlbut, who has been described as a handsome and impressive person, set about in search of some means for getting even with Joseph Smith.

In Conneaut, about fifty miles east of Kirtland, Dr. Hurlbut heard that there had been a manuscript written a few years earlier which bore a strong resemblance to the *Book of Mormon*. He took affidavits from persons who had heard the manuscript read, then hurried off to New York State in search of the manuscript itself. This was the manuscript of the recently deceased Reverend Solomon Spaulding, destined to play so large a part in attempts to show that Joseph Smith had consciously perpetrated a fraud. Hurlbut located Spaulding's papers in a farmhouse in Otsego County, but was disappointed to discover that the clergyman's romance bore only a superficial resemblance to the *Book of Mormon*.

In New York, Hurlbut did, however, make a discovery which seemed to him of equal importance. He ran into the whole tangled mass of legend and fact concerning the early history of the Smith family and Joseph's reputation as a money-grubber. From the Smiths' former neighbors he extracted additional affidavits concerning the peculiarities of the family and anecdotes recounting their search for buried gold. Armed with the statements from Conneaut and Palmyra and with the Spaulding manuscript, Hurlbut began a tour of Ohio towns, "exposing" Joseph as a fraud and a forger. He even ventured into the branches of the church in the vicinity of Kirtland.

The seriousness with which Joseph took the charges is indicated by the vigor with which he fought back. He defended himself wherever Hurlbut appeared, denying the charges and attributing them to the cunning of Satan. "I will stand," he told his members, "like the sun in the firmament when my enemies and the gainsayers of my testimony shall be put down and cut off, and their names blotted out from among men."

The energy with which he conducted his defense held most of his saints to him, and it brought such men as Brigham even more closely to his side. "He was persecuted," Brigham declared, "for the same reason that any righteous person has been or is persecuted at the present day." He was to say later; "Let any people enjoy peace and quiet . . . never persecuted for their religion, and they are likely to neglect their duty, to become cold and indifferent, and lose their faith."

Joseph's vigorous defense also moved Hurlbut to make threats against him. This was the moment Joseph had been waiting for. He took Hurlbut's threats to the county court. He won his case, and Hurlbut was put under bond to keep the peace. After the trial Hurlbut, discouraged, sold his evidence to E. D. Howe, the editor of the Painesville *Telegraph*, who had become an enemy of the Mormons when his wife and daughter had joined the church a few years earlier. Howe published the statements in book form in 1834, along with an account of the Spaulding manuscript and Joseph's trouble on the march to Missouri. The book, *Mormonism Unveiled*, remained for many years the basis for all attacks upon the prophet and the church.

One reason for the success of Joseph's defense against the Hurlbut attack was that he had by now moved far beyond the world of his early visions as Hurlbut portrayed them. Few of Joseph's followers, watching him stride through the streets of Kirtland, hearing him hurl his defiance of all persecutors from the pulpit, or recalling small acts of generosity and sympathy which he had performed for them, could long believe in the portrait Hurlbut had painted. One sight of the temple, now rising three stories above the green Ohio hilltop, did more to convince them of Joseph's divine gifts than any amount of talk about revelations and visions.

In the face of persecution—perhaps to some extent stimulated by it—Joseph called together members of the Missouri Expedition who had returned to Kirtland. From them he appointed what he called "a traveling High Council"—soon to become known more familiarly as the Twelve. They were to be, he told them, like the apostles of old, traveling throughout the world, organizing his churches and preaching the gospel. At their head he placed Thomas B. Marsh, an early convert who had had much success as a missionary in his native state of Massachusetts. Next he appointed David Patten, an active young man who had served as a dispatch-bearer between Kirtland and Missouri at the height of the trouble. His third appointment went to Brigham Young.

The new council was given great authority, which Joseph may not at first have recognized, but which he later characterized as the authority "to hold the keys of this ministry, to unlock the door of the Kingdom of Heaven unto all nations, and to preach the Gospel to every creature." While the two councils in Kirtland and Missouri were accountable to their individual stakes, the new council was accountable only to Joseph Smith. Also, since the Twelve were authorized to organize and install High Councils in other stakes, it was only logical to assume that their authority extended beyond that of such councils.

Following the silencing of Hurlbut, the saints at Kirtland entered upon their most prosperous period. The Mormons in Missouri had been taken in by the settlers of Clay County, and they were again establishing homes and communities. In Kirtland the most important activity was the completion of the temple. Sidney Rigdon had been left in charge during Joseph's absence, and progress had been made. Now all energy was put forth to complete it as soon as possible. Those members who did not work on the structure itself labored indirectly by sewing, cooking, raising crops, and donating their savings for the purchase of supplies.

All the materials for the temple's construction were supplied from the surrounding area. Timber was cut and milled. Iron was forged. Glass for the windows was made. Carpets and draperies were woven and sewn. Candelabra were forged and molded. Brick, which had been suggested in the first specifications, proved less practical than stone, so granite was cut and hauled from nearby quarries and put into place by local masons. All finishing and interior decoration were done by local craftsmen. Brigham Young, as a carpenter, painter, and glazier, was well prepared for this kind of work. He was put in charge of completing the interior, while his brother

Lorenzo worked outside, applying the finishing plaster that covered stones.

The temple was three stories high, with a steeple at the east end from which one could on a clear day see the waters of Lake Erie twelve miles to the north. The first and second stories were completely given over to auditoriums, similar except for a more elaborate finishing on the ground floor. The third floor was composed of twelve rooms, designed for meetings of the various priesthood groups—or "quorums," as Joseph called them. The largest of these rooms was reserved for Joseph's office and "translating room."

No sooner was the upper story made habitable than Joseph began to use it as a study. He had begun what he called the School of the Prophets during Brigham's first winter in Kirtland. This was a series of meetings in Joseph's home at which ecclesiastical matters were discussed and debated by the leading elders of the church. The winter after the return from Missouri, Joseph had enlarged the school to include classes in Hebrew and Greek, hiring an instructor, Joshua Seixas, who had been educated at Andover and now taught at a nearby academy. He had sent East for grammars, which he passed out to the elders. These classes were held in the unfinished upper story of the temple, and Joseph surpassed his followers in both talent and industry—even those like Sidney Rigdon and Orson Pratt, who pretended to more learning. One of his teachers, when asked later how Joseph had performed in the study of English grammar, replied, "Joseph was the calf that sucked three cows. He acquired knowledge very rapidly." Heber Kimball, on the other hand, the teacher said, "never came to understand the difference between noun and verb."

The dedication of the temple was set for March 27. It had cost the members of the church approximately seventy thousand dollars, not including the labor, which had been donated. It rose 128 feet to the tip of the steeple. Inside, the main auditorium resembled an early colonial, large-city church, except for two unusual features. Instead of a single pulpit, each end of the auditorium contained twelve pulpits, rising in tiers of three, each carved with three gilded initials. The initials symbolized the order of the priesthood that the occupant of the pulpit would represent. Although the pulpits in the east and west were identical, the west end contained the seats of the Melkizidek, or higher, priesthood (perhaps an unconscious symbolism); while the pulpits on the east seated officials of the Aaronic, or lower, order. The pews were so arranged that, by a simple shifting of benches, the congregation could face in either direction.

Outside, the building disguised its size by its excellent proportions. The rough stone had been covered with plaster, into the mortar of which the women of Kirtland had broken their finest china and glassware, so that the building sparkled under the reflected rays of the sun. It possessed the dignity of an ordinary meeting house, but its dignity was enhanced by the unique qualities that Joseph imparted to everything he touched.

The dedication ceremonies opened with a general meeting, not unlike those that had been held before in homes, in barns, in boweries, except that now every saint within walking or riding distance was present, filling the auditorium to capacity and overflowing beyond the doors and far down the hillside. Several thousand were turned away, and Joseph announced that the meeting would be repeated later for their benefit. Hymns were sung, and a few general remarks made about the construction of the building; then Joseph offered the dedicatory prayer.

The most important ceremonies—those promised by Joseph at the disbanding of Zion's Camp—began in the evening. They were confined to men, who were holders of the priesthood, and these meetings became known as "the Solemn Assembly." For years afterward it was a mark of distinction for any Mormon to remember that he had participated. They continued for several days, and, since they were secret, they gave rise to rumors over the surrounding countryside that the Mormons were engaging in horrible orgies.

Brigham Young, as a member of the ruling council, was at the forefront of these activities. The meeting began with Joseph's washing of the feet of his principal subordinates, who, in turn, washed the feet of those immediately below them. This was followed by an anointing with consecrated oil, each man receiving a blessing and a promise that what had been done was immediately "sealed" in heaven. The elders of the anointeds' quorum then crowded together, each placing his hand upon a brother's head, and Joseph spoke.

"The heavens are opened to me," he intoned solemnly, "and I behold the celestial Kingdom of God, and the glory thereof, whether in the body or out I cannot tell. I see the transcendent beauty of the gate through which the heirs of that kingdom will enter, which is like unto circling flames of fire; also the blazing throne of God, whereon is seated the Father and the Son."

The weight of hands upon their heads, the measured tones of Joseph's voice, the sense of fulfillment in the air caused many of those present to imagine that they too penetrated beyond the veil and saw visions of angels hovering over the congregation.

"Angels ministered unto them," Joseph recorded in his journal, "as well as to myself, and the power of the Highest rested upon us."

After these blessings all the quorums arose in order and presented themselves before Joseph. With hands uplifted, they asked that the Spirit of God remain with them. Petition after petition was offered by succeeding groups, some elegantly worded and expressed, some crudely, but all with the fervor of the assembly behind them. As each concluded, the entire congregation answered aloud, "Amen! Hosanna! Hosanna! Hosanna! To God and the Lamb, forever and ever, amen and amen!"

At one point there was said to have come a rushing of wind, and Joseph announced that the building was filled by hosts of angels. The women, who were excluded from the meeting, maintained that they heard the sound from their homes and rushed to the building. They thought at first fire had broken out. They saw, they reported, a pillar like fire resting on the summit of the temple.

Such an outburst of emotion came very close to the evangelism that Joseph had discouraged in the past, and it was the last official expression of such a spirit in the church. Trouble was to follow too swiftly upon this brief moment of exaltation to allow the saints to dwell on it. The emotions the solemn assembly excited were soon dwarfed by events of a very different nature, only to be recalled later in consolation or in pride. In fact, the speed with which ill fortune followed upon the heels of prosperity is indicated in a de-

scription of the time given later by George A. Smith, a cousin of
Joseph and a member of the Twelve, for he recalled in a single
breath the beginning of apostasy and pride at having participated
in the stirring events of the dedication of the temple. On the evening
when four hundred and sixteen men stayed in the temple all day,
performing the ceremonies, the women, he said, got suspicious,
"imagining some mischief was going on. Some of them were right
huffy about it." As for the men who received their endowments,
he went on, "some apostatized because there was not more of it,
and others because there was too much."

During the past five years the Mormons had shared in the general
prosperity of the frontier. They had bought land on credit and seen
its value soar. On paper, most of them were wealthier than they
had ever been or hoped to be. Outwardly the church was prosperous, for its imposing temple and printing shop seemed to make it a
good credit risk. Money was cheap and easy to obtain, so Joseph
had borrowed heavily, himself infected with the optimism of the
times. He had borrowed to allow the Missouri Mormons to purchase land. He had borrowed from Eastern bankers, from individuals and banks in Ohio, and from individual Mormons in the East. Although the members in Kirtland were poor, they were industrious
and created an atmosphere of prosperity, which added to the impression that Joseph's community was a good credit risk. Even before the temple was completed he had begun to run into trouble,
but always donations from incoming members seemed to save him.
These he attributed to the management of a watchful God.

The most serious threat had appeared in 1834. Creditors had begun to press, and Joseph and Oliver Cowdery repaired to the unfinished temple and prayed for relief. At about the same time a
wealthy New York convert sold his property and prepared to
emigrate to Missouri, where his two sons had gone with Zion's
Camp. Before he was well on his way he got the impression—as he
expressed it—that he was needed in Kirtland. He arrived in January 1835, and immediately loaned the prophet two thousand dollars to save the temple property. He also loaned the temple committee thirteen thousand dollars to aid in the construction. But

even such resources as this could not save Joseph from the final blow, which came July 11, 1836, from the office of Andrew Jackson in Washington. It was an order forbidding agents to accept anything except gold and silver for the purchase of public land.

Jackson's specie circular did not affect members like Brigham Young until later, when credit tightened and the value of their property dropped. They had land and homes, and what did it matter whether they were valued at the fifty dollars per acre they had originally been worth, or two thousand dollars, the heights to which they had recently soared? These members were aware only that they could no longer make their usual donations to Joseph and the church, donations which were not large in individual cases, but which added up to amounts often capable of satisfying the immediate needs of the community, either by fulfilling demands for interest on money already borrowed or by financing new projects such as a steam mill and the new printing plant, upon which additional money could then be borrowed.

Seemingly more important to the Mormons was the recurrence of the trouble which always seemed to emerge within the church when misfortune struck from the outside. Even during the period of relative tranquillity following the silencing of Philastus Hurlbut there had been embarrassing minor squabbles. When Brigham had gone with the members of the Twelve on their first mission to the East in 1835, he had returned to charges of overzealousness made by the Kirtland High Council, and Joseph had been forced to rule that the Twelve were accountable only to him, not to the council in Kirtland or anywhere else. This had resulted in jealousy on the part of older members of Joseph's hierarchy, particularly members of the Whitmer family, who felt that their suffering in Missouri had gone unappreciated and unrewarded.

To make matters worse, there had been a certain amount of ill feeling within the Council of the Twelve itself. Two of its members had been called before the Kirtland council to answer charges which grew out of letters they had written from their missions, criticizing the administration of affairs at home. Joseph's younger brother William, who was a member of Brigham's council, had quarreled with Joseph publicly, flouting his authority and embarrassing both the Smith family and the regular membership of the church.

In Missouri too, troubles began again. So many additional Mormons had emigrated to Clay County that the residents of Liberty, fearful that the Mormons would come to dominate the life of the area, petitioned the Mormons to locate elsewhere. Such a request the Mormons could not take lightly, for the Missourians of Clay County had befriended them at a time of desperate need. Conferences were arranged between Mormons and non-Mormons. The state government was appealed to, and a separate county north of Clay County was established for Joseph's followers. It was to be called Caldwell County. Again the Mormons who had settled in the vicinity of Liberty were forced to move on. The new county was located in what was then the northern section of Ray County, in the almost unpopulated Shoal Creek area.

Such a move demanded financial assistance, so once again Joseph was required to appeal to the Kirtland saints for aid. They had little to contribute. As a means of relieving himself of his financial burden, the prophet conceived the idea of a bank for Kirtland. It would be backed by Mormon property and by the sale of stock to members. It was to be called the Kirtland Safety Society Bank, and it would print enough bills to pay off the obligations of the church. Almost at once he sent members of the Twelve East to solicit funds. He sent one of his elders to Philadelphia to purchase plates for the printing of the bills. He sent another to Columbus, the state capital, to obtain a charter.

A few years earlier such a bank, if run on sound principles, might have succeeded. In January 1837 it would have taken a miracle greater than what Joseph had ever before accomplished. Hundreds of banks in Ohio had been established on foundations no more solid. By this time, however, the state government had begun to sense danger. It refused the Mormons' request for a charter. The plates arrived from Philadelphia, where their engraving had cost Joseph money he could ill afford to spend, but there was no bank to issue them.

In desperation, Joseph drew up new articles. He changed the ostensible aim of his company from that of a banking institution to that of a society to provide "safety" from existing banks. As an anti-banking society, he would need no charter. He still went ahead with his plan to issue bills. He had his printer alter the plates by hand, so that when they appeared they read:

THE KIRTLAND SAFETY SOCIETY
anti-BANK*ing Co.*

These bills Joseph hopefully sent out in payment of the church's debts. Prosperity was short-lived. Creditors had become suspicious of Western banks—a suspicion that was to bring on the panic of 1837. No sooner had the bills gone out than they were returned for redemption. The only way even a small portion of them could be redeemed was by calling upon members of the church to fulfill their pledges as stockholders. If they did this they would be left homeless. Besides, calling upon them now undermined their faith in Joseph as a prophet, for he had prophesied great things for a bank that had been established by divine inspiration. Even so devoted a follower as Parley P. Pratt rebelled. He had lost his home in Missouri and had just become established again in Kirtland; he could not submit his family to complete poverty again so soon.

The Kirtland bank survived under Joseph's direction for less than a month, from January to February 1837; then Dr. F. G. Williams, who had had more business experience than the prophet, took over. Even he could not stem the tide which was to bring the failure of over eight hundred of the nation's banks within a single month. In March, Joseph was brought to trial on the charge of operating a bank illegally and was fined one thousand dollars and costs. The loss of the case finished the bank and brought Joseph's enemies swarming down upon him.

In all these events Brigham Young's role had been a minor but not an unimportant one. In 1836 he made a trip to the East as a missionary and had converted most of the members of the family of his uncle Joseph Richards of Massachusetts. Among these converts was Dr. Willard Richards, Brigham's cousin, who accompanied him to Kirtland and was baptized by him on December 31. The next month Brigham and Willard went east again in search of support for the bank. They succeeded in raising ten thousand dollars, but this was not enough. In June 1837 Joseph Smith called Heber Kimball and Willard Richards to go as missionaries to England, and Heber asked if their friend Brigham Young could not accompany them on this first mission abroad.

Joseph's reply indicated the increased reliance he was putting upon Brigham Young. "No," he replied, "no, I have greater work here for Brother Brigham."

In July, Joseph suggested to Brigham that they leave Kirtland and travel to the Eastern branches to enlist support against the rebels in Ohio. Even this was difficult to do. When Joseph and Brigham arrived in Painesville, on their way to Fairport Harbor, they were recognized, and Joseph was served writ after writ for debts owed both by him and by the church. Even after they had decided to return to Kirtland, the sheriff sprang into Joseph's carriage, seized the reins, and served a final summons. The next day Brigham and Joseph drove thirty miles east to Ashtabula in order to escape notice when they boarded the steamer.

One purpose of the Eastern trip was undoubtedly to raise money. Joseph's debts at that time have been estimated as high as $150,000. No sooner were the two men away from Kirtland, however, than the split in the church, which had been threatening before their departure, broke into the open. Both of Joseph's councilors of that time, Oliver Cowdery and Dr. Williams, had deserted him, and now they began actively to campaign against him. David Whitmer became the head of a faction whose aim, openly stated, was to overthrow Joseph Smith. Many of the other former leaders became apathetic or grumbled that the church could not continue with Joseph at its head.

Brigham, hearing of these attacks, rushed back to Kirtland. He had one advantage over the attackers; that was the fact that the general membership of the church was more confused than disillusioned. Actually the financial crisis had touched them very lightly. What they had lost, they had lost on paper. When they saw

Brigham Young standing before them, accusing them of disloyalty and lack of faith, the words had a familiar ring. These were the vigorous, positive tones they were accustomed to hearing.

On September 3 a meeting was called in which the names of the authorities came up for approval. Brigham led in the rejection of any who had not remained loyal to Joseph. Such opposition made personal enemies for Brigham, but it held the rank-and-file membership of the church together. In November, Roger Orton, a high elder, was excommunicated for "abusing Brigham Young."

The height to which feeling soared at this time is indicated in an account by Joseph's mother, describing a meeting at the temple. Father Smith was in the pulpit. He said something in favor of his son and reflecting upon the later officers of the bank. One of them was in the congregation, and he rushed forward and attempted to pull the old man from the platform. Father Smith appealed to Oliver Cowdery for help, but Cowdery remained seated. Young William Smith then sprang forward and carried the attacker from the church. Whereupon, according to another reporter, "John Boynton and others drew their pistols and bowie knives and rushed down from the stand into the congregation, Boynton shouting he would blow out the brains of the first man who dared to lay hand upon him." Town policemen arrived and disarmed the disturbers, but in the scuffle they knocked down a stovepipe, which sprayed soot all over the congregation.

Many of the saints began leaving Kirtland, some apostatizing, some moving to the settlements in Missouri. Oliver Cowdery and the Whitmers departed for Far West, the new Mormon village in Caldwell County. But the plotting against Joseph continued. In December, Brigham heard that a meeting of Joseph's enemies had been called to discuss means of deposing the prophet. The gathering was to be held in the upper rooms of the temple, and Brigham made it a point to be present.

The plotters were not pleased to see him. Some of the men had supported Sylvester Smith in his charges against Joseph three years before. "I rose up and told them," Brigham wrote later, "in a plain and forceful manner that Joseph was a prophet; and I knew it; and they might rail and slander him as much as they pleased, they could not destroy the appointment of a prophet of God; they could only destroy their own authority, cut the thread which bound them to the prophet and to God and sink themselves to hell. Many were highly enraged at my decided opposition to their measures and Joseph Bump . . . was so exasperated that he could not be still. Some of the brethren near put their hands on him to be quiet; but he writhed and twisted his arms and body saying, 'How can I keep my hands off that man?' I told him if he thought it would give him any relief he might lay them on. The meeting was broken up without the apostates being able to unite on any decided measures of opposition. . . .

"This was the crisis," Brigham concluded, "when earth and hell seemed leagued to overthrow the prophet and the Church of God. The knees of many of the strongest men in the church faltered."

Brigham's family had by this time increased to five children. His first son, Joseph, was born soon after the return from Missouri. In 1836 his wife had borne him twins, Brigham, Jr., and Mary. He began to fear for their safety in Kirtland. A few days before Christmas, 1837, he heard that a plot was being laid to put him out of the way. By now Joseph Smith had returned, and Brigham decided that his usefulness to the prophet had ended. After making arrangements for his family to leave their Kirtland home by team and wagon, he fled the town on horseback the night of December 22. As he had feared, apostates set out in pursuit, but he eluded them, although it is said that they lodged at the same inn the first night. Brigham is reported to have heard, through the thin walls of the hotel, his enemies plotting his capture. He remained in his room in the morning until he had seen them ride away; then he waited for his wife and children to join him.

A few days after Brigham's departure Joseph and Sidney Rigdon called a meeting of all the Mormons remaining in Kirtland. Rigdon first addressed the confused and rebellious congregation, pleading tearfully for their support in the name of all that they had accomplished together over the past six years. A person who was present reported that on this occasion "the pathos of Rigdon's plea, and the power of his denunciation, swayed the feelings and shook the judgment of his hearers as never in the old days of peace, and when he had finished and was led out, a perfect silence reigned in the Temple until its doors had closed on him forever." Joseph made a determined battle to refute the charges of the apostates, speaking firmly as the head of the church and boldly leveling charges against his accusers. But many of the members present were his enemies; those who had remained faithful to him had mostly left the city, and they were now either in Missouri or on their way there.

The day following the meeting, he and Sidney Rigdon set out for Missouri on horseback. Sixty miles southwest of Kirtland they met Brigham Young. It was the dead of winter. They made plans to travel together, going by way of Cincinnati and Quincy, Illinois. They were almost penniless and without provisions. Sidney Rigdon's health was bad, so he stopped along the way with a daughter, to wait for spring. It took Joseph and Brigham over two months to make the journey they had made three years before in less than one. Together they entered the Mormon town of Far West on March 13, 1838. The reception they received erased the gloom from Joseph's mind. The whole town turned out to meet them. Amid cheers and music, Joseph heard his Missouri followers tell him they believed God had purposely brought the failure of the Kirtland bank. Hadn't Joseph always said that Missouri was the gathering place? Wasn't this Zion?

CHAPTER FOUR

MISSOURI

I

The Mormon town of Far West, in Caldwell County, Missouri, stood almost in the center of a rough triangle formed by the Missouri River on the west and south and the Grand River on the northeast. At the southwest angle, where the Missouri turned eastward toward St. Louis, stood the frontier cities of Independence and Liberty, one on each side of the river. Within the eastern angle, where the Grand flowed into the Missouri, was DeWitt, a settlement which still harbored some of the Mormons driven from Jackson County in 1833. At the top of the triangle, in Davies County, the Mormons established another town, which they called Adam-ondi-Ahman, for it was here (Joseph Smith announced) that Adam had settled after his expulsion from the Garden of Eden. Almost exactly between Far West and Adam-ondi-Ahman was Gallatin, the county seat of Davies County.

At the time of Joseph's arrival in 1838 there were approximately ten thousand Mormons in the Missouri settlements. The number almost doubled during the year. Joseph was soon joined in Far West by Sidney Rigdon. His second councilor, Dr. Williams, had apostatized after the bank failure, and he was replaced by Joseph's brother Hyrum. Even the Council of the Twelve had been depleted, but new appointments were made to fill the vacancies. Thomas B. Marsh was still at the head of the council, followed by David Patten and Brigham Young. The old councils of Kirtland and Independence had been dissolved. The ruling council included Heber Kimball, still away in England as a missionary; the Pratt brothers, Parley and Orson; and the fiery Lyman Wight, who had led Zion's Camp four years before.

Brigham Young settled his family on property granted him a few miles outside Far West, on Mill Creek. After the years of bickering in Ohio, the calm industry of the early spring in Missouri must have made the country seem indeed the gathering place of Israel. The land was less fertile here than in Ohio, less valuable than their first location at Independence, but it was beautiful, rolling country, surely a bequest from heaven.

Missouri must have seemed secure that spring of 1838. The Mormons had their own county, Caldwell, their own officers, their own militia. It was true that there were some isolated settlements of Mormons in other counties, but why should that matter? The saints were law-abiding citizens, and in those days it seemed unlikely that a few thousand Mormons could arouse the old antagonism. It was true, too, that the Mormons had begun to build up Adam-ondi-Ahman in Davies County, but Davies County was far to the north and sparsely settled; there were few old settlers to contend with, and the Mormons could grow up with the country.

Already Joseph had announced plans for a new temple in Far West. With the apostates absent and excommunicated, with enemies distant, it seemed now as though the gathering Joseph had talked about so much would finally begin to take shape.

It was a time for re-examination and reassessment of faith in the leadership of Joseph Smith and the religious and social principles which he had given the saints. What directions such thinking took may be judged by some of Brigham Young's later sermons.

At the center of Brigham's beliefs was Joseph's concept of the gathering of the saints. "Except ye are one, ye are not mine," the Lord had told Joseph Smith. But how was this oneness—this unity —to be accomplished? "The religion of heaven unites the hearts of the people and makes them one," Brigham said. "How is it that the Latter-day Saints feel and understand alike, are of one heart and one mind, no matter where they may be when they receive the gospel, whether in the north or the south, the east or the west, even to the uttermost parts of the earth? They receive that which was promised by the Savior . . . namely, . . . that holy unction from on high which recognizes one God, one faith, one baptism, whose mind is the will of God the Father, in Whom there dwelleth unity of faith and action, and in Whom there cannot be division or confusion; when they received this further light, it mattered not whether they have seen each other or not, having been adopted into the family of Christ through the bonds of the everlasting covenant."

In contrast with the kingdom, Brigham saw the gentile world as one of disintegration. "The world of mankind have taken a course to alienate the feelings of each other," he said; "they have destroyed the little fellowship and confidence that were formerly placed in man towards his fellow man. . . . With few exceptions, none dare trust his neighbor, and we have to restore that confidence which has been lost."

The Kingdom of God was the gathering of the saints, here and now, in the final dispensation of time, but it was also an attempt to recapture the righteousness of the City of Enoch, which was so perfect that it was gathered bodily into the heavens, as well as to obtain a foretaste of the City of Heaven. Why were the saints put here on earth? "They are here," Brigham said, "to increase and multiply, to enlarge, to gather the House of Israel, redeem Zion, build up the Zion of our God, and to promote that eternal intelligence that dwells with the gods, and begin to plant it in this earth, and make it root downward and bring forth fruit upward to the glory of God, until every obnoxious principle in the hearts of men is destroyed, and the earth returns to its paradisaical state, and the Lord comes and dwells with this people, and walks and talks with them as He did with Father Adam." This cannot be, he added, "until the people are better organized in a temporal point of view, that all their temporal actions may point to the building up of the Kingdom of God, when no man will say that aught he possesses is his own, but hold it only for the interest and good of the whole community of the saints."

He went on to say that man was fashioned in the image of God. Indeed God was our father—our actual father. Adam and Abraham and Jacob and Moses and Christ were our elder brothers. It is true that Christ was begotten in the spirit; but what is spirit? Spirit—like matter—has shape, outline, form for those who have the power to see. We have the testimony of the Scriptures that spirits have been seen by men. God was visible before the tent of Abraham; Jacob wrestled with an angel; even doubting Thomas, when he was not fully convinced that he had seen the risen Christ, was allowed to touch His wounds. What difference, then, whether such a being be called spirit or matter?

The difference was that spirit existed in eternity; matter was subject to death and corruption. Brigham devoted much thought to this subject, for it was the kind of problem that made Joseph's beliefs a living religion for him, the kind of thought that brought man nearer to the state of perfection in which God lived. He was prepared, a few years later, to discuss it with his fellow saints.

Our bodies are composed of visible, tangible matter, as you all understand; you also know that they are born into this world. They then begin to partake of the elements adapted to their organization and growth, increase to manhood, become old, decay, and pass again into dust. Now in the first place, though I have explained this many times, what we call death is the operation of life, inherent in the matter of which the body is composed, and which causes the decomposition after the spirit has left the body. . . .

What is commonly called death does not destroy the body, it only causes a separation of spirit and body, but the principle of life, inherent in the native elements, of which the body is composed, still continues with the particles of that body and causes it to decay, to dissolve itself into the elements of which it was composed, and all of which continues to have life. . . . There is not a particle of element which is not filled with life, and all space is filled with element; there is no such thing as empty space, though some philosophers contend that there is.

Life in various proportions, combinations, conditions, etcetera, fills all matter. . . . It is in the rock, the sand, the dust, in water, air, the gases, and in short, in every description and organization of matter, whether it be solid, liquid, or gaseous, particle operating with particle.

I have heard philosophers argue that because no body could move without displacing matter, therefore there must be empty space. That reasoning is nonsense to me, because eternity is, was, and will continue to be full of matter and life. We put a ship in motion on the water, and have we created an empty space? No, we have only changed the position of matter. Men and animals move upon the earth, birds and fishes cleave the elements they are organized to operate in, but do they leave a track of empty space? No, for all eternity is full of matter and life. . . . By way of illustration I will quote one passage from the Book of Job, who in his affliction was visited by several friends, and after he had concluded that they were all miserable comforters, he exclaimed, "Though worms destroy this body, yet in my flesh shall I see God." To make this passage clearer to your comprehension, I will paraphrase it, Though my spirit leave my body, and though worms destroy its present organization, yet in the morning of the resurrection I shall behold the face of my Savior, in this same tabernacle; that is my idea of the idea so briefly expressed by Job.

Of even more importance, Joseph had taught that the end was not merely spiritual existence. The journey from eternity (pre-existence), through time (this world), and into eternity (after-existence), was the progression from a spiritual existence to a material one, and from material existence to a transformation which might end even in godhood. The present world, Brigham said, "is a world in which we are to prove ourselves. The lifetime of man is a day of trial, wherein we may prove to God, in our darkness, in our weakness, and where the enemy reigns, that we are our Father's friends, and that we receive light from Him and are worthy to be leaders of our children—to become lords of lords, and kings of kings—to have perfect dominion over that portion of our families that will be crowned in the celestial kingdom with glory, immortality, and eternal lives." Again: "I believe in a God who has power to exalt and glorify all who believe in Him, and are faithful in serving Him to the end of their lives, for this makes them God, even the sons of God, and in this sense there are Gods many."

Brigham Young had spent the past year convincing his brethren that they should stand by their prophet. If you give up Joseph, he had told them, you give up the authority of heaven, you are lost, and you will sink yourselves to hell. What are a few acres of earth in Ohio or Missouri compared with the glories of eternity? Of what use to you is peace with your neighbors if thereby you lose heaven?

But not all the saints had been as loyal to their leader as was the man who was destined to succeed him. Joseph had told them for several years that Missouri was the gathering place. They had refused to listen. He had told them their society was a proving ground for faith and for the increase of knowledge. Instead of listening, they had quarreled and bickered among themselves. Now, here they were in Missouri. How had they got there? It was as though some force not their own had impelled them. Impatient at their procrastinations, the power of heaven had ejected them from the sloth and ease of Kirtland and deposited them here on the prairies—on the frontier.

Sidney Rigdon had been plunged into despair by the failure at Kirtland. Joseph had feared that his cause was lost when he left Ohio, but the welcome he received upon his arrival at Far West revived in him the old faith in himself and his followers. Within a few days he was moving about the little community with his usual assurance, his head filled with plans for the reconstuction of Zion. Rigdon too, when he arrived, had shaken off his gloom and his enfeebling illness. He was thinner, his eyes more deep-set, the gaunt look of his face more settled, his mind seething with resentment against his enemies.

Never was the contrast between the two men more marked. Joseph's mind and body were supple, resilient, youthful. Sidney was brooding, brittle, and filled to overflowing with prophetic wrath. They were agreed on one thing—the need to strengthen the defenses of the saints. The Mormons were still a minority in Missouri, and feeling in the state continued to run high against them. An old enemy from Jackson County, Lillburn Boggs, had become governor on an anti-Mormon platform. They could count on no assistance from his administration. On the other hand, they had their rights under the constitution, they were all together in one place for the first time, and they were united more than they had ever been before.

The first need was for economic order, and the stubborn hand of Sidney Rigdon may be seen in the earliest proposal—a plan very much like the one that had caused so much trouble in the early days of Kirtland. He would ask all the saints to deed their property to the church, after which it would be redistributed to them according to the size of each family. From this land, given as an "inheritance," they would henceforth pay one-tenth of the proceeds as tithing. There were objections to this proposal, partly because the saints remembered their earlier difficulties with the Order of Enoch, partly because there was difficulty determining the ownership of much of the land. A revised plan was then proposed, one which bears more closely the marks of Joseph's imagination. The saints would not be asked to transfer title, but simply to lease their land to the church. Upon this land a cooperative system of corporations would be established. The economy would be divided into bodies of farmers, mechanics, laborers, artisans, and storekeepers, with each man contributing his special skill for the common good.

As spring came to the Missouri hills, Joseph's old optimism returned. As nature renewed herself, so did the spirits of the saints. In order that they should not lose this new energy and faith, Joseph joined them in entertainments and dancing. He instituted wrestling matches for the young men, and he himself stripped to the waist and challenged all comers.

With the return of hope, the dream of Zion returned to the weatherbeaten faces of the older members; it was more deeply instilled in the minds of the young. The faith that life like this could go on again, and go on indefinitely, flooded with the tide of spring. The spirit of revelation returned to Joseph. He predicted great things for the community on the Western plains:

Let the city, Far West, be a holy and consecrated land unto me; and it shall be called most holy, for the ground upon which thou standest is holy.

It was not enough merely to till the soil and raise homes and give birth to children. "Man is that he might have joy," Joseph had taught them, but there was no joy without labor:

Therefore, I command you to build a house unto me, for the gathering together of my saints that they may worship me.

And let there be a beginning of this work, and a foundation, and a preparatory work, this following summer;

And let the beginning be made on the fourth of July next; and from that time forth let my people labor diligently to build a house unto my name;

And one year from this day let them recommence laying the foundation of my house.

While Joseph overflowed with hope and energy, Sidney Rigdon could still not contain his wrath. He had never been able to bring himself wholly to accept Joseph's levity, the wrestling, the singing, and the dancing. He saw that many of the objections to his plan for re-establishing a communal system had come from a few apostates who had hurried away from Kirtland, settled in Missouri, taken up the choicest land, and who now refused to share. He moved about the settlement, a prophet of doom, and Joseph's occasional joke at his expense served only to darken the brooding hatred he felt for all apostates and gentiles.

On June 17 he stood before the congregation at Far West and delivered himself of a portion of the animosity that had gathered within him.

" 'Ye are the salt of the earth,' " he thundered at the saints, " 'but if the salt hath lost its savor, wherewith shall the earth be salted? It is henceforth good for nothing but to be cast out and trodden under foot of man.' . . . We have proved the world with kindness, we have suffered their abuse without cause, with patience, and have endured without resentment, until this day, and still their persecution and violence does not cease. But from this day and this hour, we will suffer it no more."

He referred to the apostates who had plotted against them at Kirt-land—the Whitmers, Oliver Cowdery, and Lyman Johnson—who had run away from Kirtland, then tried to stir up dissension in

Missouri. For more than an hour he harangued, his ire growing with each sentence. Finally he concluded in a tone of passionate intensity.

"If the county cannot be freed of these men in any other way," he shouted, "I will assist to trample them down or erect a gallows on the square of Far West and hang them up as they did the gamblers at Vicksburg, and it would be an act at which the angels would smile with approbation."

His angry words aroused the congregation so that Joseph had to get up and warn them against taking justice into their own hands. Rigdon's words frightened many of the apostates away from Far West, but it did nothing to alleviate the old fears of the native Missourians, who now became more convinced than ever that the Mormons intended to use violence in the preservation of their kingdom.

With the recurrence of ill feeling between Mormons and non-Mormons, a relatively new convert came forward with a plan to form a secret military organization within the ranks of the Mormons —a picked group of militiamen to be known as the Sons of Dan, or, more popularly later, the Danites. This new convert was Sampson Avard, a man later described as "cunning, resourceful, and extremely ambitious." Avard played upon the feelings aroused by Rigdon's "Salt Sermon"—as it became known. The name of his organization was taken from a passage in Genesis which says: "Dan shall be a serpent by the way, an adder in the path, that biteth the horse's heels, so that his rider shall fall backward." The Danites were to enlist the youngest, the rashest, and the most vigorous of the Mormons as an élite corps which would serve secretly within the regular militia. They would act not as a group, but as individuals who could be called forth by their leaders to effect swift and immediate revenge for any act of violence practiced against the saints.

It seems clear that Sidney Rigdon knew more than Joseph about the activities of Avard's band, more than any of the leaders except David Patten and Lyman Wight, both of whom seem to have been members of the band. The aim of the group, in any case, came nearer to expressing Rigdon's outraged and fanatical anger than it did to representing any of the other Mormons except a few of the hot-blooded young men, who seemed determined to meet violence with violence.

Less than a month after Rigdon gave his Salt Sermon he again took the platform, to deliver a Fourth of July oration. He took as his text the lines, "Better, far better, to sleep with the dead than be oppressed among the living." As the saints grouped themselves about the liberty pole they had erected on the square, he delivered a speech which began as a mild defense of American liberties, but which grew in heat and anger as he recalled the violations of his own and his people's liberties. He told his hearers that the next band of ruffians to come against the Mormons would find themselves engaged in a war of extermination. "For we will follow them till the last drop of blood is spilled, or else they will have to exterminate us; for we will carry the seat of war to their own houses and their own families, and one party or the other shall be utterly destroyed. Remember it then, all men! We shall never be aggressors; we will infringe on the rights of no people, but shall stand for our own until death." Finally, in a full burst of enthusiasm, he announced, "We this day then proclaim ourselves free, with a purpose and a determination that never can be broken— No never! no never!! no never!!!"

The crowd, carried away by his words and his feeling, broke into cheers and shouts of "Hosanna, hosanna to God and the Lamb!"

Three days after the speech a violent thunder-and-lightning storm appeared and rattled the surrounding countryside. In Far West a brilliant flash appeared, thunder cracked, and when the saints again looked toward the public square they saw their liberty pole in splinters. Descriptions of this event appear in most Mormon journals. One Mormon recorded that Joseph Smith was among the first to reach the scene. He walked round and round the pole, examining the damage. Finally he looked at his awestruck people and said, "As that pole was splintered, so shall the nations of the earth be."

A fear closer to the minds of the saints was expressed by someone far back in the crowd of onlookers. As the curious stood, examining the pole, turning over in their minds the words of their prophet, his call came ringing above their heads.

"Farewell!" he shouted. "Farewell to our liberties in Missouri!"

2

A state election had been scheduled for August 6. In Davies County the gentiles had announced that no Mormon in that county would be allowed at the polls. On the morning of the day, thirty Mormons, most of them young men, arrived at the polls in Gallatin for the election. About a hundred Missourians were there before them, listening to one of the candidates, William Peniston, fulminate against the Mormons from the top of a whisky barrel.

"They are thieves, and knaves, and dupes," Peniston shouted. "If they continue to pour into the county, no man's rights or his property will be safe."

One of the Mormons made a move toward the polls. His way was barred. "Mormons don't vote no more'n niggers," a Missourian told him.

When the Mormon moved again, he was knocked down. As he got to his feet he raised his hand to his face. This was the Danite signal of distress. The remainder of the Mormons had moved beside a pile of ash billets of a size convenient for use as clubs. Now each picked up a club and jumped to his brother's defense. The fight was violent but short. Within a few seconds nine of the Missourians lay stretched on the ground; the others ran. The thirty Mormons walked into the polls and cast their votes.

This was not an unusual incident for a frontier polling place, particularly with whisky flowing and feelings running high. What was different in Davies County was that the antagonists were Mormons and gentiles. When news of the fight, including the rumor that two Mormons had been killed, reached Far West, Joseph Smith took a company of the Caldwell militia and rode toward the northern border of the county. Missourians elsewhere heard that two gentiles had been killed by Mormons. When Joseph reached the border of the county with his troops, he discovered that both stories were exaggerations, but he continued on to the home of the nearest justice of the peace and obtained the following certificate:

I Adam Blak a Justice of the Peace of Davies County, do hereby Sertify to the people coled Mormin, that he is bound to suport the Constitution of this State, and of the United State, and he is not attached to any mob, nor will he attach himself to any such people, and so long as they will not molest me, I will not molest them. This is the 8th day of August 1838.

No sooner had Joseph left Black's house than the justice rushed to Gallatin and announced that Joe Smith had arrived with a troop of horsemen from Caldwell County, and had threatened him and coerced him into signing a document saying that he would protect the Mormons. Joseph himself went to Adam-ondi-Ahman, where he met Lyman Wight, who had settled nearby, and proposed a meeting between him, as the Mormon leader in Davies County, and the newly elected state officials, with a view to working out ways to preserve the peace.

The meeting was held, but rumor had already spread beyond the confines of the county. Everywhere in Missouri the old settlers heard the exaggerated accounts of the fight at Gallatin; then of Joseph Smith's marching across the border of the county with a company of militia. Even in faraway Jackson County men began to gather and to revive the old talk about getting rid of the Mormons. In Carroll County mobs gathered and threatened the smaller Mormon settlements near DeWitt. Two days later William Peniston, the candidate who had provoked the affray at Gallatin, swore out a writ for Joseph's arrest, charging him with violating the county border and coercing a justice of the peace.

Throughout the Mormon county of Caldwell the air became charged with the old tension. Mormon families who lived out of town began moving down the roads leading to Far West. Most of them merely repeated the old rumors, but some brought reports of new terrors, of threats uttered by bands of horsemen who had ridden into their yards and told them to get moving. In a few cases there had been beatings; a few had their houses or barns burned to the ground. Now they were on the road again, but this time they had Far West as a sanctuary, where they might rally to defend themselves.

On August 30 Governor Boggs ordered out the state militia. For a time it seemed as though this action might enforce peace. The commanding officer was General Atchison of the law firm which the Mormons had earlier engaged. He convinced Joseph Smith that he had nothing to fear from a trial over Peniston's charges, and Joseph agreed to go to Davies County under his protection.

The trial was held just across the border in Davies County. No decision was handed down, but Joseph was put under a peace bond by the judge.

Meanwhile the Mormons were attacked by strong forces at their two principal settlements in Carroll and Davies counties, DeWitt and Adam-ondi-Ahman. Little damage was done in the attacks, but the attackers settled down to besiege the two communities, content to keep them from bringing in supplies from their fields or reinforcements from Caldwell County. When Mormons did venture outside to forage food for their families, they were beaten by the Missourians.

Joseph did not make an immediate attempt to relieve his brethren at these settlements, because he had promised General Atchison that he would use his militia only in self-defense. Atchison's law partner, Colonel Doniphan, was at that time making a strong effort to persuade the old settlers of Davies County to sell out to the Mormons. He seemed on the verge of success until events in Carroll County defeated him. The settlers of Carroll County demanded that the Mormons vacate DeWitt by October 1. When the saints refused, the Missourians resumed their attack. They outnumbered the Mormons ten to one, and the Mormons, who feared their enemies across the river in Jackson County more than they did the forces they faced, finally capitulated. They had no choice but to abandon their homes and property—some of which they had owned since the expulsion from Independence three years before. They were driven from the town and allowed to flee northwestward, into Caldwell County and Far West.

The Missourians' success in Carroll County emboldened the old settlers of Davies County and broke down the efforts of Doniphan to conciliate.

"To hell with compromise!" they shouted. "To hell with Doniphan's peace settlement!"

It was at this time that Brigham moved his own family into Far West. He was there when the DeWitt settlers made their pathetic entry into the city, and his own anger matched that of the prophet. This was what happened, Joseph noted bitterly to his council, when the Mormons withheld their forces and attempted to come to terms with the gentiles. He called all the saints together and addressed them in the strongest language he had yet used. He began by reviewing their troubles in Missouri. Then he related all the attempts the Mormons had made to come to a peaceful settlement.

"The latest reply of Boggs to our petition is to tell us to fight our own battles," he told them, his voice charged with anger. "And that, brethren, is exactly what we intend to do."

He went on to say that Doniphan had authorized their army to serve as a regiment of the state militia. Tomorrow he planned to march them to the relief of the settlers of Adam-ondi-Ahman.

The Mormons were two hundred and fifty men by the time they reached Davies County. Gentile spies rushed through the county, announcing that Wight and Hinkle (the military leaders of the Mormons in Davies and Carroll counties) were marching against them with fifteen thousand men. The Missourians' opposition before Adam-ondi-Ahman vanished. The Mormons marched unopposed into their second largest stronghold.

But the anger that the Mormons had been building up against their enemies could not be satisfied with so easy a victory. The bulk of the forces went out in search of the gentile opposition. They marched through three settlements, including Gallatin, repaying the Missourians in kind, looting and firing stores, homes, and barns, before their anger spent itself. Members of the military force, many of whom had lost homes and property to their enemies, considered their own acts and booty no more than just repayment for what they had suffered.

When they returned with their loot, many of their own people were appalled and frightened. Thomas B. Marsh, Brigham's superior as President of the Twelve, let it be known that he did not approve such retaliation, and he left the church.

The attacks on the gentile settlements brought about still more reprisals, and within a few days almost every Mormon home lying beyond the protection of the army was leveled by gentile mobs. In Far West the next night, after everyone except a few guards had gone to bed, the big bass drum in the square sounded an alarm. Men tumbled from their beds and hastened toward the central meeting place, imagining that there was an attack on Far West itself. There was not. Reports had come that the Davies County militia had illegally crossed the border into Caldwell County and captured two Mormons. Rumor said that they were to be shot at eight in the morning.

Joseph called for volunteers to go to the rescue. In a few minutes forty mounted men, under the command of David Patten, who had earned the nickname "Captain Fearnot," were on their way to Crooked River, where the enemy troops were said to be encamped. The distance was twenty miles, and they reached the camp-ground just before sunup. They dismounted and started for the gentile camp on foot. As they approached, a shot rang out, and one Mormon fell. The remainder divided into two groups and charged from opposite directions. In the fight that followed, two more Mormons and one gentile were killed. One of the Mormons was their leader, David Patten, whom the Mormons even today look upon as their first martyred apostle.

No sooner had the battle ended than a rumor spread that the entire gentile company of fifty men had been wiped out by the Mormons. Frantic appeals were sent to the governor. Governor Boggs, although he had done nothing to halt the depredations against the Mormons, now replaced General Atchison (whom he may have considered too friendly to the Mormons) with General John B. Clark and ordered the entire force of the Missouri militia to march against the Mormons at Far West.

His order—which has since become known as "the extermination order"—stated that the Mormons must be treated as enemies of the state. "They must be exterminated or driven from Missouri, if necessary for the public good." The Mormons, unaware of the order, made preparations for the defense of their homes. They knew that something unusual threatened. They tore down cabins and threw up breastworks about the settlement. They reorganized their own forces. When word was brought that the gentile militia was approaching, the Mormons were astonished at the size of the force. Estimates ran as high as ten thousand men. The first group to arrive and face the city was a company under the command of Major General Lucas, one of their old enemies from Independence. He was soon joined by companies under Doniphan and Clark.

Learning that Doniphan was present and realizing that the Mormons had no chance against such a force, Joseph decided to sue for a peaceful settlement. Fearing what might happen if he entered the enemy camp in person, he sent Colonel George M. Hinkle, his former commander at DeWitt, to learn General Clark's terms. What happened in the camp of the militia after Hinkle's arrival has never been told. He was probably offered his own safety in exchange for a betrayal of the Mormons. He returned to Far West and announced that Lucas would meet with Joseph and a certain number of Mormon leaders under a flag of truce. When Joseph and his men arrived in Lucas's camp they were shown an agreement that Hinkle had signed which stipulated that all the Mormon leaders would be surrendered to stand trial for treason, that all Mormon property would be confiscated to repay the gentiles for their losses, that all Mormon arms would be surrendered, and that all Mormons would move peacefully from the state. Joseph was astonished. He protested that Hinkle had no authority to sign such an agreement. Nevertheless, he and his leaders were seized and put under arrest. Among them were Sidney Rigdon and Hyrum Smith, Joseph's two councilors in the first presidency. Lyman Wight was there, as was Parley Pratt, both well known to the Missourians. Brigham Young was not, nor was Heber Kimball. Brigham's activities had been too little noticed by the gentiles, and Heber had just returned from his mission abroad. The prisoners were told that they would be tried by court martial the next morning.

Parley P. Pratt described the first night's imprisonment:

In the camp we were placed under strong guard, and were without shelter during the night; lying on the ground in the open air, in the midst of a great rain. The guards during the whole night kept up a constant tirade of mockery, and the most obscene blackguardism and abuse. They blasphemed God; mocked Jesus Christ; swore the most dreadful oaths; taunted Brother Joseph and others; demanded miracles; wanted signs, such as: "Come on, Mr. Smith, show us an angel." "Give us one of your revelations." "Show us a miracle." "Come, there is one of your brethren here whom we took prisoner yesterday in his own house, and knocked his brains out with his own rifle, which we found hanging over his fireplace; he lays speechless and dying; speak the word and heal him, and then we will believe." "Or, if you are apostles or men of God, deliver yourselves, and then we will be Mormons."

When they stood before the court martial in the morning, the charges against them were reviewed summarily; Lucas found them guilty of treason and sentenced them to death. He sent Doniphan the order:

Sir—You will take Joseph Smith and the other prisoners into the public square of Far West, and shoot them at 9 o'clock tomorrow morning.

Doniphan knew the Mormons well. He replied in terms which halted the hot-headed Lucas:

It is cold blooded murder. I will not obey your order. My brigade shall march for Liberty tomorrow morning at 8 o'clock, and if you execute these men, I will hold you responsible before an earthly tribunal, so help me God.

In Far West the Mormons were left in ignorance concerning their leaders. In the morning the soldiers entered the town and ordered all the men into the public square. They lined them up and marched them to a nearby ravine, where they were told that if they tried to escape they would be shot. The warning was reinforced by

artillery pieces on both hillsides, and a strong guard was placed
about the men. During the remainder of the day they were taunted
and ridiculed, not only by the gentile soldiers but by some of their
apostate brethren. William McLellin, who had been a member of
the Twelve and who was later to sue for reinstatement in the
church, came up to Heber C. Kimball.

"What do you think of Joseph Smith, the fallen prophet, now?"
he asked. "Has he not led you blindfolded long enough? Look and
see yourself poor, your family stripped and robbed, and your brethren in the same fix. Are you not satisfied with Joseph?"

"Yes," Heber replied angrily. "I am more satisfied a hundredfold
than I was before; for I see you in the very condition that he foretold you would be in—a Judas to betray your brethren."

General Clark arrived in the afternoon. He moved the Mormons
into a hollow square formed by his companies of militiamen. He
read a list of fifty-six men whom, he said, he would hold prisoner.
The remainder would be free to go, but they were not to assemble
in groups of more than five at a time. If they did they would be attacked. He read them the agreement signed by Hinkle, and there
was a murmur of surprise. This was the first time most of them had
heard of it.

"There is no alternative for you but to flee," the general told
them. "You need not expect any redress. There is none for you."

He left no doubt in their minds about his own attitude toward
them or their leaders:

If you remain—if I am called here again . . . do not think I will
do as I have done now. You need not expect any mercy, but extermination, for I am determined the government order shall be
executed. As for your leaders, do not think, do not imagine for a
moment, do not let it enter your minds, that they will be delivered
and restored to you again, for their fate is fixed, their die is cast,
their doom is sealed.

Once again the Mormons were disarmed and at the mercy of
their enemies. General Clark was right on one count; there was no
alternative for them but to flee. But where to flee? And how? Many
of their men were still prisoners, and those who were not were de-

fenseless. During the first week after General Clark's arrival, several thousand Missourians visited the city of Far West. Mormon women were dragged from the streets into the schoolhouse, tied to benches, and raped. Cattle and hogs were shot for sport, then left to rot in the streets. Heber Kimball reported that "one mobber drove up, and finding no convenient place to fasten his horse to, shot a cow that was standing near, while a girl was milking her, and while the poor animal was struggling in death, he cut a strip of her hide from the nose to her tail, to which he fastened his halter."

3

General Clark, in his determination to destroy the Mormons, made one serious mistake. He did not include the name of Brigham Young among those who were to be taken prisoner. With Joseph and the first presidency under arrest, with David Patten dead and Thomas B. Marsh an apostate, Brigham was now the leading authority of the Mormon church.

On the night following Joseph's arrest Brigham received a message saying that Hyrum Smith was in the city for a few minutes and wanted to speak with him. The gentle Hyrum had won the sympathy of one of the guards, and he had been allowed to return briefly to Far West to see how his family fared and to obtain clean linen. Brigham met him in the shadow of the trees on the square. Hyrum brought word from the prophet. Joseph said he did not know how long he would be kept prisoner. He placed the saints in Brigham's hand. Brigham should be their protector. Nothing could be gained now by fighting. They must attempt to get away from Missouri.

Brigham assured Hyrum that he would look after the members of the church. He would keep them together, and he would lead them north into Iowa Territory or east into Illinois. He would send Heber Kimball to check on the movements of the prisoners, to get word from them or to them, if the occasion arose. He would do what he could to effect their release.

Hyrum Smith left Brigham Young with a heavy burden. A few weeks before, there had been approximately twenty thousand Mormons in the state of Missouri. How many had deserted or apostatized Brigham could not know. His first problem was to organize those who were now in Far West. Then he would get word to the outlying settlements. Preparations must be made hastily, for winter was approaching. It would take the utmost in good will and cooperation if the saints were to move again. Even then, there would be heartache, suffering, and perhaps death traveling the trail with them.

In the days following General Clark's address, Brigham began calling the elders together a few at a time. He told them they must pledge themselves to get all their brethren out of Missouri. He made a count of those who had teams and wagons. They would go first, then return to assist others. The saints would pool their resources, and the responsibility of no man would end until the last Mormon was out of Missouri.

As preparations were under way, Brigham's brother Joseph came in with a tale of horror perpetrated by the Missourians at Haun's Mill, a Mormon settlement on Shoal Creek. Joseph Young had been on his way to Far West with a company of emigrants from Kirtland when he was first accosted by the gentiles. A group of Missourians had ridden up to the train, asked them if they were Mormons, and, when they answered that they were, had threatened them and ordered them to leave the state.

"Wherefore?" Joseph had asked them.

"Because you are damned Mormons."

"We are law-abiding Americans," he replied, "and have given no cause for offense."

"You are damned Mormons. That's offense enough," the Missourians told them. "Within ten days every Mormon must be out of Missouri, or men, women, and children will be shot down indiscriminately. No mercy will be shown. It is the order of the governor that you should all be exterminated; and by God you will be!"

Joseph's company had halted at Haun's Mill to debate what to do. The Mormons at the mill felt safe, because just a few days before they had made an agreement with the local Missouri settlers that there would be no violence on either side. Joseph's company pulled up a short distance beyond the mill and encamped. Almost immediately the settlement was attacked without warning. Joseph was near enough to view the whole tragedy.

On that fatal afternoon, he said, "the banks of Shoal Creek, on either side, teemed with children sporting and playing, while their mothers were engaged in domestic employments. Fathers or husbands were either on guard about the mills or other property, or employed in gathering crops for winter consumption. The weather was very pleasant, the sun shone clearly, and all was tranquil, and no one expressed any apprehension of the awful crisis that was near us—even at our doors."

Joseph was sitting before the open door of a cabin, a child in his arms, his wife standing beside him. At about four in the afternoon he noticed a body of men riding swiftly toward the settlement. As they approached they seemed to him to form themselves "into a three-square position—forming a vanguard in front." A Mormon who also saw them approaching shouted a warning to his brethren, then ran forward to sue for peace; but the horsemen did not stop. Many of the Mormons ran into the blacksmith shop; others fled to the woods. The Missourians opened fire, first aiming at those who were fleeing; then they rushed to the blacksmith shop and began firing through the crevices between the logs into the bodies crowded within. Joseph Young reported that there were two hundred and forty of the attackers, and that they seemed determined to leave none of the Mormons alive.

Among those who fled into the woods was Amanda Smith, and she left a moving account of her own experience:

I seized my two little girls and escaped across the mill-pond on a slab walk. Another sister fled with me. Yet though we were women, with tender children, in flight for our lives, the demons poured volley after volley to kill us.

A number of bullets entered my clothes, but I was not wounded. The sister, however, who was with me, cried out that she was hit. We had just reached the trunk of a fallen tree, over which I urged her, bidding her to shelter there where the bullets could not reach her, while I continued my flight to some bottom land.

When the firing had ceased I went back to the scene of the massacre, for there were my husband and three sons, of whose fate I as yet knew nothing.

As I returned I found the sister in a pool of blood where she had fainted, but she was only shot through the hand. Farther on was lying dead Brother McBride, an aged white-haired Revolutionary soldier. His murderer had literally cut him to pieces with an old corn-cutter. His hands had been split down when he raised them in supplication for mercy. Then the monster cleft open his head with the same weapon, and the veteran who had fought for his country, in the glorious days of the past, was numbered among the martyrs.

Passing on I came to a scene more terrible still to the mother and wife. Emerging from the blacksmith shop was my eldest son, bearing on his shoulder his little brother Alma.

"Oh, my Alma is dead!" I cried in anguish.

"No, mother; I think Alma is not dead. But father and brother Sardius are killed."

What an answer was this to appal me! My husband and son murdered; another little son seemingly mortally wounded; and perhaps before the dreadful night should pass the murderers would return and complete their work.

But I could not weep then. The fountain of tears was dry; the heart overburdened with its calamity, and all the mother's sense absorbed in its anxiety for the precious boy which God alone could save by his miraculous aid.

The entire hip joint of my wounded boy had been shot away. Flesh, hip bone, joint and all had been ploughed out from the muzzle of the gun which the ruffian placed to the child's hip through the logs of the shop and deliberately fired.

We laid little Alma on a bed in our tent and I examined the wound. It was a ghastly sight. I knew not what to do. It was night now.

There were none left from that terrible scene, throughout that long, dark night, but about half a dozen bereaved and lamenting women, and the children. Eighteen or nineteen, all grown men excepting my murdered boy and another about the same age, were dead or dying; several more of the men were wounded, hiding away, whose groans through the night too well disclosed their hiding places, while the rest of the men had fled, at the moment of the massacre, to save their lives. . . .

Yet was I there, all that long, dreadful night, with my dead and my wounded, and none but God as our physician and help.

Oh my Heavenly Father, I cried, what shall I do? Thou seest my poor wounded boy and knowest my inexperience. Oh Heavenly Father direct me what to do!

And then I was directed by a voice speaking to me.

The ashes of our fire was still smouldering. We had been burning the bark of the shagbark hickory. I was directed to take those ashes and make a lye and put a cloth saturated with it right into the wound. It hurt, but little Alma was too near dead to heed it much. Again and again I saturated the cloth and put it into the hole from which the hip-joint had been ploughed, and each time mashed flesh and splinters of bone came away with the cloth; and the wound became as white as chicken's flesh.

Having done as directed I again prayed to the Lord and was again instructed as distinctly as though a physician had been standing by speaking to me.

Near by was a slippery-elm tree. From this I was told to make a slippery-elm poultice and fill the wound with it.

My eldest boy was sent to get the slippery-elm from the roots, the poultice was made, and the wound, which took fully a quarter of a yard of linen to cover, so large was it, was properly dressed.

It was then I found vent to my feelings in tears, and resigned myself to the anguish of the hour. And all that night we, a few poor, stricken women, were thus left there with our dead and wounded. All through the night we heard the groans of the dying. Once in the darkness we crawled over the heap of dead in the blacksmith shop to try to help or soothe the sufferers' wants; once we followed the cries of a wounded brother who hid in some bushes from the murderers, and relieved him all we could.

Next morning brother Joseph Young came to the scene of the massacre.

"What shall be done with the dead?" he inquired, in horror and deep trouble.

There was not time to bury them, for the mob was coming on us. Neither were there left men to dig the graves. All the men excepting the two or three who had so narrowly escaped were dead or wounded. It had been no battle, but a massacre indeed.

"Do anything, Brother Joseph," I said, "rather than leave their bodies to the fiends who have killed them."

There was a deep dry well close by. Into this the bodies had to be hurried, eighteen or nineteen in number.

No funeral service could be performed, nor could they be buried with customary decency. The lives of those who in terror performed the last duty to the dead were in jeopardy. Every moment we expected to be fired upon by the fiends who we supposed were lying in ambush waiting the first opportunity to dispatch the remaining few who had escaped the slaughter of the preceding day. So in the hurry and terror of the moment some were thrown into the well head downwards and some feet downwards.

But when it came to the burial of my murdered boy Sardius, Brother Joseph Young, who was assisting to carry him on a board to the well, laid down the corpse and declared that he could not throw that boy into this horrible grave. . . .

There he lay until the next day, and then I, his mother, assisted by his elder brother, had to throw him into the well. Straw and earth were thrown into this rude vault to cover his body. . . .

The crawling of my boys under the bellows in the blacksmith's shop where the tragedy occurred, is an incident familiar to all our people. Alma's hip was shot away while thus hiding. Sardius was discovered after the massacre by the monsters who came in to despoil the bodies. The eldest, Willard, was not discovered. In cold blood, one Glaze, of Carroll county, presented a rifle near the head of Sardius and literally blew off the upper part of it, leaving the skull empty and dry while the brains and hair of the murdered boy were scattered around and on the walls.

At this one of the men, more merciful than the rest, observed: "It was a d——d shame to kill those little boys."

"D——n the difference!" retorted the other; "nits make lice!"

Of the thirty-eight residents of the settlement, seventeen were killed and fifteen seriously wounded. Despite Amanda Smith's fears, she remained on with a few other women to nurse the wounded. The Missourians sent word that if these Mormons were not out of the state by a certain date they would be killed. On the date specified, fifty armed men appeared. Amanda wrote:

I met them at the door. They demanded of me why I was not gone. I bade them enter and see their work. They crowded into the room and I showed them my wounded boy. They came, party after party, until all had seen my excuse. Then they quarreled among themselves and came near fighting.

At last they went away, all but two. These I thought were detailed to kill us. Then the two returned.

"Madam," said one, "have you any meat in the house?"

"No," was my reply.

"Could you dress a fat hog if one was laid at your door?"

"I think we could!" was my answer.

And then they went and caught a fat hog from a herd which had belonged to a now exiled brother, killed it and dragged it to my door, and departed.

These men, who had come to murder us, left on the threshold of our door a meat offering to atone for their repented intention.

Such tales as this Brigham heard in the midst of his preparation to leave the state. He decided to move toward Quincy, Illinois, a city above St. Louis, where he had heard there were expressions of sympathy for the Mormons. It was two hundred and fifty miles to Illinois, and the weather had turned cold.

The exodus from Missouri was the first test of Brigham Young's leadership. Fortitude and self-denial he had shown before. In Kirtland he had thrown the weight of his power of persuasion to the support of the prophet. Now he needed what he could not have known he possessed, a genius in organization sufficient to transport almost twenty thousand poverty-stricken men, women and children across a hostile territory in the cold of an approaching winter.

One of the first accidents occurred in his own family. Mary Ann and the children started out ahead, while Brigham remained behind to direct the operation. The roads were rutted and icy. Before they had gone far in the jolting wagon, his young daughter Mary was thrown from the top of the load. Her head fell beneath the wagon, and one of the wheels passed over it. Mary Ann leaped to the ground and discovered that her child's skull had been crushed. Taking her baby in her lap, the mother patiently molded the small broken skull back into shape, then continued the journey. Mary survived, but she was never well afterward, and she died a few years later.

In Far West, Brigham continued to keep track of the movements of Joseph Smith and the other prisoners, who were chained together in a single unheated cell in Richmond jail. They remained outwardly calm, but Joseph's real feelings had been expressed in a letter to his wife: "Oh Emma for God's sake do not forsake me nor the truth but remember me, if I do not meet you again in this life may God grant that we meet in heaven. I cannot express my feelings, my heart is full. Farewell, oh my kind and affectionate Emma, I am yours forever your husband and true friend."

Sidney Rigdon stood the imprisonment least well. He lay on the floor, shaking with fever, his gaunt frame unable to stand the rigors of the life into which his religion had led him. His mind escaped often into a more peaceful past, and then his companions heard him recalling scenes from the quiet days in Ohio, when the spirit had filled him only with exultation.

The gentile guards mocked their charges. They related accounts of their looting and raping at Far West and Haun's Mill. At one time their language became so foul that Joseph arose in a rage.

"Silence, ye fiends of the infernal pit! In the name of Jesus Christ I rebuke you, and command you to be still; I will not live another minute and hear such language. Cease such talk, or you or I die this instant!"

Parley P. Pratt remembered the incident as a moment of "dignity and majesty." The guards were, for the time being, restrained.

The charges brought against the prisoners were, "treason, murder, arson, burglary, robbery, larceny, and perjury." The judge assigned to their case was Austin A. King, a man who had but a week before written a letter to a Missouri newspaper accusing the Mormons of murder. Joseph's principal accusers were apostate Mormons such as Avard and Hinkle. Others had been members of the Missouri mobs. Whenever a loyal Mormon attempted to testify, he was immediately arrested or he was silenced by the judge.

"If a cohort of angels were to come down and declare you innocent," Joseph's attorney, Doniphan, told him, "it would make no difference, for King is determined to see you in prison."

The judge's chief interest seemed to be in the charge of treason. At one point in the hearing the Mormons were asked if they believed in the statement from the sixth chapter of Daniel, that the Kingdom of God would subdue all other kingdoms and stand forever. When the prisoners answered yes, they did believe that, Judge King turned eagerly to his clerk and said, "Write that down. It's a strong point for treason."

Doniphan, who despite threats of assassination continued to fulfill his legal contract with the Mormons, observed laconically, "Judge, you'd better make the Bible treason."

Doniphan could supply only six Mormons to testify, three of them women, but they had no sooner begun to speak favorably of Joseph Smith than they were interrupted by shouts of, "Put him out!" "Kick him out!" "God damn him, shoot him!" "Kill him, damn him, kill him!" "He's a damn Mormon!"

The most damaging testimony came from the apostates Hinkle and Avard. They testified that the Mormons had organized a secret military force to exact vengeance from their persecutors in the state.

Ten of the Mormon leaders were indicted. Six of them, including Joseph and Hyrum Smith and Sidney Rigdon, were moved to Liberty, in Clay County. They arrived November 30, 1838, and there they were destined to remain during the winter months, for their trial could not take place until April 1839.

The months between November and April were exactly the months of the Mormon exodus. Brigham Young did not leave until February, and when he did he passed many a weary Mormon caravan still on the road. Having completed the organization from the western end, he was now hurrying to Quincy to rally the saints who had already arrived in Illinois. He settled his family in a small town near Quincy, then continued his efforts to collect money and equipment to keep the emigration moving. On March 18 he called the Council of the Twelve together and told them to locate near Quincy for the present. He also read them a letter from Isaac Galland, a land agent, who had property he wanted to sell in Lee County, Iowa. Finally he reminded them that Joseph had prophesied the previous July that the cornerstone for the temple at Far West would be laid one year from that date. He astonished them with a proposal that the Twelve should return to Far West, hold a meeting on the temple site, and that they should lay the stone as Joseph had predicted.

Not all the apostles were convinced that so hazardous a project should be attempted. Most of the saints were away from Missouri now; let them not tempt fate any further. Even Joseph Smith's father was of the opinion that the Lord would not require so arduous an enterprise, considering their present condition; but Brigham, more than anyone else, recognized the temper of the incoming saints. What they needed now was a glimmer of hope, and words would no longer suffice.

On April 18 Brigham left Quincy with Orson Pratt, Wilford Woodruff, John Taylor, George A. Smith, and Alpheus Cutler, in two carriages bound again for the land of their enemies. On the way they met John Page, who was still en route to Illinois. His wagon was bottom-side up, all its contents spilled, including a barrel of soft soap. Page was squatting beside the road, scooping up the soap with his hands.

"Will you come with us?" Brigham asked.

Page said he didn't see how he could. He had to get his family to Illinois.

"I want you with us," Brigham told him.

"How long will you give me to get ready?" Page asked.

Brigham told him five minutes. Page's fellow apostles helped him to right and load the wagon. He drove it down the hill and set up a camp for his family. In little longer than five minutes he was on his way with them.

On the road they met company after company of departing Mormons. To each they gave news of their brethren in Illinois, while from them they received the rumors from Missouri. Each caravan the apostles met departed a little less dispirited than it had been upon meeting. Brigham told them the folks in Illinois were friendly and sympathetic. There were plans afoot to buy property. Zion would grow again and prosper.

The apostles reached Far West on April 24. They camped in a grove outside of town, and here they met first with the committee Brigham had appointed to remain and attend to the removal of the destitute, then with Heber Kimball, who gave them their first news of Joseph's trial. He told them, too, of events in Jefferson City, where members from the eastern counties were pressing for an investigation. It had been learned that at least one member of the legislature had been involved in the Haun's Mill massacre. The legislature had appropriated two thousand dollars to assist the Mormon emigration.

Two thousand dollars! Brigham could feel nothing but contempt for such paltry measures to assuage the consciences of the Missourians.

At daybreak on the morning of April 26 the Mormons assembled at the temple site. Prayer was offered, first by Brigham, then by each of the Twelve in the order of his standing. At the conclusion of their prayers, just as dawn was breaking, the assembled members sang their song in celebration of Zion—"Adam-ondi-Ahman."

> This earth was once a garden place,
> With all her glories common;
> And men did live a holy race,
> And worship Jesus face to face—
>   In Adam-ondi-Ahman.
>
> We read that Enoch walked with God,
> Above the power of Mammon;
> While Zion spread herself abroad,
> And saints and angels sang aloud—
>   In Adam-ondi-Ahman.
>
> Her land was good and greatly blessed,
> Beyond old Israel's Canaan;
> Her fame was known from east to west,
> Her peace was great, and pure her rest
>   Of Adam-ondi-Ahman.
>
> Hosanna to such days to come—
> The Savior's second coming,
> When all the world in glorious bloom
> Affords the saints a holy home,
>   Like Adam-ondi-Ahman.

The singing concluded, Alpheus Cutler, who had been appointed master workman for the temple, laid the southeast cornerstone in position. Joseph Smith's prophecy had been fulfilled.

On April 6 Joseph and his fellow prisoners had been removed from the Liberty jail and taken to Davies County for trial. Here the Mormon attorneys argued for a change of venue. They pointed out that it was in Davies County that the trouble began, but that there were no longer any Mormons there, only Missourians hostile to the prisoners. By now the lust for Mormon blood had receded. Since the legislative proceedings at Jefferson City in which it had come to light how cruel the measures were that the mobs had taken to expel the Mormons, the state authorities had become fearful of a full-scale investigation. Joseph's presence in prison had become less a satisfaction than an embarrassment. The change of venue was granted. The judge, in giving instructions for the prisoners' transfer, told the guards not to transport the prisoners to Boone County, the site of the new trial, but to "do as you please with them."

The guards, who, according to Hyrum Smith, had been drinking heavily, did not know whether this was an invitation to do away with their charges or encouragement to let them escape. Hyrum offered them a disguised bribe. They took Joseph's note for four hundred dollars, ostensibly in payment for their horses, then exchanged clothing with their prisoners and set them free. A few days later Heber Kimball redeemed the note from money collected by Brigham Young. By this time Joseph and Hyrum Smith were riding swiftly toward Illinois.

Brigham Young heard about the release while he was still in Missouri. By the time he got back to Quincy, Joseph was again at the head of the church. He had met Isaac Galland, the land agent, and begun negotiations for property on both sides of the Mississippi River, a few miles north of Quincy. Of the United States government, to whom he meant to appeal, Joseph wrote: "O Columbia, Columbia, how art thou fallen! The land of the free, the home of the brave!—the asylum of the oppressed—oppressing thy noblest sons in a loathsome dungeon, without any provocation, only that they have claimed to worship the God of their fathers, according to his own word, and the dictates of their own consciences!!!"

To his own people he wrote: "The keys of the kingdom have not been taken away from us, for verily thus saith the Lord, 'Be of good cheer, for the keys that I gave unto you are yet with you. . . . Zion shall yet live, though she seem to be dead.' "

CHAPTER FIVE

NAUVOO

I

When Brigham returned from Missouri with his fellow members of the Twelve, he found that Joseph had already purchased a farm for himself at Commerce, a small village lying on the east bank of the Mississippi, and he had moved his family there, begun a series of complicated dealings with the land agent Isaac Galland, and invited the saints to follow and take up land. Commerce was beautifully situated on the bend of the river, its land sloping gradually from the river bank to a height of about five hundred feet a half-mile east of Joseph's property. Brigham moved his own family northward and settled them in an abandoned military barracks on the Iowa side of the river. Almost the whole body of Mormons followed, and within a few weeks they had formed the beginnings of two flourishing communities, the larger one at Commerce, a smaller one at Montrose, Iowa, on the west bank.

Joseph's dealings with Isaac Galland began auspiciously. He negotiated first for $18,000 worth of land on the Illinois shore and $80,000 worth of property in Iowa across the river. The Mormons had left Missouri with only as much property as they could load into their wagons, but with them they carried the deeds to their land. These Joseph exchanged for the land in Illinois and Iowa. He then negotiated two further purchases worth $9000 and $53,000, signing the notes himself. He laid his Illinois community out in regular lots, as he had done at Kirtland and Far West, and charged each able-bodied Mormon $500 for them; those Mormons who had suffered the most in the Missouri persecution received their lots free. In all these dealings Isaac Galland acted as agent. He even joined the church and convinced Joseph that his actions were motivated only by good will and sympathy for the Mormons.

To see Joseph during those months in Illinois, no one would have imagined that he had just come from six months' imprisonment. Again his mind expanded with the old dream of a Zion laid out in regular squares, dominated by a great temple. The village of Commerce he renamed, for, he said, "It is a beautiful site, and it shall be called Nauvoo, which means in Hebrew a beautiful plantation." He had the land surveyed, locating the proposed temple on the brow of the hill, where it would overlook both the town and the river. He apportioned the lots below it impartially to the followers who flocked to him for advice and instruction.

Brigham Young's decision to purchase property on the west bank came from his belief that the Mormons would find it easier to settle the almost virgin land of Iowa than they would the Illinois property, where the situation was comparable to that in Missouri. The Iowa property had become known as the "half-breed tract," for it had been set aside by the government for the descendants of mixed marriages, but little of it had been taken up and actually settled. It had been sold and resold, traded at first by the original grantees for whatever they could get—a gun, a horse, blankets and supplies— sometimes sold to several buyers at the same time. It soon became clear that Galland's rights to this land could never be proved. Eventually almost all the Mormons who had settled on the Iowa side of the river, including Brigham's family, were forced to abandon their property and move back across the river into Illinois.

In Nauvoo the rights were also confused, but they proved finally to be secure. The greatest trouble the Mormons had was not in gaining title to the Nauvoo property, but in paying the exorbitant interest charged for the loans Joseph had negotiated through Galland. The situation was not improved when Galland absconded with one of the interest payments, amounting to several thousand dollars, and Joseph had to call upon the saints in the East, many of whom were selling their property and emigrating to Illinois, to assist him in paying off these debts.

Yet Nauvoo prospered, as had Kirtland and the Missouri settlements. Two hundred and fifty houses were built at Nauvoo alone during the first year. Unfortunately, the lowlands near the river were swampy and malarial. Fever broke out the first summer. The Mormons, weakened by persecution and their strenuous winter march, succumbed in great numbers. Among the victims were Joseph Smith's father and his younger brother, Don Carlos.

The residents of Illinois, aware of the injustices practiced upon the Mormons both in Independence and in the northern Missouri counties, were at first sympathetic and friendly. Rivals of the Missourians in the heated race for national recognition, they welcomed this influx of new settlers, particularly since they knew of the Mormons' reputation for industry and sobriety. Families in Quincy and the surrounding towns had taken in Mormon families and helped care for them when they arrived, destitute and suffering, from Caldwell County. Illinois newspapers had joined the Mormons in calling for a national investigation of the Haun's Mill massacre. The Illinois legislature, when it met, was quick to grant every request by the Mormons in their petition for a city charter for Nauvoo.

While still in Missouri, Joseph Smith had received Heber Kimball's report on the success of his mission to Great Britain. Converts in England had flocked to the Mormon call. Heber had left Willard Richards in charge of the rapidly growing branches across the Atlantic, and now the prophet was anxious to see the work prosper even more. He saw rightly the British conversions as a new reservoir of strength for the Mormon cause. Even at the moment when many of the saints were still suffering from the ravages of fever, he called Brigham and other members of the Twelve to him and announced that the Lord desired their presence in England. None of them had built a suitable home for his family; none had sufficient funds to undertake such a journey. Never mind, Joseph told them, the Lord would provide. They were to start at once.

Brigham's journal records the day of departure:

September 14, 1839—I started from Montrose on my mission to England. My health was so poor that I was unable to go thirty rods, to the river, without assistance. After I had crossed the river I got Israel Barlow to carry me on his horse behind him to Heber C. Kimball's, where I remained sick 'till the 18th. I left my wife sick, with a baby only ten days old, and all my children sick and unable to wait upon each other.

On September 17 Mary Ann heard that Brigham was lying ill at the Kimballs'. She crossed the river from Montrose and hired a boy to drive her the mile to the Kimball house. Although Brigham had not fully recovered, he was preparing to leave the next day. He did not even have an overcoat in which to begin his long trip across country. His wife insisted that he take something to protect him from the cold, and he picked up a ragged quilt and threw it across his shoulders.

The journey eastward was made in slow stages. Brigham traveled with George A. Smith, and he had but $13.50 in his purse. The two missionaries went first to Kirtland, where Brigham's brother John still lived, and he remained with his relatives for several weeks, visiting members who had not emigrated, urging them to a firmer faith, and recounting events of the past year in Missouri and Illinois.

Brigham possessed, when he got to Kirtland, only "a York shilling," he reported, but the saints took up a collection, and he was able to make the next stage of his journey by steamboat from Fairport Harbor to Buffalo. He left Kirtland on November 22, and arrived in Buffalo on the twenty-seventh. From there he traveled eastward into Massachusetts, stopping often to preach in branches he had helped establish as a missionary on earlier visits. In West Stockbridge he was conducting a meeting with George A. Smith when some local boys sneaked into the room and threw sulphur on the stove. They had to raise windows and open doors to get rid of the stench.

Brigham reported:

George A. said it was the first time he had been permitted to visit the state of Massachusetts. He had heard from his childhood of the refined morals, high state of Christianity and perfect order that reigned predominant in this state, and of the great missionary exertions made to civilize, moralize and Christianize almost every portion of the world. He said he had traveled in the west, north, and south; met in congregations of savages of the forest, and he had never seen so mean a breach of good order and decency before in his life. His first impression was that some sectarian preacher, a wholesale dealer in fire and brimstone, in making an exposition of his creed, had got so near hell that he had been unable to take all the brimstone away. At least, he considered himself in no danger of catching the itch in Massachusetts, for the smell of brimstone indicated it was thoroughly cured.

Brigham reached New York City, finally, on January 31, 1840. His problem now was to raise money for the passage to England. He located Parley P. Pratt, who had brought his family East with him, and whose home at 58 Mott Street provided a central meeting place for the missionaries. Part of Brigham's passage money came from donations from the saints, part from working at odd jobs as a carpenter and glazier. One of the members gave him an old "satinette" overcoat to replace the quilt which had served during the journey from Nauvoo. Brigham was ready to sail by March 9.

"We engaged passage for Liverpool on board the Patrick Henry," he reported,

a packet ship of the Black Ball line, Captain Delino, and paid eighteen dollars each for a steerage passage, furnished our own provisions and bedding and paid the cook one dollar each for cooking. Brother H. C. Kimball and myself occupied a lower berth, Brother Parley and Orson Pratt, the one over us, Brother George A. Smith and R. Hedlock, an upper berth at their feet; two Englishmen occupied the berth below. The brethren in New York furnished us with an ample supply of provisions by donation. The sisters made us ticks and filled them with straw for our beds and filled some bags with straw for our pillows.

The *Patrick Henry* docked at Liverpool on April 6. A few days later the apostles met at Preston for a conference. There were seven of them present, and their first business was to ordain Brigham's cousin, Willard Richards, to their council, bringing the re-

Joseph Smith, probably from a daguerreotype made at Nauvoo in 1843.
(Reprinted by permission of *The Improvement Era*)

Joseph Smith, from a lithograph made about 1850. (From *Route from Liverpool to Great Salt Lake Valley* by Frederick Piercy, Liverpool, 1855)

The Kirtland, Ohio, temple. Completed in 1837, it was the first of such temples built by the Mormons. It is still standing and in use as a church

Joseph Smith in his last public address as Lieutenant General of the Nauvoo Legion. (Reprinted by permission of *The Improvement Era*)

Nauvoo from an early print, with the temple dominating the right center.
(Reprinted by permission of *The Improvement Era*)

Ruins of the temple at Nauvoo after the exodus. (From *Route from Liverpool to Great Salt Lake Valley* by Frederick Piercy, Liverpool, 1855)

OLIVER COWDERY.

DAVID WHITMER.   MARTIN HARRIS.

Three leaders of the early Church of Jesus Christ of Latter-day Saints,
from a contemporary postcard

Brigham Young's house at Nauvoo. Built by him after his return from England, it is still in use as a family dwelling

Room in which Joseph and Hyrum Smith were held at Carthage, Illinois. (From *Route from Liverpool to Great Salt Lake Valley* by Frederick Piercy, Liverpool, 1855)

Kanesville. (From *Route from Liverpool to Great Salt Lake Valley* by
Frederick Piercy, Liverpool, 1855)

Great Salt Lake City in 1853. (From *Route from Liverpool to Great Salt
Lake Valley* by Frederick Piercy, Liverpool, 1855)

organized total in England to eight. It was also decided that a periodical should be established and edited by Parley P. Pratt, to be called the *Latter-day Saints Millennial Star*. A hymn book was to be prepared and printed, because, as Brigham reported to Joseph Smith in his first letter, "when we arrived here, we found the brethren had laid by their old hymn books, and they wanted new ones." John Taylor was to select and edit the hymns.

The work of the apostles succeeded even beyond the expectations raised by the success of the earlier missionaries and the continued ministrations of Willard Richards. When they arrived there were approximately fifteen hundred Mormons in Great Britain. By the time Brigham left, a little more than a year later, the number had risen to five thousand, and within the next decade they were to reach an all-time high of thirty thousand.

Brigham and his companions preached in the churches and in homes when they were invited, on street corners and in parks when they were not. The message which Brigham took to England, as he explained later, was "that there are doubtless millions of just as honest people among the several religious denominations as are amongst the professedly Latter-day Saints. But they have not the gospel, they are in darkness with regard to the plan of salvation, and their teachers are blind guides, totally unable to give the people the living word, the way of life."

Such words did not fall pleasantly upon the ears of the Anglican, the Methodist, or the Presbyterian ministry, and the missionaries found their greatest opposition among the clergy. An incident which Brigham related to illustrate both their difficulty and their success occurred in Manchester on November 8. "I had organized the priesthood in Manchester," he said, "to meet every Sabbath morning and distribute themselves throughout the different parts of the city to preach in the streets. In this way they occupied about forty preaching stations, at each one of which the congregation were notified of our regular meetings in Carpenter's Hall. This so annoyed the sectarians, particularly the Methodists, that they made complaints to the mayor, who issued an order to have all the street preachers arrested. I went to the priesthood meeting in the morning and felt impressed to tell the brethren to go home. The police, who had been instructed to arrest all street preachers that morning, took up twenty, who all proved to be Methodists. When the magistrate learned they were not 'Mormons,' they were dismissed."

Most of the Mormon conversions were made among the poorer classes. As Brigham explained, "We gather those who are poor, who wish to be redeemed; who feel the oppression the high and the proud have made them endure. . . . Take those who are in the enjoyment of all the luxuries of this life, and their ears are stopped up; they cannot hear."

Preaching and proselyting did not occupy all the time and energy of Brigham and his companions. Willard Richards had been a relatively new convert at the time he came to England. He had kept in touch with the various branches organized before Heber Kimball's departure in 1838. Now Brigham undertook to establish councils and organize the local missionaries. Conferences were held in all the principal cities of England, Scotland, and Wales, and here authority was established and the affairs of the various branches put in order. Brigham also undertook to begin the orderly emigration of those members who wished to gather with the saints in Nauvoo. He chartered vessels to carry none but Mormon passengers, and arranged the details so well that Parliament later investigated his plan to see if they could not learn from it a more efficient means of sending out their own people to the colonies.

On April 20, 1841, on his return voyage to New York, just two weeks after he had held his final conference in Manchester, attended by more than six thousand persons, Brigham wrote in his journal a summary of his activities in England:

It was with a heart full of thanksgiving and gratitude to God, my Heavenly Father, that I reflected upon his dealings with me and my brethren of the Twelve during the past year of my life, which was spent in England. It truly seemed a miracle to look upon the contrast between our landing and departing from Liverpool. We landed in the spring of 1840, as strangers in a strange land and penniless, but through the mercy of God we have gained many friends, established churches in almost every noted town and city

in the kingdom of Great Britain, baptized between seven and eight
thousand, printed 5,000 Books of Mormon, 3,000 hymn books,
2,500 volumes of the Millennial Star, and 60,000 tracts, and emigrated
to Zion 1,000 souls, established a permanent shipping agency, which
will be a great blessing to the saints, and have left sown in the
hearts of many thousands the seeds of eternal truth, which will
bring forth fruit to the honor and glory of God, and yet we have
lacked nothing to eat, drink or wear; in all things I acknowledge
the hand of God.

2

During Brigham's absence his family had been given a plot of
ground in Nauvoo and had settled into a small unfurnished log
cabin. The house, Brigham reported, was "Situated on a low, wet
lot, so swampy that when the first attempt was made to plough it
the oxen mired." He set about to see that the land was drained, and,
when it was, he had one of the most valuable properties in the city,
midway between the river and the temple lot at the crest of the hill.

Nauvoo had flourished during his twenty-two months' absence.
An orderly procession of houses dotted the hillside rising from the
Mississippi, and at the summit work had begun on the new temple.
Crops had been good the past year, and the saints were beginning to
lose their bitter memories of Missouri.

Yet they were running the danger of repeating the errors made
at Kirtland. Even more than in Ohio and Missouri, they were becoming a close-knit and self-contained community. In January 1842,
James Gordon Bennett, the editor of the New York *Herald*, wrote
an editorial which, while in praise of Joseph Smith and the Mormons on the surface, struck a note which already had caused un-
easiness among the non-Mormons of Illinois:

Here is a new prophet starting into existence in the green valleys
and lovely little hills of the town of Manchester, in Ontario County,
New York—leaving New York as Moses left Egypt—wandering
over the wild prairies of the west, as the great Jewish lawgiver wandered over the wilderness of Zion—and ultimately establishing a
holy city and a new religious empire on the Mississippi, that num-

bers 10,000 persons in the city and 30,000 beyond its limits—with a splendid temple for public worship—and a military organization of 1500 "pretty well" disciplined troops.

This presents a germ of religious civilization, novel, affecting, inviting, wonderful, and extraordinary . . . all the priests and philosophers of the day may take a lesson from Joe Smith, who seems to have hit the nail exactly on the head, by uniting faith and practice —fancy and fact—religion and philosophy—heaven and earth, so as to form the germ of a new religious civilization, bound together in love and temperance—in industry and energy—that may revolutionize the whole earth one of these days. Joe Smith is evidently no fool—he knows what he is about. Go ahead, old boy.

At first the gentiles were content to watch and marvel at the progress of Nauvoo, much as they had the progress of Kirtland. It very soon became the largest city in the state of Illinois; not only the largest, but the most colorful and prosperous.

In part its color was an extension of the colorful personality of Joseph Smith, who combined the temporal and the ecclesiastical in a manner new to American society. Typical of such a blend were the ceremonies marking the laying of the cornerstone for the temple, which took place on the eleventh anniversary of the founding of the church, April 6, 1841.

The ceremonies began early in the morning, with the full militia —known now as the Nauvoo Legion—lined up for review. Joseph strode on the parade ground, his tall figure dressed in a resplendent scarlet and blue uniform with gold epaulets. He was accompanied by four aides-de-camp and twelve specially selected guards, all equally well uniformed. The military band met him with a flourish of trumpets, then, as he took his place on the reviewing stand, it struck up a march and paraded before him and the troops. The artillery fired a salute, and the fifteen hundred members of the Legion presented arms.

Throughout, the ceremonies were marked by similarly impressive pomp, which included the presentation to the Legion of a large silk flag made for it by the ladies, a military review, a general parade, an oration by Sidney Rigdon, and the laying of the cornerstone by Joseph Smith.

Flushed with the success of his foreign mission, Brigham may not have been much astonished by the progress made at home. He was not averse to such ceremonies as those performed by the Legion, and he believed that the Mormons, after their Missouri experiences, deserved all the encouragement such outward signs of well-being could bring them. He must have been struck, however, with the contrast between the conditions of his own family, in their poor log cabin on the hillside, and the elaborate uniforms of the Legion officers, not to mention the imposing red-brick dwellings that were beginning to rise above the green sod of Nauvoo. Joseph too must have been aware of this discrepancy, for within ten days of Brigham Young's return from England he communicated to him the following revelation:

Dear and well-beloved brother, Brigham Young, verily thus saith the Lord unto you, my servant Brigham, it is no more required of your hand to leave your family as in times past, for your offering is acceptable; I have seen your labor and toil in journeying for my name, I therefore command you to send my work abroad, and take special care of your family from this time, henceforth and forever.

On September 2 Brigham was elected to the town council to replace Joseph's brother, Don Carlos, who had died; on November 8 Joseph called upon him to dedicate the new baptismal font, just completed in the lower story of the temple.

The prophet also reaffirmed the place of the Council of the Twelve in the authority of the church: "To stand in their places next to the First Presidency." The reasons for this announcement seem clear, although they have never been adequately explained. During Brigham's absence important changes had been made in the administration of the church. Sidney Rigdon, who had been ailing since his return from Missouri, had been partially replaced in the first presidency by that newcomer to the Mormon cause, John Cook Bennett. For him, in addition to making him second in command of the Nauvoo Legion, Joseph had created a special office called "assistant to the president." Bennett had also been elected mayor of Nauvoo, as well as appointed chancellor of the proposed, though not yet existing, University of Nauvoo. Also, Joseph's brother Hyrum had been released from the presidency in order to replace his father, who had died of fever, as the Presiding Patriarch—the office responsible for bestowing the official blessings and prophecies upon individual members of the church. The position as second councilor to Joseph had been taken by William Law, an early Canadian convert who had only recently come to Nauvoo from near Toronto at the head of a caravan of Canadian Mormons.

The rapid elevation of these relative newcomers, Bennett and Law, was typical of Joseph's tendency to accept all men too rapidly, to trust them too early, and to exalt them before they had proved their loyalty. Even now the presidency and the council were concerned with the unfortunate result of that tendency in the case of Isaac Galland, the land speculator, who had professed conversion to the church during the period of his dealings with Joseph Smith, had been raised to an office of responsibility for the settling of their land claims, and had absconded with money entrusted to him for the payment of interest on Mormon loans.

The year and a half following the apostles' return from England was one of the most prosperous and peaceful periods in Mormon history. The population of Nauvoo by the middle of 1841 had been 3000. By the end of the year it approached 10,000. The lower areas of the city had been drained, and the threat of malaria had disappeared. Industries arose, their development speeded by the arrival of trained craftsmen—weavers, dyers, tanners—from Great Britain. The walls of the new temple continued to rise.

One of the members described the plan of the temple for the benefit of the English branches. "The temple is up as high as the caps of the pilasters, and it looks majestic," he wrote. "This splendid model of Mormon grandeur exhibits thirty hewn-stone pilasters, which cost about three thousand dollars apiece. The base is a crescent new moon; the capitals near fifty feet high; the sun, with a human face in bold relief, about two and a half feet broad, ornamented with rays of light and waves, surmounted by two hands holding two trumpets."

The temple was being constructed of white limestone. It was 128 feet long by 83 feet wide; 60 feet high in the building itself, surmounted by a tower and steeple to rise almost 200 feet. It would contain two stories in the clear, and two half-stories in the recesses over the arches: "four tiers of windows, two gothic and two round." A temporary font in the basement had already been constructed, and it was in use for baptisms.

With the near-completion of the temple came the final development of the Mormon ceremonies—or endowments. A note in Brigham Young's journal, under the date of May 4, 1842, reports that he met that day with Joseph Smith, in the company of Hyrum Smith, Heber C. Kimball, Willard Richards, and a few others, "where Joseph taught the ancient order of things for the first time in these last days, and received my washings, anointings and endowments."

Joseph Smith, as always in times of peace and prosperity, had turned his thoughts again to ecclesiastical matters. Chief among these was the problem of marriage. While he was translating the Old Testament in Kirtland, his interest in two ancient customs had been aroused. First was the temple worship of the Hebrews, reflected tentatively in the construction of the first Mormon temple; second, the marriage relationship of the prophets, put forth cautiously as a Mormon model to only a few chosen companions. In his mind the two seemed intimately related, but the logical relationship, in terms of a religious creed, came to him only gradually. It was not to complete itself until this period in Nauvoo.

Polygamy, Joseph knew, was a dangerous doctrine, despite the example of the Old Testament fathers, but his own nature predisposed him to look with favor on it. Joseph saw heaven as a place of genuine reward. Like the prophet of Islam, Mohammed, with whom Joseph was often to be compared, he saw paradise very much as the Moslem conceived it:

> . . . a blissful abode
> Gardens and vineyards
> Damsels with swelling breasts of suitable age
> And a brimming cup.

One of Joseph's own followers put into words what the Mormons have always considered the essence of Joseph's beliefs: "Man is that he might have joy." Yet the doctrine could not, Joseph knew from the beginning, be put forward as the gratification of sensual desires.

Non-Mormon historians have seen in Joseph Smith's concern with polygamy a reflection of the early-nineteenth-century concept of "spiritual wifeism"—the doctrine of spiritual affinities, preached and practiced as a very real physical relationship by John Humphrey Noyes in his Oneida Community, expressed in a more spiritual form by the Shakers and the community at New Harmony, Indiana. Noyes had written in 1836:

The marriage supper of the Lamb is a feast at which every dish is free to every guest. In a holy community there is no more reason why sexual intercourse should be restrained by law, than why eating and drinking should be.

Certainly Joseph knew the doctrine, and the fact that it was in the air may have had something to do with his own first interest, but good sense led him to a less idealistic, a more reasonable, expression of that interest.

The culminating incident which brought Joseph his final clue, the key idea which made his doctrine of plural wives possible within the theological framework he had already established, probably resulted from his meeting with John Cook Bennett in Nauvoo. At the time of the meeting, Joseph had just escaped from prison, the Mormons were in need of men of influence to establish their new community, and Bennett's recommendations must have seemed to him excellent. Bennett was secretary of the Illinois Medical Society and quartermaster general of the Illinois militia. He was a man of worldly dignity and manner. He was well acquainted with Illinois politics, and to prove it he adroitly steered the Nauvoo city charter through the state legislature.

More important for the present discussion is that Bennett was a member of the Masonic Order, although even then (a fact which Joseph did not know) he was on the point of being expelled from an Ohio lodge. Though Joseph had spoken disparagingly of secret societies in the *Book of Mormon*, he was now in search of sources of influence. Much of the Mormons' trouble in Missouri, he believed, had come from a lack of influence in high places. On the frontier the most successful and powerful men were Masons. Some of his own leaders, such as Brigham Young, Heber Kimball, and Joseph's brother Hyrum, were former Masons. Bennett convinced him that it would be to the benefit of the Mormons to establish a Masonic lodge in Nauvoo.

The benefit Joseph derived seems to have been quite different from what he anticipated. At that time the Masons were almost the only organization on the frontier with a fully developed ritual. That Joseph recognized the psychological value of ritualistic symbols is obvious from his beginnings in Kirtland. The use of secret oaths, penalties, signs, grips, and secret means of recognition he had seen as an important means of binding his people together. The Masons then taught that their doctrine and ritual derived from the guildsmen who came up from Egypt to labor on Solomon's temple. Mention of Solomon led Joseph back to his former concern with Hebraic religion—in this case, the forms of temple worship. He must have startled Bennett when he came up with his own explanation: Masonry was essentially right, but it represented a corruption of the true forms. The original ceremonies had been disclosed to Adam at the time of his expulsion from the Garden of Eden. They embodied the promises made to our first parents, including knowledge of their own fall from grace and the assurance of eventual redemption. They included the forms practiced by the ancient prophets down to and including the time of Christ and the apostles. They contained the marriage ceremony, sanctioned by God and practiced by all peoples of the true religion of God in all the dispensations of time, a ceremony which allowed more than one wife in the present, just as it had in the past.

The orthodox Mormon view is somewhat different from this. According to it, Joseph received the sanction of plurality during the Kirtland period in answer to one of his pleas for information concerning God's view of marriage. He was told that the time was not yet ripe for such a revelation, and that the details would be supplied at a later date if the saints showed themselves worthy of it.

Details were apparently supplied during the period of Joseph's association with Bennett, probably during the months when Brigham and the apostles were away on their missions, and it was these details that Joseph taught them in May 1842, in preparation for the completion of the temple.

An expression of this orthodox view is contained in a speech made by George A. Smith later in Salt Lake City, describing events in Kirtland and Nauvoo:

Now if the Lord had considered it wisdom, on the day of the Kirtland endowments and great solemn assembly, to come forward and reveal to the children of men the facts that are laid down plainly in the Bible, and had told them that without the law of sealing [the Mormon term for marriage] no man could be exalted to a throne in the celestial kingdom, that is, without a woman by his side; and that no woman could be exalted in the celestial world without she was exalted with a man at her head; that the man was not without the woman, nor the woman without the man in the Lord; had He revealed this simple sentiment, up would have jumped some man saying, "What! Got to have a woman sealed to me in order to be saved, in order to be exalted to thrones, dominions, and eternal increase?" Yes. "I do not believe a word of it, I cannot stand that, for I never intended to get married, I do not believe in any of this nonsense." At the same time, perhaps, somebody else might have had faith to receive it. Again up jumps somebody else, "Brother Joseph I have had two wives in my lifetime, cannot I have them in eternity?" No. If he had said yes, perhaps we should all have apostatized at once.

We then passed from the year 1837 until the year 1843, when the Lord concluded that the people who had been gathered from Missouri, had been made acquainted with the principles of His kingdom so long, that they must have become strong enough to reveal one sentiment more.

Whereupon, the prophet goes up on the stand, and, after preaching about everything else he could think of in the world, at last hints at the law of redemption, makes a bare hint at the law of sealing, and it produced such a tremendous excitement that, as soon as he had got his dinner half-eaten, he had to go back to the stand and unpreach all he had preached, and left the people to guess at the matter.

The official Mormon historian, Brigham H. Roberts, reports that "as early as 1831 the rightfulness of a plurality of wives under certain limitations and special conditions was made known to Joseph Smith." But he adds, "It was in the Nauvoo period that the doctrine of salvation for the dead was fully developed."

The important thing is that with the acceptance by Joseph Smith of the principle of polygamy came the final revelation of the temple rituals, which have a superficial resemblance to Masonic ceremonies, but which are essentially a marriage rite—what the Mormons call a "sealing." In the original endowments at Kirtland, only men participated. With the working out of Joseph's doctrine of salvation, the role of women increased. Adam was the first father, and to him was given Eve. With the temptation and the fall came the necessity of the generations of man and the redemption of Christ. Up to this point the Mormon doctrine differed little from most conventional Christian beliefs. Its principal difference consisted in the manner in which it conceived of eternity, or the stage beyond the present world.

In a true nineteenth-century manner, Joseph had conceived of the hereafter as a continuation of his community of saints—a kind of religious Utopia. This being the case, what happened to the family relationship? The Scriptures said, as rival clergymen pointed out, that women were not to be given or taken in marriage in the hereafter. True, Joseph replied, but that did not imply that marriages contracted on earth did not continue into the hereafter. In fact, according to his view, it was this continuing relationship which formed the basis of life in the hereafter. Given the importance of continuing the generations of Adam, marriage and procreation were the first of the duties necessary to salvation. Man's mission was to clothe the spiritual children of God in "tabernacles of flesh," in order that God's plan might be worked out. Joseph went even further, concluding that if men were the actual children of God, God Himself must have had a mate. As he argued, such a belief did not so much degrade the idea of God as it exalted the condition of man. The Mormons restate this belief in one of their most memorable epigrams: "As man is, God once was; as God is, man may become." A Mormon poetess, Eliza R. Snow, has celebrated Joseph's concept of the married God in a famous Mormon hymn, originally entitled "Invocation; or, the Eternal Father and Mother," more recently known as "O! My Father":

> O! my Father, thou that dwellest
>   In the high and holy place;
> When shall I regain thy presence,
>   And again behold thy face?
>
> In thy glorious habitation,
>   Did my spirit once reside?
> In my first primeval childhood,
>   Was I nurtured by thy side?
>
> For a wise and glorious purpose,
>   Thou hast placed me here on earth;
> And withheld the recollection
>   Of my former friends and birth.
>
> Yet oft-times a secret something
>   Whispered, "You're a stranger here";
> And I felt that I had wandered
>   From a more exalted sphere.
>
> I had learned to call thee Father,
>   Through thy spirit from on high;
> But until the key of knowledge
>   Was restored, I knew not why.
>
> In the heavens are parents single?
>   No; the thought makes reason stare.
> Truth is reason; truth eternal
>   Tells me I've a mother there.
>
> When I leave this frail existence—
>   When I lay this mortal by,
> Father, mother, may I meet you
>   In your royal court on high?
>
> Then at length, when I've completed
>   All you sent me forth to do,
> With your mutual approbation,
>   Let me come and dwell with you.

The ritual introduced by Joseph Smith in 1842 was primarily a marriage ceremony in which marriages could be consummated not only for "time," but for "eternity" as well. To know how much Joseph borrowed from Masonry, one would have to be a Mason as well as a Mormon (and the Mormons, of course, deny that there was any borrowing). There are similarities that cannot be denied. For instance, the baptismal font, which Joseph constructed after the model of the fountain described as Solomon's in the Old Testament, symbolized the twelve tribes of Israel by the twelve oxen that support it. The Mormon undergarments which are supplied in the temple ceremony, which symbolize the garments given to Adam and Eve, and which thus represent God's promise to man, bear the square and compass reminiscent of Free Masonry. If such details were borrowed, they were not taken until Joseph Smith's fertile imagination had thoroughly incorporated them into the Mormons' peculiar system of religious belief.

The fact that participants in the Mormon ceremonies swear an oath to preserve their secrecy has led many writers to conclude that these ceremonies also include sexual initiation. Apostates who exposed the mysteries hinted at unnatural sex relations. In actual fact, the rites are an allegorical portrayal of the Mormons' concept of the plan of salvation, portrayed in stages from the creation of the world to the final fulfillment. They include the washings and anointing of the Kirtland period, and add to them oaths of loyalty and secrecy, as well as pledges of chastity and faithfulness. Concluding as they do with the ceremony of marriage, they bring the life of the devout Mormon into a close and actual relation to the abstract plan.

Along with the ceremony performed for the living, came the concept of proxy performance for the dead. Joseph's first concern with this principle of his religion came from the words of the Apostle Paul: "Else what shall they do that are baptized for the dead, if the dead rise not at all? Why are they then baptized for the dead?" Joseph's theory of heaven and earth included the belief that all beings who had not accepted the true church on earth continued their existence in a realm called paradise—a concept very similar to the Roman Catholics' view of purgatory. Not until the dead had accepted the truth, and had it confirmed through baptism and their endowments on earth, were they released to gain their final celestial inheritance. Continuing ceremonies, which are performed to this day in the Mormon temples, are held in the names of deceased progenitors.

Joseph's revelation expresses the purpose of the gospel as ushering in the fullness of time, "which dispensation is now beginning to usher in, that a whole and complete and perfect union, and welding together of dispensations, and keys, and powers, and glories should take place, and be revealed from the days of Adam even to the present time." This revelation was given in two parts, in September 1842, and Brigham Young said of it, "The doctrine of baptism for the dead is the greatest doctrine, one of the most glorious doctrines that was revealed to the human family; and there are light, power, glory, honor, and immortality in it."

Likewise the doctrine of marriage—"celestial marriage," as the Mormons prefer to call it: if baptism is performed in order to bind in heaven that which has been acknowledged on earth, what of marriage vows, if the marriage relation is to continue into the hereafter? It was not until such a question was answered that the doctrine of polygamy, or plural marriage, was made public, or divulged even to selected members of the church. The doctrine of "salvation for the dead" finally came to mean both the ceremonies of baptism and marriage. In the Mormon catechism, the problems would probably be stated somewhat as follows:

Question: What is the purpose of marriage?

Answer: To raise up souls unto God and to provide means for their development in intelligence, knowledge, and well-being.

Question: Is it for this world alone?

Answer: No. For the development of the soul is eternal.

Question: Is it, then, for eternity?

Answer: Yes. For we are God's children, here and in the hereafter.

Question: If a man have one wife upon earth, and she dies, is he entitled to marry again?

Answer: Yes. For it is his duty to raise up souls to God.

Question: What, then, becomes of the second wife in the hereafter?

Answer: She remains his wife still, for she has been sealed for time and eternity; God would not be so cruel as to ask him to put her by.

Question: Is not, then, the true system of marriage one of plurality of wives?

Answer: Yes, if the participants are prepared for the responsibility which plural marriage bestows.

Question: And if the husband dies, is the wife allowed to marry again?

Answer: Yes. For her obligation remains, to raise up souls to God.

Question: To whom, then, will she belong in the hereafter, to her first or her second husband?

Answer: To her first, for to him she was married for eternity. To the second, she can only be married in this world.

Question: To whom will the children belong?

Answer: To her first husband, for to him pertain all the rights of eternity.

Question: Is there any evidence in the Scriptures that plural marriage is acceptable to God?

Answer: Yes. For the Old Testament teaches that Abraham and Jacob and many of the ancient prophets took more wives than one, and God found them acceptable in His sight.

3

By 1843 Joseph had both doctrinal and scriptural support for a system of polygamous marriage which he had probably begun to practice secretly as early as 1836, and which he was to continue to the day of his death. Fawn M. Brodie, his most thorough biographer, lists forty-nine documented instances of Joseph's polygamous alliances, and she suggests that there may have been many more, although a few seem to have been made with older women for the purpose of celestial reward only.

Parley P. Pratt, in describing a long conversation he had with Joseph Smith on a visit to Philadelphia in 1840, says, "He taught me many great and glorious principles concerning God and the heavenly order of eternity. It was at this time that I received from him the first idea of eternal family organization, and the eternal union of sexes in those inexpressibly endearing relationships which none but the highly intellectual, the refined and pure in heart know how to prize and which are the foundations of everything worthy to be called happiness." The more practical Brigham Young testified to his reaction when the doctrine was first announced to him. "I was not," he said, "desirous of shrinking from any duty, nor of failing the least to do as I was commanded, but it was the first time in my life that I ever desired the grave, and I could hardly get over it for a long time."

Not all Joseph's followers could be won over to polygamy, and it is likely that the doctrine of plural marriage caused more apostasies than we know of in the Nauvoo period. Sidney Rigdon and William Law were opposed, as was Joseph's strong-willed wife, Emma. When Hyrum Smith asked Joseph to write down the revelation on polygamy, he thought that with words in writing he could convince Joseph's wife.

"I will take it and read it to Emma," he told his brother, "and I believe I can convince her of its truth, and you will hereafter have peace."

Joseph was doubtful. "You do not know Emma as well as I do," he told his confident brother.

Nevertheless, he did allow Hyrum to use his more gentle method of persuasion. Hyrum carried the document to Emma, certain that she would endorse it finally, as his own wife had. Instead she flew into a rage, plucked the sheaf of paper from his hand, and flung it into the fire.

"In all my life," he told Joseph when he returned, "I have never been so abused by a woman."

Joseph's experience with Emma was only the beginning of the

scandal which the introduction of so unconventional a system of marriage was destined to bring upon the church. Apostates and non-Mormons presented the sensational aspects. Devout Mormons, of necessity sworn to secrecy, did not speak up for several years. One of the earliest rumors of Joseph's attention to a woman other than his wife arose in Ohio in 1832, when it was said that the leader of the mob that tarred and feathered him at Hiram was Eli Johnson, who, among other things, resented Joseph's attentions to his sister Nancy. Nancy married Orson Hyde, one of the Council of the Twelve, in 1834; but it is possible that Joseph never lost interest in her, for rumor continued to link her name with his, and by 1842, in Nauvoo, some were saying that Joseph had taken her for his celestial wife while her husband was away on his mission.

Rumor also explained the growing coldness between Joseph Smith and Sidney Rigdon by whispering that the prophet had attempted to obtain Rigdon's young daughter, also named Nancy, as one of his celestial wives. In this instance Joseph and his assistant John C. Bennett were said to have been rivals for Nancy Rigdon's favor, with the girl seeming to prefer the dapper Bennett. Joseph made the mistake of putting his desires into writing, and Nancy carried the letter to her father, who read it with profound shock, then with a growing fury. Joseph at first denied everything, but, when confronted by the letter, attempted to excuse himself by explaining that he had merely been testing Nancy's virtue.

One account of a courtship in Nauvoo at this time involves Brigham Young as the suitor. The girl was Martha Brotherton, a young English convert, who later went to St. Louis and signed an affidavit to the truthfulness of her report. It tells how Heber Kimball and Brigham came to her and announced that Joseph Smith wished to see her at the tithing office. When she arrived, Joseph and Heber left Brigham alone with her.

According to her report Brigham asked her whether "if it were lawful and right," she would accept him as her husband. When she demurred, saying that perhaps she might in that case, but, as he knew, it would not be "lawful and right," he told her of Joseph Smith's revelation permitting plural marriages, adding that "whoever is the first that is willing to take up the cross will receive the greatest blessing, and if you accept me I shall take you straight to the celestial kingdom."

According to the account, Martha did not consent to marry Brigham. Both Brigham Young and Heber Kimball denied that there was any such interview. Whether it did or did not take place is immaterial, for other interviews of a similar nature certainly did. Brigham married his first polygamous wife, Lucy Ann Decker, in 1842, when she was twenty years old and he was forty-one. The next year he married two, Harriet Cook and Augusta Adams, the first nineteen years old, the second forty-one.

It would be wrong to conclude from these facts that either Joseph or the men who followed his teachings were reckless libertines. There were undoubtedly a few men in Nauvoo at the time who welcomed Joseph's doctrine as license for gratifying libidinous desires, but this was not the general attitude. That Joseph Smith was capable of promulgating such a doctrine as polygamy should not surprise us. That he should practice it without at least a show of doctrinal support would have been contrary to his nature. The same is true of the greatest number of his followers. If they had not believed themselves to have been acting under divine sanction it would be difficult to account for the continuing influence they had upon their followers.

In later years men were to characterize the practice of polygamy as a responsibility and a trial, not as a sexual privilege. On the whole, the history of Mormon plural marriage (contrary to much belief) provided testimony of circumspection and moderation in wedlock, not the contrary.

With the beginning of the practice in Nauvoo in the 1840s, however, the days of peace and quiet for the Mormons were again ended. Efforts to keep polygamy secret were in vain. In addition to the social and political differences which had arisen in Ohio and Missouri, in addition to charges of lawlessness and murder, there was now the charge of sexual aberration. The Mormons by 1843 were stronger than they had ever been before, but their peace and security hung by a slender thread. For the gentiles in Illinois, rumors which came to them from apostates only intensified the fear and wonder which they had begun to feel toward this peculiar community. Perhaps the Missourians had not been wrong after all in expelling them, the gentiles began to tell themselves. Newspapers outside Nauvoo began the attacks; then politicians—seeing the way the wind was blowing—suggested that the trouble all came from the city charter the Mormons had been granted. They put forward measures to revoke it. Even the Masons, with whom the Mormons had affiliated in 1842, and particularly the lodges in Quincy and Warsaw, began to grow cool toward their brother Masons in Nauvoo and Montrose, and by the end of 1843 the Mormons' dispensation had been recalled by the headquarters of the Grand Master for the State of Illinois.

Not all these events were the result of the institution of polygamy, but polygamy was the decisive factor in the change of sentiment. As in Missouri, the Mormons had unwittingly sown the first seeds of dissension almost as soon as they entered the state. Once again they would reap the whirlwind.

CHAPTER SIX

THE MARTYRDOM

I

During Brigham Young's absence in 1840 and 1841, events in
Nauvoo seemed to be following an orderly and auspicious pattern. Reports from home were only a little less optimistic than
those sent from England to America. Politically the Mormons were
in a favorable position, wooed by both the Whigs and the Democrats. In the fall of 1840 Joseph Smith had been served with a writ
on the old Missouri charges. The case was heard by a rising young
politician, Stephen A. Douglas, who ruled that Joseph had been
illegally held in Missouri, so need not be returned for trial. About
the same time the Nauvoo charter was granted by the state legislature, one of the affirmative votes being cast by a then little-
known politician named Abraham Lincoln.

The city charter granted the Mormons almost unlimited authority and accompanied it by state aid in arming and maintaining the
Nauvoo Legion as a branch of the state militia. The necessity for
such broad powers seemed as obvious to Brigham Young as it did
to his fellow Mormons, for elsewhere it had always been their enemies who had the sanction of the law. In Nauvoo they wanted
power to enact their own legislation as well as to enforce it. In 1842
the city council passed a law granting their court the right to examine all writs served upon anyone within the limits of the city and

either to try or to dismiss the accused according to the court's judgment. What this meant to the Mormons was that none of their members could be seized by writ and whisked away for trial by an unfriendly court. To the gentiles, it seemed that the Mormons were
attempting to evade due process of law.

When newspapers in neighboring communities attacked such
powers as the Mormons had granted themselves, Joseph Smith
called for a decision by two prominent attorneys who were candidates of the opposing parties in a coming state election. Anxious not
to alienate so large a body of voters, both candidates assured the
Mormons that they were within their rights.

By encouraging both parties to seek their support, however, the
Mormons were unknowingly guaranteeing themselves the enmity
of whichever party did not receive their votes. As it turned out,
Joseph Smith went even further, throwing the entire support of
the Mormon vote except his own to the Democratic candidate upon
the basis of a secret pledge of support. By this act, as Governor
Thomas Ford remarked later, "they made their continued existence
in the state a political issue." Since the Mormons had, in an earlier
election, voted Whig, their wholesale switch now to the Democrats
not only seemed a betrayal to the Whigs but opened the eyes of
many people to the threat they posed as a political influence in the
state of Illinois.

Moreover, the Mormons' city by 1842 contrasted strangely
in its orderliness and growth with the gentile villages that surrounded it. Most of the homes were built of brick, surrounded by
gardens and trees which gave, as one visitor described it, "every
dwelling . . . the character of a snug country residence, with
more marks of simple taste and refinement than you meet along
your high roads in Pennsylvania." By contrast, most frontier villages
had a temporary, makeshift appearance, and this was true of the
Illinois towns in the vicinity of Nauvoo.

Brigham's home, which he labored on from the time that he returned from England until he moved into it in May 1843, was constructed of red brick and was 22 feet long by 16 feet wide, "two

stories high, with a good cellar under it." It was so substantially built that more than a hundred years later it still served as a family dwelling.

Such signs of prosperity, coupled with the fact that Nauvoo, in its rapid growth, was eclipsing all other cities in the state, created jealousy and made every uncommon event within the Mormon community cause for rumor and alarm.

Sometime before 1842 word began to circulate in the vicinity of Nauvoo that the Mormons were practicing polygamy. On June 23 of that year John Cook Bennett was excommunicated from the church for what the knowing said was licentious and adulterous behavior. On July 8 the *Sangamo Journal* released an extra in which it announced that Bennett, the former assistant to the President of the Mormon Church, was preparing a series of articles to expose the Mormons. They would clothe rumor in fact and suspicion in certainty.

The articles appeared and were indeed a sensation. They caught the interest of newspapers from one end of the country to the other. At the conclusion of the series they appeared in a book entitled *The History of the Saints: or, an Exposé of Joe Smith and Mormonism.*

Bennett's break with the church precipitated an even graver crisis than Hurlbut's defection in Ohio or the Avard-Hinkle apostasy in Missouri. A peculiar combination of fact and fancy, his writing contained enough verifiable information to lend authority to what he said. He accused Joseph Smith of plotting to set up an empire in the West with himself as emperor, supported by the Danites and by a system of terror and assassination. Bennett also revealed the practice of polygamy, presenting it as an elaborate system of immorality cloaked in mystical religious rites and headed by Joseph Smith and his leading elders.

Bennett opened his first letter to the *Sangamo Journal* by saying, "I write you now from the Mormon Zion, the city of the saints, where I am threatened with death by the Holy Joe and his Danite band of murderers." Members of the Nauvoo Legion, he said, had taken an oath to protect the prophet under all conditions, wrong or right. A picked group of Danites, known as the Destroying Angels, had taken it upon themselves to seek out and destroy the particular enemies of Joseph Smith.

Of polygamy, he said that the women of Nauvoo were divided into orders, known as "the Cyprian Saints," "the Chambered Sisters of Charity, or Saints of the Green Veil," and "the Cloistered Saints, Saints of the Black Veil." The first order consisted of ladies of easy virtue, who would at all times be at the service of the church leaders. The second order consisted of more discreet and less generous women, but female saints who would occasionally bestow their favors upon the leaders outside of marriage. The third and highest order was made up of women who went through a marriage ceremony and became "spiritual wives." "When an Apostle, High Priest, Elder, or Scribe conceives an affection for a female," Bennett wrote, "and he has satisfactorily ascertained that she experiences a mutual claim, he communicates confidentially to the Prophet his *affaire du cœur*, and requests him to inquire of the Lord whether or not it would be right and proper for him to take unto himself the said woman for his spiritual wife. It is no obstacle whatever to this spiritual marriage if one or both of the parties should happen to have a husband or wife already united to them according to the laws of the land."

In his opening pages Bennett claimed that he had joined the Mormons and become a friend and associate of Joseph Smith with the aim of exposing him. He filled the early sections of his book with affidavits testifying to his own good character. The fact is that Bennett's character was such a mixture of competence and rascality that he had, even before he joined the Mormons, compiled elsewhere a remarkable record of deceit, while at the same time rising to high office wherever he went.

Hyrum Smith had brought the first word of Bennett's deception when, after a trip to the East, he had revealed to Joseph that Bennett, who posed in Nauvoo as an extremely eligible bachelor, had deserted a wife and children. Further information became available when application was made for the installation of the Masonic lodge in Nauvoo, and it turned out that Bennett, who was the applying secretary, was even then under sentence of expulsion from a lodge in Ohio. His record as founder and head of medical colleges in almost all the Western states in the years before he joined the Mormons, impressive as it may have seemed to the unknowing, shows him as an adventurer who remained in one place only long enough to reap the first harvest, then moved on to further opportunities.

When Joseph drew up his first notice of excommunication he did not realize the full extent of Bennett's debauchery, which had been accomplished in his name. He called in a number of Mormon women, whose names had been linked in rumor with Bennett, and discovered that his councilor had not only seduced them or attempted to seduce them in the name of their religion, but that, as a medical doctor, he had promised to perform abortions for any who became pregnant.

What happened in the meeting between the two men, when Joseph confronted Bennett with the charges, has been reported only by Bennett. Joseph, he said, called him to his office and, when he had entered, locked the door and put the key in his pocket. He then drew a pistol and placed it before him.

"The peace of my family requires," he said, "that you should sign an affidavit, and make a statement before the next city council, exonerating me from all participation whatever, whether directly or indirectly, in word or deed, in the spiritual wife doctrine, or private intercourse with females in general, and if you do not do it with apparent cheerfulness, I will make catfish bait of you, or deliver you to the Danites for execution tonight—for my dignity and purity must and shall be maintained before the public."

On May 19 Bennett appeared before the city council and announced his withdrawal. He was voted public thanks for his service to the community.

"I know what I am about," he said, "and the heads of the church know what they are about, I expect; I have no difficulty with the heads of the church. I publicly avow that anyone who has said that I have stated that General Joseph Smith has given me authority to hold illicit intercourse with women is a liar in the face of God."

In spite of the fact that, a few days later, Joseph Smith softened toward Bennett and came to his defense, Brigham Young and his council would not be placated, and on June 23, 1842, the excommunication became final.

The degree of seriousness with which the authorities took the public attack of Bennett when it appeared can be estimated by the fact that the Council of the Twelve, including Brigham, who had earlier been assured by Joseph that he need no longer travel, prepared again to go forth on missions to combat the charges.

Also at this time, partly as the result of Bennett's exposé, several important Mormons left the church, and they greatly hindered the labors of the missionaries by verifying a portion of Bennett's charges. One of these men, Francis Higbee, had been a close friend of Bennett, and Joseph had, as an aftermath of the Bennett hearing, included him in many of the charges made against Bennett. As a result, Higbee sued Joseph for libel. In the presentation of evidence he dragged into the open much that Joseph still hoped might be kept secret. Others who defected were William Law, Joseph's recently appointed second councilor; his brother, Wilson Law, an ex-general of the Nauvoo Legion; and Dr. R. D. Foster, a wealthy convert. Joseph's differences with these men, who were merchants and builders, began in a quarrel over whether their labor and materials should be applied to the construction of the temple or to that of private dwellings and stores, but ended in a dispute over the practice of polygamy and the truth or falseness of Bennett's charges.

Again, to add to Joseph's troubles, an attempt had been made in May on the life of Governor Lillburn Boggs of Missouri. About his feelings toward Boggs, who had been an enemy of the Mormons since the first mobbings in Independence, Joseph had made no secret. It was said he had predicted that Boggs would die within a year. Also, a Mormon newspaper in Nauvoo, upon hearing of the attempted assassination, had commented, "Boggs is undoubtedly killed according to report; but who did the noble deed remains to be found out." It was rumored in Illinois that at the moment when the shooting had taken place Joseph's friend and bodyguard, Porter Rockwell, had been absent from the city. The event occurred at a propitious time for John Cook Bennett, for he was able to include in his book the charge that Rockwell had shot Boggs, and he even made a trip to Jefferson City to lay his purported evidence before the authorities in Missouri.

Bennett's accusations undoubtedly began the myth that Porter Rockwell was a hired killer for the prophet and the church, a charge that would continue to be made for many years. Rockwell was a powerful, vigorous man with a black beard, and he wore his hair so long it was said he could conceal a revolver in it. Joseph, it is reported, had promised Rockwell protection so long as his hair remained uncut. The bodyguard was a crack shot, one of a group of young Mormons, including the later notorious William Hickman and John D. Lee, who dressed in white uniforms and served as the prophet's guard of honor when the Legion was on parade.

The governor of Illinois issued a writ for the arrest of Joseph and Rockwell. They submitted to the Nauvoo court for a review of the evidence, and were released at once. Rockwell left for Philadelphia, and Joseph went into hiding, swearing that he would never allow himself to be returned to Missouri for trial. Although few people believed that Smith could be convicted of the attempt to murder Boggs, Joseph was confronted by a dilemma: if he did not give himself up, his guilt would be assumed by his gentile enemies; if he did, he might well experience treatment similar to that which he had known before in Missouri. Residents of the communities surrounding Nauvoo were clamoring for the withdrawal of the Nauvoo charter, which they said had allowed Joseph to evade the law. He went into hiding for four months; then, when the newly elected Governor Ford took office in January, he gave himself up to the state authorities. After a sensational trial at Springfield, where Joseph by the magnetism of his personality not only succeeded in convincing the court of his innocence but proved a social success as well, he was released on January 11, 1843.

By June, however, the Missouri authorities, aided by the imaginative evidence furnished by Bennett, succeeded in obtaining another writ on the old charges of treason and murder. This time they took Joseph by surprise while he was visiting in nearby Dixon, hoping to obtain his release from Illinois quickly and hurry him off to Missouri for trial. Joseph, who was locked in the upper room of a tavern, got word to some of his followers, and they raced off to Nauvoo to spread the alarm.

A mass meeting was called by Hyrum within half an hour at the Masonic Hall. Three hundred volunteers offered to go to the relief of the prophet. A dispute arose as to how such an expedition was to be financed, and some of the lukewarm members of Joseph's council announced they would not leave Nauvoo until sufficient means had been raised.

Again it was Brigham Young who took upon himself the burden of Joseph's defense. "I told the brethren to get in readiness," he recorded, "and the money would be forthcoming." Within two hours he had taken up a collection of more than seven hundred dollars to finance the expedition.

Meanwhile, in Dixon, Joseph had preached through the window of his prison to the curious townspeople who, once word had spread that Ol' Joe Smith the prophet was there, held prisoner, flocked to listen. Few of them had any love for the Missourians from across the river, and Joseph won their sympathy by recounting events of the persecution a few years past. Finally someone humorously called for a sermon on marriage. Joseph obliged, and, as he reported, "My freedom commenced from that hour."

Having won the sympathy of the crowd, Joseph gained time, but he was not freed. Stephen A. Douglas was holding court in Quincy, and the Illinois officials decided to take him there for a hearing. On the road with the sheriffs, Joseph saw a band of horsemen driving furiously toward his carriage. For a moment he thought they were from Missouri; then he recognized members of the Nauvoo Legion.

"I am not going to Missouri this time," he exclaimed. "These are my boys."

He persuaded the attorney to turn and conduct the hearing in the Nauvoo court—not too difficult to do now that his Mormon support was on hand. They were met at the outskirts of the city by most of the population, which Brigham Young described as "multitudes of the brethren and sisters," who filled the air with cheers as expression of "the devotion and good feeling in the hearts of the saints towards their prophet."

The trial was held July 1, with Brigham Young sworn as one of the witnesses to testify to the events which had occurred in Missouri. The result was a foregone conclusion. Joseph was released, and the Missouri officers returned empty-handed.

2

Events during the fall of 1843 were to simmer rather than boil, with the most important of them occurring in the caucuses and backstage consultations of the two principal political parties. On the surface Nauvoo seemed calm, prosperous, and self-sufficient. Beyond the borders of Illinois, however, Bennett's charges had produced a nationwide scandal. Once again the Twelve were called to travel in defense of the church.

On July 7 Brigham Young started on a preaching tour which took him, by way of St. Louis, Pittsburgh, and Baltimore, to the Eastern states and lasted three months.

In a meeting in New York City on August 26, at which all the Twelve were present, Brigham delivered his principal sermon. His subject was the necessity of spiritual sight. "Place a man in this room who is ignorant of science," he said, "and take everything out that he can see, and ask him if there is anything in the room. He will say no, only we two. I tell him that there are millions of live animals in the room, that we even breathe them, and I will show him by the aid of a microscope that there are live animals in a drop of water, which appear to be eight feet long, but he won't believe it, until he sees them through the magnifying glass. So with the unbeliever in revelation—he does not believe in God, in angels, or in spirits, because he cannot see them; but let him have spiritual glasses, or obey the commandments of God, get the Spirit of God, and then he can see the truth."

When Brigham returned to Nauvoo in October, the atmosphere

seemed charged with anticipation, whether of good or bad he could not tell. Joseph had demonstrated the effects of the Mormon vote in the recent elections. The Democratic candidate for the legislature, backed by two thousand Mormon votes, had won by a plurality of eight hundred votes, and thus owed his election to a sudden switch of the Mormons from the Whigs to his party.

On January 3, 1844, William Law, Joseph's apostate councilor, appeared before the city council and complained that "Joseph had administered a secret oath to the police and instructed them to kill him." The police were called in, and they denied the accusation.

On February 21, at a meeting between Joseph and the Twelve, an exploring company was chosen to go to California "to select a location for the settlement of the saints."

By March, Brigham had heard so many complaints in his dual capacity as city councilman and spiritual adviser that he decided to preach a sermon on the subject of complainers. "If any of you wish to know how to have your bread fall butter side up," he told the saints, "butter it on both sides." Also in March, Joseph became convinced that a conspiracy existed among the Laws, Higbee, and Foster to take his life.

During recent months Joseph had written to the two leading aspirants to the United States Presidency, Henry Clay and John C. Calhoun, asking them what pledges of protection they would offer the Mormons if they were elected. Both wrote evasive answers, Clay replying that he could "enter into no engagements, make no promises, give no pledges to any particular portion of the people of the United States," Calhoun stating that the Mormons' case against Missouri was a matter between them and the state administration and did not come under the jurisdiction of the federal government. Joseph, in a gesture of disgust, announced that he would himself be a candidate for President, and asked for volunteer missionaries to travel throughout the states, organizing the various branches to place his name on the ballot, and 344 men offered their services. At the same time he said that all North and South America constituted the land of Zion.

There is little reason to believe that he had any hope of success, but he did wish to test the voting power of the church when its membership was placed squarely behind a particular candidate. He possessed a vigorous missionary organization, which could be turned into electioneers almost without change.

Joseph's political platform was serious enough. He took note of the most pressing national problems. He expressed himself as favoring abolition of slavery through the purchase of slaves by the government, the establishment of a national bank, and the expansion of the country into Oregon and Mexico. More revealing than his formal statement was an ironic notice run in the Mormon periodical *Times and Seasons*, which disarmingly took account of practically all the charges made against the Mormons by their enemies.

Gentlemen, we are not going either to "murder exGovernor Boggs," nor a Mormon in this state, "for not giving us money"; nor are we going to "walk on water"; nor "drown a woman"; nor "defraud the poor of their property"; nor "send destroying angels after General Bennett to kill him"; nor "marry spiritual wives"; nor commit any other outrageous act this election, to help any party with; you must get some other person to perform these kind offices for you in the future. We withdraw.

Before Joseph's campaign was well under way, an event occurred which was to wreck it, and alter forever the fortunes of the Mormon church. On June 7, 1844, less than six weeks after Brigham Young and the members of the Twelve had left on their electioneering missions, the apostates in Nauvoo, headed by William Law and Robert D. Foster, published the first issue of a newspaper called the Nauvoo *Expositor*. Here, on their own ground, the Mormons were attacked on the basis of polygamy, were charged with grasping for political power, and were accused of dishonest financial maneuvering. To Joseph the act was more than a betrayal of him personally; it was treason against a whole society. At his direction, the Nauvoo council met and declared the newspaper a public nuisance and a threat to the peace of the city. The marshal was ordered to destroy the press.

Nothing Joseph could have done could have more effectively brought his enemies down upon him. The right to freedom of utterance—the freedom of the press—was the right frontier Americans had learned most jealously to guard. It did not matter that in Missouri the enemies of the Mormons had destroyed the presses of *The Evening and the Morning Star*, or that just a few years earlier the residents of Alton, Illinois, just down the river from Nauvoo, had destroyed the press of the abolitionist editor, Elijah Lovejoy, and riddled his body with bullets. This was the excuse the gentiles had been waiting for.

"War and extermination is inevitable," shrieked a front-page editorial in the neighboring Warsaw *Signal*. "CITIZENS ARISE. ONE AND ALL!!! Can you *Stand* by and suffer such INFERNAL DEVILS! to Rob men of their property and rights, without avenging them? We have no time for comment; every man will make his own. LET it be made with POWDER AND BALLS!!!"

Within a few days the countryside around Nauvoo had taken up the challenge. Almost no excuse short of murder would have served so well as a rallying cry. Armed mobs appeared and roamed the roads, threatening Mormons wherever they found them. A committee from Carthage, the county seat, waited upon the newly elected Governor Ford and demanded that he call out the militia.

Governor Ford refused at first, but as rumor upon rumor came to his office he decided to pay a visit to the county and see with his own eyes how serious the trouble was. He knew that the owners of the *Expositor* had gone to Carthage and issued warrants for the arrest of Joseph Smith and his councilmen. He knew that Smith had invoked his power of habeas corpus under the Nauvoo charter and gained his release.

On June 21 the governor arrived in Carthage, twenty miles southeast of Nauvoo. He found that the anti-Mormons had called up the militia without his authority. He sent word to Nauvoo that the Mormons should deliver representatives to the county seat to present their side of the story. Between the charges and countercharges, the governor could make little sense of the whole affair. He believed that a wrong had been perpetrated in the destruction of the press, but he could not understand the intensity of the emotions that had been aroused by it.

As he reported later, the atmosphere was confused by rumor, "artfully planned and executed by tact. It consisted in spreading rumors of the most fearful character." As examples:

On the morning before my arrival at Carthage, I was awakened at an early hour by the frightful report, which was asserted with confidence and apparent consternation, that the Mormons had already commenced the work of burning, destruction, and murder; and that every man capable of bearing arms was instantly wanted at Carthage for the protection of the country. We lost no time in starting; but when we arrived at Carthage, we could hear no more concerning the story. Again: during the few days that the militia were encamped at Carthage, frequent applications were made to me to send a force here and a force there and a force all about the country to prevent murders, robberies, and larcenies which, it was said, were threatened by the Mormons. No such forces were sent; nor were any such offenses committed at that time except the stealing of some provisions, and there was never the least proof that this was done by a Mormon. Again: on my late visit to Hancock County, I was informed by some of their violent enemies that the larcenies of the Mormons had become unusually numerous and insufferable. They indeed admitted that but little had been done in this way in their immediate vicinity. But they insisted that sixteen horses had been stolen by the Mormons in one night near Lima, in the county of Adams. At the close of the expedition, I called at this same town of Lima and upon inquiry was told that no horses had been stolen in that neighborhood, but that sixteen horses had been stolen in one night in Hancock County. This last informant, being told the Hancock story, again changed the venue to another distant settlement in the northern edge of Adams.

Governor Ford sent word to the Mormons that if their leaders would surrender to him he would assign men to protect them and guarantee them a fair trial. To this the Mormons at first agreed, but as the time came for them to appear, memories of Missouri returned to check their too hasty response.

It is said that Joseph Smith had a premonition that death threatened him this time. The night before he was to report to the governor, he and his brother Hyrum, Willard Richards, and John Taylor crossed the Mississippi into Iowa, determined to start at once for the Rocky Mountains. The next morning one of his elders came to see him to tell him that his wife Emma wanted him to remain. Besides, he told Joseph, the city was leaderless with all of the apostles away. What would they do if Joseph too deserted them? Joseph turned to his brother Hyrum for advice.

"Let us go back and give ourselves up, and see the thing out," Hyrum is reported to have told him.

Joseph replied, "If my life is of no value to my friends, it is of no value to myself. If you go back, I will go with you, but we shall be butchered."

The four men returned that day to Nauvoo and, with a Mormon escort, rode to Carthage and gave themselves into the hands of Governor Ford. They were quartered that night at a hotel.

Well might Joseph have remembered Missouri when, the next day, he was paraded before the curious eyes of the assembled troops and townspeople. The governor had appointed the Carthage Greys as escort. He introduced Joseph and Hyrum to the soldiers as "the generals Smith," whereupon some of the officers of the militia drew their swords and announced that they would introduce themselves to the damned Mormons in a different manner. Unable to control them, the governor had them put under arrest for their offensive speech. They later apologized and were released.

Joseph had come to Carthage with two charges against him: inciting to riot, because of the destruction of the *Expositor;* and treason, because the gentiles maintained that he sought to establish a kingdom of his own at Nauvoo. At the hearing that morning, he was bound over to the court on the first charge, and bail was set at seventy-five hundred dollars. Nothing was said about the second charge. No sooner had he arrived back at the hotel, however, than he was rearrested on the charge of treason and sent to jail without a hearing. He and his brother were not placed in the regular cell-room on the second floor of the jail, but in an adjoining room containing a double bed, a table, and a few chairs. They were also allowed to receive some of their Mormon friends as visitors. The governor later claimed that the Smiths were placed in jail for their own protection, and it is possible that the illegal arrest was intended to safeguard them. He planned to ride to Nauvoo the next day to investigate the charges there, but before departing he visited Joseph and discussed the accusations made against him. It is said that the governor and the prophet agreed on all points except the destruction of the press.

"The press of the United States is looked upon as the great bulwark of American freedom," Ford is reported to have said, "and its destruction in Nauvoo was represented and looked upon as a high-handed measure, and manifests to the people a disposition on your part to suppress the liberty of speech and of the press."

"Could we suffer a set of worthless vagabonds to come into our city," Joseph asked, "and right under our own eyes and protection, vilify and calumniate not only ourselves, but the character of our wives and daughters, as was impudently and unblushingly done in that infamous and filthy sheet? There is not a city in the United States that would have suffered such an indignity for twenty-four hours." He added, "There may have been some better way, but I confess I could not see it."

When Joseph learned that the governor was going to Nauvoo he asked to be allowed to accompany him, for he had heard rumors of threats against his life. The night before, he had become alarmed at activity outside the jail. There had been whispered consultations; then a shot was fired beneath his window. He had sent one of his companions to inquire. A guard told him, "We have had too much trouble to get old Joe here to let him ever escape alive, and unless you want to die with him you had better leave before sundown."

Joseph's messenger had carried this threat to the governor, who replied, "You are unnecessarily alarmed for your friends, sir, the people are not that cruel." Again the next day he refused to take the threats seriously. Before leaving Carthage, he discharged most of the militia. He left the jail where Joseph was housed under the guard of the Carthage Greys.

The Mormons at Nauvoo had been asked to disarm, and they had done so, despite their memories of what had happened twice before when they had acceded to such requests. The governor rode into the city accompanied by a troop of dragoons. He addressed the people in a public meeting and recounted all the accusations made against them, and urged them to submit peacefully to his plans for ending trouble in the county, and when he asked for a show of hands to indicate how far he could count on their support, every hand went up.

As an added precaution, perhaps, the governor at the end of the meeting had his company of horsemen dash through the main streets of the city, performing their sword exercises, passes and guards, cuts and thrusts, as though suggesting that if the Mormons did not submit peacefully this was the kind of power he had at his command to use against them. After a stay of only a few hours, he left the city.

Back at Carthage, Joseph sat in the jail with Hyrum and the only two apostles who had not been away from Nauvoo at the time of his arrest, Willard Richards and John Taylor. In his belt Joseph had a revolver that one of his brethren had given him earlier. Throughout the day they had carried on a quiet though apprehensive conversation.

At one point Willard Richards said, "Brother Joseph, if it is necessary that you die in this matter, and if they will take me in your stead, I will suffer for you."

John Taylor's proposal was somewhat different. Less mild-mannered than either Willard or Hyrum, he suggested, "Brother Joseph, if you will permit it, and say the word, I will have you out of this prison in five hours, if the jail has to come down to do it."

Taylor's proposal was to go to Nauvoo, collect a sufficient force, and return to liberate the prophet. Joseph refused his offer and asked him instead to sing a song that was a favorite of his. Taylor sang:

> A poor, way-faring man of grief
> Hath often crossed me on my way;
> Who sued so humbly for relief,
> That I could never answer, Nay.
>
> I had not power to ask his name,
> Whither he went, or whence he came;
> Yet there was something in his eye
> That won my love, I know not why.

When he had finished, Hyrum asked him to sing it again, but Taylor replied, "Brother Hyrum, I do not feel like singing."

"Never mind," Hyrum told him; "commence singing and you will get the spirit of it."

A few minutes later John Taylor looked out the window of the jail to see a group of men approaching. They had their faces smeared with lamp-black, and they were armed. Briefly they clustered about the Carthage militiamen who had been left as guards. There were a few words and some laughter; then the guards were led away. At the same time others forced open the front door of the jail and came rushing up the stairs to the second floor and the room in which Joseph was held. A shot was fired through the lock of the door; then a second through one of the panels.

The second shot struck Hyrum Smith full in the face. Before he could fall, a shot from outside, through the open window, struck him in the back. He fell, exclaiming, "I am a dead man!"

Joseph rushed to him. "Oh, my poor, dear brother Hyrum!" he exclaimed.

He pulled his revolver from his belt. Striding to the door, he fired three shots through it into the mob. John Taylor followed him and began parrying the revolvers at the partly open entrance with a heavy walking-stick. As the pressure increased, the door began to yield. Taylor turned and ran to the window. Before he could leap, a ball struck him in the thigh. Another came through the window and struck him in the chest. The second shot was deflected by a gold watch in his vest pocket, and the force of it dropped him to the floor inside the window.

Joseph, it is said, gave the Masonic signal of distress, but there was no response. He tried to leap from the window. As he did so, shots from inside and outside the building struck him at the same moment.

"Oh, Lord, my God!" he exclaimed.

His body crumpled on the window ledge, then slowly toppled outside, falling to the path on the east side of the building.

Governor Ford received word of the assassination on the road from Nauvoo and hurried on to Carthage. He spoke with the grieving Willard Richards, the only person in the room with Joseph who had not been wounded or killed, and asked him to write a public letter to the Mormons in Nauvoo, asking them to remain calm. Willard wrote, saying that he had pledged his word that there would be no reprisals.

The bodies of the two martyrs were returned to Nauvoo the next day. As the wagon carrying the remains reached the eastern edge of the city, at about three in the afternoon, it was met by the entire population of Nauvoo, who waited for it to pass, as one reporter said, "amid the most solemn lamentations and wailings that ever ascended into the ears of the Lord of Hosts." One member recorded in his journal: "I felt as though I could not live. I knew not how to contain myself. . . . And I hope to live to avenge their blood; if I do not, I will teach my children to never cease to try to avenge their blood and then teach their children and children's children to the fourth generation as long as there is one descendant of the murderers upon the earth."

But the calm voice of Willard Richards prevailed, and no vengeance was attempted. The bodies lay in state, and more than twenty-five thousand of the prophet's followers filed past for the last sight of the man who had led them for almost fifteen years. When the burial took place, and the throng watched the pine coffins being lowered into the dark Illinois soil, only a chosen few knew that the bodies of the dead martyrs were not in them—that the boxes were filled only with sand. At midnight the night before, ten men had secretly removed the bodies and buried them in the basement of the unfinished Nauvoo House, across the street from Joseph's first home on the banks of the Mississippi. The Mormons were fearful that, even in death, the prophet might be the object of further attacks by their enemies.

For the time being the gentiles believed they had accomplished their aim. With the destruction of Joseph, they believed they had assured the downfall of his church. What they did not know was that Joseph had prepared for just such an event, and that his death, far from destroying the faith of his followers, would come to serve as a source of additional strength. Unwittingly the mob had provided Joseph with the final correspondence between his church and the original church of Christ—martyrdom.

3

Brigham Young was in New England when he heard the first rumor that Joseph was dead. He had heard such reports too often in the past to believe them without confirmation. Nevertheless, he said, he had had a premonition several days earlier that Joseph was in danger. Brigham was in Peterboro, New Hampshire, when he finally saw a letter which provided the facts of the slaying. Joseph had told him many times that he did not expect to live past forty. He had died at thirty-nine. Brigham must have been stunned by the news, but characteristically he reports, "The first thing I thought of was whether Joseph had taken the keys of the kingdom with him from the earth."

Brigham and Orson Pratt were sitting in the home of a member of the Peterboro church. Each was in deep thought. Brigham was leaning back in his chair. With Joseph gone, what had happened to the authority which he had received to govern the church? Suddenly Brigham brought the palm of his hand down on his knee.

"Brother Orson," he said, "the keys of the kingdom are right here with the church."

This was July 16, three weeks following the murder. Brigham and Orson hurried to Boston, where they met Heber Kimball and Wilford Woodruff and held council. The pressing problem was, who was to succeed Joseph? Who possessed the keys to the kingdom of heaven? Was it Sidney Rigdon, who had been longest in the first presidency as Joseph's councilor? Rigdon had recently been all but released from his official duties, and he had moved to his old home in Pittsburgh to recover his health. Joseph's other advisors, John C. Bennett and William Law, had apostatized, and Law was thought to be one of Joseph's murderers. Hyrum Smith had been a councilor to Joseph until his appointment as patriarch, but Hyrum was dead. At one time Joseph had given indication that he wished his eldest son, young Joseph, to succeed him, but the boy was now only twelve years old. Could a twelve-year-old boy be invested with the high priesthood and set at the head of the church?

These were all considerations to be weighed by members of the church. But the solution of the problem seemed clear. As the keys to the original church had been entrusted to Peter and his fellow disciples, so the authority of the Latter-day Saints was invested in Brigham and the members of the Twelve. Even if Sidney Rigdon or young Joseph turned out to have valid claims, the authority would still have to come to them through the Council of the Twelve Apostles. Their duty now was to hurry back to Nauvoo and to see that the succession to leadership, however it was decided, was accomplished in an orderly manner.

Before they could get there Sidney Rigdon had arrived from Pittsburgh. With him he brought a revelation which he claimed to have had, calling upon him, as "guardian," to head the church. In a meeting with Willard Richards and the wounded John Taylor, in company with Parley P. Pratt and George A. Smith, who had returned about the time Rigdon did, he revealed the contents of the order he claimed to have had from heaven.

"Gentlemen," he began in his remarks to them, "you are used up; gentlemen, you are divided; the anti-Mormons have got you; the brethren are voting every way, some for James, some for Deming, some for Coulsen and some for Bidell. The anti-Mormons have got you; you can't stay in the country. Everything is in confusion; you can do nothing. You lack a great leader; you want a head; and unless you unite upon that head, you're blown to the four winds. The anti-Mormons will carry the election. A guardian must be appointed."

Nothing Rigdon could have said would have been more typical of him or more certain to arouse the antagonism of those whose support he needed to become head of the church.

To his charges, George A. Smith replied, "Brethren, Elder Rigdon is entirely mistaken. There is no division; the brethren are united; the election will be unanimous, and the friends of law and order will be elected by a thousand majority. There is no occasion to be alarmed. Brother Rigdon is inspiring fears there are no grounds for."

Rigdon insisted upon setting a date for the saints to make their decision. August 8 was finally decided upon. On August 6 Brigham Young, Heber Kimball, Lyman Wight, Orson Hyde, and Wilford Woodruff arrived, having traveled night and day by railroad, stage, and steamboat. In a meeting with Rigdon the next day, Brigham heard the old man announce again that he proposed to be a guardian of the people.

"In this," he said, "I have discharged my duty and done what God commanded me, and the people can please themselves whether they accept me or not."

Brigham arose and replied. "I do not care who leads the church, even though it were Ann Lee," he said; "but one thing I must know, and that is what God says about it. I have the keys and the means of obtaining the mind of God on the subject." He went on to say that he knew that their lives would be threatened as Joseph's and Hyrum's had been, but that the power of the priesthood would remain. "Joseph conferred upon our heads all the keys and the powers belonging to the Apostleship which he himself held before he was taken away, and no man or set of men can get between Joseph and the Twelve in this world or in the world to come."

He asked them, "How often has Joseph said to the Twelve, 'I have laid the foundation and you must build thereon, for upon your shoulders the kingdom rests'? . . . My private feelings," he said in conclusion, "would be to let the affairs of men and women alone, only go and preach and baptize them into the Kingdom of God; yet, whatever duty God places upon me in His strength I intend to fulfill it."

The decisive meeting of the full membership of the church at Nauvoo was held in the open air, on a meadow overlooking the river, directly below the unfinished temple. No meeting hall was large enough to hold the numbers expected to attend. After a two-hour appeal by Rigdon, in which he tried to convince the saints of the validity of his revelations calling him to leadership of the church, the meeting was adjourned until afternoon.

Just before two o'clock the saints began solemnly to reassemble. As soon as they were all together, Brigham Young arose on the platform. Many in the gathering had not known before that he was back in the city. His first words caught them unawares.

"Attention all!"

He commented on the size of the crowd—multitudes, he said, as great as in the days of Benjamin. "For the first time in my life," he said, "for the first time in your lives, for the first time in the Kingdom of God, in the nineteenth century, without a prophet at our head, do I step forth to act in my calling in connection with the Quorum of the Twelve, as apostles of Jesus Christ unto this generation."

Mormon history and legend agree that the effect of Brigham Young this day was electrifying. George Q. Cannon, the youngest member of the Twelve, commented, "If Joseph had arisen from the dead, and again spoken . . . the effect would not have been more startling." Orson Hyde said Brigham was an excellent mimic; it would have been possible for him to imitate the voice and the inflection of Joseph— "But how," he asked, "could a man several inches shorter have imitated the very stature of the dead prophet?"

Different versions of this event have been told many times by eye-witnesses or their descendants, who remember having heard it from their parents. A common account relates that a woman was seated in the congregation nursing a child. She had her eyes upon the baby when Brigham arose to speak. At the sound of his voice, she looked up, startled, almost dropping the child. It was the voice of Joseph she heard, and it was Joseph she now saw speaking from the platform.

This myth—this miracle—was among the first to grow up about the person of Brigham Young. Joseph, the prophet, had returned to indicate his desires in the matter of authority; his mantle had fallen upon the shoulders of Brigham Young, the logical leader, the president of the Quorum of the Twelve.

When the question was put, the authority of the Twelve was sustained by an almost unanimous vote. The apostles of the new dispensation, like those of old, were the rock upon which the church had been built. Joseph's influence was not lost; it returned, purified and intensified, his image living in the memory of the saints as a force even greater than that he had enjoyed in his lifetime, sanctified, almost deified.

CHAPTER SEVEN

THE EXODUS

I

The secret of Brigham Young's strength as a leader of the Mormons lay in his insistence that the structure of authority set up by Joseph Smith be maintained. With this reasoning, he held the body of the church together. He understood, too, the necessity of continuous labor. He believed that work on the temple should be pushed forward at all costs. Missionary labors must continue. The fall harvest, which had been delayed, must be gathered and stored. Insofar as possible, life should go on as usual.

Brigham's reasons for insisting on the construction of the temple were clear. The ceremonies would bind the saints even closer in a common cause; the labor itself provided a goal and would take the Mormons' minds off the troubles that continued to plague them; most important, Joseph's doctrine of celestial marriage depended upon the rites that the prophet had disclosed to only a few of his leading elders. Before the full membership of the church could receive their endowments, the temple was necessary.

There were two reasons why missionary work became urgent after the death of the prophet; first, the saints in the East and in England must know that the work of the church had not ceased with Joseph's death; second, dissenters had come forward with claims that they were Joseph's chosen successors. Brigham sent Parley P. Pratt to New York and Wilford Woodruff to England to reassure the saints and to combat the false charges made by the apostates.

The persecution before Joseph's death and the period of mourning and indecision afterward had taken important days of the growing season in and about Nauvoo, and rations were short. When Bishop Whitney, who had charge of supplying the temple workers, complained to the council that he hadn't enough supplies to keep the work going, Brigham ordered him to give all he had, promising that the Lord would provide more. One day a missionary came in with twenty-five hundred dollars contributed by members of the outlying branches. When the council met to consider the use of the money, the Bishop declared that "the law was to lay the gold at the apostles' feet."

"Yes," Brigham replied, "and I will lay it at the bishop's feet."

He opened the mouth of the sack, grasped it by the bottom, and scattered the money across the floor. "Now," he said to Bishop Whitney, "go and buy flour for the workmen on the temple, and do not distrust the Lord any more."

Despite Brigham's hurry to speed work on the temple, he seemed to realize that the days of the church in Illinois were coming to an end. In a social gathering held in the first part of January 1845, he and Heber Kimball again took up the problem of settling in country far to the westward. They decided to ask the saints elsewhere to provide their Illinois brethren with teams and wagons to outfit a preliminary expedition to the Rocky Mountains. A committee was appointed to study the resources of the Far West.

Brigham Young's days were now filled with meetings, with giving counsel to individual members, and with correspondence with his missionaries. Few of the Mormons who saw him striding through the streets of Nauvoo or watched him giving instuctions to the temple workers on the hill doubted his energy or the source from which it came. The Mormon editor Phelps had once christened Brigham, "The Lion of the Lord," and now he seemed more a lion than ever, with his powerful shoulders and the wind from the river whipping his tawny locks about his face. When he discovered a missionary from one of the rebellious factions in the city trying to tempt the saints away from the influence of the Twelve, his gray eyes would flash with anger. He had built his personal creed upon the belief in absolute loyalty to Joseph, and now that the church had been entrusted to him, he demanded the same loyalty from his followers.

At the time of his death, Joseph Smith had come to take a much more moderate view of revelation than he had in the early days. Religious and secular forms of Mormon society had become established in the peace and prosperity of Nauvoo. At first Joseph had been satisfied to make his own decisions as to whether revelations of others than himself expressed the spirit of truth. Later he had established an orderly manner of deciding. If any Mormon claimed to have received knowledge by revelation, such knowledge was placed before the lowest order of the priesthood. Once passed by them, it went on to the higher priesthood, then to the high council, and finally to the first presidency. If there was no objection made by any quorum, then the revelation was ruled "of God."

Following Joseph's death there was a flood of claims to the power of prophecy and the gift of revelation. The first was that of Sidney Rigdon. An Eastern member then claimed that he had been told by the Lord that he was Ephraim, "born again among the gentiles." A seventeen-year-old boy came forward in Nauvoo to announce that Joseph himself had, before his death, transmitted to him the powers of prophecy and translation.

Sidney Rigdon, after his revelation was rejected by the council and, in effect, by the membership of the church when they voted not to accept him on the terms he proposed, unsuccessfully attempted to head a reorganization of the church in violation of the decision of the people and the advice of the council.

James Strang, one of the most colorful claimants to prophetic power, had been baptized only in February and was little known in Nauvoo. Before that he had been an aspiring poet, a frontier schoolmaster, a lawyer, and an itinerant preacher. After his baptism he had requested that he be allowed to head a colony of Mormons in Wisconsin, and the letter of appointment which he received from Joseph Smith he later represented to be an appointment as Joseph's successor to the entire church.

At the beginning of Strang's curious career it seemed likely that he might combine all the dissident elements of the church. Associated with him at one time or another were William Smith, William E. McLellin, John E. Page, William Marks, and even John Cook Bennett, all of whom had held responsible positions during Joseph's lifetime. He made overtures to Emma Smith and Joseph's mother, Lucy, as well as to Sidney Rigdon and Lyman Wight. His strength lay partly in his personality, for he was a tall, handsome man, robust, with a flowing black beard; also in the fact that he began by disavowing polygamy, thereby putting himself on the side of Emma Smith (who had since Joseph's death denied that her husband preached the doctrine of plural wives) and all who were in opposition to Brigham Young.

Among Strang's first acts was the announcement that he had received a divine revelation granting him all of Joseph's authority and gifts. He even produced a set of metal plates, which he maintained was an addition to the *Book of Mormon*. Probably under the influence of John Cook Bennett, he came to dress himself in regal robes, and he had himself crowned Emperor of the Kingdom of God; he changed his mind about polygamy and took extra wives. Such excesses and inconsistencies led to his eventual failure. They lost him his most influential followers and forever alienated Emma Smith, thereby giving rise eventually to what was to become the most successful of the schismatic branches of Mormonism, the Reorganized Latter-day Saints Church, which in 1860 put Joseph's and Emma's oldest son, young Joseph, at its head. Strang himself finally led his dwindling following from Wisconsin to Beaver Island in Lake Michigan, where, after a brief and harassed existence as the ruler of the Kingdom of St. James, he was killed by an assassin in 1856.

In the fall of 1844 Brigham arose in conference to state his own beliefs on the doctrine of revelation. "Every member has the right of receiving revelation for himself, both male and female," he announced. "It is the very life of the church. . . . No man preached

a gospel discourse, nor ever will, unless he does it by revelation.
. . . It is the right of an individual to get revelation to guide himself. It is the right of the head of a family. It is the right of an elder
when he builds up a church to get revelation to guide and lead that
people until he leads them and delivers them to his superiors."

In other words, revelation was much like what we have come to
call "inspiration." It might legitimately be received for guidance
only within the sphere of each man's already established authority.
Insofar as the church as a whole was concerned, Brigham left no
doubt. "If you don't know whose right it is to give revelation, I
will tell you. It is mine."

Regardless of the claims of Rigdon and the early claims of Strang,
regardless of Emma Smith's reluctance to say whether or not she
accepted the leadership of the Twelve, the thing that damned them
all in the eyes of Brigham was their opposition to Joseph's doctrine
of polygamy. The temple ceremonies and the whole concept of salvation for the dead, which had been Joseph's final contribution to
Mormon doctrine, depended on it. Brigham's one idea seemed to
be to preserve the church as Joseph had established it.

The principle of celestial marriage had been a long time in the
making, and it was not easy to preach, as Joseph had discovered. It
needed time for the saints to get used to the idea, and it needed the
temple ceremony to dignify its practice. As Brigham expressed it,
"The whole subject of the marriage relation is not in my reach,
nor in any other man's reach on this earth. It is without the beginning of days or end of years; it is a hard matter to reach. We can
tell some things with regard to it; it lays the foundation for worlds,
for angels, and for the Gods; for intelligent beings to be crowned
with glory, immortality, and eternal lives. In fact, it is the thread
which runs from the beginning to the end of the holy Gospel of
Salvation—of the Gospel of the Son of God; it is from eternity to
eternity."

If, as Joseph had said, celestial glory depended upon the principle
of celestial marriage, then Brigham knew that those who rejected
it were rejecting the prophet and the gospel. Besides, there were
other practical reasons to consider. What about the wives Joseph

and Hyrum had taken? What about Brigham's own wives, and Heber Kimball's, and Willard Richards', and Parley and Orson Pratt's? Were they to be abandoned now? What about the children? Were they to be accounted bastards? Also, in Nauvoo, as in most religious communities, there was a predominance of women. If the saints were to move again—particularly if they were to move into the wilderness of the West—who would become the protectors of these extra women?

In an article in the *Millennial Star* printed in England in the spring of 1845, just about the time the temple was nearing completion, eleven months after Joseph's death, Parley P. Pratt outlined a theory of "Celestial Family Organization" which sounded very much like a public introduction of the doctrine of polygamy as Joseph had taught it. Yet a few months later he appeared again, this time with an article entitled "The Fragment of an Address," in which he warned the Mormons to "beware of seducing spirits and doctrines of evil, as first introduced by John C. Bennett under the name of the 'spiritual wife' doctrine; and still agitated by the Pittsburgh Seer and his followers under the same title." He then went on significantly to say, "If a man has a wife according to the law of God and the regulations of the church, she is his REAL wife, body, soul, spirit, heart, and hand, and not his 'spiritual wife.'" These words were not so much contradictory as they were intentionally ambiguous.

Writers on Mormonism have cited such statements as deception —denials of plural marriage at a time when the leading elders were practicing it; and this it was to the degree that Brigham and his elders knew that a public acknowledgment of polygamy at the time might very well prevent the Mormons from leaving Illinois at all. They were even then in the process of negotiating with state officials and with the federal government in an attempt to leave the state peacefully. Such seeming denials were not contradictory to the doctrine. They were practical diplomacy, designed to give the saints time to discover a place of refuge, far from the confines of gentile prejudice and hatred.

Despite harassing opposition, they made good progress during the summer of 1845. Speeches and publications of the Mormons for this period reflect a growing self-confidence. The branches were told to send their tithing to Nauvoo to assist with the building of the temple, and they did. The young grain was thick in the fields and promised a good harvest.

A young British convert heard Brigham speak for the first time and reported his words to his brethren across the sea: "Is there any poor man here without money, without meat, and without work, let him come to me and I will keep him. I will not promise to give him money, but he shall have plenty of meat, and if he wants a coat he shall have one, if he wants a hat he shall have one, or anything else, and he can stay till something better turns up."

"Can you imagine any of our English priests speaking such words as these?" the Englishman asked.

He quoted Brigham's advice to the bishops: "Do you bishops attend to the poor as you ought to do? I fear some of you do not. I know there are some good ones, but those of you who do not, resign your offices to those who will attend to them, and if you do not, cursed be you in the name of the Lord from this time, and the curse shall follow you wherever you go."

Brigham heard that some of the saints objected because he had removed the old wooden baptismal font from the basement of the temple and replaced it with a new one of polished marble. This they considered extravagance. Brigham replied by recalling an incident from the Kirtland days. "A very pious lady came to see the temple. She walked up and down in the house with her hands locked together, and after the escape of one or two of the sectarian's most sanctified groans, she exclaimed, 'The Lord does not like such extravagance.' Poor thing. I wonder how she will walk upon the streets when they are paved with gold. She could not bear to see the temple of God adorned and beautified, and the reason was because she was *full of the devil.*"

Brigham had inherited the kingdom from Joseph Smith, but it was not his kingdom any more than it had been Joseph's. Behind it, he firmly believed, was a force greater than either of them. Joseph, he had said, "was the instrument made use of." Now he had become an "instrument," not wholly in the way that Joseph had been, for Joseph was a prophet, but similar insofar as he had received the keys from the prophet.

"I am here," he once said, "to school my brethren, to teach my family the way of life, propagate my species, and to live, if in my power, until sin, iniquity, corruption, hell, and the devil, and all classes and grades of abomination are driven from the earth."

2

Governor Ford regarded the murder of Joseph Smith as a violation of his trust in the citizens of the state. He had not trusted the Mormons before; now he could not trust the anti-Mormons. When a committee from Warsaw, whose residents everyone believed to have been most responsible for the murder, wrote him in the summer of 1844, asking him to drive the Mormons from the state, the governor replied with some spirit that he had not the authority to order them out, and he implied that the Mormons, despite his lack of sympathy with them, had behaved much better than those who had opposed them. He demanded that the Warsaw militia surrender their arms. They refused, and he attempted to obtain a company of United States troops to send into Hancock County to preserve the peace while he sought out the leaders of the mob and brought them to trial.

In September, he received word that the Hancock County militia had announced a "Grand Military Encampment." He heard that locally the encampment was spoken of as "the great wolf hunt"— that its object was to bring the militia together to drive the Mormons from the state. The governor hurried to the county, countermanded the orders, and forced the Warsaw militia to surrender its arms. Fearing for his own safety, he wrote to Brigham Young, as the new commander of the Nauvoo Legion, asking him to hold his own troops ready to protect the governor if necessary.

The anxiety the governor felt at this time, he expressed in a letter to the Mormons: "You may be disposed to ask, what use is there for law and government if these things be so? I answer you that cases like the present do not seem to be fully provided for in our constitution; they were not anticipated to occur."

Governor Ford was determined to bring the murderers of Joseph and Hyrum to trial. At the time he wrote to the Mormons he was attempting to serve writs upon the suspects, one of whom was the editor of the Warsaw *Signal*; another was a prominent member of the state legislature. The suspects fled to Missouri, then sent word back that their flight was the result of fear that they would be brought to trial in Nauvoo. Given assurance that they would not, they returned and surrendered to the governor.

The trial was held in the spring of 1845, but long before it began, the results could have been predicted. The acquittal, handed down by a non-Mormon jury and judge, combined with the growing strength of the Mormon community, left matters pretty much as they had been before the surrender of Joseph and Hyrum.

The Mormons' belief in Joseph as a true martyr was now justified. In words addressed as much to his enemies as to his friends, Brigham stated his own attitude before a Sunday meeting in Nauvoo. "I swear by the God of heaven that we will not spend money in feeing lawyers. All the lawsuits that have been got up against the saints have been hatched by fee lawyers, tavern keepers, etcetera. I would rather have a good six-shooter than all the lawyers in Illinois."

A few days after the conclusion of the trial, the capstone of the temple was raised and set in place. The building was now finished except for the roof and the steeple. The framework of the roof was in place, and timbers had been set up to raise the steeple. Brigham expected to have the attic story finished in about five weeks. "We have paid nearly $4000 this spring for lumber (pine boards, etc.) and near $1000 for lead and tin, and as yet lack nothing," he wrote to Wilford Woodruff in England. "There is the most perfect union prevailing among the saints, and every man seems determined to do all he can to roll on the work of the Temple as fast as possible."

An uneasy peace between the Mormons and the gentiles was maintained during the summer while the crops were in the ground, but with the approach of autumn the anti-Mormons renewed their activity. In September, they attacked a Mormon settlement near Lima, firing 150 dwellings and driving the inhabitants from their land. Brigham sent word to all Mormons living outside Nauvoo to move into the city, where they would have the protection of the Legion.

The building of the temple had taken four and a half years and had cost the Mormons many thousands of dollars and hours of labor. Yet, even before its completion, the Mormons had made plans to leave it. Brigham hoped that, by announcing the Mormons' intention to leave, an attack on Nauvoo could be prevented.

A month before the dedication of the temple the Twelve had met and prayed that the Lord would grant them "wisdom to manage affairs in regard to western emigration." The Mormons were advised to begin looking for buyers of their property if they wished to be among the first to leave Illinois. A company of fifteen hundred persons had been proposed as an exploring party. Now the remainder of the saints were organized into companies by hundreds. Every house in the city was turned into a workshop for the construction of wagons, the repair of harness and equipment, and the packaging of possessions.

On November 30 Brigham reported:

Every hundred have established one or more wagon shops: wheelwrights, carpenters and cabinetmakers are nearly all former wagon makers, and many not mechanics are at work in every part of the town preparing timber for making wagons. The timber is cut and brought into the city green; hub, spoke, and felloe timber boiled in salt and water, and other parts kiln dried; shops are established at the Nauvoo House, Masonic Hall, and arsenal, nearly every shop in town is employed making wagons. . . .

Very few sales of property are being made, the citizens of the country around instead of aiding us to sell our property, are using their influence to discourage sales and the authorities constantly haunt us with various writs; efforts are making to bring us into collision with the authorities of the United States by means of vexatious writs from the federal courts. The brethren are doing their utmost to prepare amidst all the discouragements that surround us for a general exodus in the spring; but from the manner that our

neighbors have kept their faith, it is very apparent that as soon as
the strength of Israel is gone, the remainder will be in danger of
violence, from our cruel persecutors, the promises of governors,
generals, judges, conventions of citizens, and mob leaders, and their
hounds to the contrary notwithstanding.

Brigham was not unaware of personal danger. The mob had killed
Joseph Smith with the hope that the death of the prophet would
mean the end of Mormonism. Yet here were the Mormons, more
than a year later, stronger and more unified than ever. One evening
when Brigham was in the temple conducting the endowment ceremonies, his carriage driver came to him and told him that a United
States marshal had come to apprehend him and take him to Carthage.
He looked about for a means of escape. "Nothing came to my mind
what to do," he reported, "until I looked across the room and saw
Brother William Miller leaning against the wall."

Miller was about the same size and build as Brigham. Brigham
walked up to him. "Brother Miller," he said, "the marshal is here
for me. Will you go and do just as I tell you? If you will, I will serve
him a trick."

Miller agreed. Brigham took off his coat and put it on Miller. He
handed him his hat and told him to accompany the driver to the
carriage. He told the driver, "When you get there, look toward
Brother Miller, and say to him, as though you were addressing me,
'Are you ready to ride?' "

Miller and the driver did as they were instructed, and William
Miller, accompanied by the marshal and his posse, rode off to Carthage. Here Miller was identified by an ex-Mormon, and the angry
marshal was forced to release him.

The anti-Mormons had again brought up the old charges that the
Mormons had manufactured counterfeit money in Nauvoo. It was
a charge that could have been made in every river town the length
of the Mississippi. Counterfeit bills flooded the frontier, and the
river towns were notorious as the source, because there a bogus
money-maker could elude arrest by rowing quickly from one state
into another. It is possible that counterfeit money had originated in
Nauvoo, even that it had been manufactured by someone who had

joined the church in order to cloak his activity. Joseph Smith and Brigham Young had both vehemently denied any knowledge of it. However, more than one recent convert had been excommunicated when it was discovered that his conversion had been no more than a mask to hide some unlawful action.

The Mormons prided themselves on the law-abiding nature of their members. There were few taverns in Nauvoo, and no brothels. In fact, one of the charges made by the gentiles had been that the Mormons did not allow a gentile resident freedom to engage in his accustomed vices. It seemed to the Mormons a bitter irony now that charges of harboring vice should be used as an excuse for the gentiles to get their hands on Brigham Young.

In February word came that Brigham was to be taken on these charges. Although the thermometer stood at twelve degrees below zero, he decided to leave the city. He would take with him members of his family and those members who seemed in the greatest danger of being held responsible.

On February 15 Brigham led the departure of two thousand Mormons. They left hurriedly while the ice of the river was still frozen solid enough to hold the heavy-laden wagons. Where they were going they did not know, except that it was again westward. Even in Brigham's mind their goal was known only by a name he had read on a rudely inked and uncertainly constructed map.

Behind them they left homes and thriving farms and businesses. In eight years they had transformed a sleepy village into the largest city in Illinois, but it was a city in a state that could no longer hold them. Perhaps this time, if they went far enough, they could find a peace less deceptive than that of Illinois. As their wagons climbed the Iowa bluffs strong gusts of wintry wind caught their wagon-covers, billowing them out and whipping them down with reports like pistol shots.

The caravan had not traveled far when messengers left behind by Brigham rode up to the wagons to report that the gentiles, instead of being appeased by their departure, had become emboldened. Mormons who wandered beyond the limits of the city had been shot at; some had been captured and beaten with their own ox-goads. In panic, many of their brethren were leaving the city, inadequately prepared for either the cold or the length of the journey. Wearily Brigham sent back word to them—"Be of good cheer!" They were escaping bondage like the Israelites of old, and a way would be opened for them. He gave instructions for them to keep order, to obey the counsel of those who had been put in charge. He would keep messengers like Porter Rockwell and Howard Egan moving between the companies. He would send help wherever possible when it was needed, but they were to look first to their own leaders for advice and assistance. Each man was to care first for his own family. Leaders of groups of ten were responsible for families left in their care; likewise, leaders of fifties and hundreds.

In Nauvoo, Brigham had left a committee in charge to care for the remaining saints and to do what they could to dispose of the church property. Few of the Mormons had been able to sell their property, and those who had had been at the mercy of the purchasers, so that each house and farm had been traded for little more than a wagon and team of oxen or for a few necessary supplies. Much of the land was simply abandoned, although with the hope that Brigham's committee might eventually be able to dispose of it. By May there were lines of Mormon wagons scattered from Keokuk, on the Mississippi border of Iowa, three-quarters of the way to the Missouri River in the west. Only a handful of Mormons remained at Nauvoo, yet the persecution increased. The Nauvoo Legion no longer existed to protect them, so citizens within the city, Mormons as well as non-Mormons, formed themselves into a military posse. The non-Mormons were mostly settlers who had bought Mormon property cheaply. Since they insisted upon defending it, they were classified with the Mormons by the anti-Mormons, who daily raided the fields and outlying houses. Finally the anti-Mormons became convinced that the Mormons could no longer protect themselves. They formed themselves into a military force and announced that they would attack the city.

Hastily the Mormons threw up breastworks east of town. This time they fought. They held the gentiles at bay for two days, but the forces outside the city grew stronger as word flew from settlement to settlement that the gentiles had the Mormons cornered. The energy of the Mormons was gradually exhausted. They finally surrendered and were given twenty-four hours to leave. The non-Mormons who had joined with them were caught and thrown into the river.

"That is what you get for dealing with Mormons," they were told. "We'll make Mormons of you! How's that for a baptism?"

Since most of the Mormons who had remained were the aged and the ill, their suffering was greater than that of those who had left in midwinter. Thrown without shelter or possessions on the Iowa shore, many of them died and were buried where they lay. Brigham's committee did what it could to help. Brigham himself, as soon as he heard, stripped members farther west of teams and wagons and sent them in relief, but for many the assistance came too late.

Earlier Brigham had sent some of his elders to the Eastern states in search of help. One of them, Elder Jesse Little, stopped in Philadelphia, where he met Judge John Kane, a federal judge, and appealed to him for advice on how to sue for justice in Washington. Judge Kane was the father of Elisha Kane, a well-known American arctic explorer, and Thomas Kane, who had just graduated from law school and was now serving as his father's clerk. Elder Little's story aroused the interest and sympathy of young Thomas Kane, and he immediately set out to investigate the matter for himself.

Arriving in Nauvoo just after the last of the Mormons had been driven out, Kane described its awesome appearance:

I saw on the Left Bank of the Mississippi a large and gay city which shone brightly in the sunshine as when I first . . . came in sight of it. Its houses were all new, mostly of a cheerful red brick with pretty garden plots around them—and a splendid marble building with gilded cupola rose above them all with the dignity of proud beauty. As I drew near I was surprised to see in this new city no sign of life.—No one appeared on the shore of the river— it was a pleasant morning and not nine o'clock yet but not a woman could be seen in any of the green gardens. I got out of my little boat in which I crossed from the Iowa side and everything was [so] still that I heard the flies buzz and the river ripple in the shallow. After a while I thought I heard the sound of human voices—I listened and a minute after heard it repeat so clearly that I knew it to be the distant sound of boisterous laughter. Guided by my ferryman I went to whence it proceeded and found it made by a large number of drunken men who were carousing in the porch of the splendid marble building I had noticed when I first drew near the spot. They had several jugs of strong waters of various kinds of which they were drinking heavily; inside also which proved to be the Mormon Temple others like them were to be found . . . beastly intoxicated, who had much defiled it with their vomit and filth and I found the building so greatly defiled with their filth that much vomit was observable in the upper story of its steeple where orgies were not omitted. . . . In addition to these degraded beings, I beheld around and in the Temple—and in [the] house neighboring to it . . . many others who seemed their friends. Inebriety at least partial was evidently no stranger to their faces—they were armed to the teeth, and had besides rifles, pistols & knives—muscats & cannon marked as property of the U. S. I was not without apprehension for my life when several of them for whose sobriety I would not now answer altercated violently with me because I had entered the Silent City without a passport from one of their leaders . . . whose description given by them failed answerably in no respect [to] that of a bandit chief. They dismissed me however as I did not attempt to withstand their evil humour and left me free to wander where I wished.

Kane also reported that in walking through the streets of the deserted city he felt he should tread on tiptoe, "as if walking down the aisle of a country church, to avoid rousing irreverent echoes from the naked floors." Upon his return to the Iowa shore, he "found as many as six or seven hundred still remained . . . being those too sick or too poor to be able to proceed further. . . . They had been reduced to great strait of wretchedness, from their extreme poverty and the exposure to which they have been subjected."

Unlike the temple at Kirtland, which still stands, the Nauvoo temple was burned by the marauders before the last of the Mormons had left their heart-rending encampment on the Iowa shore. The Mormons could see the flames rising as they huddled in misery and gazed across the water. Only the front wall and a portion of the side wall were left standing. Later a tornado was to weaken what remained. The walls were toppled with dynamite to prevent their

accidentally falling and injuring someone. The property was purchased by a group of French Icarians under Etienne Cabet a short
time after the Mormons left, but their communistic experiment
failed within a few years. Their failure supplied John Taylor, the
Mormon apostle, with some of his most telling arguments when, in
Paris as a Mormon missionary, he debated Mormonism with members of a Fourierist society. The Mormons, he said, built Nauvoo
from the ground up and created a prosperous and thriving community. The French communists had moved into a ready-made city
—yet what do I hear everywhere in France? Taylor asked. Give us
aid! Send us assistance! That is the word out of Nauvoo under your
system. Eventually the brick and stone from the temple went into
the construction of a Catholic girls' school, St. Mary's Academy,
erected near the temple site.

Nauvoo, which at the height of its prosperity under the Mormons
contained 25,000 inhabitants, became a sleepy river village, and in
the 1950 census reported a population of 1242.

3

Of all the journeys made by the Mormons, the most difficult and
the least known was the movement in the dead of an Iowa winter
across the rolling plains from Nauvoo to what the Mormons called
Winter Quarters, on the present site of Omaha, Nebraska. William
Clayton, an English convert who served as Brigham Young's secretary and was in charge of moving the church property and records,
left an account of the daily progress in the winter of 1846 that records the suffering, the disappointments, and the frustrations of
the trek. Clayton was a musician as well as a scribe, and he composed during this time what has become the Mormons' most prized
hymn—"Come, Come Ye Saints":

> Come, come ye saints,
> No toil nor labor fear,
> But with joy wend your way;

Though hard to you
This journey may appear,
Grace shall be as your day.

'Tis better far for us to strive
Our useless cares from us to drive;
Do this, and joy your hearts will swell.
All is well! All is well!

Clayton tells us that Brigham ordered the brass band, of which Clayton was a member, to remain together and to play nightly for the cheer of the saints. Occasionally the band played also for residents of the scattered Iowa settlements. Sometimes a collection would be taken up to pay the musicians; at other times their pay would be corn and potatoes, and on one occasion they received only a pail of honey. More than once the Mormons were told to move on; the settlers had heard about them from Missouri and Illinois and wanted nothing to do with them.

Brigham's system for moving so large a body of men, women, and children so great a distance was to establish camps at various places across the territory. At each camp a certain number would halt, prepare the land for planting, and then move on. Others would follow, putting in crops from the seeds they had brought with them. Later companies would harvest the crop and carry it with them to Winter Quarters. This way, Brigham reasoned, the saints could augment their short supply of provisions. The most permanent of these camps were at Garden Grove and Mt. Pisgah, and they served the Mormon emigration not only during the Nauvoo exodus but for years afterward.

Brigham also insisted that when a company left camp their departure should be accomplished in an orderly manner. After all, there were more than 20,000 Mormons on the march. The wagons were appropriately spaced so that they would not compete with one another for feed and camp grounds. As the wagons moved forward he sent scouts ahead to search out the best route. Eliza R. Snow, who had been one of Joseph Smith's wives, and was later to be sealed to Brigham Young, described in her journal the first evening's encampment of one of the companies.

It was impossible for us to move in a body; and one company filed off after another; and, on the first of March we broke camp and moved four or five miles and put up for the night, where at first view the prospect was dreary enough. It was nearly sunset—very cold, and the ground covered with snow to the depth of four or five inches; but with brave hearts and strong hands, and a supply of spades and shovels, the men removed the snow, and suddenly transformed the bleak deserted scene into a living town, with cloth houses, log-heap fires, and a multitude of cheerful inhabitants.

But there was more suffering than cheer during most of the journey. On that first night out of Nauvoo, nine children were born, "and from that time," the journal reports, "as we journeyed onward, mothers gave birth to offspring under almost every variety of circumstances imaginable, except those to which they had been accustomed; some in tents, others in wagons—in rain-storms and in snow-storms. I heard of one birth which occurred under the rude shelter of a hut, the sides of which were formed of blankets fastened to poles stuck in the ground, with a bark roof through which the rain was dripping. Kind sisters stood holding dishes to catch the water as it fell, thus protecting the new-comer and its mother from a shower-bath as the little innocent first entered on the stage of human life; and through faith in the great ruler of events, no harm resulted to either."

A constant watch was maintained because the Mormons were still apprehensive that they might be pursued. Also, they were crossing territory not too distant from their old enemies in Missouri, and rumors of an intended attack by them were heard daily.

Brigham Young's company reached the bank of the Missouri River in June, having traveled more than three and a half months and averaged only about one hundred miles a month. Behind them were the bulk of the emigration, on the plains, in the encampments, putting in crops, or simply struggling through the spring rain and mud. Brigham paused and told his companions to get crops in and houses up, for food and shelter during the next winter. When the first companies had left Nauvoo it had been hoped that many of the Mormons could remain there a while in peace and that the temple and other church property could be sold to help defray the expenses of travel and settlement. Brigham's only hope now lay in his appeal to Washington for assistance in collecting damages from the citizens of Illinois or in aiding them to settle in the Far West; for the last of his people had been driven from the city, and those who had not died from the intense cold of late winter and early spring were even now attempting to rejoin those who had left earlier. By the time Brigham arrived at the Missouri he was on the border of Indian territory, but he felt that the Mormons would be safer in negotiating a treaty with the Indians across the river than in remaining on the east bank, subject to gentile opposition still. Here he first indicated the manner in which he planned to deal with the Indians. He asked for an audience with Big Elk, chief of the Omahas.

"We are on a journey to California," he told the chief, "and with your permission we would like to winter here. We can do you good. We will repair your guns, and make a farm for you, and aid you in any other way that our talents and circumstances will permit. We should like to get some honorable men to watch our cattle. We will assist you for any favors you may be willing to confer on us. Can you furnish someone who will watch our cattle and keep them safe? Have you any objection to our getting timber, building houses, and staying here until spring or longer? The government is willing if you are. Would you like to have some of our mechanics repair your guns? Do you feel disposed to be on amicable terms with us? Are you willing we should sow wheat here this fall and plant corn next year? I will be glad to have you express yourselves freely on these subjects."

To this Big Elk replied, "My son, thou hast spoken well. I have all thou hast said in my heart. I have much I want to say. We are poor. When we go to hunt game in one place our enemies kill us. We do not kill them. I hope we will be friends. You may stay on these lands two years or more. Our young men may watch your cattle. We would be glad to have you trade with us. We will warn you of danger with other Indians."

Brigham had scarcely reached the Missouri, with the bulk of the emigration still trailing behind, when he was visited by an Army

officer. War with Mexico had broken out, and the government requested that the Mormons supply a battalion of five hundred of
their younger men to march into Mexican territory. The government agreed to pay in advance a portion of the money that would
be owed the soldiers, and the Army would, of course, provide them
with provisions and clothing during the terms of their enlistment.
It was agreed that the battalion would be discharged in the West,
presumably not too far from where the Mormons hoped eventually
to settle. These were advantages, to be sure; but there were disad-
vantages as well. The loss of their youngest and strongest men
would leave the Mormons without sufficient teamsters, road-
builders and bridge-builders, scouts and watchmen. The families of
most of the men who enlisted would have to be cared for by those
who remained. But also the enlistment was a means of partial deliverance from their most serious problem—a lack of money with
which to defray the expenses of the migration.

Brigham knew that the Mormons had no choice. With Heber
Kimball and Willard Richards he returned along the trail, enlisting
men to join the battalion. His feelings were expressed when he met
William Clayton on the road before Winter Quarters and told him,
"This is a good prospect for our deliverance and if we do not do it
we are doomed." The problems he still faced were emphasized by
Clayton, who commented in his journal, "I am now destitute for
help. Edward Martin is advised to go and leave his family in my
charge. I have still four yoke of oxen missing and I don't know
where to find them."

In contrast to the cooperation which Chief Big Elk had given
Brigham, Thomas H. Harvey, local agent for the Department of
Indian affairs offered only fumbling obstructionism. Suspicious of
the Mormons, he could not understand why Brigham made such
thorough plans if all he intended was to winter on the Missouri
River. He was a man of little imagination, and he seems to have had
no understanding of the problem of moving so great a body of people into an unsettled country. In the sparsely settled stretches of
southern and western Iowa, Brigham had found no government
bureaucrats to prevent his setting up temporary settlements on land

not yet pre-empted. When he reached Indian territory, however, he found in Harvey a man fearful of responsibility, who would neither absolutely deny the Mormons' rights nor grant them his permission to settle or to travel in Indian lands. He sent letter after letter to Washington, each one conveying his own attitude of suspicion of Brigham's intentions and each requiring months of uncertain waiting for a reply. Meanwhile the Mormons, who had expected assistance from Washington, not petty obstruction, were left at a crucial moment of their history in uncertainty.

Young Thomas Kane of Philadelphia, his interest further aroused by the glimpse he had had of the Mormons driven from Nauvoo, had traveled from St. Louis up the Missouri to the Mormon encampment. He had arrived ill with fever, and he was nursed back to health by Brigham's wife Mary Ann. In gratitude, he undertook to represent the Mormon cause to the Commissioner of Indian Affairs in Washington. He wrote:

I have been requested by the Mormon Council through a special messenger to urge strongly upon your immediate consideration two requests preferred by them to the President last Fall.

The first relates to their sojourn on the Omaha lands on the Western side of the Mo. near old Council Bluffs. You are aware that when the prairie grass began to fail last year the Mormon emigrants moving in scattered parties with different degrees of expedition, halted to winter at various points, along their line of march between Nauvoo and their place of destination beyond the Rocky Mts. The principal of the places of wintering thus established was this [the east side] of the Omaha country and here they put in very large crops of grain and potatoes to recruit their nearly exhausted stock of provisions. As these must be gathered in the approaching summer and autumn unless hundreds are to die of starvation, and as the harvesters must remain on the farm of the settlement till the season for travelling is gone by, it follows that it is impossible for the whole body to be . . . off before next spring. The men who continue on their journey till late this summer (for the Mormons dragging along with them their all, furniture, herds, feeble & poor, move very slowly) will have no time on their part to make proper preparations for their families before the approach of Winter. They are going among the most untamed and ferocious of our Indians, and though for their advance of the young & hardy, they can as they doubtless will, build such stockade fort with block houses as may be large enough to guard them & their limited ration of provisions, they know it would be utterly impossible to do this for all the sick & old and women & children of their horde which now number over 20,000 in motion.

They will therefore have to leave the greater part of them at their Omaha town as an Asylum for passing the winter. Here they have built nearly a thousand houses which have sheltered since last fall 15 thousand souls. They have it perfectly well fortified on all sides and under its protection are the rush bottom peculiar to the Mo. where their cattle can find fattening pasture from Nov. to April. During the absence of the fighting men of the church on pioneer duty a few can here ensure their safety and provide for the comfort of all the dependent members of the Community. For these reasons, the Mormons ask you to allow them to hold this post till next Spring (May or June 1848) shortly after which time their treaty with the Omahas expires, and they ask a formal permission to this effect or such license as you have power to bestow. . . .

Kane also requested that one of the Mormons be made a representative of the Indian Bureau, with power to engage in treaties with the Indians farther west during the journey to the Rocky Mountains. Both requests were eventually denied, but the correspondence took so long that the Mormons, although they lacked peace of mind concerning their rights on the Missouri, had time to complete arrangements for moving most of their members westward—which was the substance of their first requests. In the end they were forced to desert Winter Quarters and build a new town, which they named Kanesville, in honor of Thomas Kane, on the east bank of the river; but this did not happen until the bulk of the emigration had moved on to the westward.

Meanwhile, at Winter Quarters, Brigham Young divided the large encampment into wards, each under the direction of a bishop, and regular services were resumed. He organized a high council for over-all administration. He ordered that each able-bodied man contribute the tenth day of his labor, or an equivalent, for the support of the poor and to assist the families of the Mormon Battalion members. However, all was not solemn duty. Brigham instituted concerts and entertainments of various kinds in order to keep the minds of the saints from dwelling on their troubles or remembering too poignantly their former prosperity. On one occasion the church historian records that, "President Young told the brethren and sisters he would show them how to go forth in the dance in an acceptable manner before the Lord. President Young then knelt down and prayed God in behalf of the meeting, imploring his blessings upon those present and dedicating the meeting and house to the Lord. At the sound of the music the President then led forth in the dance."

Thomas Kane recorded the number and condition of the Mormons during the fall of 1846 as follows:

	Souls	Families
On the edge of the Settlements of Iowa & Missouri and partly employed in work there—several small bodies and scattered families of five persons. Of these one body near Bonaparte Iowa since broken up, run by count in Sept. 638 persons.	1,000	200
Near the edge of the settlements on a small water course	100	20
Proceeding Westward		
Twenty miles Soap Creek	100	20
Head of Chariton or Chariton Pt.	50	10 or 12
On the White Breast or Sein Blanc (here is a crop put in)	75	15
Garden Grove (heavy crop)	400	80
Mt. Pisgah (do. do.)	1,000	200
On creek E. of Indian Town called Cent Deux or One Hundred and Two by Traders	200	40
On E. Nishnabotna at Indian Town on W. Nishnabotna &. ———	50	10
On Branch of Keg Creek	125	25
On Keg Creek or Caque	100	20
Near the Missouri & Bluffs E. side	750	150
Near the mouth of the Poncah R., W. side of the Mo. (This is a couple of hundred miles off the line described)	1,000	200
Under estimate of the Main Camp taken one month since	11,250	2,250
Total	16,000	3,200

Kane's figures must be considered little more than a rough estimate, since not even Brigham Young could have known exactly how many Mormons were on the trail behind him. Some few deserted and moved into Missouri, resettling on the land they had left earlier. Missionaries from James Strang's schismatic sect were active and tempted a few others into Strang's colony to the north. A number of families remained in various Illinois communities. The total figure seems not too far off, since it has since been assumed that between 18,000 and 20,000 eventually followed the lead of Brigham Young into the West.

Most of the Mormons arrived at Winter Quarters between June and September 1846. Many died on the way and were buried beside the roadside; many others survived until they reached the Missouri, but expired from hardship and privation soon after. Brigham Young suffered continuous illness during the winter. His robust body, which had filled out in Nauvoo, lost so much weight that he said he could wrap his greatcoat twice around him. Nevertheless, he remained so active that Heber Kimball complained that he was endangering not only his own life but the lives of the saints. His trouble was, he told Brigham, that he insisted upon taking too much of the responsibility on himself.

In February 1847, just a year after he had crossed the Mississippi from Nauvoo, Brigham wrote a letter to one of his elders in the East, describing their settlement. "Winter Quarters," he wrote, "is platted in 41 blocks, numbering 20 lots to a block, 4 rods by 10 covered by about 700 houses divided into 22 wards, with 22 bishops and counsellors over whom preside a municipal High Council of 12 High Priests. The health of the camp is good as could reasonably be expected and a general good feeling prevails; all are anxious to remove west. Many will go this season, and their places will be filled by others coming on, ready to follow the season following. The more the travel, the better the road, and the more grain ahead, the lighter the load."

To a merchant who wrote, asking about the possibility of opening a store and trading with the Mormons, Brigham sent the following advice:

The variety of articles mentioned in your letter are all desirable in their place and it takes a general assortment to accommodate all people, of which yourselves as merchants must be well aware, and in general terms can only say on this point, that we are like other people, and a variety of such articles as are needed for convenience in families, and will be light, durable and portable will meet with the readiest sale and in general the botanic medicines will be the ones most called for. This place will be under the watch of vigilant police, and we shall not expect Indians to come within our stockade, or that any disorderly conduct will be tolerated here, consequently we shall object to your bringing any spiritous liquors to this place to sell or give away. We must also object to your trading with the Indians or having any intercourse with them to call them into the city, or anywhere in the vicinity, for we have plenty of them without their having any additional incentive to visit our borders.

Relations with the Indians were not easy, as the Omahas, a friendly race, were constantly being attacked by the more warlike Sioux. If a Mormon's stock was stolen he could not know whether it had been taken by the Omahas, with whom Brigham treated, or by their enemies. Brigham had to warn his people that if they committed any acts of violence against the Omahas they would be subject to Indian justice, just as the Indians were held responsible to the Mormons for what they did in the Mormon settlement.

Brigham's letter concluded:

We shall also object to your having or harboring about your premises, persons of any description, engaging in gambling or conniving in any form. We do not state these objectionable points because we suppose they are countenanced by you, but simply that you may know our principles, which, when once known to all men, might save some the trouble of leaving, for it is easier for those who do not approve of good order and wholesome regulations, to keep away, than be obliged to go after they have once arrived.

This was the time, Brigham knew, when the final test had been put to his followers. A few had wandered off with Lyman Wight to Texas, where they were to develop a small independent colony. A handful had followed Sidney Rigdon back to Pittsburgh. Emma

Smith and her mother-in-law Lucy, as well as Joseph's young sons, remained in Illinois. Those who stayed with Brigham were now genuinely the Camp of Israel. They had taken their first step into the wilderness. As children of Israel, they had faith that a way would be opened to them.

CHAPTER EIGHT

THE TREK

I

One historian of the Mormons divided the early history of the church into two periods. The fourteen years of Joseph's leadership he called the period of spiritual development, with the establishment of the creed and the ordering of the priesthood. The period under Brigham Young he called the "materialistic," with less emphasis upon revelation, more on "reason and common sense"—a greater concern for the material prosperity of the Mormons. This is only partly the case. There were always the rational justification and the concern for the material community in Smith's doctrine; and, despite the necessity to engage in practical affairs, Brigham's first impulse was always to regulate matters in terms of the Kingdom of God.

It has been suggested that if Brigham had not joined the Mormons and associated with Smith, he might have become one of America's famous exploiters—a Gould, a Fisk, a Huntington, or an Andrew Carnegie, all men of humble origin who rose to heights of power. Certainly Brigham possessed characteristics similar to these men, the same restless energy and vitality, the same courage and quickness of decision, the same sensitivity to the timbre of American aspirations. Where he differed (and it is an important difference) was in the fact that he tied his fortunes to Joseph's concept of a community of saints, not to the spirit of the individual entrepreneur, demonstrating the truth uttered by Walt Whitman, who wrote, "The common ambition strains for elevation, to become some privileged exclusive," but, "The master sees greatness and health in being part of the mass."

Joseph Smith's vision was one that conceived of a union of all humanity, both lineally in historical time (from the present back to Adam) and laterally in terms of the Kingdom of God on earth. In a council of the leaders at Winter Quarters in the early part of 1847, Brigham related a dream he had had the night before. "I dreamed," he said, "that I went to see Joseph. He looked perfectly natural, sitting with his feet on the lower rounds of the chair. I took hold of his right hand and kissed him many times and said to him, 'Why is it that we cannot be together as we used to be? You have been from us a long time, and we want your society and I do not like to be separated from you.'

"Joseph, rising from his chair and looking at me with his usual earnest, expressive and pleasing countenance, said, . . . 'It is all right; we cannot be together yet; we shall be by and by; but you will have to do without me awhile, and then we shall be together again.' . . .

"I said, 'Brother Joseph, the brethren you know well, better than I do; you raised them up, and brought the priesthood to us. The brethren have a great anxiety to understand the law of adoption or sealing principles; and if you have a word of counsel for me, I should be glad to receive it.'

"Joseph stepped toward me, and looking very earnestly, yet pleasantly, said, 'Tell the people to be humble and faithful, and be sure to keep the spirit of the Lord and it shall lead them right. Be careful and not turn away the small still voice; it will teach them what to do and where to go; it will yield the fruits of the kingdom. Tell the brethren to keep their hearts open to conviction, so that when the Holy Ghost comes to them, their hearts will be ready to receive it. They can tell the spirit of the Lord from all other spirits; it will whisper peace and joy to their souls; it will take malice, hatred, strife and all evil from their hearts; and their whole desire will be to do good, bring forth righteousness and build up the Kingdom of God. Tell the brethren . . . to keep the spirit of the Lord; and if they will, they will find themselves just as they were organized by our Father in Heaven before they came into the world. Our Father in Heaven organized the human family, but they are all disorganized and in great confusion.'

"Joseph then showed me the pattern, how they were in the beginning. This I cannot describe, but I saw it, and saw where the priesthood had been taken from the earth and how it must be joined together, so that there would be a perfect chain from Father Adam to his latest posterity."

If it had been Ralph Waldo Emerson instead of Joseph Smith whom Brigham saw in his dream, the advice would have been not too different: the small, still voice, the hearts open to conviction, the whispers of peace and joy, the highest form of earthly society an image of the soul of God. Joseph Smith and Brigham Young did not know Emerson's writings, but they had breathed the same nineteenth-century American air; they were affected by the same need to reconcile matter and spirit. One difference between them (and a small one) was that Emerson's vision was that of the poet, the thought made concrete in the images of the poem or essay; Joseph Smith's was that of the prophet, with the need to translate the vision into act. Both views represented a break with the absolutism of traditional religion.

It is this side of Mormonism which non-Mormon writers have always failed to see. Thinking in terms of nineteenth-century American individualism, they have been led to regard Joseph Smith and Brigham Young as opportunists, differing from the opportunists of the financial or political realms only in the means they chose to pursue. In Whitman's terms, Joseph and Brigham sought greatness not in privileged exclusiveness, but in working for the welfare of the mass, which was the community of saints. Individualism, Whitman said, is only half of man's dream. "There is another half, which is adhesiveness or love, that fuses, ties and aggregates, making the race comrades and fraternizing all. Both are to be vitalized by religion. . . . For I say at the core of democracy, finally, is the religious element."

The Mormon persecutions have also been seen as a progress by elimination, a process of "the survival of the fittest." This is, in part, true. Persecution may have eliminated many of the Mormons least able to survive physical hardship, but the greatest number it eliminated were those who were weak in the dream of heavenly communion. At all times there had been concern for the ill and infirm among the Mormons. In an epistle issued at Winter Quarters, Brigham outlined plans for the beginning of emigration to the Far West: "The widow and fatherless must not be forgotten. Let as many of them be taken as can, and that all who remain be amply provided for."

It is significant, too, as a reflection of the sense of responsibility which played so important a part in plural marriages, that so many of them took place during the period of the final persecution at Nauvoo. Brigham had taken five additional wives under Joseph's direction before the prophet died. One of them, Clara Decker, he married just preceding his final mission to the East, and it was she who was destined to accompany him in the first company to leave Winter Quarters. In the year following Joseph's death, Brigham married five more, including two of the women who had been sealed to Joseph Smith. In 1846, just before leaving Nauvoo, he married eight women, including two more of Joseph's widows. During the trip across Iowa, he married twice.

Most historians have pointed facetiously to these many marriages as indications of Brigham's excessive virility. There can be no doubt about his manliness, for the wives he married during these two years presented him, eventually, with forty-seven children. But there were other reasons too. In the case of the four widows of Joseph, it was Brigham's obligation under the system not only to make himself responsible for their welfare, but also "to raise up children unto Joseph." Although Brigham eventually married six of Joseph's widows, who bore him a total of ten children, these children would remain as Joseph's progeny in another existence.

As is the case with all Mormon doctrine, the marriage principle grew from a combination of theory and necessity. Had sexuality been the only justification for the practice of polygamy, the thousands of Mormons who came finally to accept it could never have been won to such a belief. Many of Brigham Young's marriages were performed at a time when Mormon society was again harassed by gentile persecution and when Brigham himself was in constant danger, the last possible time when he would ordinarily have thought to add to his responsibility. They were performed because the year 1846 provided the last possibility for the performance of the temple endowments. They were performed also as a means of supplying protection and care for superfluous women in a society which was to spend the next two or three years in temporary encampments in Iowa, Nebraska, and the Western plains country.

The urge behind the rationalization of Mormon marriage is seldom discussed. Mormon polygamy has been called "Puritanical" by one historian, emphasizing the sense of duty and obligation which accompanied it. In another sense it was anti-Puritanical, although springing from the same source. Perry Miller, an authority on Puritan thought, has written: "The Puritans were gifted—or cursed—with an overwhelming realization of an inexorable power at work not only in nature but in themselves, which they called God." The Mormons, many of whom were descendants of the Puritans, shared this sense, and it was heightened in them, as it had been in the Puritans, by their nearness to actual nature. The Puritans reacted to it by proscription, particularly in sex. The Mormons accepted. For them this "inexorable power" was the power of the universe—the power of God. Whatever was truly "natural" was truly of God.

Except for the terms in which it is stated, some such view would seem to be behind the twentieth century's preoccupation with the subject of sex. Today's frankness would have shocked the nineteenth century, with its mantle of Victorian respectability, even more than the Mormons shocked them, not only by polygamy, but by their frankness in talking about it as a sexual relationship. Heber C. Kimball is reported once to have said, in addressing a group of departing missionaries: "Let truth and righteousness be your motto, and don't go into the world for anything but to preach the gospel, build up the Kingdom of God, and gather the sheep into the fold.

You are sent out as shepherds to gather the sheep together; and remember that they are not your sheep; they belong to Him that sends you. Then don't make a choice of any of those sheep; don't make selections before they are brought home and put into the fold. You understand that. Amen."

The Western frontiersman called himself a "child of nature," half horse and half alligator, rivaling in his description the marvels of nature. He could create a ballad about Brigham Young and his many wives, and sing it with gusto:

> Brigham Young was a Mormon bold,
> And a leader of the roaring rams,
> And a shepherd of a heap of pretty little sheep,
> And a nice fold of pretty little lambs,
> And he lived with his five and forty wives,
> In the city of the great Salt Lake
> Where they woo and coo as pretty doves do,
> And cackle like ducks to a drake.

Mormons were as much children of nature as the frontiersman, although they named their father God, and created a heaven in the image of the world as they knew it. A God without a sense of humor was an inconceivable God—and what better subject for humor than the facts of nature?

The Mormons needed a sense of humor almost as much as faith during the end of 1846 and the beginning of 1847. Brigham Young's energies were divided between attempts to settle his people safely in Iowa and Nebraska encampments and his plans for the migration to the West. He had counseled his earliest companies to build shelters firm enough to serve the emigration for several years. The seven hundred houses he had listed as being constructed the first summer were not the enduring brick homes the Mormons had built in Nauvoo, but they were probably as well built as the usual settler's log cabin on the frontier. He advised his followers to plant early and carefully, to raise as much as possible, and to conserve and store all that was not absolutely necessary to their subsistence. As soon as the weather permitted, he planned to set out with a pioneer company, to be composed of men he trusted and knew he could depend upon. They were to be followed as soon as practicable by all who could assure themselves of food and supplies to last them eighteen months. They were to take with them as many of the families of men who had enlisted in the Mormon Battalion as possible. In a letter to one of the missionaries in February, Brigham said: "I feel like a father with a great family of children around me, in a winter storm, and I am looking with calmness, confidence, and patience for the cloud to break, and the sun to shine, so that I can run out and plant and sow and gather in the corn and wheat and say: 'Children Come Home, winter is approaching again and I have homes and wood and flour and meal and wheat and potatoes and squashes and onions and cabbages and a joyful feast to all who will come and partake.' "

On March 24 Brigham sold his grist mill for two thousand dollars, which enabled him to pay the debts on it. On the twenty-sixth he called a special conference, in which he gave his final instructions to the whole camp at Winter Quarters. He told them how to care for their houses, how to plant their crops, and how to deal with the Indians. On April 1 he wrote a long letter to the committee in the East, asking them to procure a printing press and type, "whereby we can furnish our children with books, and the saints with new things to feast the soul."

2

On April 16 the pioneer company was on the road west. It was made up of 143 men and boys, 3 women, 2 children, 72 wagons, 93 horses, 52 mules, 66 oxen, 19 cows, 17 dogs, and an unknown number of chickens. They were as well equipped as they might be, considering the circumstances. "The men carried rifles and small weapons, and a cannon was taken along to overawe hostile Indians. In their covered wagons were plows, and other implements, seed grain, and a year's supply of provisions." They also had with them the bell from the temple at Nauvoo and a case of surveyor's instruments which Parley P. Pratt had recently brought with him when he returned from a mission.

Of the entire country between the Missouri River and California, a traveler who crossed it in 1851 wrote: "It is of no account; the soil is poor, sandy, and too dry to produce anything but this little short grass, and, when it does rain, in three hours afterward you could not tell that it had rained at all." Although this description was later to be proved wrong, most travelers then accepted it; and the only emigration of consequence before the Mormons had turned north to Fort Hall when it came up against the Rockies in western Wyoming, and then had headed for Oregon. Of the few emigrants to California before 1849, most had gone by ship, either around the Horn or by taking a second vessel after crossing the Isthmus of Panama. None of the Mormons had been so far west, and almost the only travelers through the central Rockies had been fur trappers and such explorers as Bonneville and Frémont. Today the nearest parallel to the route followed by Brigham and his pioneer company is the Union Pacific railroad from Omaha across Nebraska and Wyoming to Echo Canyon in Utah; the nearest present-day highway is Highway 30.

In the Mormon company, bugles sounded each morning at five. Two hours were allowed for breakfast and prayers. During the day the company traveled in a close file, most of the men walking beside the wagons with their weapons loaded and clearly visible. At night the wagons were drawn into a tight circle—or a semicircle if the company camped on a river bank. Usually the animals were pastured within the circle to keep them from wandering or being stolen by Indians. The men would retire for prayers by groups at eight-thirty, and they were expected to be settled by nine. Fifty of them had been appointed as guards, with twelve of these standing duty each half-night. At one time, while they were traveling on the prairies, in Indian country, the company drove five wagons abreast.

The Mormons sighted their first buffalo at the head of Grand Island on April 30. Hunters from the camp rode after them and succeeded in bringing down eleven, which were added to the meat larder. On May 4 the travelers were delayed when they came upon a band of about four hundred Indians, who followed them curiously from a distance, until Brigham, becoming alarmed, ordered the cannon to be fired. The Indians disappeared, but they set fire to the prairie ahead, causing the company to halt until the wind shifted and drove the flames away from them.

Brigham's organization of the company seems almost faultless. The conduct of his followers was less so. Early in the journey, some of the men were careless in penning their stock at night. Their horses wandered away, and valuable morning hours were spent searching for them. The spirit of the camp was lighter than Brigham felt it should be. Most of the men were free of any family responsibility, and a few of them seemed to feel that they were on a pleasure outing. Cards appeared in the wagons at night, and an occasional bottle of whisky. There was music around the fire at night, by Brigham's direction; and some of the younger men took to dancing with each other in a parody of their amusement at Winter Quarters the winter before.

So long as the fun remained within bounds, Brigham remained silent. When it didn't—when it endangered the safety of the company or caused unnecessary delays—he resorted to strong language.

During the days, he rode at the head of the column, preceded only by the scouts and hunters. As the pioneers traveled along the Platte River they came upon buffalo so numerous that Brigham estimated them in the hundreds of thousands. Several times the company was forced to pause while the shambling herds crossed the trail before them. At the sight of so much sport, the younger men could not contain their enthusiasm. They chased after the shaggy beasts, whooping and shouting as they shot them down.

On May 18 Brigham called the whole camp together for a strong rebuke. "You are not," he told them, "to kill any more game. We have more on hand now than we can take care of." He reminded them of the companies to follow—their own families. They would need meat. He told them: You are "servants of God going forth to seek out a resting place for the saints."

After leaving Grand Island, they broke a new trail. Instead of taking the route followed by the Oregon settlers on the south bank of the river, they remained on the north, thus establishing what became known as the Mormon Trail, or the Old Mormon Road. Along this route they established a regular postal system to guide the companies that would follow. The longest letters were written out, then inserted in a notch cut in a board slab and nailed to a fifteen-foot pole, which they planted alongside the trail. Occasionally they scribbled terse messages on a shaved board or the bleached skull of a dead buffalo. Such messages might consist of the date, the distance traveled that day, and the Mormon byword: "All is well."

On the plains before Fort Laramie, Brigham celebrated his forty-sixth birthday. The trials and illness of the year before had thinned his stout body. He wore his hair even longer than he had before. His health, he reported at this point, was better than it had been when the journey began.

As they approached Laramie, the first inhabited place they had seen since leaving Winter Quarters, the spring green of the prairies was replaced by the blended purple and green of the desert. Mountains appeared in the distance, their peaks seeming to float in the clear air. William Clayton had constructed an ingenious machine of wooden cogs attached to one of the wagons to measure the distance, and he estimated they had come 522 miles. Here the nights were cold and the days hot. They had climbed to an altitude of almost 7000 feet on the long, gradual slope before the fort.

The arrival at Fort Laramie was made with some anticipation. Here the pioneers expected to meet members of a company of Mormons from Mississippi, who had journeyed west by a southern route and had spent the past winter at Pueblo on the Arkansas River. They expected also to meet some of the battalion members who had been left at Pueblo because of illness. As it turned out, only a few families of the Mississippi company had arrived at the fort. They reported that the main body would be along in a few days. Brigham waited three days, utilizing the time to ferry their wagons from the north bank of the Platte to the south and setting up forges and bellows to make necessary repairs of their equipment. When the company had not arrived by June 4, Brigham pushed on, leaving detailed instructions for them at the fort.

"If experience has not already taught you," he wrote, "we would say, keep a sharp lookout for buffalo, Indians, and bears, all of which may be met and endanger the life and liberty of men, women and children, beasts and property. Be wise, and watch as well as pray continually, and having done all you possibly can, and exercised all the skill, wisdom and prudence and care and strength that you possess, should you be overtaken with accidents or losses of any kind, take the spoil thereof patiently and cheerfully, and murmur not for Christ's sake."

He also left messages for them along the trail. The company, under the direction of Captain James Brown, arrived soon after Brigham's departure and immediately set off in his wake. Composed of families with all their possessions, the Mississippi company could not make as fast time as the pioneers, so did not overtake them until the journey's end, six weeks later.

One hundred and twenty-four miles west of Laramie the trail crossed the Platte again, and here (where the river was generally shallow enough to ford) spring rains had swelled the flow, so that it was necessary for Brigham's company to empty their wagons and float their goods on a leather boat across the river. As luck would have it, a company of emigrants on their way to Oregon was at the swollen ford. They offered Brigham a dollar and a half a wagon if his men would transport them across the river. They paid the toll in flour at two dollars and fifty cents per hundredweight. Since flour was selling at Fort Laramie at ten dollars a hundredweight, this was a bargain for the Mormons. They moved the company across the river and divided the earnings equally among all members of their camp. Before leaving the river Brigham selected ten men to remain behind with the boat, to operate a ferry at similar rates for any other companies to follow.

On June 26 they passed the Continental Divide, which marked the entrance to the South Pass. Near here they met a trapper, Pegleg Smith, who had been one of Ashley's men in the fur trade, but who now operated a trading post near Fort Hall on the Oregon trail. He gave an adverse report on the valley, and proposed another, eighty miles to the north—Cache Valley, so called because it had been the winter rendezvous of the Mountain Men and had been utilized for storing their furs.

"He so far made an impression on the camp," one of the men reported, "that we were induced to enter into an engagement with him to meet us at a certain time and place two weeks afterward, to pilot our company into that country." For some reason the trapper failed this appointment, which led the Mormon to conclude, "I have ever recognized his failure to do so as a providence of an allwise God."

Two days after their meeting with Smith, they came across Jim Bridger, who now conducted a trading post about a hundred miles east of the Great Salt Lake. Bridger told Brigham Young that it would be unwise to take a large population into the Great Basin until it was determined that grain could be grown there. So positive was he that it could not be done that he offered to give one thousand dollars for the first bushel of corn to be raised in the Salt Lake Valley.

On July 3, on the banks of Green River, Brigham Young met Samuel Brannan, leader of the New York branch of the church, who, at Brigham's advice, had taken his colony of Mormons from New York and sailed with them around the Horn to California. Brannan had been delighted by the country around San Francisco, where he had settled his company, and he had pushed on east to intercept Brigham. He hoped to convince him that California was the place for the Mormons to settle.

Brannan, who was an impetuous and positive man, told Brigham that his company had one hundred and fifty acres of wheat growing, besides potatoes and other crops, and his people were just waiting for the emigrating saints to come and settle among them. He lauded the climate and the resources. He reported that the Mormon Battalion was now at the Pueblo de Los Angeles, having completed one of the longest military marches in history, so that it could easily be gathered.

Brigham listened to Brannan's enthusiastic report but was firm in his refusal. "Let us go to California," he told Brannan, "and we cannot stay there over five years; but let us stay in the mountains, and we can raise our own potatoes and eat them; and I calculate to stay there."

Brannan had not experienced the persecutions in Missouri and Illinois. He was not wholly aware of the danger of settling where others were already established.

From the Green River Brigham sent five members of his company back to guide the companies who were following, and in a letter sent with them he recounted Brannan's enthusiasm for California and concluded, "But our destination is the Great Basin or Salt Lake for the present, at least, to examine the country."

In the same letter he announced a malady that had recently struck the camp:

The cold frosty nights of the mountain pass, followed by warm days and the great dust of the succeeding plains, tend to produce sickness, such as fever, head and back ache, etc. about the time travellers arrive at Green River, to prevent which, let every soul be very careful for clothing and keeping warm over the mountain pass, and particularly as night approaches, keeping out of the evening air, as much as possible, and out of the dust. To accomplish which the camp can separate into small parties, and keep a short distance apart, and should your camp be too large for convenience, you might divide, keeping one or half a day's distance apart, over the sand hills. The sheep should be started separate from the herd, very early in the morning, to prevent their becoming deceased through snuffing too much dust.

Beyond Green River the company approached the mountains. At the left were the high Uintahs, with snow still visible on their peaks; ahead, the Wasatch Range, into the fastness of which the company was to go. The Oregon companies had already turned to the northwest, toward Fort Hall, over the well-marked trail that would skirt the mountains and the lava plains at the north end of the basin. The Mormons continued due west, over a trail which was no more than a thin line on Frémont's map.

As they entered Echo Canyon the terrain became rocky and abrupt. The fever increased, and Brigham himself became ill. On July 19, on the banks of the Weber River, with the rocky cliffs of the mountains rising high above them, with only a few precipitous canyons opening out from them, Brigham sent several members of the company ahead to seek the best route. The remainder would follow more slowly after them.

This small advance party entered the Great Basin of the Wasatch on July 22 through a narrow defile, since known as Emigration Canyon. Willard Richards, Orson Pratt, and George A. Smith, who were of the party, wrote a report which they sent by messenger back to Brigham Young:

> The brethren have done a great deal of labor on the road, and there is much more that ought to be done. . . . The 2nd division overtook the 1st this forenoon. Since that we have opened a road thru the kanyon where it is uncertain whether man or beast ever trod before unless it be a bear or a rattlesnake, for we saw a bear's track and killed 2 rattlesnakes, and one since we arrived in camp. Also one scorpion has been seen here. We are now about 4 miles within the long sought valley. . . . Timber can hardly be said to be scarce in this region, for there is scarcely enough of it to be named, and sage is as scarce as timber, so that if you want to raise sage and greasewood here, you had better bring the seed with you from the mountains. . . . Mammoth crickets abound in the borders of the valley. There are some sand hill cranes and hawks. Feed abundant and of the best quality. Water in the creeks passably good.

Brigham had considered both the Salt Lake Valley and the Valley of the Utah Lake, forty miles to the south. His reason for favoring the Salt Lake country was that here he had heard that the Indians were less warlike than they were farther south.

When Brigham did come within sight of the valley on July 24, he was still ill with fever and lying on a bed in Heber Kimball's wagon. Legend reports that he raised himself up and gazed silently at the scene before him. "Yes," he is supposed to have said. "This is the place. Drive on."

At the spot where the wagon is supposed to have halted, the Mormons a hundred years later erected their most imposing monument, a tall shaft rising at the mouth of Emigration Canyon, popularly known as "the this-is-the-place monument."

From his point at the mouth of the canyon, Brigham would have seen the valley stretching twelve or fifteen miles to the shimmering whiteness of the Great Salt Lake in the distance. To his right was the rounded hill which he would climb in a few days and give the name of Ensign Peak. Across the valley to the left a mountain curved to a point, like an extended arm, dividing the Salt Lake Valley from Utah Valley to the south. In the southwest, beyond the silver glint of a river (soon to be named the Jordan) and bordering Salt Lake on the south, rose another mountain, hiding beneath its shallow covering of topsoil the largest deposit of open copper in the world, a fact which Brigham was never to know. Beyond the lake in the west spread the blank whiteness of the salt flats.

The valley itself would have been still green, but even then touched with yellow in anticipation of the dry season to follow. There were few trees in the valley (legend says there was one), but near the river and creek beds were willow and berry bushes. It was a scene of lonely splendor, particularly to a traveler who had just penetrated the rocky fastness behind him.

By the time Brigham entered the valley the first companies had already plowed several acres of the semi-desert soil and planted seed potatoes and grain. They had diverted water from the canyon streams and had begun the system of irrigation that was to bring life to this western land.

On July 28 Brigham recorded in his journal: "Some of the brethren talked about exploring the country further for a site for a settlement; I replied that I was willing that the country should be explored until all were satisfied, but every time a party went out and returned I believed firmly they would agree that this is the spot for us to locate."

Members of the company were mixed in their first reactions. William Clayton wrote in his journal the day of their arrival: "Most of the brethren express themselves well-pleased with the place, but some complain because there is no timber." Harriet

Young, the wife of Lorenzo, who was ill with fever when she arrived, expressed herself more directly: "Everything looked gloomy, and I felt heartsick."

Brigham's company had corralled their wagons a little below what is now known as City Creek Canyon, at approximately the spot where the present Salt Lake City and County building stands. Within four days the temple site was selected—a plot of forty acres, later reduced to ten; and a city two miles square was laid off after the model of Kirtland and Nauvoo. Companies were selected to investigate Bear River Valley and Cache Valley in the north and Utah Valley in the south. Peach and apple seeds were planted, along with more potatoes, turnips, and grain. The surrounding hills were explored for timber and sites for dams and mills.

The land upon which the Mormons stood had, when they began their journey, been Mexican territory. It was not to be formally ceded to the United States until a year later, at the treaty of Guadalupe-Hidalgo, which ended the Mexican War. The Mormons were not to possess legal title to it for many years, but they worried no more about it than did other settlers who moved onto the frontier from the East. The continent was, for most Americans, "God's country," but it seemed more literally so to the Mormons, who believe they had been guided westward by supernatural powers. They had no doubt that the Constitution, based upon natural law (which was God's law), would eventually uphold their rights.

The day after his arrival Brigham climbed the peak to the north of his camp. Here he was with the vanguard of his people, a minute speck among the rocks and crags that rose several thousand feet above him and stretched in a mighty chain from north to south. Below him in the valley his settlement was no more than a dot upon vast stretches of uninhabited desert reaching east and west. The gentile settlements were more than a thousand miles behind him; westward were seven hundred dreary miles to California. Certainly here the saints would be safe from any enemy, for there were only wild beasts and Indians, and what were these to the Mormons, compared with the dangers of civilization?

In the first real burst of optimism and hope in this new homeland, Brigham turned to his companions and remarked, "Give us ten years in this place, and we'll ask no odds of Uncle Sam or the devil."

3

The first homes in Salt Lake were built in the shape of a fort, called "the Old Fort," on what is now known as Pioneer Square. They were built of "Spanish bricks"—or adobes, fashioned from the claylike soil on which they stood—with rough-hewn lumber and logs hauled from the mountains for door and window frames. Before Brigham left his little colony for the return trip to Winter Quarters, there was one death, that of a three-year-old child, son of one of the Mississippi emigrants, who drowned in City Creek; there was one birth, recorded August 9, a girl named in honor of Queen Elizabeth and the Mormon leader: Young Elizabeth Steele. John Steele, the father, had been detached from the battalion at Pueblo.

With the Pioneer Company and Captain Brown's company of Mississippi emigrants and battalion members, the colony in Salt Lake now numbered four hundred and fifty. Although Brigham didn't yet know it, there were many more saints on the way West than he had planned to send this first year. He had thought one hundred families the most the country could provide for, but his instructions had been disregarded, and there were now nine companies on the plains between Winter Quarters and Salt Lake—a total of more than four hundred families, with five hundred and sixty-six wagons and five thousand head of stock.

Brigham remained in the valley until late August, assisting with the construction of the fort, directing the planting and the exploration of the surrounding country. He organized a High Council, with John Smith, the uncle of Joseph, as president. He sent Captain Brown to California to tell the battalion members that he would see that their families all came West with the first companies from Winter Quarters. Then, with the members of the Twelve, he gathered up all available teams and wagons and began the long journey back to the Missouri River.

On September 9, while in camp en route, he sat down and wrote an epistle to the saints he had left behind in Salt Lake Valley, outlining in detail the thoughts and feelings that had possessed him during the days and nights since his departure:

To the Saints in the Great Salt Lake City, Great Basin, N.A. Greetings:

Beloved: We have now fulfilled the mission, one which we were set, by selecting and pointing out to you a beautiful site for a city, which is destined to be a place of refuge for the oppressed, and one that is calculated to please the eye, to cheer the heart, and fill the hungry soul with food. . . .

While with you we used the utmost diligence to erect a fort of sufficient size to contain houses for all who will be at the city the coming winter, and we hope the brethren will not release their exertion until the fortification is completed, and the houses therein with all their necessary fixtures for health and convenience. We would recommend a high and strong fence within the enclosure, and about two rods distant from the houses which will form a yard of sufficient extent to contain all your cattle and horses, should any alarm demand their security, otherwise you had better yard your cattle without the walls, so as to keep the fort as clean as possible; also in the corner of this enclosure all your hay may be stacked with safety, for it is wisdom that you should cut some hay that your stock may be provided for, in case of deep snow, Indian alarm or any other contingency.

If all things remain quiet until spring, as we anticipate, we recommend that the cattle yard within the fort be plowed and prepared in the best possible manner for gardens and a just portion thereof allotted to each family for a garden, so that your women and children may plant and till, and water and gather the fruits thereof without being exposed abroad; for this and all domestic purposes, you will turn a portion of the City Creek within the walls of the Fort and pass it around at a convenient distance on every side.

Your fortification is sufficiently extensive to supply all your necessary conveniences in houses, yards, etc., unless the emigration exceeds our expectation, and this was planned in wisdom, that you might have all the time possible for cultivating the soil and raising an abundance of grain, . . . and should you spend the coming year in fencing individual lots, and building your homes thereon, it will be impossible for you to furnish your families with bread and supply the demands of the emigration.

The land bordering on the west line of the city, is at present designed for common pasturage, that on the south and east for farming, so far as it shall be needed. . . .

We feel that it is necessary to urge upon you the importance of planting and sowing in their appropriate time and season, every kind of grain, fruit and vegetable, that will yield sustenance to man and beast etc. . . . not forgetting the flax, cotton, or any other kind of seed at your command, from which you may raise those commodities that are absolutely indispensable for your future clothing, and there is and will be in your midst abundant means for such manufactures as soon as raw material can be produced. The culture of rice should not be neglected.

We would remind the brethren that it does not injure the young and tender corn to be nipped by the Frost, and that repeatedly, provided the embryo of the tassel is not destroyed; and [the] same principle is good in relation to many of the grain and vegetables; and as you are located in a new country and untried climate, and as we know the drouth to be great in the latter part of the summer, we recommend that you begin to plant and sow such seeds as soon as the snow is gone in the spring, or even before spring, so that we may know by experience whether it is possible to ripen grain in the valley before the summer drouth shall demand the labor of irrigation; therefore we wish the brethren to begin their farming and gardening as early as possible and continue it so long as they have seed, and keep a record of the time and manner of sowing, planting and cultivating, and also of the weather daily, that we may learn by experience and records the best time and method.

Should irrigation be found necessary, the City Creek will yield an abundance of water for that purpose, and it is wisdom that you should provide for such contingency. We would therefore recommend that you prepare pools, vats, tubs, reservoirs, and ditches at the highest points of land in your field or fields that may be filled during the night and be drawn off to any point you may find necessary, through a tight and permanent gate prepared for that purpose when it shall have become sufficiently warm, so as not to check vegetation.

It is important that you secure what timber you will want for farming utensils, mechanic tools etc. and fuel for the coming winter before the snow falls upon the mountains, which we anticipate will be early; and in selecting your fire wood, . . . choose that which is dry and not suitable for timber of any kind, and we wish all the green timber and shrubbery in and about the city to remain as it is, unless you find time to trim it and that it may grow tall and straight; and we also wish the green timber and young trees in the mountains to remain as they are, particularly the sugar maple, many of which are large enough to be transplanted in the city, when time will permit, which will be valuable for shade, and from which we will hereafter receive an abundant harvest of sweet, particularly until such time as the sugar cane can be introduced, and be very careful and not let a fire run through the grass of the valley, or the woods of the mountains, as it would be one of the greatest calamities which might befall you through carelessness.

The fall is the time for you to secure your year's stock of salt from the Salt Lake; and we recommend that you procure good timber and erect a substantial bridge over the Western Jordan [river] before the water rises, which will give you easy access to the Lake which is a pleasant place of resort and its water very healthy for bathing, as well as the warm springs on the north of the city.

Not neglecting your plowing and sowing, when the rains commence this fall, it is desirable that one or more saw mills should be put in operation as speedy as possible; and place should also be provided for the carding machine by the time of sheep shearing, and a grain mill will be indispensable for the comfort and convenience of the city as soon as grain shall ripen. . . .

When the Lamanites [Indians] are about, you will keep your gates closed, and not admit them within the walls; so far as you do come in contact with them, treat them kindly; but do not feed them or trade with them, or hold familiar intercourse with them in the city; but if you wish to trade with them, go to their camp and deal with them honorably. . . .

Should the brethren at any time discover any specimens or beds of chalk, lime, coal, iron, lead, copper or any other minerals, we wish they would report the same to the council, who will keep a record of the same with the specimens, the place where found, and by whom, which record may be of great worth hereafter. . . .

As soon as you are located within the fort, let a sufficient number of rooms be appropriated for schools, furnished with the best teachers, or furnish your children with teachers at home, and give every child among you an opportunity of commencing his education anew, and see that he attends to it, and that individual who has the opportunity to educate his children and does not, is not worthy to have children, and teach your children the principles of the Kingdom that they may grow up in righteousness. . . .

Should the brethren of the Battalion arrive among you before you return, it is our council that those who have no families, or their families are with you, go immediately to work to assist in raising grain, etc., and that those whose families have not arrived, to go to them as soon as they can cross the mountains in safety. . . .

We have no land to sell to the saints in the Great Basin, but you are entitled to as much as you can till, or as you need for your support, provided you pay the surveyor for his services, while he is laboring for you; and at a future day will receive your inheritances on the farming lands as well as in city lots; and none of you have any land to buy or sell more than ourselves; for the inheritance is of the Lord, and we are his servants, to see that every one has his portion in due season. . . .

Your present location is designed to you for a city of refuge, a place of rest, therefore see to it that ye pollute not your inheritance, for if you do, you must expect that the judgment of heaven will be poured out upon you, not as hitherto, while you have been surrounded by gentiles, whom the Lord has permitted to scourge you by their laws, and contrary to their laws, but if ye shall defile your inheritances, while you have the privilege of keeping the law of God, you can expect nothing less than the judgments and pestilence the most dreadful, for the Lord God will have a holy people, and they shall build up a holy city unto him, even the lots of their inheritance, or he will remove them out of the place and call others who will do his work according to His holy commandments.

We therefore intreat you in the name of Jesus, to give diligent heed unto all your ways, and as you are at a place of rest, rest yourselves, and let the earth rest, and let your cattle and horses and everything about you rest one day in seven, and honor the sabbath of the Lord by assembling yourselves together and administering to each other in every word and ordinance pertaining to that Holy Day, and profane not the name of Jehovah at any time. . . .

This epistle was written before Brigham had discovered the great number of his people who had already begun to emigrate from Winter Quarters. It was sent back by him with the first Mormons he encountered. Meeting the companies in the mountains, he was at first angry that his counsel had been disregarded, then sympathetic when he saw how anxious they all were to reach their new city of refuge. He gave them advice and his blessings, then added to the original letter to the council in Salt Lake, giving more information for the accommodation and the assimilation of the many who would be arriving unexpectedly this year.

Brigham concluded this addition to his epistle by exhorting his followers ". . . to remember at all times, that when we left you to return to Winter Quarters, the oracles of the Church left, and returned with us; and that this is your oracle and guide until you see us or hear from us again; therefore, let no one undertake to overturn or overrule this letter, but let it be read in the congregation of the saints every sabbath day; which if ye do, and recite accordingly, ye shall be blest and the spirit of the Lord will rest down upon you, your souls will be filled with light and knowledge, your hearts will rejoice; and the small still voice will be whispering within continually: this is the way, walk ye in it; which voice follow at all times, and you will never go astray; but the riches of heaven and earth will be multiplied unto you, and we bless you with these blessings in the name of Jesus Christ—Amen."

CHAPTER NINE

CITY OF THE SAINTS

I

When the companies which followed the Pioneer Camp came into the valley, two additional forts were built—called the South and North Forts—connected with the Old Fort by gates through which the people went to and from their fields outside. On October 3 Brigham's young wife Clara wrote a letter which was taken to Winter Quarters by one of the returning members of the Mormon Battalion. "I felt very lonesome after you left," she told Brigham, "it seemed to me that I was a lone child, though in a pleasant land."

By the end of October three thousand persons had arrived. In this valley which twenty-five years before had never known the tread of a white man's foot a flourishing community began to rise.

Those early days were filled with labor. In the evenings the council met by the light of a smoky lantern to consider infractions of the regulations set up by Brigham and to administer justice in the disputes that arose. Laws were passed concerning the distribution of farmland, the control of cattle, the construction of grist mills, saw mills, and a planing mill. Trade was limited to the few men who had had experience with the Indians. A company was sent to California to buy cattle and seeds for the spring planting.

Despite Brigham's foresight and the council's best efforts, problems arose. A few of the company were dissatisfied with the location of the fort, and some of them talked about moving away and locating by themselves. A few considered going on to California. There were disputes over property.

But, on the whole, the community knew that its safety depended upon cooperation. The saints were too far away from neighbors to depend upon anyone for assistance. If they were to survive, it must be by their own efforts. The first four ordinances of Great Salt Lake City were passed in December, and they reflected the problems of the isolated little community—indolence, disturbing the peace, immorality, and theft. The punishment for the last three charges included "a certain number of lashes on the bare back, not exceeding thirty-nine," in addition to fines up to one thousand dollars. For indolence, the most serious offense of all, the law provided that the judges should take charge of the property of the offender and administer it for the benefit of his family, and at the same time should assign work to the convicted person.

Fortunately the winter of 1847-48 was reasonably mild, but it was more severe than the Mormons had expected. Supposing that they had settled in a semi-desert region, they constructed the houses of the fort with flat roofs. When the snow came, it piled high on the roofs, then melted and leaked through into the dwellings. Eliza R. Snow wrote in her journal:

I stayed with Clara Decker Young who came with the pioneers. She was living in a log-house about eighteen feet square, which constituted a portion of the east side of the fort. . . . This hut, like most of those built the first year, was roofed with willows and earth, the roof having but a little pitch. . . . We suffered no inconvenience from this fact until about the middle of March, when a long storm of snow, sleet and rain occurred, and for several days the sun did not make its appearance. The roof of our dwelling was covered deeper with earth than the adjoining ones, consequently it did not leak so soon, and some of the neighbors huddled in for shelter; but one evening, when several were sitting around, the water commenced dripping in one place, and then in another; they dodged it for awhile, but it increased so rapidly that they finally concluded they might as well go to their own wet houses. After they had gone I spread my umbrella over my head and shoulders as I ensconced myself in bed, the lower part of which, not shielded by the umbrella, was wet enough before morning. The earth overhead was thoroughly saturated, and after it commenced to drip the storm was much worse indoors than out.

In April and May the little colony emerged from the winter struggle to labor under a clear blue sky—a sky so unexpectedly brilliant that it seemed the surrounding mountains were mere silhouettes. There were still too little to eat, so hunting and fishing parties were sent to the nearby canyons and streams. The Mormon leaders, following Brigham's instructions, drove the saints to exertions of which they had not believed themselves capable, chastising those who complained, praising the industrious, and always warning their followers that the second winter would be no easier than the first. By the end of this summer they expected a population of at least ten thousand persons in the valley.

By June the wheat planted during the fall and winter had begun to head, the vegetables were green, a few of the small fruit trees had begun to leaf. The spring soil seemed richer than even the most optimistic had dared to hope. It demanded water from the mountain streams and intensive cultivation with the hoe and shovel, but when such labor was supplied, the earth responded almost as it had done in Illinois.

Then suddenly, just when the crops were at their most promising, disaster struck the Mormon settlement. The green fields were invaded by hordes of creeping and flying insects. They were giant crickets—since known in the West as "Mormon crickets," as large as small mice—and they came in droves like an invading army, destroying whatever living lay in their path. They clung to leaf and stem with a ravenous grasp, eating until the last green stock had been reduced to nothing but a wilted shred. At first the Mormons tried beating them to death. They wielded wet rags, switches, boards from their wagons, anything they could lay their hands on. Still the crickets advanced across the fields. Someone got the idea of diverting water from the irrigation ditches and drowning the insects, and this worked better than anything else; but eventually the streams became choked with their black bodies, and these provided a bridge whereby others might cross. Hundreds seemed to appear for each that was beaten to death or drowned in the ditches.

Finally there seemed nothing to do but pray, and the Mormons prayed, still fighting and struggling against the invaders.

Then, once again, the western sky became darkened, and the discouraged saints believed an even greater disaster was to strike. When they discovered that the newcomers were seagulls flying in from the lake to the west, the Mormons thought they were coming only to complete the destruction. "Not this," they prayed, "not all the labors of these months gone for nothing." Without food, how could they survive in this wilderness? What had they done to deserve further persecution—this time from Nature herself?

But a miracle occurred—at least what the Mormons have always considered a miracle. The gulls did not attack the crops. They fell upon the insects and began to consume them. Sometimes they ate so rapidly that they could not digest what they had killed, so they simply disgorged and began again. Not until the pests were completely destroyed did the gulls cease their feasting; then all but a few of them flew off to the west. Not all the crops had been saved, but neither had they been totally destroyed. This evidence of what they believed to be heavenly intervention the saints took to be both a warning and a sign that they were under the surveillance of a great supernatural power. They took hope again and returned to work with a new faith and a new energy.

Brigham Young arrived in Salt Lake City again in September, and with him came additional thousands, in company after company that rolled down into the city from the mouth of Emigration Canyon. He had not planned to hurry the movement so rapidly, but the federal agent in Nebraska had finally decided that the Mormons' presence on Indian land constituted a danger to the peace of the frontier. He insisted that Winter Quarters be abandoned, and the saints were forced to move back across the river into Iowa. Here they established Kanesville, named in honor of their friend from Pennsylvania who had come to their aid the year before. Many of the Mormons were, understandably, reluctant to remain on the Missouri River to build up temporary homes again if there was any chance of emigration, so Brigham had, even against his better judgment, brought more of them with him than he believed the country

could comfortably contain. But, he reasoned, there would be dis-
comfort, even suffering, in any case; and he believed that the sooner
the Mormons were gathered in a single place the better off the
church would be.

The winter of 1848-49 was unusually severe. Many of the newcomers had no opportunity even to provide shelter before the fall
storms struck. Hundreds of Mormons were still camped in wagon-
boxes or in tents when the intense cold and the snow closed the
mountain valleys. Cold and hunger were a common condition; illness and death became the fate of many. As a result of the heavy
immigration and the short harvest, an inventory made in February
showed that there remained no more than twelve ounces of corn
per day for each person until the fifth of July—the first date that
they could reasonably expect to harvest any of their next year's
crops. One woman reported later that she wore out five lace veils
that winter, using them to sift the coarse corn meal that was doled
out to her.

And then another miracle occurred with the gold rush in
the spring, and, strangely enough, the discovery of gold in California was not only tied up with the later fortunes of the saints in Utah,
it was also related to events which were occurring among the Mormons in California. The year before, when Samuel Brannan had returned, disappointed, to California, Brigham had told him to advise
all the young unmarried members of the battalion to remain on the
coast for the time being. They were to find work, save as
much money as they could, and bring it with them to Utah when
he sent them the word.

Brannan was a born leader, but he was of an erratic and unstable
temperament. Several times he had been expelled from the church,
then allowed to resume membership. After each period of disfavor
he confessed his error and then worked himself back into a position
of importance. Upon his return from the Salt Lake Valley he discovered that some of the Mormon Battalion members had found
work east of San Francisco at a mill run by Captain Sutter. Brannan
himself was at the mill on January 24, 1848, when Henry W. Bigler,
one of the Mormon workmen, recorded in his journal: "This day

some kind of metal was found in the tail race that looks like gold."
It was the first written record of what was to become the gold rush
of 1849.

In an attempt to check the swelling enthusiasm among his workmen, Captain Sutter and his foreman, Marshall, swore them all to
secrecy. However, Samuel Brannan was not a man to keep such
news to himself, and neither did he believe, as Brigham Young came
to believe the next year, that gold-seekers were "gainsayers in behalf of Mammon." He hurried off to San Francisco.

"Gold! Gold! Gold!" he is said to have shouted, striding through
the streets of the little city, swinging his hat and holding aloft a
bottle of yellow dust, "which he displayed to the gaping crowds
that gathered round him." He published word of the strike in the
California Star, which the New York Mormons had established on
their arrival; and it was this announcement, picked up by the
Eastern papers, that set off the biggest rush in the nation's history.

With the opening of the road across the mountains came the first
trickle of what was to become a flood of emigrants rushing to the
scene of the strike. The Mormon city was in its direct path. When
the gold-seekers arrived in Salt Lake City they were intent upon
only one thing—to get to California as quickly as possible. To these
men who had already traveled several thousand miles, the Mormon
city seemed near the end of their journey. Despite the fact
that they had more than seven hundred miles of blistering desert
and high mountains to cross, many of them traded their heavy out-
fits for light wagons, or they simply abandoned their property and
continued on horseback.

No longer did the saints have to subsist on the small, bitter roots
of the sego lily, which had been so great a part of their diet the
winter before. They traded one fat horse for two lean ones that
could be fattened or for a span of mules or oxen. They traded livestock for flour, for clothing, for dress-goods, and for wagons. A
kind of prosperity came over the community that was both to sustain and to weaken it over the next few years. Most Americans would have called it "luck," but the Mormons knew better, for

An early portrait of Brigham Young, probably as he was in about 1850

Brigham Young when he was about seventy years old

Beehive House, Brigham Young's second residence in Salt Lake City. Behind it, and barely visible in the picture, is the White House, occupied before Beehive House was built. At the right is the Eagle Gate, formerly the entrance to the Young estate. To the right of the gate was the Young family schoolhouse, where Brigham's children were taught

Lion House, Brigham Young's third Salt Lake City residence, with the Utah State Capitol in the background. Each gable marks an apartment occupied by one of Brigham's wives. At one time the White House, the Beehive House, and the Lion House, were occupied simultaneously by the Young Family

Mrs. Ann Eliza Young, the apostate wife of Brigham Young, who lectured widely against Mormonism during the 1870s. (From her book, *Wife Number 19*)

A DESPERATE ATTEMPT TO SOLVE THE MORMON QUESTION

The result of their labor is here—and what 's more,
We 'll remark that in Utah they laugh at all four.

Four artists who differ in style and in mind
This cartoon on the Mormons have jointly designed.

Anti-Mormon cartoons. (From *Puck*, April 27, 1904)

"Taking Leave of Brigham Young," drawing from an unidentified contemporary magazine, showing Brigham as he probably looked during the last ten years of his life

Salt Lake City about 1890, with the not quite completed temple to the right of center. The domed building at the right of the temple is the tabernacle

The Manti Temple. (Reprinted by permission of *The Improvement Era*)

The Brigham Young Monument at Salt Lake City by Dallin, with the temple
in the background. (Reprinted by permission of *The Improvement Era*)

The Mormon Temple at Berne, Switzerland. (Reprinted by permission of *The Improvement Era*)

Brigham Young had told them, "The Lord takes care of His own, though how He chooses to do it is His business, not ours."

2

Freed from the burden of poverty, if not actual starvation, the Mormons in the next few years built up an attractive city on the foothills of the Wasatch Range. "Great Salt Lake City," wrote a visitor a few years after the Mormons' arrival, "presents a very singular appearance to the eye of the stranger. It is built of adobe or sun-dried brick, and is of a uniform lead color." The only exception was Brigham's house, which he constructed of lumber sawed by his own mill in Cottonwood Canyon, and painted white. It was located in the center of town and was taller than the surrounding houses, so that it became a landmark for travelers—the first thing to be seen and noted as they entered the valley.

After the disastrous trial of Spanish-type roofs the first winter, all houses now were constructed with English-style roofs and gables. Mark Twain, who was an early visitor to the city, referred to the "block after block of trim dwellings built of 'frame' and sun-burned brick—a great thriving orchard and garden behind every one of them."

No less interesting than the houses were the small irrigation streams running down each of the streets and used to water the orchards and gardens. Twain called them "street-streams winding and sparkling among the garden beds and fruit trees." These streams all flowed from central canals, directed above, or sometimes through, the city to the farmlands outside. The water was crystal clear and made a pleasant murmur as it traveled over the smooth pebbles and rocks of the stream-bed. Each central canal was controlled by a water-master, and each property-owner possessed a certain share in the water rights. His portion of water was parceled out to him at certain stated and well-regulated intervals.

The same was true of the farmlands below and to the north and south of the city. "The Mormon farmer," wrote a visitor, "is subject to some heavy drawbacks. The necessity of irrigation imposes no trifling addition to his labors; water ditches are to be cut over and through his land, and great care is necessary in their proper management. In some places where water is not abundant, the neighbors use it alternately, and spend the night as well as the day distributing the precious moisture over their fields."

In the center of the city was the "Temple Square." This ten-acre tract was very early surrounded by a brick wall, eight feet high, built, it was said, as a make-work project by Brigham Young. The square contained at first a "Bowery"—an outdoor meeting place where services were held in the open air, with the congregation protected from the sun by a covering of green boughs over a framework of timbers. Later a "Tabernacle" was constructed, not yet large enough to accommodate all the members (it seated three thousand)—a predecessor to the later, unique building which has become the chief tourist attraction of the city. It was not to be long before work was begun on the temple itself. To serve until that time, an "Endowment House" was built, where the necessary ceremonies could be performed until the temple was completed.

Main Street, which ran south from the Temple Square, contained most of the stores and a hotel owned by Brigham Young. "Its architecture," reported a visitor, "was nothing to boast of, being that of a town whose citizens are still in the first stage of doing, and have not yet reached the second one of considering how to do. The shops were consistent with the hotel, and like it might have been transported from the principal street of any prosperous Eastern village. There were some brick, some wooden, and numerous adobe houses, generally two stories in height, and without decoration. The commercial fronts displayed their wares through no ambitious plates of French glass, but announced them on shingles or handbills, and by the still more straightforward methods of samples at the doorways."

Main Street and all the other principal streets of the city were 125 feet in width, an unusual feature in a nineteenth-century American city. Streams of water ran down each side of them.

As early as 1849 a petition for statehood was sent to Congress, asking that the area be designated the "State of Deseret"—its name, derived from the *Book of Mormon*, meaning Land of the Honey-bee—and that it comprise all the area south to the Rio Grande, north to Canada, and west to the Pacific Ocean. This ambitious request was not honored, but in the summer of that year the United States Government sent Captain Howard Stansbury to make a topographical survey of the region, and a year later the Territory of Utah was designated to include an area now making up the states of Utah and Nevada, as well as parts of Colorado and Wyoming. The Congress appointed Brigham Young governor of the territory, and many of the first offices were awarded to Mormons. Federal funds were appropriated for salaries and other expenses of government, and a special appropriation for a library was also approved. In June 1850 Brigham established the first newspaper, *The Deseret News*, with Willard Richards as its editor.

Brigham followed strictly the forms of priestly government set up by Joseph Smith in organizing the various ecclesiastical divisions of the Mormon territory. At each settlement a High Council was selected to have jurisdiction over the spiritual welfare of the stake; bishops were appointed to each ward. Storehouses were set up by the bishops, and they served both as repositories for tithing, which was paid usually in produce or labor, and as trading posts where one type of goods could be bartered for another.

An early visitor to Utah described the Mormons as "a strange, harsh, hardy, severe looking people. In some respects they re-sembled an old Puritanical audience. The men were tanned, hard, muscular mountaineers; they looked sombre, though happy and content as ordinary people. The old women were the only persons who looked really happy; they smiled benignly, seemed to enjoy their religion and to be perfectly satisfied of their own perfect righteousness. The young girls, less than fifteen years old, did not seem much more morose, or rather unanimated, than retiring back-woods children ordinarily do. . . . The people were dressed very cleanly but in simple stuffs."

The most common dress for the men was a coarse, dark homespun suit. The women generally wore muslin sunbonnets and dresses that fell straight from their shoulders to their feet, with only a little gathering at the waist. A few of the young men might wear buckskin jackets and trousers. An old lady might be seen in a silk cap or hood, brought with her across the plains or got in exchange from some passing emigrant from the East. "The people complain of want of clothing," our visitor reported, "but I think their dressing will compare favorably with other people so far removed from a market and manufactories."

Brigham Young, who combined in his office both the spiritual and the temporal leadership, was now at the height of his energy. Although he had never completely lost the rustic quality which life on the frontier had made a part of his personality, responsibility had added a firmness of bearing that impressed everyone who met him. Richard Burton, the British explorer and writer, meeting Brigham in the early days in Salt Lake City, described him as having the appearance of "a gentleman farmer in New England. . . . Of his education, I cannot speak, 'Men not books—deeds not words' has ever been his motto; he probably has . . . 'A mind uncorrupted by books' . . . he converses with ease and correctness, has neither snuffle nor pompousness, and speaks as an authority on certain subjects."

Another visitor, who had been raised in the same section of New York State from which Brigham came, reported that "Brigham's manners astonish any one who knows that his only education was a few quarters of such common-school education as could be had in Ontario County, Central New York, during the early part of the century. There are few courtlier men living. His address is a fine combination of dignity with the desire to confer happiness, of perfect deference to the feelings of others with absolute certainty of himself and his opinions. He is a remarkable example of the educating influence of tactful perception wedded to entire singleness of aim, without regard to its moral character."

That Brigham could be mild as a dove or raging as a lion we know from testimony of those who were assisted by him and those whom he chastised. As an administrator he had bursts of impatient anger that made him often appear despotic, particularly to those against whom his anger was directed or to those who heard only one side of the story. To the great majority of the Mormons he was their protector and spokesman, and his success lay partly in his singleness of purpose, which was to build up the Kingdom of God.

In exhorting the saints after the difficult winter of 1848 he said, "We have been kicked out of the frying pan into the fire, out of the fire into the middle of the floor, and here we are and here we will stay. God has shown us that this is the spot to locate His people, and here is where they will prosper; He will temper His elements for the good of the saints; He will rebuke the frost and the sterility of the soil, and the land shall become fruitful. Brethren, go to, now, and plant out your fruit seeds."

After experiencing two winters of hunger and privation, some of Brigham's followers considered going to California. But Brigham opposed it. Speaking to his followers, he said that "some were murmuring and had not faith to go to work and make their families comfortable; they had got the gold fever and were going to California." He added, "Some have asked me about going. I have told them that God appointed this place for the gathering of the saints, and you will do better right here than you will by going to the gold mines. Some have thought they would go there and get fitted out and come back, but I told them to stop here and get fitted out. Those who stop here and are faithful to God and His people will make more money and get richer than those that run after the god of this world."

Nowhere was Brigham's tact and leadership better shown than in his dealings with the Indians. "They are the seed of Abraham, and God is ever their God," he wrote of them. "Moreover, a pacific policy is the cheapest of any; it is preferable to clothe and feed than fight them. We make innumerable efforts to enlighten the pagan nations of distant lands. Are not the Indians, who live in the midst of us, worth as much as they? Bestow on them your faith and your prayers. At the same time be on guard against their savage nature, and show them that you are their superiors by your virtue."

In a specific situation, such as the one at Fort Utah (later Provo) in 1853, Brigham issued these instructions: "Let any man, or company of men be familiar with Indians, and they will be more familiar; and the more familiar, you will find the less influence you will have with them. If you would have dominion over them, for their good, which is the duty of the elders, you must not treat them as your equals. You cannot exalt them by this process. . . . You have been too familiar with them. Your children have mixed promiscuously with them, they have been free in your houses, and some of the brethren have spent too much time in smoking and chatting with them instead of teaching them to labor. Such a course has encouraged them in idleness and ignorance, the effects of which you begin to feel."

The chief of the Utes was a leader as colorful in many ways as Brigham, but much less predictable. He was named Wakara (sometimes spelled Walkara), the whites called him Walker, and he had by far the most influence over his braves of all the Utah Indian chiefs. Brigham treated him as a leader and as a friend. But Walker's "savage nature" is indicated by an incident at one of his first meetings with the Mormons. He had come to trade, and as a final item he brought forth a young Indian girl of nine or ten, whom he had captured from the neighboring Santa Clara tribe in the south. What would the Mormons offer for her as a slave? The Mormons' only interest was in saving the girl from starvation or death at the hands of her captors, for she had been badly mistreated. They offered a horse and a sheep. Walker was not satisfied. In a fit of anger, and to show the Mormons that they must meet his price hereafter, he leaped upon the child with his tomahawk. After felling her with a blow to the head, he chopped her to pieces as she lay quivering on the ground. If he could not have his price, he told the Mormons, neither could they have the girl. When the Indians later offered to trade their captive children, the Mormons met their price.

Brigham taught his followers caution in dealing with the Indians. Give them no opportunity to steal, he told the saints; it is the nature of the Indian to steal, and they steal even from each other. He also forbade his followers to take revenge into their own hands, telling them to petition the local chief whenever any crime was committed against them. Later, when Walker attacked the Mormons, and the Mormon militia retaliated and drove the Indians into the mountains, Brigham refused to allow his soldiers to follow and annihilate them as they wished to do. Instead, he wrote a letter to Chief Walker:

Captain Walker:—I send you some tobacco for you to smoke in the mountains when you get lonesome. You are a fool for fighting your best friends, for we are your best friends, and the only friends you have in the world. Everybody else will kill you if they could get a chance. If you get hungry send some friendly Indians down to the settlements and we will give you some beef-cattle and flour. If you are afraid of the tobacco which I send you, you can let some of your [Mormon] prisoners try it first, and then you will know it is good. When you get good-natured again, I would like to see you. Don't you think you should be ashamed? You know I have always been your best friend.

Conditions which caused the most serious difficulty between Indians and whites on the frontier were a dilemma for both sides. The Indian tribes depended for their livelihood upon the control of large tracts of land, where they would be free to follow the migrations of the game they hunted. When either the land or the supply of meat was interfered with, they were threatened with starvation. If they moved away from their own lands, they encroached upon other tribes and were killed by them. If they remained on the land pre-empted by the whites, they were reduced to begging, stealing, or trading at terms disadvantageous to the whites. Brigham's policy of indulgent paternalism was the only possible solution and the one which eventually became the policy of the United States Government.

Brigham Young's talents were never better displayed than in his organization of the Mormon emigration from Europe. Such emigration was resumed almost before the Utah colonies had become established. No sooner were most of the Mormons across the plains than members of the Twelve were again sent abroad, this time not only to England but into France, Germany, Italy, the Scandinavian countries, and even Palestine.

On October 6, 1849, the Perpetual Emigrating Fund Company was organized to assist the movement of converts from Europe to Utah. As early as Brigham Young's presidency of the British Mission in 1839-40, he had chartered vessels to transport Mormon converts across the Atlantic. Now, with the additional problem of getting the emigrants across almost the whole of the North American continent, he set up a transportation company, financed by what was called the Perpetual Emigrating Fund, which would supply ship passage to either New York or New Orleans, rail or boat passage from there to the frontier, and finally teams and wagons as transportation across the plains. Money was advanced to pay the costs of any worthy convert who was too poor to pay his own way. Upon his arrival in Utah, the convert was given a job and land, from the proceeds of which he was expected to repay the amount advanced. This money would then go back into the fund to assist the next worthy member. In England the fund was administered by the president of the mission, who in 1849 was Franklin D. Richards, a nephew of Willard Richards and a member of the Council of the Twelve. Other authorities were stationed at the docks in New York and New Orleans, on the Mississippi River in Iowa, and at Kanesville on the Missouri, to see that the immigration functioned smoothly.

In the first ten years of settlement in Utah, almost twenty thousand immigrants came from England alone. At one point, a third of all British immigrants to the United States were Mormon converts. The news of their departure from England was generally headed in the Mormon periodicals: GOING HOME TO ZION. The authority for such a "gathering" came from one of Joseph Smith's revelations:

And the time cometh, and that speedily, that the righteous must be led up as calves to the stall, and the Holy One of Israel must reign in dominion, and might, and power, and great glory. And He gathereth His children from the four quarters of the earth; and He numbereth His sheep, and they know Him; and there shall be one fold and one shepherd.

By 1851 there were thirty thousand Mormons settled in the territory, only five thousand of whom were in Salt Lake City. Colonies had been established at Ogden, Provo, Payson, Nephi, Bountiful, Tooele, Manti, and Parowan, stretching three hundred miles along the west slope of the mountains. Typical of Brigham's activities in these days is a description he sent to one of his apostles in the East:

I have been all the day crowded with an anxious inquiring people to allot them their inheritances, to set out their farming land, to oversee the building of a clerk's office and a Council House, to manage the adobe yards, to watch over the people and keep them from oppressing each other, to prepare houses for my family to occupy during the winter, and sending off parts of my teams to different parts of the valley.

Brigham would stand up at a public meeting in the Bowery and announce that machinists and miners were needed in the settlements in Iron County. He would call for carpenters and shoemakers for Sanpete County. A miller might be needed at Payson, weavers at Bountiful. In each case he would extol the virtues of the colony. At other times he could be more direct. From his leaders he would "appoint" someone to go to a particular settlement to administer to the spiritual needs of the saints. If a member threatened to "get out of line" in Salt Lake, he might be "called" to settle in one of the more distant and difficult colonies. There was occasional grumbling at such calls, but few Mormons refused to go.

Brigham made periodic visits to all the settlements, inspecting their progress, advising them, and bringing them news of their brethren in Salt Lake. He took his councilors with him, Heber Kimball and Willard Richards, traveling in a train of carriages and supply wagons. Often they would be met at the outskirts of a village by escorts of horsemen, sometimes by a band of musicians; and occasionally the entire settlement would be on hand to greet them, lining the roadway into town. Important visitors to the territory were sometimes invited to accompany the party.

During a visit to Provo, Mrs. Thomas L. Kane was a member of the party, and she described a dinner given by one of the Mormon families for Brigham's company:

What had we for dinner? What had we not! Turkey and beef, fresh salmon trout from the lake, wild duck, chicken pie, apple fritters, wild plum, cranberries-, and currant-jellies, a profusion of vegetables; and then mince pies (drawn from the oven *after* the grace was said!), smoking plum-puddings for us, and wholesome plain ones for the children (who preferred the *un*wholesome!); pears, peaches, apples, and grapes, pitchers of cream and scarcely less creamy milk, cakes, preserves, and tarts numberless, and tea and coffee. All were served and pressed upon us by our active hostess, for whom a seat was reserved at President Young's right hand—to which she was invited once in five minutes, replying, "Immediately, Brother Young," "Directly, Sister Lucy," as she flew off, to reappear with some fresh dainty.

The same reporter described a visit to Parowan, two hundred miles south of Provo, near where Brigham hoped to develop the iron ore his colonists had discovered. The people, she said, "talked away to Brigham Young about every conceivable matter, from the fluxing of an ore to the advantages of a Navajo bit, and expected him to remember every child in every cotter's family, and he really seemed to do so, and to be at home, and be rightfully deemed infallible on every subject. I think he must make fewer mistakes than most Popes, from his being in such constant intercourse with his people. I noticed that he never seemed uninterested, but gave unforced attention to the person addressing him, which suggested a mind free from care. I used to fancy that he wasted a great deal of power in this way; but I soon saw that he was accumulating it. Power, I mean, at least as the driving-wheel of his people's industry."

Mormonism was never a "bookish" culture, and was even less so under Brigham Young than in the days of Joseph Smith. Education came through social intercourse, practical experience, and religious observance. There were few tradesmen or strictly professional people. Everyone tilled his own plot of ground and cared for his own stock. When a doctor in the East wrote to Brigham, asking what possibilities there might be in Salt Lake for practicing his profession, Brigham replied that the Mormons thought little of one who could not build his own house, irrigate his own land, and raise up a crop of wheat, corn, beans, peas, and potatoes. If the doctor wanted to come under these conditions he would be made welcome, but if he had any thought of accumulating wealth, Brigham told him, he would be wasting his time.

Even their religious services took a practical turn that puzzled many visitors. Since there was no professional "ministry" in the church, all meetings were conducted by laymen, who were usually farmers or tradesmen. A sermon might be more concerned with problems of irrigating the earth than with how to achieve heaven; it might deal with child-rearing, the baking of bread, or how to cut cloth for a coat.

Yet as the Mormons achieved a measure of security they turned naturally toward the refinements of civilized life. By 1855 there was a Philharmonic Society in Salt Lake, a Polysophical Society, the Universal Science Society, the Deseret Theological Institute, and the Horticultural Society of the State of Deseret. From the beginning there were musical organizations—church choirs, orchestras, and brass bands—in each settlement. One of the first public buildings to be erected was a social hall, where balls and concerts were held and dramatic pieces presented. A university was conceived of in the earliest legislation, although it was not to become a reality for many years. The Salt Lake Dramatic Association was incorporated on the same day as the Perpetual Emigrating Fund Company. A library was established in Salt Lake. Of the musical fare in the Salt Lake Valley, a French visitor, Jules Rémy, reported in 1856, "The music, we should observe to the credit of the Mormons, was very good, and better than one meets with in most provincial towns in Europe."

For the ordinary Mormon—particularly those in the outlying settlements—such organizations probably had little meaning. He and his whole family would spend long days in the fields in the summer; in the winter there would be improvements on homes and property demanding his attention, in addition to hunting and trapping. His only diversion came from attending church services on Sunday or from what entertainment could be provided within the family. Where he differed from pioneer settlers elsewhere was in his relation to his church. As a member of the priesthood, he had definite obligations. He might be the bishop of a ward or a member of the stake High Council, in which case his duties would be those of an executive and teacher. Since the ecclesiastical authority was the most important in his community, he might have to take time off from his own work during the week to legislate—to plan; or he might be called to sit as a judge in some dispute between his neighbors, or, if a young man, to care for the meeting hall, assist in the sacrament service, or even preach. The women, who had been formed into a female "relief society" by Joseph Smith in Nauvoo, had their own concerns, mostly related to caring for the poor or the afflicted.

A Mormon's first duty was to his family, the second to his church —which was, in fact, simply an extension of his family. His day would begin with prayers at daylight and end with a family prayer soon after dark. Sometimes the prayers, particularly if delivered by the head of the household, would become miniature sermons recounting the family problems and invoking divine guidance in solving them. Such lives could, and sometimes did, become somewhat grim, depending upon the temperament of the family. On the whole, however, the Mormon household was not noted for grimness. Both Joseph Smith and Brigham Young approved of such entertainments as music, dancing, and dramatics.

Brigham Young's attitude toward recreation was never in doubt. "We say to the Bishops and to everybody, exercise yourselves, provide innocent amusement for the youth, attract the minds of the children, and get the upper hand of them and be on the lead." He added, "A gathering and social spirit seems to be the order of heaven—of the spirit that is in the gospel we have embraced." Of education, he said, "Our education should be such as to improve our minds and fit us for increased usefulness; to make us of greater service to the human family; to enable us to stop our rude method of living, speaking, and thinking."

3

Mormon society, for a few years following the first difficult winters, exuded an air of hope and confidence. Speeches from the rostrum of the Bowery or the Tabernacle spoke of the miracle that had been wrought in establishing, within a few years in an isolated desert country, a network of industrious settlements, free from the evils of the gentile world. The Mormons felt happy and secure in their villages and in their faith. George A. Smith, in a speech celebrating the seventh anniversary of their entrance into Salt Lake Valley, told the Mormons: "Like the pilgrim fathers who first landed upon Plymouth Rock, we are here pilgrims and exiles from *liberty;* and instead of being driven into the wilderness to perish, as our enemies had designed, we find ourselves in the middle of the floor, or on the top of the heap."

In the same meeting, a young Mormon boy arose and addressed Brigham Young "in behalf of the young men" of the church. "Born among mobs and cradled on the billows of persecution," he said, "we have learned to appreciate the banquet of peace that we enjoy in the valleys of Ephraim. Our cities arise in beauty and grandeur; our villages multiply; our fields teem with plenty; our flocks and herds abound; all nature seems to smile on us; in fact the wilderness and the solitary places have been made glad, and the desert has blossomed as a rose."

A year earlier Brigham had warned his people against the dangers of complacency. The church had become prosperous and strong, he said, not because it had always been so, but because it had been persecuted. "We are the happiest people when we have what are called trials," he said, "for then the Spirit of God is more abundantly bestowed upon the faithful."

The complacent, he told them, were those who denied Joseph Smith and remained in Missouri. They were those who remained in Illinois or who dropped out during the march across Iowa. They were also those in Utah who were growing prosperous and neglecting their duties. In 1847 he had said, "Give us ten years in this valley, and we will ask no odds of Uncle Sam or the devil." The ten years were almost up. Were the saints better prepared now than they had been when they entered the valley? They were more prosperous, and Brigham had little contempt for prosperity; but along with prosperity had come a dangerous laxness. He had told his followers that the devil, when he could no longer attack them through their enemies, would find means to get to them through their own weakness. Perhaps that time had come. At least Brigham seemed to sense a serious weakness in his saints that increased as their sense of security increased.

During the early years in Utah there were few gentiles near enough to challenge the Mormons. There was a handful of federal officials who resented their appointments to such primitive and obscure posts and who disliked the atmosphere of a community in which there was no worldly society and in which they were doomed to be looked upon as interlopers. There were a few businessmen, the inevitable camp followers of the frontier, who appeared as though sprung from the soil whenever a settlement was established. There were the gold-seekers, who paused briefly in their headlong rush to California, refreshed themselves with the Mormons' illegal whisky known as Valley Tan, ogled the Mormon women, made jokes about polygamy, then disappeared into the westward deserts.

Even the Indians, who might have constituted a threat to the peace of the Mormons, remained friendly. They seemed satisfied to trade with the Mormons, and some even joined the church, impressed by the Mormons' claim to knowledge of their ancestors. They learned to distinguish between the Mormons and the gentiles, calling the latter Amerikats and generally fearing them, while they regarded the Mormons as their friends.

Memories of persecution grew dim in the minds of the older saints. A new generation was coming of age, less inclined to the extreme piety of its elders, more accustomed to the vigorous life of the frontier. Incidents of theft increased in the territory; cases of bickering came more and more often into the bishops' courts. Prosperity brought with it pride, and pride engendered ambition. All this Brigham felt to be a dangerous relaxation of his people's will to perfection, a softening of the moral muscles. Most of the offenses committed in the settlements were too trivial or insubstantial to result in apostasy or to give cause for excommunication. Perhaps for this very reason—because of their elusiveness—they must have seemed an even greater threat to the spiritual health of Mormondom than if they had been overt actions, easily detected and speedily punished.

CHAPTER TEN

THE DEVIL
AND UNCLE SAM

I

What Brigham saw as the remedy for this chronic moral illness of the Mormon community came suddenly and almost accidentally. Willard Richards died in 1854, and his position as councilor to Brigham had been filled by a young apostle, Jedediah M. Grant. Grant, as a boy of eighteen, had accompanied Joseph Smith and Brigham Young into Missouri as a member of Zion's Camp in 1834. He later became an effective missionary, particularly in the Southern states, where he acquired a reputation as a fiery and effective exhorter. In 1851, when Salt Lake City was incorporated, he had been elected its first mayor. In 1856, after his rise to the top level of Mormon leadership, Grant's preaching took on additional force and vigor. Filled with warnings of hell-fire and damnation, his sermons stirred congregations to sudden and dramatic recognition of their sins, real or imagined, and an equally forceful desire to repent. After each sermon he would himself lead them to the nearest body of water and remain waist-deep in the cool stream until all erring members had submitted themselves for rebaptism.

Brigham saw this enthusiasm as an answer to the problem of complacency. He had always been suspicious of revivalism, but now the effectiveness of Grant's preaching seemed a means of effecting desired reforms within the church. In a letter to Orson Pratt he explained the purposes of the reformation as he saw them:

"The Reformation," as it has been called, has begun—not a change in our religion, not of the principles revealed from the heavens through Joseph—but a change in the practices and an arousing of the people from habits of lethargy: and its salutary influences are already perceptible. We have appointed two or more home missionaries to each ward in the city, and drawn up a list of questions to be asked the Latter-day Saints. Those missionaries go from house to house, and examine every individual therein separately; and, as a consequence, we have had this people examining themselves minutely; much honest confession and restitution have been made. The catechism has been as a mirror to the Saints, reflecting themselves in truth.

Seen in historical perspective, the reformation seems, on the whole, to have done the Mormon cause more harm than good. Perhaps it did, as Mormons claim, reawaken the saints, arouse them to a sense of greater responsibility and a heightened energy. It instituted a system of home missionary activity which eventually became less a means of exerting pressure to conformity than it was a method of discovering those in the congregation deserving of assistance because of illness or poverty. It unquestionably purged the church offices of lazy administrators. On the other hand, it led Mormon leaders to unrestrained expressions of beliefs similar to those preached by Sidney Rigdon in the early days of Far West, which could be misinterpreted in the East and thus provide fresh subjects for gossip and sensationalism in the newspapers. It provided incidents excessive enough to appear humorous to those who did not participate in the spirit of the movement—humorous even to the Mormons themselves when the enthusiasm had died down.

One such occasion was a meeting held in the Social Hall in Salt Lake City, attended only by male members of the church who were holders of the priesthood. In the excitement of speeches by Jedediah Grant and Heber Kimball, Brigham arose and asked all members present who had committed adultery to stand up. To his surprise and chagrin, three-fourths of the men got to their feet. A bishop arose and asked if the men had not misunderstood Brother Brigham's question. He thought that the elders did not understand that the question referred only to the time since they had repented of sin and joined the church. Brigham replied, yes, that was the intended meaning of his question; but when he put it to them again, in this modified form, the men all remained on their feet.

T. B. H. Stenhouse, a leading figure in Mormonism who later apostatized and wrote a book vigorously attacking Brigham Young, was among the first to report this incident. He testified that the meeting actually took place as reported, but he doubted the actual guilt of most of the confessors, writing that during his twenty-five years' association with the Mormons, "he never knew of more than two or three cases of this kind, and the transgressors were immediately excommunicated. . . . There has always been a dreadful horror of the crime of adultery in the minds of the Mormons."

When Brigham realized the dangers of an emotionalism that led men to make confession beyond the bounds of reason, he hurried to advise them to repent and be rebaptized, informing them that when their sins were washed away by the waters of baptism, "you can truly say that you are not guilty of the sins inquired by the catechism, though you may have committed them."

Already the interest of the outside world in the Mormons, and many of the old animosities, had been revived by their success in Utah. Efforts to achieve statehood for Utah had been defeated in Congress. The open practice of polygamy (which had been announced by Brigham in 1852) had become a scandal, and efforts were now made to depose Brigham as territorial governor on the old grounds that the Mormons represented a theocracy and were, therefore, traitors to the nation.

The particular aspect of the reformation which aroused the gentiles most was the emphatic declaration of the hitherto little-known Mormon doctrine of blood atonement. This theological concept is another example of the Mormons' peculiar blending of Old and New Testament doctrine. It expresses the familiar belief in the atonement of Christ as a blood sacrifice for the sin of Adam and combines it with the Hebraic injunction, "Who so sheddeth man's blood, by man shall his blood be shed." The murder of innocence was an unforgivable sin, as testified to in the Old Testament, but

THE DEVIL AND UNCLE SAM

so was the denial of the Word of God, as proposed by Paul in the New Testament. For either of these sins, the Mormons said, final absolution can come only through blood sacrifice.

Jedediah Grant's most famous utterance concerning the principle of blood atonement was made in a conference in Salt Lake City in 1856. "I say," he shouted in an excess of passionate revivalism, "there are men and women that I would advise to go to the President immediately, and ask him to appoint a committee to attend their case; and then let a place be selected, and let that committee shed their blood."

Brigham Young's views were somewhat more temperate, but no less clear. "There are sins that men commit," he announced from the rostrum of the Tabernacle, "for which they cannot receive forgiveness in this world, or in that which is to come, and if they had their eyes open to see their true condition, they would be perfectly willing to have their blood spilt upon the ground, that the smoke thereof might ascend to heaven as an offering for their sins; and the smoking incense would atone for their sins, whereas, if such is not the case, they will stick to them and remain upon them in the spirit world."

The words sound like an announcement of, or an invitation to, ritualistic murder. Such the gentiles and the apostates took them at once to be. But there was no rash of killings in Utah.

In calmer moments following the reformation, Brigham challenged anyone to prove that he, or any Mormon leader with his approval, ever shed, or ordered to be shed, the blood of any single person, Mormon or gentile. He did not deny that murders were occasionally committed by Mormons ("The net cast forth into the sea brought forth evil as well as good fish"), but he did deny the accusations that were brought against him with great assurance in the early days of Salt Lake City, that the saints ordered their enemies to be slain and that the slayings were carried out by that same band of Danites whom the settlers of Missouri maintained had been established to seek vengeance against them.

What testimony there is to the truthfulness of Brigham Young's assertion resides in the fact that no accusation ever made against Brigham could be made to stand up in court, while many of the charges have been proved false or exaggerated.

A later president of the church, in describing the doctrine of blood atonement, presents it as a purely symbolic concept; and it is no doubt in this light that the Mormons understand it today. Yet it is clear that certain Mormons, under the stimulation of the reformation, did on occasion shed the blood of an apostate, possibly with the benevolent hope that they were thus sparing him the torments of hell. It is true, too, that Utah is the one state in which the execution of prisoners by shooting is still practiced, and that is because Mormons, as late as the beginning of the century, still quietly maintained that the shedding of blood was the only adequate atonement for the crime of murder.

Typical of the exaggerated gentile accusations that followed the reformation period—typical too of the manner in which the imagination created fiction from the Mormon mysteries—is this passage from an anti-Mormon book:

I deem it proper to state . . . that the mysteries of the second anointing of the Endowments, among other inhuman ceremonies, are supposed to be defiled by the monstrous rite of offering human sacrifices, or at least, that the doctrine is fully taught there. Enough has already transpired among the women to justify this conclusion. Those who have not taken this anointing, and but a comparatively small number have taken it, are very alarmed about this, as they know what to expect. They are always upon the rack, as they are liable to be called upon at any time to go to the Endowment rooms for that purpose.

The same author also wrote:

The Mormons recognize the *right*, and inculcate the *duty* of the father to slay his daughter or her lover, as a last resort, to prevent her marriage with a "Gentile."

Even more fanciful is an account from another early book:

Mrs. Maxwell had two sons, aged respectively fourteen and sixteen years. Their father urged them to go through the Endowment House and become Mormons, bound by all the oaths of the church.

Mrs. Maxwell objected, and in order to prevail over her sons she told them the secrets of the Endowment House.

The penalty for revealing these secrets is dismemberment of the body, the throat cut, and the tongue torn out.

Mr. Maxwell overheard his wife, being in an adjoining room, and forthwith he informed the Elders, who sent for the unfortunate woman and her two sons. They were taken into what is called the "dark pit," a blood-atoning room under Brigham Young's house. The woman was then stripped of all her clothing, and then tied on her back to a large table. Six members of the priesthood then performed their damnable crime; they first cut off their victim's tongue, they then cut her throat, after which her arms and legs were severed.

The sons were compelled to stand by and witness this dreadful slaughter of their mother. They were then released and given twenty-four hours to get out of the Territory, which was then an impossibility. The sons went directly to the house of a friend, to whom they related the butchery of their mother, and obtaining a package of provisions they started; but on the following morning they were both dead.

They had met the Danites.

It seems difficult to conceive that such accounts were taken seriously, but obviously they were by many people; for there are accounts of travelers' fearing to pass through the Mormon country on their way to California.

One Utah killing which has been often cited as an example of official Mormon murder occurred in Springville, a settlement six miles south of Provo, in the spring of 1857. The murdered man was an official in the church, William R. Parrish, who, it was rumored, had "fallen away" and intended to move himself and his family to California. When visited by the bishop and asked the series of questions put by the home missionaries, Parrish was said to have given unsatisfactory replies. Two Mormons were delegated to spy on him, under the pretense that they were helping him to leave the territory. An ambush was arranged, but plans went awry and one of the spies was killed by a Mormon named William Bird, who also killed Parrish and his son.

The facts in this case, so far as they can be ascertained, seem to be that several local Mormons were guilty of plotting to take the life of a prominent apostate. When a federal judge later investigated the case, he discovered that Mrs. Parrish had appealed to Brigham Young, who told her he "would have stopped it had he known anything about it," but advised her to drop her investigations. On the basis of this fact, the judge charged later before the House of Representatives, "I am justified in charging that the Mormons are guilty, and that the Mormon Church is guilty of the crimes of murder and robbery, as taught in their books of faith."

Another murder which particularly aroused the gentiles occurred in Salt Lake City. It was the killing of Dr. J. King Robinson, who had come to Utah to practice his profession. Dr. Robinson had married the apostate widow of a former prominent Mormon and was at the time of his death engaged in a lawsuit with city officials over the ownership of the warm springs at the northern outskirts of Salt Lake, where he and the chaplain of the military post near the city planned to construct a hospital. The doctor was waylaid one night and beaten to death near his home, and the gentiles concluded that it was because he had chosen to come into conflict with Mormon officials.

The majority of the Mormons were not of such character as to give rise to suspicion of murder; they were in fact pious, sincere, somewhat fanatical believers in law and order. Describing an evening in Salt Lake City in the summer of 1860, Richard Burton wrote:

Long after dark I walked home alone. There were no lamps in any but Main Street, yet the city is as safe as St. James's Square, London. There are perhaps no more than twenty-five or thirty constables or policemen in the whole place, under their captain, a Scotchman, Mr. Sharp, by name as well as nature so; and the guard on public works is nominal. Its excellent order must be inferred to the perfect system of private police, resulting from the constitution of Mormon society. . . . During my residence at the Mormon city not a single murder was, to the best of my belief, committed: the three days which I spent at Christian Carson City witnessed three.

It is possible that Brigham came later to regret the emotional intensity of the reformation. If so, he never admitted it, but he must have seen the harm it did, if only in intensifying the feelings be-

tween Mormons and gentiles by giving the non-Mormons grounds
for their suspicions and fear. He must have seen, too, that it was
contrary to his own deepest feeling and contrary to the spirit of the
religion he had inherited from Joseph Smith. About polygamy and
the principles of the Kingdom of God, which were to become
sources of even more serious conflict between his people and the
outside world, he had no regrets.

In any case, the movement was not long-lived. Jedediah Grant
died in December 1856. His death, it was said, came as a result of
spending long hours in the water, rebaptizing repentant sinners.
Even if Grant had lived, it seems doubtful that the excitement
among the Mormons could have continued for long. What did continue was the fallacious image of the Mormons it presented to the
world.

2

The open practice of polygamy by the Mormons was looked
upon by the gentiles as the final outrage of a benighted people. The
first word of it trickled back following the heavy migration of the
Gold Rush in 1849 and 1850. In 1851 the first federal appointees
arrived in the newly organized Territory of Utah.

When the gentile officials arrived, attempts were made to continue the successful relations which the political achievement in
Washington seemed to promise. Brigham, as governor of the territory, held a dress ball, fêting the new arrivals, and an era of good
feeling between Mormons and non-Mormons seemed to have begun. In Philadelphia, before the Pennsylvania Historical Society,
Thomas Kane delivered a highly favorable report of his experiences among the Mormons, which, because of his name and the
reputation of his family, was widely reported across the country.

But such a condition was too good to last. Associate Justice
Perry E. Brocchus, one of the federal appointees, met with the
Mormons in the Bowery to discuss a proposal to send a block of
Utah marble as the Territory's contribution to the building of the

Washington Monument. He was introduced to the saints by Brigham Young, who little anticipated the storm that was blowing up. Judge Brocchus began mildly enough, thanking the Mormons for their kindness to him during a recent illness. Then, unexpectedly, he turned to Brigham Young and began an attack on him for certain remarks Brigham had recently made in criticism of President Zachary Taylor, who had opposed the Mormons' petition for statehood. Brigham had announced Taylor's death to his people by saying, "Zachary Taylor is dead and gone to hell, and I am glad of it." Judge Brocchus remarked that, unless the stone could be sent in perfect sincerity and loyalty, it had best not be sent at all.

This was not an unreasonable request, but it was critical of Brigham, and the Mormons received it in utter silence. The trouble came when the judge turned his attention to the Mormon women present.

"In order to make this presentation acceptably," he went on, "you must become virtuous, and teach your daughters to become virtuous, or your offering had better remain in the bosom of your native mountains."

At these words, men throughout the congregation leaped to their feet, clamoring to reply. Brigham quieted them, but he himself trembled with anger as he turned upon the offending speaker.

"Be ashamed," he cried, "you illiterate ranter, . . . standing there, white and choking now at the hornet's nest you have stirred up—you are a coward, and that is why you have come to praise men that are not, and why you praise old Zachary Taylor."

As for Mormon womanhood, Brigham said, nowhere were there women more virtuous than among the Mormons. "What you have been afraid to intimate about our morals," he went on, "I will not stoop to notice, except to make my particular personal request to every brother and husband present not to give you back what such impudence deserves. You talk of things 'you have on hearsay' since your coming among us. I'll talk of hearsay, then—the hearsay that you are discontented, and will go home, because we cannot make it worth your while to stay. What it would satisfy you to get out of us I think it would be hard to tell; but I am sure that it is more than you'll get. If you or anyone else is such a baby-calf, we must sugar your soap to coax you to wash yourself on Saturday nights. Go home to your mammy straight away, and the sooner the better."

Brigham said later that if he had but crooked his little finger the congregation would have torn the judge to pieces. During Brigham's reply Heber Kimball stood up and tapped him on the shoulder, interrupting to remark that not only was old Zach Taylor in hell, but that Judge Brocchus was undoubtedly well on his way to joining him there.

In order to understand the force of Brigham's anger, it is necessary to understand the Mormons' determination not to be preached at or dictated to by the gentiles in their own homeland. Judge Brocchus and his associates were, from that time, ostracized by Mormon society, which was in 1851 practically the only society of the territory. Within a few months the three gentile judges packed up their things, including the money appropriated for the government of the territory, and returned to Washington.

Their arrival at the capital caused great excitement, not without some censure of them for deserting their posts. At least partly in self-defense, the judges maintained that Utah Territory was a lawless society, governed by a fanatic autocracy under Brigham Young, and that they had fled in fear of their lives. They reported, too, that what rumor had said was true—the Mormons *were* openly practicing polygamy.

By August 1852 Brigham had decided to make the doctrine of plural marriage public. He chose as the occasion a special conference in which 107 missionaries were chosen to travel throughout the world. On the second day of the meetings Brigham called upon Orson Pratt, who had a reputation as an explicator of doctrine, to announce the theory of marriage and set down the lines upon which it was to be defended. Joseph Smith's revelation of July 12, 1843, was read, enunciating the principles of the celestial relationship: ". . . if any man espouse a virgin, and desire to espouse another, and the first give her consent; and if he espouse the second, and they are virgins, and have vowed to no other man, then is he justified; he cannot commit adultery, for they are given unto him; for he cannot commit adultery with that that belongeth to him and to no one else."

Despite Pratt's lack of preparation for this particular meeting, he had been called on before by the authorities to explain to many a doubtful saint, including his fellow apostles, the grounds upon which polygamy was practiced. That the announcement that day was intended not only for the assembled missionaries, but for the world at large, is clear from the concern he showed for the legality of the practice.

"I believe," he said, referring to the courts of the land, "that they will not, under our present form of government (I mean the government of the United States), try us for treason for believing and practicing our religious notions and ideas. I think, if I am not mistaken, that the Constitution gives the privilege to all of the inhabitants of this country, of the free exercise of their religious notions, and the freedom of their faith and the practice of it. Then, if it can be proved to a demonstration that the Latter-day Saints have actually embraced, as a part and portion of their religion, the doctrine of a plurality of wives, it is constitutional. And should there ever be laws enacted by this government to restrict them from the free exercise of their religion, such laws must be unconstitutional."

The report of this meeting was published in an extra put out by the church newspaper, *The Deseret News,* thus assuring its republication in the Eastern press.

By openly acknowledging the practice of polygamy Brigham had taken some of the wind out of the judges' sails. The announcement provoked vehement protest in the East, but at least now the gentiles could not claim that the Mormons were surreptitiously practicing something they dared not openly defend. So far as the outside world was concerned, Brigham reasoned, the question was no longer a moral, but a legal, issue, in which was involved the constitutional guarantee of religious freedom.

Brigham must have hoped that most politicians would consider Utah Territory not worth the trouble it would be to fight the Mormons, and in this he was partly right: many did not. However, he had not reckoned with the zeal of reformers, such as Harriet Beecher Stowe, who soon bracketed polygamy with slavery—those "twin relics of barbarism" which must be swept from the face of the American earth. He had not counted, either, on the annoyance that could be caused him by the presence in Salt Lake City of a small group of federal officers, generally inferior men of lofty ambition, who had been scraped from the bottom of the political barrel.

Political appointments in a territory such as Utah presented a particular difficulty. These jobs were not sought after by competent men, partly because of the low salaries (a judge was paid $1800 a year), partly because they provided little chance for advancement. In some federal posts there were the inducements of social prestige; but social life in the Western communities was primitive, and in Utah there could be little satisfaction in a position which set one off as an outsider—a gentile. After 1852, when the Mormons became a political issue in the nation, such officers could expect active opposition and dislike.

Federal judges would have had a difficult time in Utah in any case. In other territories they provided means for guaranteeing law and order. In Utah, Brigham believed the Mormons could settle their own difficulties. For minor misdemeanors he had set up what he called the Bishop's Court, where disputes could be settled by bringing opposing parties together under the watchful eye of an ecclesiastical authority. Also, in the Utah courts presided over by the federal judges cases would often involve disputes between Mormons and gentiles, with a natural preponderance of Mormons available for jury duty, so that an accused gentile might fear that he was not having a fair hearing, an accused Mormon might be charged with having been let off lightly by his fellow Mormons.

Before 1854 there were too few gentiles in Utah to constitute a serious problem to Brigham Young; but in the fall of that year a detachment of several hundred United States troops was called to service in California and chose to winter in Salt Lake City en route. The troops were under the command of Colonel E. J. Steptoe. At about the same time Brigham's term as governor was due to expire, and reformers in the East began to urge that President Pierce appoint a non-Mormon in his place. Colonel Steptoe was proposed as a satisfactory candidate for the position, but he declined and even headed a petition urging the reappointment of Brigham Young, with whom he had maintained friendly relations during the winter. This petition was granted, Brigham was renamed governor, and eventually the federal troops moved on.

No sooner had the soldiers left, however, than it was discovered that several Mormon girls, and even some Indian squaws, had been the victims of seduction. A few Mormon young women had been persuaded to accompany the soldiers to California. Hearing of this, Brigham arose in a meeting to complain about the conduct of the soldiers and to warn Mormon girls against the attractions of strangers in the city.

"If any wish to go to California to whore it," he told his people angrily, "we will send a company of them off; that is my mind, and perhaps some few ought to go, for they are indeed bad enough."

The incident caused considerable glee among the enemies of the Mormons in the East. The reformers saw it as an indication that Mormon women sought to escape the fetters of polygamy; others as a joke on Brigham Young and his elders. The New York *Herald* editorialized:

This is momentous news and very significant withal. It shows that Mormon women are ripe for rebellion, and that a detachment of the regular army is a greater terror to the patriarch of the Mormon Jerusalem than Indians or drouth or grasshoppers. It indicates the way, too, for the abolishment of the peculiar institution of Utah. The astonishing results of the expedition of Colonel Steptoe, in this view, do most distinctly suggest the future policy of the government, touching the nest of the Mormons. It is to send out to the Great Salt Lake, a fresh detachment of young, good-looking soldiers and at the end of two or three months, order them off to California and replace them by a new detachment at Salt Lake City and so on until those Turks of the desert are reduced, by female desertions, to the standard Christian regulations of one wife apiece.

After 1854 relations between Mormons and gentiles in Utah Territory became steadily worse. One notorious cause was first the presence in Utah, then the resignation, of a federal judge named W. W. Drummond, who came to Utah with a mistress, whom he insisted should sit beside him as he tried his cases, sharing his bench and sharing the contempt he openly expressed for the Mormons. Drummond had deserted a wife and children in Illinois, where his reputation was so bad that his fellow lawyers questioned his fitness for the Utah appointment. When such a man ventured to lecture the Mormons on the virtues of monogamy their outrage passed the bounds of that aroused by Judge Brocchus or by other judges whose frustration came from their inability to do business with the Mormons. Drummond was cursed in the tabernacle by Heber Kimball, whose picturesque manner of speech was not tempered by his excess of anger.

He ". . . is the poor curse," Kimball shouted, "who has written the bigger part of those lies which have been printed in the states; and I curse him in the name of Israel's God, and by the Priesthood and authority of Jesus Christ; and the disease that is in him shall sap and dry up the fountain of life and eat him up. Some of you may think he has not the disease I allude to; he is full of pox from the crown of his head to the point of its beginning. That is the curse of that man; it shall be so, and all Israel shall say, Amen."

Judge Drummond, who was to leave his post in 1856 and make unfounded charges which were to bring the Mormons into conflict with the United States government, boasted to Jules Rémy that "Money is my God, and you may put that down in your journals if you like."

Brigham Young summed up his own reasons for objecting to the federal soldiers and officials who were in Utah between 1852 and 1855:

Now I will tell you one thing that I am opposed to; it is to a man's coming here as an officer, with a bit of sheepskin in his pocket having some great man's name to it, and saying, "I am a gentleman, I am a high-minded gentleman; can you tell me where I can find a woman to sleep with me tonight?" and setting up gambling shops, and drinking and carousing, and stirring up strife, and hatching up law-suits; hunting up disaffected spirits, and then lecturing the people on morality, wishing them to become like other communities, and saying to Mrs. Such-a-one or Miss Such-a-one, "Won't you ride with me—won't you take a sleigh-ride tonight with me? I am a high-minded gentleman." A prudent father, or husband, says, "Come home here; this is your place; you have no business with strangers." What is the result of this? Why, from most of the high-minded gentlemen you can hear, "God damn the Mormons. They are opposed to the Federal Government, because they will not let us sleep with their wives and daughters." I am opposed to such men, and am after them with the forked arrows of the Almighty. To what extent? Let them intrude upon the chastity of my family, and so help me God, I will use them up. [All the congregation said, "Amen."] Such characters may cry, "Aliens, aliens; the Mormons are hostile to the government," and they may cry it until they are all in hell.

With the increasing flood of anti-Mormon literature in the East, an image of Brigham emerged which had little relation to reality; he was depicted as a lecher, a murderer, and a tyrant. Judge Drummond had fled the state, shouting accusations at the Mormons. He claimed that Brigham kept his people in bondage and the gentiles in fear for their lives. Brigham, he said, vowed that he could not be removed from office, and he had ordered all records of the federal courts destroyed. Judges who had been in Utah earlier remembered slights, real or imagined, and wrote books, articles, and letters to the newspapers. Even the conservative *New York Times* urged the necessity for doing something about what it called "the Utah situation." It berated President Pierce for delay and urged the incoming president, Buchanan, to replace Brigham as governor, even if it meant sending an army to Utah to do so.

During the spring of 1857—Brigham's tenth year in the valley—Mormon news vied for the most prominent positions in Eastern newspapers with the war in Nicaragua, trouble in Kansas, the Dred Scott decision, and a spectacular murder in Manhattan. The editor of the *Times* did pause occasionally to wonder why the reports of his "special correspondent," sent him via California, did not agree with accounts brought east by the first parties to come directly from Salt Lake in the spring. The correspondent wrote that Utah was an armed camp, that Mormons who wished to leave were prevented by force, that life for the gentile was a perpetual nightmare of fear. He said that Brigham Young had made preparations to flee upon the approach of federal authorities. Carriers of the first mail reported that life in Salt Lake was calm, that the harvest the previous year had been good, that Brigham Young had gone to one of the outlying settlements for a few weeks to improve his health. Yet even the popular Colonel Thomas Kane, whose explorer brother had died that year and was mourned in all the newspapers, was attacked when he came again to the defense of Brigham Young and the Mormons. A letter-writer to the *Times*, who presented himself as a former resident of Salt Lake City, reported, among other things, that he had been told by a daughter (it was a daughter-in-law) of Brigham Young, "If Salt Lake City were roofed over, it would be the biggest whore-house in the world."

One of the most interesting accounts of that year was the report of a speech made by a still-young politician, Abraham Lincoln, in reply to Stephen A. Douglas, who had talked on what he called "the burning questions of the day," which included the Mormon problem. Douglas had proposed that Utah Territory be annexed to New Mexico, or one of the other neighboring territories, and governed by the officers of that territory. Lincoln pointed out the undemocratic nature of such a proposal and suggested that the question of polygamy had been exaggerated to serve political ends. After all, he said, there is nothing in the federal Constitution to prohibit the practice of polygamy.

From the point of view of the government, the great difficulty was that no competent politician desired the Utah office. One candidate after another turned it down. Brigham's term as governor had expired in 1854. He had not been reappointed, but he had continued to serve, even though his drafts for the cost of government had not been honored.

Brigham Young's speeches, reproduced in full in the New York papers from the files of *The Deseret News*, made little attempt to disguise the Mormons' determination to stick up for their rights. In 1953 he had said, and it had been widely reported, "We have got a territorial government, and I am and will be governor, and no power can hinder it, until the Lord Almighty says, 'Brigham, you need not be governor any longer.'" In February 1855 he said that for a governor ". . . to come here and infringe upon my individual rights and privileges, and upon those of my brethren, will never meet my sanction, and I will scourge such a man until he leaves." Such words made it easier for his enemies, both in Salt Lake and in the East, to get a sympathetic hearing.

Typical of the manner in which Mormon news was reported was the account of the murder of Parley P. Pratt, the Mormon apostle, in 1857. He was killed in Arkansas by Hector McLean, the former husband of one of his wives. The newspapers presented the case as one where a Mormon "missionary" converted a married woman, seduced her into becoming his polygamous wife, assisted her in kidnaping her children, and was justly shot to death by the wronged husband. The story, coming as it did at the height of the anti-Mormon feeling, was displayed prominently in this form in papers all over the country. Although it was denied at once by the Mormons and by the former Mrs. McLean, who had been estranged from her husband and a member of the Mormon Church in California before meeting Pratt, it is this account which remains the most generally reproduced version of the slaying, even today.

Brigham Young expressed his view of the impasse between the Mormons and the outside world as a parallel to the Old Testament story of Joseph and his brethren. "They persecuted him, and lied to to their father about him," he said, "and succeeded in a measure in estranging the feelings of the father from the young child. So it is with the government and us. We have pleaded time and time again, and we will plead, saying, 'Spare us, love us; we mean to be one of the best boys you've got; be kind to us, and if you chasten us, it may be said that we have kissed the rod and reverenced the hand that gave it, and tried again; but be merciful to us, for do you not see that we are a dutiful child?' But no, Tom, Bill, Dick, Harry, and the rest of the boys are eternally running to the old man with lies in their mouths, and he will chasten little Joseph. And though the old fellow has not come out in open war upon him, and arrayed the force and arms of the government to kill the boy, yet he sleeps in his chair, and dreams it over, and talks in his sleep, saying, 'Go it, boys.' What will become of little Joseph? . . . I will tell you what this will amount to, they will pound and abuse little Joseph until his affections are entirely weaned from his parent, and from his brethren, and he becomes an independent boy."

This parable in which the Mormons play the role of Joseph in Egypt had a special meaning for Brigham's followers, for the Mormons considered themselves the descendants of Joseph. They had been driven into exile, but they would, they believed (and still do believe), eventually provide succor for their parent and elder brothers. They were not only Israelites, they were the chosen among tribes. The present was the moment when they had been sold into Egypt, and Brigham concluded his address by emphasizing this point. "If this is not Egypt enough," he asked his saints, "where will we find it?"

CHAPTER ELEVEN

THE HANDCARTS

I

The American push westward has been called "the march of empire"—the fulfillment of destiny. The frontier has also been seen as a catch-all for the defeated and indolent, the misfits and the lawless. Yet the West had one appeal which has been too little emphasized; it was the appeal of nature, a return to some ancient beginning where men were what they seemed, equal in fact amidst the forces that surrounded them. Herman Melville said that "the Western spirit is, or will be, the true American one." He conceived of American political institutions as fitting the circumstances that prevailed on the frontier, differing essentially from those of the Old World in that, instead of seeming "intensely artificial," they seemed "to possess the divine nature of a natural law."

Brigham Young would have approved of Melville's description, had it been applied to his people, for the Mormons' belief was that their religion represented a oneness with nature that was a oneness with God, and that theirs was a community of saints organized according to natural (which is to say, divine) law. Yet Brigham recognized that this was an idealized description. For Brigham, Satan still held sway over this world, diverting the energies and the affections of his people, stirring up antagonism on the outside. In his view the temptations and the persecutions of Satan would bring the Latter-day Saints to a greater understanding of God's grace, thus

multiplying their virtue. No one living on the frontier could fail
to know that the storms of nature were as common as her blessings
and that, if natural law were the equivalent of divine law, God was
as stern a taskmaster as nature.

The winter of 1855-56 had come as one warning of nature's
power. It was the most severe the saints had yet experienced in the
mountains. The snow came early, and, when it did not snow, freez-
ing rain pelted the fields. The crops were frozen in the ground, and
many of the saints suffered from a lack of adequate food and shelter. The most serious loss, however, came from a circumstance that,
even after nine years' experience in the valley, had not been fore-
seen. So much of the livestock froze or starved to death that the
whole plan of immigration which had annually transported thousands of converts into the territory might have to be abandoned.

For several years the higher northern valleys had been used as
winter pasturage for the stock—particularly for the animals which
Brigham Young utilized in transporting the immigration from the
Missouri River to Salt Lake Valley. This year the fury of the storms
covered the land in deep layers of ice and snow. The storms began
earlier in the season than they did in the southern valleys, and they
continued until late in the spring. Horses, mules, and oxen slowly
starved, then froze to death. Heber C. Kimball described the conditions in a letter to his son, who was serving as a missionary in England:

My cattle, sixty head of them, were put in Cache valley with the
church cattle, and those of other individuals, numbering about two
thousand five hundred head, with some forty or fifty horses, some
six or eight of which were mine. When the snow fell in that valley
about ten inches deep, the fatter portion of the cattle broke and
came over into Box Elder and Weber valleys, and scattered hither
and thither. It is supposed that one-half of those two thousand five
hundred are dead. Whether mine are all dead I know not. My John
horse fled out of that valley down on the Weber and died. Old Jim,
Elk, Kit and Kurley remained in Cache valley, and they were with
about forty head of other horses when last seen, but they have not
been heard of for a considerable time, and whether living or dead
we know not. The snow is about waist deep in that valley. Week
before last, Heber and some other boys started to go there, but

when they got to the divide between that valley and Box Elder, the snow was about twelve feet deep, and they were obliged to return. . . .

He goes on with a sad partial list of the dead cattle and horses— most of the Carr boys' and Daddy Stumps' cattle dead, fourscore or so of Brother Brigham's, seven hundred head belonging to Brothers Hooper and Williams, six or seven hundred of the herd of the Gentile Kerr, and many others.

What could it mean unless it was an evidence of God's displeasure? The suffering added intensity to the spiritual rebirth that was expressed in the reformation. Meanwhile, what would become of the emigrating saints, who were already planning their move from the old world to the new?

Earlier Brigham Young had considered the possibility of walking his companies across the plains, as a way of moving more of them at smaller cost. Now the plan seemed particularly attractive to him. As a matter of fact, most of the companies had walked a great deal of the distance in the past, utilizing the wagons only as carriers for goods and supplies. Why could they not, this year, construct small handcarts, in which the personal supplies could be transported as easily as in a baby carriage? The heavy supplies could still be transported by a few wagons per company. There could be one cart to a family, and the whole group could be organized into companies by hundreds.

The total plan as it was worked out demanded the usual machinery of the Perpetual Emigrating Fund Company in Europe. In addition, it needed shops for the construction of the carts and depots stocked with adequate supplies and provisions. Brigham sent members of the church to St. Louis to purchase lumber and other materials. He decided upon Iowa City, Iowa, as the starting point and dispatched carpenters, blacksmiths, and presiding elders there to oversee the construction of the carts and the organization of the companies. He gave John Taylor in New York responsibility for the movement from the East Coast to the plains of Iowa.

No sooner was the Handcart Plan announced abroad than the mission office in Liverpool was flooded with applications. Since the cost was now lower than before (the entire trip from England to Utah could be made for ten pounds), the huge backlog of poor members, who had been unable to emigrate earlier, saw the possibility of this year gathering with the saints in Zion. About thirteen hundred signed up and were accepted in England. They were advised to travel "light," without trunks or chests, and most of them carried their few possessions in cloth or oilskin bags.

The degree of their enthusiasm is suggested in a song they composed to sing while crossing the plains:

> Hurrah for the Camp of Israel!
> Hurrah for the handcart scheme!
> Hurrah! Hurrah! 'tis better far
> Than wagon and ox team.
>
> Oh, our faith goes with the handcarts,
> And they have our hearts' best love;
> 'Tis a novel mode of traveling,
> Devised by the gods above.
>
> And Brigham's their executive,
> He told us the design;
> And the saints are proudly marching on,
> Along the handcart line.
>
> Who cares to go with the wagons?
> Not us who are free and strong;
> Our faith and arms with a right good will,
> Shall pull our carts along.

That not all were happy at the prospect of walking halfway across a continent is suggested by a letter written from America by the sister of one of the leading British elders:

On the 18th of April we received your letter dated March 29. We had been anxiously expecting to hear from you, and I can say that when we did hear, we felt somewhat surprised to find that we had to go by hand-carts. Father and Mother think this cannot be done, and I am sure I think the same, for mother cannot walk day after day, and I do not think any of us will be able to continue walking everyday. We think it will be better to remain . . . at St. Louis for a time until we are able to help ourselves to wagons.

The saints began to assemble at Iowa City late in May. The first group to arrive was divided into five companies, and the first of these set out across the sparsely settled plains on June 9. The remaining companies followed at spaced intervals. They took approximately three weeks to reach Florence, Nebraska, on the Missouri River.

Five hundred miles west, a member of one of these companies recorded in his journal: "We averaged twenty miles a day for the past weeks, and are determined to travel that or more every day until we reach Great Salt Lake City." He then went on to describe their manner of travel. Provisions were hauled in a wagon and rationed out every other day, each adult receiving one pound of flour, with portions of tea or coffee, sugar, and rice. They had with them eighteen cows that gave milk, and they had killed three buffalo for meat. They also had with them enough beef cattle to last to Utah if they slaughtered one each week. "One sister that has walked all the way from Iowa City," the account concluded, "is seventy-three years old. There are in the company those still more advanced in years, who ride in the wagons."

That the plan was workable under favorable conditions seemed now apparent. The first two companies arrived in Salt Lake City on September 26. On September 30 Wilford Woodruff wrote to Orson Hyde in England describing their arrival:

Having heard the night previous that they were camped between the two mountains, President Young and Kimball, and many citizens with a detachment of Lancers and the brass bands, went out to meet them and escort them into the city. They met the companies at the foot of the Little Mountain . . . and after meetings and salutations were over . . . the escort was formed. . . . I must say my feelings were inexpressible to behold a company of men, women, and children, many of them aged and infirm, enter the City of the Great Salt Lake, drawing 100 hand-carts . . . with which they had travelled some 1400 miles in nine weeks, and to see them dance with joy as they travelled through the streets, complaining of nothing, only that they had been detained by the ox teams that carried some of their provisions. . . . There has never been a company enter these valleys that has had the honors and respect paid them that the hand-cart companies have.

Thus the handcart migration started out with the success which Brigham Young had always attributed to the special protection which God had accorded the saints. But by the time the last two companies had arrived in Iowa City, prepared to begin their journey, something had happened to the plan of organization. The lumber which had been supplied them was green, so that the carts were heavier than usual. As they were pushed over the hot countryside of late July boards shrank and iron rims fell off the wheels, causing delays, and supplies diminished faster than had been allowed for. Whereas the earlier companies had taken three weeks to reach the Missouri River, these late ones took almost six. They did not get to Florence until the middle of August.

Still, their spirits were not so low that they did not want to continue. Franklin D. Richards, who had been released from his missionary duties with the sailing of the last shipload of emigrants, met the fifth and final company on the Missouri River and was astonished to find them still there. He wrote back to England on September 3: "Except for the lateness of the rear companies, everything seems . . . propitious for a safe and profitable wind-up of the emigration at the far end."

He also shared the emigrants' faith that a divine providence would see them through. "It certainly would warm your heart with melting kindness," he wrote, "to pass along the line of a camp going by hand-carts, and receive the cordial shakes of the hand, with a fervent 'God bless you,' as I did when I visited Edward Martin's train, several of whom expressed their thanks in a particular manner for being permitted to come out this year."

The fall storms made an even earlier appearance than they had the year before. Soon after the first of October snow fell in the mountains and across the plains. "Our emigration is late," Brigham wrote anxiously to England; "the last two companies, consisting of over 900 souls, have not yet arrived."

He soon realized that help would be necessary. In a general conference on October 6 he opened the meeting by announcing that all blacksmiths in the congregation would be excused immediately to shoe horses for the wagons setting out to attempt the dangerous crossing of the mountains to meet the incoming saints. His son Joseph would go along to guide them to a meeting with the handcarts.

"Let this be a lesson to us in the future," he said, "not to start companies across the plains so late. It is a great mistake."

2

The most comprehensive account of the final companies of handcart emigrants is a narrative written by a Mormon named Chislett. His company, under the leadership of James G. Willie, was composed of five hundred persons. It was made up primarily of English and Scottish Mormons, although there were many converts from the Scandinavian countries and a few Germans.

"We started from Florence about the 18th of August," he wrote, "and travelled in the same way as through Iowa, except that our carts were more heavily laden, as our teams could not haul sufficient flour to last us to Utah; it was therefore decided to put one sack (ninety-eight pounds) on each cart in addition to the regular baggage. Some of the people grumbled at this, but the majority bore it without a murmur. Our flour ration was increased to a pound per day; fresh beef was issued occasionally, and each 'hundred' had three or four milch cows. The flour on the carts was used first, the weakest parties being the first relieved of their burdens."

The greatest trouble came from broken axles. Dust picked up by the loose-fitting rims of the wheels would settle in the axles and grind out the wood—the wheels would weaken and break. Some of the travelers cut up their boots and nailed the leather to the worn axles; others pounded their tinware flat and affixed that. They had no lubricant, so they dipped into their small supply of bacon and soap to grease their wheels.

At first the company averaged fifteen miles per day, never traveling less than ten miles, sometimes as many as twenty when there were no breakdowns. On Wood River the country came suddenly alive with herds of buffalo. Animals and men alike became nervous as the shaggy beasts lumbered across their trail. One evening at dusk the Mormons heard a roar across the prairie. They looked up to see a herd of buffalo rushing straight toward them. It turned before it reached the camp, but the emigrants' cattle broke and stampeded from the camp. The men, already weary from the long day's exertion, set out after them. It was dark long before they had found a few of the animals and driven them back to camp. Thirty head were still missing. They spent three days searching, then reluctantly yoked up what remained of the oxen. There were not enough to move the heavy wagons, so they added their beef cattle and milk cows; but many of these were young and wild, unaccustomed to harness, so that they jerked and pulled to free themselves. Finally the saints, recognizing the need to get on, wearily accepted another sack of flour each for their handcarts, and the thin column again moved off across the sandy plain.

But the progress was slow. The old breakdowns recurred. When a cart collapsed it was difficult for the owner to see the long line move on without him while he remained behind with a few crude tools, struggling to repair the damage. Knowing that he would be hours late reaching camp that night, he would be tempted to leave the cart where it stood and to set off on foot and without provisions.

One evening when they were camped on the North Bluff Fork of the Platte River, an outfit of carriages and light wagons drove in from the east. The occupants were the apostle F. D. Richards and a group of young missionaries, including sons of Brigham Young and Heber Kimball. The missionaries and emigrants camped together that night, and in the morning a general meeting was called. Apostle Richards addressed them and counseled them to be faithful, prayerful, and obedient to their leaders. He ended by prophesying in the name of Israel's God that "though it might storm on your right and on your left, the Lord will keep open your way before you and get you to Zion in safety." Chislett records that the people were much moved by this prophecy and responded with a hearty "Amen, while tears of joy ran down their sunburnt cheeks."

Franklin Richards also advised them to cross here to the south side of the river, where traveling would be easier. He and his company waited while the emigrants pulled their carts through the mile-wide river. When they left, the next day, they promised to attempt to procure provisions for the travelers at Laramie and to see that help was sent out from Salt Lake City to aid them through the mountains.

The company reached Laramie about the second of September, but there were no provisions for them. A meeting was called, and Captain Willie announced that at the present rate of consumption their supplies would be exhausted while they were still several hundred miles from their destination. Rations were again cut, and the Mormons resolved to put forth every effort to travel faster. Their allowance was now three-quarters of a pound of food apiece each day.

At Independence Rock the captain of the company received a letter sent by courier. It told them that they could expect to meet assistance by the time they reached the South Pass. But an examination of their supplies showed that they did not have enough to last that long. There was nothing to do except to cut the rations still more. They decided that the average could not be more than ten ounces per person, so they apportioned it to allow men who pulled the carts twelve ounces, old women and old men nine ounces, and children from four to eight ounces.

As the company traveled up the Sweetwater River, the nights, which had grown gradually colder, now became severe. Supplies of clothes and bedding were insufficient for the climate. "Instead of getting up in the morning strong, refreshed, vigorous, and prepared for the hardships of another day," Chislett said, "the poor 'Saints' were to be seen crawling out from their tents looking haggard, benumbed, and showing an utter lack of that vitality so necessary to our success."

The first effect of such hardships was that the older travelers began to succumb to fatigue, to lose spirit and courage. They died, Chislett said, like lamps whose oil had been depleted, whose wicks grew gradually dimmer, until they expired altogether. At first stops were made to perform decent burials. As deaths grew more frequent and the rigors of the weather increased, haste and fear forced the survivors to be more perfunctory.

"These men," Chislett explained, "were worn down by hunger, scarcity of clothing and bedding, and too much labour in helping their families. Weakness and debility were accompanied by dysentery. This we could not stop or even alleviate, no proper medicines being in the camp; and in almost every instance it carried off the parties attacked. . . . I have seen some pull their carts in the morning, give out during the day, and die before next morning . . . with the calm faith and fortitude of martyrs."

Each day increased the labors and responsibilities of those remaining. Pelted by the snow, which soon arrived to add to the weariness and the discouragement, men would have to work long after the day's march to pitch tents for women left without husbands and children left without fathers. As they moved doggedly on, the storms became so intense that they could make scarcely any progress against the snow piled about the wheels of their carts.

Finally, as they paused one day at noon to rest, they heard a shout. Through the storm they saw the blurred form of a light wagon coming toward them, bearing Joseph Young and Stephen Taylor. The men stopped to tell the company that a train of supplies and assistance was on its way. They then hurried off to look after the Martin company, which was still farther behind. News of this relief spurred the hopes and energies of the saints. They made the best time that afternoon they had made for several weeks. When a team couldn't pull a load through a snowdrift, they doubled up, hitching and rehitching. When a man fell behind, another would go back to assist him.

They found a better camp than usual that night, a space partly protected by a bank of willows; but the wind still howled and the snow still eddied about their beds. They built fires and warmed and partially dried themselves, ate from their small supply of provisions, and offered up prayers for the hope they had suddenly been promised. During the night the snow settled down to a steady fall. By morning it covered the ground to a depth of more than twelve inches. When the roll was taken, five members of the company failed to respond. The extra exertion had been too much for them; they had died in their sleep.

The heavy snowfall had also made their cattle restless. Some had already strayed, and they were never found. Others were lying dead in the camp. The company's supplies were down to a few pounds each of sugar and dried apples, about a quarter of a sack of rice, and a small amount of hard bread. As the storm continued, it was decided to remain in camp until the relief train reached them. Captain Willie and a companion set out to seek it through the blinding storm.

"They were absent three days—three days which I shall never forget," Chislett reported. "The scanty allowance of hard bread and poor beef . . . was mostly consumed the first day by the hungry, ravenous, famished souls."

We killed more cattle and issued the meat; but, eating it without bread, did not satisfy hunger, and to those who were suffering from dysentery it did more harm than good. This terrible disease increased rapidly amongst us during these three days, and several died from exhaustion. Before we renewed our journey the camp became so offensive and filthy that words would fail to describe its condition. . . . During that time I visited the sick, the widows whose husbands died in serving them, and the aged who could not help themselves, to know for myself where to dispense the few articles that had been placed in my charge for distribution. Such craving hunger I never saw before, and may God in his mercy spare me the sight again.

As I was seen giving these things to the most needy, crowds of famished men and women surrounded me and begged for bread! Men whom I had known all the way from Liverpool, who had been true as steel in every stage of the journey, who in their homes in England and Scotland had never known want; men who by honest labour had sustained themselves and their families, and saved enough to cross the Atlantic and traverse the United States, whose hearts were cast in too great a mould to descend to a mean act or brook dishonour: such men as these came to me and begged bread. I felt humbled to the dust for my race and nation, and I hardly know which feeling was strongest at that time, pity for our condition, or malediction on the fates that so humbled the proud Anglo-Saxon nature. . . .

The relief train had also stopped when the storm began. Not realizing the extreme need of the handcart companies, it was waiting for the weather to clear when Captain Willie found it; but the men immediately hitched up their teams and pushed on through the deep snow. They reached the emigrants' camp on the evening of the third day. The storm had stopped by then, the sky had cleared, and the weather had turned much colder.

The relief train brought flour, potatoes, onions, warm clothing, and bedding, which were immediately distributed. "That evening," the Chislett narrative concludes, "for the first time in quite a period, the songs of Zion were to be heard in the camp, and peals of laughter issued from the little knots of people as they chatted about the fire. The change seemed almost miraculous, so sudden was it from grave to gay, from sorrow to gladness, from mourning to rejoicing. With the cravings of hunger satisfied, and with hearts filled with gratitude to God and our good brethren, we all united in prayer, and then retired to rest."

When the full extent of the tragedy became known, Brigham Young got up in the tabernacle and reprimanded Franklin D. Richards and his assistant, Daniel Spencer, for not advising the last companies to halt for the winter. "If there had only been someone, even a little bird," he said, "who might have whispered to Brother Franklin and Brother Daniel that it was too late in the year to send men, women, and children onto the plains and into the mountains." He also said, "We cannot yet tell you what it costs to come through in that way; but we know that it is going to cost those on the other side of the mountain cold feet and a great deal of affliction and sorrow, unless we help them."

Eventually more than one hundred horse and mule teams went to their assistance, but not before there had been much suffering and many deaths in the last two companies. Of the last company alone, which totaled four hundred immigrants, sixty-seven died of exposure or illness. Wilford Woodruff reported to the Mormons in England that many of those who arrived had frozen feet and hands. "We were relieved in our minds and made happy to see them, not withstanding their sufferings, unequalled by any previous emigration."

Brigham Young has been criticized for the failure of the hand-cart scheme, mostly by non-Mormon writers quick to leap upon any sign of fallibility in the prophet who claimed that what he did he did only through the power of God. Certainly there were mistakes made, particularly in the organization of the companies at the eastern end: Apostle Richards, with an excess of zeal, undoubt-edly allowed too many to emigrate from England under an untried plan; Apostle Taylor did not take proper precautions in supplying the materials for the handcarts. Neither of these mistakes would have been serious, however, if the weather had followed its usual pattern. During all but one of the nine years the Mormons had been in the valley, the snow and the cold had come much later than they did that year. Brigham had taken a risk and lost. Unfortunately it was a risk involving the lives of human beings.

The Mormons themselves were less critical than outsiders, and this has always seemed a puzzle to non-Mormons. The saints them-selves were not unaccustomed to adversity. They saw the tragedy of the handcart companies as another sign that they had grown slack in their duties. The event occurred at the height of the reformation, just a few months before the death of Jedediah Grant, when the Mormons had been aroused to a feverish awareness of their own unworthiness to inherit the Kingdom of God. The tragedy of the handcarts was just another instance of God's warning His people, and what more natural way than through the vicissitudes of the ele-ments? There is little doubt that many a Mormon envied his broth-ers and sisters who had died on the plains, for they were assured a high place in the hierarchy of heaven. That Brigham Young shared this view there can be no doubt, for he stood up before his people and told them that he pitied more the members of the church who had remained comfortable in the city and neglected their duties than he did those who had died on the plains for their faith. In an age of reason, such a statement appears fanatical; but to fail to understand it is to fail to understand the Mormons.

3

It was during the trials of the handcart companies that feelings against the Mormons was rising to a climax in the Eastern states. Earlier in the fall A. W. Babbitt, the Mormon representative to Washington, was killed by Indians near Fort Laramie on his way from Salt Lake City to the national capital. Babbitt had been in and out of favor with the authorities of the church many times, beginning as early as the Kirtland days. Shortly after his death the rumor was started in the East, and given prominent space in the Eastern press, that he had quarreled with Brigham Young and that Brigham had ordered his death. It was also rumored in the East that Captain Gunnison, a surveyor originally with the Stansbury expedition, who had been killed by Indians on the Sevier River in 1853, had really been put to death on orders of Brigham Young. Investigations were eventually made of both charges, but neither motive nor evidence for them was ever discovered. They may well have been based on rumors set afoot by either Judge Kinney or Judge Drummond at a time when the East was willing to believe any charges brought against the Mormons.

Early in the spring of 1857 Brigham Young announced that no emigration from the East would be sponsored during the coming year. This word was sent out by the first mail, which left the city in April. The incoming mail a little later brought from John Taylor copies of the newspapers that had appeared during the winter, containing devastating reports of the campaign being waged against the Mormons in the East. On June 14 Brigham had a selection of the articles from these papers read from the pulpit in a public meeting at the Bowery.

The saints heard these accounts with an anger tinged with resignation. They had heard such charges made so often in the past. The charges were that the Mormons held their own people captive in the territory, that they practiced a licentious system of cohabitation in which young girls were forced into wedlock with old men who held them as virtual slaves, and that the life of no gentile was safe in the Mormon domain. The most serious charge in the eyes of Eastern editors stemmed from the report of Judge Drummond that the Mormons were disloyal to the United States and wished to set up their own empire in the West, with Brigham Young eventually to be crowned its emperor, where the laws of the government would be flouted at Brigham's will and where justice would be impossible for anyone outside the Mormon Church.

On July 24, the anniversary of the Mormons' tenth year of residence in Utah, Brigham invited more than two thousand persons to a celebration in Big Cottonwood Canyon, in fulfillment of a promise he had made a year before, when he had sponsored a similar celebration. Present were Captain Ballo's Band, the Nauvoo Brass Band, the Great Salt Lake City and Ogden City martial bands, the Springville Brass Band, and the Ogden City Brass Band. There was a company of light artillery, a detachment of four platoons of lifeguards, and one platoon of the lancers—all attached to what was still known as the Nauvoo Legion. A campground had been established on the shores of a small mountain lake, where three spacious boweries had been constructed. Participants filled the whole basin surrounding the lake. Above them rose rocky summits, towering into the summer blue of the sky. In the center of the campground and from two nearby peaks United States flags whipped in the breezes that blew up the canyon walls.

Brigham Young believed that the Mormons had reason for celebrating this occasion. Ten years marked a long period of hardship and struggle, and it represented the first time the Mormons had been allowed to remain so long in one place. Settlements now stretched from the Salmon River in the north to the Grand Canyon in the south, from Fort Bridger in the east to California in the west. In Salt Lake his people had constructed a thriving city, in the center of which excavations had been started for the foundations of a temple, larger and more impressive than the one that had been destroyed at Nauvoo. An architect had been appointed and sent to Europe to study its famous buildings, then called back to begin his work. Emigrants had poured into the territory, not only from the East and the South, but from England, Sweden, Denmark, Norway, Germany, Switzerland, and France.

The mood of this Pioneer Day (as the celebration is still known) was both sobered and heightened by events of the past year. The families assembled on the morning of July 24, and the choir sang, "On the Mountain Top Appearing":

> On the mountain top appearing,
> Lo, the sacred herald stands,
> Welcome news to Zion bearing,
> Zion, long in hostile hands.
>
> Mourning captive! Mourning captive!
> God himself shall loose thy bands.

About noon, as the games and activities of the saints were in progress, four horsemen rode into camp, among them Porter Rockwell, who had gone East with the first mail delivery of the year. They brought disturbing news. President Buchanan had finally been moved by the emotional appeals of the reformers and the Eastern press. He had ordered an army of twenty-five hundred troops of the United States government to Utah. Its publicly stated purpose was to put down the rebellious saints and install a new governor of the territory. The army had already left Fort Leavenworth and was now marching across the prairies.

Outside Brigham's tent the Mormons could be heard shouting in holiday pleasure. Were these the rebels President Buchanan had in mind? It was the old story all over again, but this time the Mormons were not threatened by the mobs of Jackson County or the governor of Illinois. This time it was the military power of the United States arrayed against them.

Brigham kept the news to himself during the remainder of the day, and the celebration continued as planned. Inside his tent he conducted hasty conferences with his leaders. Some news was allowed to leak out when his councilor, Daniel H. Wells, made "a few remarks in relation to the latest tidings from the States" that evening. Brigham seemed to feel that this news was too important to break to such a special gathering of his people, even though they numbered in the thousands. Perhaps he wished also to be straight in his mind about the course he would take. In any event, the full force of the announcement he reserved for the following Sunday—two days later. When he finally got to his feet in the Bowery on Temple Square, he faced a curious and excited congregation. Rumor had spread and multiplied. Now the Mormons waited to see what Brigham would say. How would he meet this new threat to their existence?

CHAPTER TWELVE

THE UTAH WAR

I

In 1857 Brigham Young had just turned fifty-six. His rugged face had begun to soften but still retained the rough cast that had marked him as a young man. He was less robust in health than he had been. He had high blood pressure, which sometimes resulted in dizzy spells. He had put on weight during the ten years in Utah and, despite his modest stature, gave the impression of a large man when he stood on the platform in the Bowery. His blue-gray eyes glistened when he spoke; his thin, straight lips curled into a dry smile when he joked. One eyelid drooped a little and often gave his face a quizzical expression. His hair still hung, western fashion, over his ears, and he had not yet begun to wear the chin-beard which was later to soften the lines of his face. Usually he dressed in a heavy black homespun frock-coat over a satin-lapelled waistcoat. His linen was kept clean, but not always tidy. A large gold watch-chain dangled across his stomach, and he fingered it casually when he spoke.

As Brigham contemplated the approaching United States army, he must have thought back to the days of Joseph Smith. Joseph's first advice when confronted by the enemy had been to turn the other cheek, to rely upon legal means of redress, and to trust in the Lord. After his experiences in the jails of Missouri, he made some revisions. "Be not the aggressor," he had told the saints; "bear until they strike you on one cheek; then offer the other, and they will be sure to strike that; *then defend yourselves,* and God will bear you off, and you shall stand forth clear before his tribunal." But, he had added, "If mobs come upon you anymore . . . dung your gardens with them. We don't want any excitement; but after we've done all, we will rise up Washington-like, and break off the hellish yoke that oppresses us, and we will not be mobbed."

Now Brigham stood before his congregation assembled in Temple Square. "What is now the news circulating throughout the United States?" he asked them. "That Captain Gunnison was killed by Brigham Young, and that Babbitt was killed on the plains by Brigham Young and his Danite band. What more? That Brigham Young has killed all the men who have died between the Missouri River and California. . . .

"If this was not the Kingdom of God upon the earth," he asked his saints, "do you think that the world would be arrayed against it? No. . . . All hostility towards us arises from the fact that we have the eternal priesthood. The kingdom of heaven is here, and we are in it, and they are angry at us solely for that."

Brigham spoke in an even tone, with less anger than he usually showed when he preached on such a subject. The spirit of envy and worldly greed was arrayed against the Spirit of God, he told them. "I am not going to interpret dreams; for I don't profess to be such a prophet as were Joseph Smith and Daniel; but I am a Yankee guesser; and I guess that James Buchanan has ordered his expedition to appease the wrath of the angry hounds who are howling around him. He did not design to start men on the fifteenth of July to cross these plains to this point on foot. . . .

"But," he went on, "woe, woe to that man who comes here to unlawfully interfere with my affairs. Woe, woe to those men who come here to unlawfully meddle with me and this people. I swore in Nauvoo, when my enemies were looking me in the face, that I would send them to hell across lots, if they meddled with me; and I ask no more odds of all hell today. If they kill me, it is all right; but they will not until the time comes; and I think I shall die a natural death; at least I expect to."

On August 9 he again appeared before his people and asked, "What are we going to do under these circumstances?" Then he replied, "Live our religion!" He asked again, "Are we going to contend against the United States?" The answer was "No." But he went on, "Do I expect to stand still, sit still, or lie still, and tamely let them take away my life? I have told you a great many times what I have to say about that. I do not profess to be as good a man as Joseph Smith was. I do not walk under their protection, nor into their prisons as he did. And though officers should pledge me their protection as Governor Ford pledged protection to Joseph, I would not trust them any sooner than I would a wolf with my dinner."

The government's complaints were not to be fully expressed until December 8, when Buchanan delivered his first message to Congress and charged that Brigham Young's power in Utah Territory had been absolute over both church and state. He portrayed the Mormons as religious fanatics who believed that Brigham held the governorship by divine appointment and who would "obey his commands as if these were direct revelation from heaven." He pointed out that the federal judges and all other federal officers except two Indian agents had left the territory in fear for their personal safety, and said that the only government remaining in Utah was the despotism of Brigham Young. The Mormons, he complained, seemed determined to resist. "This being the condition of affairs in the territory, I could not mistake the path of duty. As Chief Executive Magistrate, I was bound to restore the supremacy of the Constitution and laws within its limits. In order to effect this purpose, I appointed a new governor and other federal officers for Utah, and sent with them a military force for their protection, and to aid as a *posse comitatus*, in case of need, in the execution of the laws."

Brigham, who had charged that one motive for the expedition was the graft made possible by the contract for the movement of supplies for the troops, had struck nearer the truth than the President. Secretary of War John B. Floyd was later asked to resign his office as a result of scandal over his Army contracts.

Not that rumor and graft were all that was behind the Utah expedition. Some historians have suggested that Floyd, in conjunction with Southern senators, urged the military expedition in order to lessen the pressure of the government against the issue of slavery. With several thousand United States troops isolated in the West, the government's military power was decreased. Others have suggested that President Buchanan himself was in a mood to use forceful measures in putting down what he considered a rebellion, because he feared secession by some of the Southern states and he wanted them to know that he was capable of acting with speed and dispatch.

The first official word Brigham received from the government came on September 8, when an advance officer of the Army, the Assistant Quartermaster, Captain Stewart Van Vliet, arrived in Salt Lake City. He had been sent to determine whether the Mormons would agree to accept the troops, to provide for them when they arrived, and to supply a suitable site for their encampment. Brigham replied flatly that the Army could not count on the Mormons for supplies, and he further added that they *could* count upon the Mormons for supplying the strongest opposition to their entrance into the territory.

In a meeting in the Tabernacle on September 14, in the presence of Captain Van Vliet, Brigham stood at the rostrum and reiterated his position.

"I have been in this Kingdom a good while—twenty-five years and upwards, and I have been driven from place to place; my brethren have been driven, my sisters have been driven; we have been scattered and peeled, and every time without a provocation on our part, only that we were united, obedient to the laws of the land, and striving to worship God. . . .

"This people are free; they are not in bondage to any government on God's footstool. We have transgressed no law, and we have no occasion to do so, neither do we intend to; but as for any nation's coming to destroy this people, GOD ALMIGHTY BEING MY HELPER, THEY CANNOT COME HERE."

Captain Van Vliet was received with all the courtesy Brigham was capable of—which was a good deal—but he was given no encouragement to hope that the Mormons would not resist the entrance of the troops. When he stated that the Army wanted nothing more than to install a new governor, Brigham asked skeptically why it was necessary to send a force of twenty-five hundred soldiers merely for that.

"I believe you tell the truth—that you believe this—" he told the captain in their private conference, "but you do not know their intentions as well as I do."

"The greatest hold the government has upon you," Van Vliet said, "is the accusation that you have burned the United States records."

Brigham told him that this was a charge made by the notorious Judge Drummond. He took the captain to the court library and showed him that all was intact—nothing, so far as Van Vliet could see, had been disturbed.

Captain Van Vliet mentioned the accusation that the Mormons held their own people captive in the territory—that they would not allow them to leave if they wished.

To this, Brigham offered to provide free transportation and the best of supplies to anyone who desired to leave Utah Territory, on the condition that the government would provide similar means to all those in the East who wished to migrate to Utah.

"And we will gain a thousand to their one," he added.

Captain Van Vliet became convinced of the good intentions of Brigham Young and the Mormons and the lack of any necessity to bring the army into the valley. He proposed to return to Washington with a Mormon representative and to attempt to convince Congress and the President that it would be more practical to send a peace commission to talk with Brigham Young than it would be to insist upon the entry of the army.

In fact, the captain became so convinced that the Mormons were in the right that he told Brigham, "If the government pushes this matter to the extent of making war on you, I will withdraw from the Army, for I will not have a hand in shedding the blood of American citizens."

On September 15, the day after his meeting with Van Vliet, Brigham declared martial law in the territory. As early as August he had ordered members of the militia, still known as the Nauvoo Legion, to scout the approach of the United States troops. On August 27 Colonel Robert T. Burton had come, with a scouting party, within sight of the advance supply trains of the army near Pacific Springs. On September 22, when two infantry regiments halted at Devil's Gate, Burton was camped less than a mile away, and from this time on he sent word by express runners to Brigham Young in Salt Lake notifying him of every movement of the troops. The mountains provided a natural fortress, and the Mormons set up defenses at strategic points at the canyon entrances. These were manned by members of the Legion, which had been mobilized for the defense of Zion.

The federal army, as appointed in Washington, was to have been under the command of General W. S. Harney, but the advance troops were under the direction of Colonel E. B. Alexander. Harney was eventually recalled—before he had ever joined his troops—and appointed to the governorship of Kansas. Alexander would later be reinforced by troops under the command of Albert Sidney Johnston, then a colonel, but promoted to general and placed above Alexander before the end of the campaign.

On September 29 Brigham sent a letter to Colonel Alexander, quoting the act of Congress of September 19, 1850, which provided that a governor should be appointed for the Territory of Utah, who should also be commander of the militia, to serve for four years and until a successor was appointed, or until he was removed by the President. He added:

I am still the governor and superintendent of Indian affairs for this territory, no successor having been appointed and qualified, as provided by law; nor have I been removed by the president of the United States.

By virtue of the authority thus vested in me, I have issued, and forwarded you a copy of my proclamation forbidding the entrance of armed forces into this territory. This you have disregarded. I now further direct that you retire forthwith from the territory, by the same route you entered. Should you deem this impracticable, and prefer to remain until spring in the vicinity of your present encampment, Black's Fork or Green River, you can do so in peace and unmolested, on condition that you deposit your arms and ammunition with Lewis Robinson, quarter-master general of the territory, and leave in the spring, as soon as condition of the roads will permit you to march; and should you fall short of provisions, they can be furnished you, upon making the proper application therefor. General Wells will forward this, and receive any communication you have to make.

Very Respectfully,
Brigham Young
Governor and Superintendent of Indian Affairs,
Utah Territory.

Colonel Alexander replied that Brigham's desires ran counter to the orders he had received, but he did say that he would forward the letter to his superiors.

Soon after this Van Vliet's report was delivered in Washington, and its contents caused consternation in the East. There had been grumbling about the manner in which the military expedition had been managed, with delays in departure and delays in establishing the command. Complaints were made that the army had been started too late in the year, that the troops had been given too little rest since returning from a campaign against the Seminoles in Florida, and that the command had been disrupted by the retention of General Harney in Kansas. Now the Eastern newspapers recorded the return of Van Vliet, who spoke favorably of the Mormons and suggested that there were ways other than military force by which the aim of the government could be accomplished. With our army facing a terrible winter on the Western plains, what do we hear? the newspapers asked. Word of a peace commission to be sent to pacify the Mormons! It was all very confusing.

2

Brigham Young could not know of these shifts of opinion in the East during the fall and winter of 1857-58. News had to come into the territory by way of California, and even this route was dangerous and slow. Brigham had ordered two Mormon settlements on the east side of the mountains to be destroyed: Fort Bridger, which the Mormons had purchased a few years before, and Fort Supply, which they had constructed at a cost of fifty thousand dollars. Both settlements were in the path of the army, and they were burned to the ground. He ordered his settlers to return to Salt Lake from Carson in Nevada and San Bernardino in California.

He also devised a means of harassment to delay the army without coming into actual conflict with it. In an order to the commanding general of the Legion he wrote that the Mormons were to ascertain the route of the soldiers and use every means of annoying and delaying them. He suggested stampeding their animals and setting fire to their supply trains. He advised burning the country before and to the sides of the army, particularly setting the fires to windward, so that the flames might cause the wagons to retreat. He told them to destroy the fords at the rivers and blockade roads by felling trees across them. In conclusion, he wrote: "Keep your men concealed as much as possible, and guard against surprise. Keep scouts out at all times, and communications open. . . . Keep me advised daily of your movements, and every step the troops take, and in which direction."

The first person to find occasion to follow these directions was a young major in the Legion named Lot Smith. Smith was one of that band of young Mormons who, having come of age on the frontier, had learned to adapt himself to it in a way that most of the soldiers in the United States Army had not. One story about Lot Smith tells of a time when he was away as a missionary in Lower California. He was taken by a friend to see a bullfight. During the intermission after the first bull had been killed, Lot jumped into the arena and announced loudly that he considered bullfighting a cowardly sport.

"You shouldn't kill the bull," he told them. "To show your pluck, you should ride him."

"Ride him?" the Mexicans replied. "No one can ride a bull."

"I can," Lot declared.

The Mexicans brought another bull into the ring in order to try this American braggart. Lot jumped on his back and did succeed in remaining on him a short time. The story, as it was told later, says that the bull dumped him squarely into the canopied box of the ruling family, where he was received as a hero.

The first Army supply train that Lot Smith came upon in the fall of 1857, he merely ordered to turn about and "go the other way till you reach the States." The captain of the train ordered the wagons turned, but as soon as Lot and his men were out of sight he again reversed his direction and continued on. Lot came upon him again, and this time he confiscated all their supplies. Later in the afternoon his scouts brought him word that another train, this one containing twenty-six wagons, was approaching. Deciding that his force of twenty-four men was large enough to confront the train, Lot followed the wagons until they had stopped and set up camp. Riding into the encampment at dusk, he was surprised to discover that a second company had joined the first, and the small Mormon band was confronted with double the number of wagons and men it had anticipated. Lot had noticed, however, that the rear of his column extended into the darkness behind him, so that the federal teamsters could not know how few men he had with him. He asked for the captain of the train and announced calmly that he was going to burn their wagons.

He fashioned a torch and lighted it in the campfire, then gave it to one of the drivers and told him to apply it to the first wagon. He did this, he explained, because he wanted the gentiles to spoil the gentiles. Both trains, consisting of seventy-four wagons and their contents, were completely burned out.

Brigham Young kept about eight hundred men in the mountains, but as a result of his "scorched-earth" policy and Lot Smith's depredations there was little danger that the inadequately provisioned army would attempt to force its way into the valley that fall. Colonel Alexander's troops had first tried to move on to Fort Hall, north of the Mormon settlements on the Oregon Trail, but when this proved impossible because of bad weather and the condition of their stock, they retraced their steps and set up camp in the ashes of Fort Bridger. When Colonel Johnston arrived in November, he established the camp on Black's Fork, two miles above Bridger, and named it Camp Scott. With him, living in dugouts, were the newly appointed governor, Alfred Cumming, and the federal judges.

The Mormons in the settlements beyond the mountains went about their business much as they had in other years. Brigham Young had advised his followers to harvest their crops and to plant wheat for the coming spring. We will get together a three-year supply, he told them, and then if we have to leave here and hide out in the mountains, at least we will not starve. Except for a small force of soldiers guarding Echo Canyon and other entrances to the basin, there was little military activity. Yet Brigham kept his people psychologically in readiness.

"If they [the troops] come here," he said to them in one address, "I will tell you what will be done. As soon as they start to come into our settlements, let sleep depart from their eyes and slumber from their eyelids until they sleep in death, for they have been warned and forewarned that we will not tamely submit to being destroyed. Men shall be secreted here and there and shall waste away our enemies."

He told his followers that if the soldiers persisted for another year the Mormons would lay waste all they had built up, so that the soldiers, if they got to the valley, would find nothing but heaps of ashes and ruins. The Mormons, he said, could disappear into the mountains and, if need be, live among rocks and in caves. He requested the bishops to see that people in their wards were provided with two or three years' provisions.

Once during the winter, hearing that the federal army was without salt, Brigham sent them a gift of eight hundred pounds from the salt-beds of the lake. Colonel Johnston indignantly rejected it, saying, "I will not accept a present from an enemy of my government." He considered the Mormons rebels, he told Brigham's messengers, and he would deal with them henceforth only under a flag of truce.

Brigham must have known that the Mormons could not fight the whole United States. His only hope was to prolong the contest until the country wearied of the cost and the misery. As the winter wore on, he seemed more and more disposed to seek means other than fighting.

As early as January 6, 1858, he had written a letter to the head of the Eastern Mission in New York, in which he said:

We have an abundant supply of grain and cattle, and if necessity compels us to flee to the mountains, bread and beef will appease our hunger. . . . Rather than see my wives and daughters ravished and polluted, and the seeds of corruption sown in the hearts of my sons by a brutal soldiery, I would leave my home in ashes, my gardens and orchards a waste, and subsist upon roots and herbs, a wanderer through these mountains for the remainder of my natural life.

Some writers have seen this wavering between war and exile in Brigham's mind as a sign of weakness. The facts seem to indicate rather that it was statesmanship. The world outside knew less about the conditions of the Mormons than Brigham knew about them; the Mormons knew the country better, and Brigham understood the price it would cost to subdue his people once they had burned their towns and scattered throughout the territory. He felt sure that the President of the United States had not anticipated such resistance, and he was reasonably certain that President Buchanan did not want to commit his troops to actual warfare.

The turning point in the conflict came on the twenty-fifth of February, when an ostensible stranger by the name of Osborne arrived in Salt Lake City from the west. The name Osborne was a disguise for Colonel Thomas Kane of Philadelphia, the same man who had come to the Mormons' aid before. Colonel Kane, although he was then in ill health, had gone to President Buchanan and proposed himself, and been accepted, as a mediator between the federal government and the Mormons. To avoid unnecessary delays and the publicity of an official appointment, Kane had traveled incognito, armed only with letters from the President.

The troops had been sent, Kane assured Brigham, merely to guarantee the installation of Cumming as governor. He also told Brigham that, on the whole, he approved the Buchanan administration, and that he believed the differences between the Mormons and the administration could be worked out without bloodshed.

Despite Kane's proved friendship for the Mormons, Brigham remained skeptical of the government's intentions. He asked Kane if the Utah representative to Congress, who had gone east to replace Babbitt, had been seated.

"Yes," Colonel Kane told him. "He was opposed by the Arkansas member and a few others, but they were treated as fools by more sagacious members; for, if the delegate had been refused his seat, it would have been tantamount to a declaration of war."

"I suppose," Brigham said, "the Cabinet are united in putting down Utah?"

Kane replied that he did not think so.

The colonel remained in Salt Lake City until March 8, meeting with Brigham privately and also with other Mormon officials. No definite plan was adopted. Brigham assured Kane that he would accept the new governor if he came peacefully, without the troops. He had no objection to receiving the peace commission. Brigham's advice, finally, was merely that Colonel Kane should go to the army encampment and "do as the Spirit of the Lord led him." If you do, Brigham told him, all will be right. But, he insisted, if it was decided that the army must enter the valley, the Mormons would leave.

When Colonel Kane left the city he traveled with a Mormon escort to within twelve miles of the army camp. He then continued on alone on horseback. Upon his arrival he immediately went into conference with Governor Cumming. Johnston, who believed he was putting down a rebellion, was offended because Kane had not reported to him instead of to Cumming. He was also suspicious of Kane, as he would have been of anyone friendly to the Mormons. When Kane proposed taking Cumming to Salt Lake City to meet with Brigham, Johnston objected and favored a continuation of the military campaign. As a military man, he wanted to bring the Mormon rebels to their knees. He also feared that the Mormons might seize the new governor and hold him hostage.

Governor Cumming agreed to the proposal, however; and Johnston's authority did not extend to ordering him to remain in camp. Cumming and Kane set out on April 5. At Echo Canyon, which marked the entrance to the Mormon stronghold, they were met by an escort of Mormon guards. A few miles farther on they were joined by a full company of uniformed Legionnaires. Obviously Brigham Young wished to impress the governor with the extent of the Mormons' determination, and Governor Cumming expressed himself as astonished at the military manner of the Mormon troops. The militia presented themselves to him, however, as a formal guard of honor, and the governor seemed pleased at the respect shown him. At Farmington, the first Mormon settlement on the west side of the mountains, where the party stopped overnight, the governor was serenaded by a band of Mormon musicians who, out of respect to him, passed over the martial Mormon airs and played such traditional numbers as "Yankee Doodle" and "Hail Columbia."

Next morning, as the party approached Salt Lake City, a disquieting sight met their eyes. All roads were filled with Mormons, their wagons piled high with goods and supplies, all moving southward. Cumming stopped and asked some of them what they were doing, and the Mormons replied that they were leaving their homes until it was clear that the army would not march into the Salt Lake Valley. When the governor reached Salt Lake City itself, he found that all the inhabitants had left. Their homes were boarded up, the chimneys cold and smokeless. The streets were deserted. Even Brigham Young was in Provo, forty miles south, where the saints had established a rendezvous.

During Kane's absence Brigham had announced publicly that he would not "war with the people of the United States, but let them destroy themselves." First the Mormons would remove all foodstuffs from the city, then the women and children. Enough men would be left behind to set fire to the homes in case the army entered. When he learned that the governor had arrived, he returned on April 13 to meet with Kane and Cumming. After several meetings, in which Cumming satisfied himself that most of the charges against the Mormons were unfounded, the governor wrote to General Johnston:

I have been everywhere recognized as the Governor of Utah, and so far from having encountered insults and indignities, I am gratified in being able to state to you that in passing through the settlements, I have been universally greeted with such respectful attentions as are due to the representative of the executive authority of the United States in the Territory.

Cumming also verified Van Vliet's report that the court records and books had not been destroyed as Judge Drummond had charged. The new governor was disturbed by the movement of the Mormons from Salt Lake City, somewhat offended by what seemed a lack of trust in himself, but Brigham refused to recall his people until he was convinced that the government was acting in good faith. Twenty-five thousand of the forty-five thousand inhabitants of the territory had moved from their homes and made preparations to burn them if the army approached.

Brigham Young attempted to keep Johnston beyond the mountains. He offered to supply the soldiers so long as they remained outside of Utah. Johnston insisted that his orders were to establish his forces where they could serve as protectors of the federal officials. This stalemate was not broken until June, when two men, constituting the peace commission, arrived from Washington and began negotiating with Brigham Young and his leaders in Salt Lake City.

3

Brigham Young and Alfred Cumming had conducted their meetings in a growing atmosphere of mutual respect. There was little of that present in the conferences between Brigham and the peace commissioners, Powell and McCullough. Neither side wished to give the impression of surrender. The honor of the government needed to be preserved, and Brigham could not back down from the strong words he had uttered to his people. During one of the

meetings Porter Rockwell entered and whispered something in
Brigham Young's ear. Brigham turned to the governor.

"Are you aware," he asked, "that those troops are on the move toward the city?"

"It cannot be," the governor replied.

Brigham looked about the room.

"Is Brother Dunbar present?" he asked.

"Yes, sir," someone replied.

"Brother Dunbar, sing 'Zion,' " Brigham told him.

The Welsh convert arose and sang the hymn which expressed
the Mormons' determination to defend themselves. According to
one historian, "Interpreted, this meant, 'Stop that army or our peace
conference is ended.' "

> Up, awake, ye defenders of Zion!
> The foe's at the door of your homes;
> Let each heart be the heart of a Lion,
> Unyielding and proud as he roams.
>
> Remember the wrongs of Missouri;
> Forget not the fate of Nauvoo.
> When the God-hating foe is before you,
> Stand firm and be faithful and true.
>
> By the mountains our Zion's surrounded;
> Her warriors are noble and brave;
> And their faith on Jehovah is founded,
> Whose power is mighty to save.
>
> Opposed by a proud boasting nation,
> Their numbers, compared, may be few;
> But their union is known through creation,
> And they've always been faithful and true.
>
> Shall we bear with oppression forever?
> Shall we tamely submit to the foe,
> While the ties of our kindred they sever
> And the blood of our prophets shall flow?
>
> No, the thought sets the heart wildly beating;
> Our vows at each pulse we renew:
> Ne'er to rest till our foes are retreating,
> And to be ever faithful and true.

After the meeting one of the commissioners and the governor took a stroll together.

"What will you do with such a people?" the governor asked, his tone expressing both admiration and concern.

"Damn them, I would fight them if I had my way," the commissioner replied.

"Fight them, would you?" the governor said. "You might fight them, but you would never whip them. They would never know when they were whipped."

The commissioners had brought with them a lengthy presidential proclamation, which they read to the Mormon leaders. In it were recited the grievances of the government against the Mormons. It then offered them "pardon and amnesty" if they would allow the troops to enter and promise to abide by the laws.

After the document had been read, Brigham got to his feet. "I have listened very attentively to the commissioners," he stated, "and I will say, as far as I'm concerned, I thank President Buchanan for forgiving me, but I really cannot tell what I have done.

"It is true," he continued wryly, "Lot Smith burned some wagons containing government supplies for the army. This was an overt act, and if it is for this we are to be pardoned, I accept the pardon."

More seriously he warned the commissioners that the Mormons had accepted government guarantees of protection before—in Missouri and Illinois. Both times they had ended by losing lives and property.

In reply, the commissioners declared that they had not come with the intention to wage war, but as an indication of President Buchanan's desire for peace. It was agreed finally that the army might enter the territory, but with the understanding that it would not encamp in the vicinity of Salt Lake City. General Johnston chose Cedar Valley for the encampment, a dry, barren retreat about twenty-five miles southwest of Salt Lake City, and, at the request of the commissioners, issued a proclamation, declaring "that no person whatever will be in anywise interfered with or molested in his person or rights, or in the peaceful pursuit of his avocation."

Brigham had not yet recalled his saints to their homes. He still maintained men in the city to put the torch to their homes in the event that the army violated its agreement. A reporter for the New York *Herald* reported the passage of the federal troups through Salt Lake City on the way to their new encampment. The caravan contained three thousand men, six hundred wagons, and approximately six thousand cattle, horses, and mules. Dust swirled behind them. Their drums beat a monotonous, somewhat weary, march step. As they entered the city all except a knot of gentiles standing in the street near Brigham Young's residence were out of sight of the marching soldiers.

"We were particularly struck by its quietness," the *Herald* reporter wrote. "There was none of the hum and stir of business that characterize gentile towns. The streets were deserted, the city was deserted. Though surrounded by houses we were nevertheless in a place of desert loneliness. The quietness of the grave prevailed where it seemed that thronging thousands and rushing commerce ought to pour their tides along. The windows had been taken out of the major parts of the houses; the doors were locked; everything had been made ready for burning, as the Mormons tell us, if peace had not been achieved before the arrival of the troops."

This was no triumphal entry. The army band played, but there were few to hear. The scattered gentile cheers were drowned by the thump of marching feet. Johnston had given orders that there was to be no halt made in the city itself. Not a man broke ranks until the army had traversed the city and reached the Jordan River west of the town. The soldiers made their first night's encampment on the opposite bank of the river, thus fulfilling an agreement made between Brigham Young and the commissioners.

The next Sunday, Brigham stood before his displaced congregation in the Bowery at Provo. "What is the present situation of affairs?" he asked, obviously not dissatisfied with his policy thus far. "For us the clouds seem to be breaking. Probably many of you already learned that General Johnston passed through Salt Lake City with his command under the strictest discipline. Not a house, fence, or sidewalk has been impinged upon by any of his command. Of course, the camp followers are not under his control, but as far as the command is concerned, while passing through the city, he has carried out his promises to the letter.

"As soon as General Johnston finds a place to locate his command —when we get news what he is going to do with his troops—we will go home."

Then he added a word of warning. "Women, do not induce your husbands to go home just yet, but wait until the proper time. . . . If any of the sisters say they have not a house to live in, they can go a short distance from their wagons and get bushes to make a comfortable shade."

Brigham's stipulation had been that the army should not remain in the vicinity of the city. The troops moved on to Cedar Valley on July 6. As soon as the army departed the saints returned, let the air and sunlight back into their darkened homes, then moved in again with their families.

The "Utah War" brought Buchanan little credit in the East. Even the newspapers, which had continued to question the wisdom of the government expedition, granted a grudging admiration for the way the Mormon "prophet," Brigham Young, had come out in his brush with Uncle Sam. In Utah, it added another chapter in the Mormon myth of Brigham's infallibility. The war, it was estimated, had cost the government at least fifteen million dollars. The Mormons were uneasy with troops still in the territory, but many a Mormon found himself enriched by trade when he undertook to supply the soldiers with necessities. Also, coming events were to work even more to the advantage of the Mormons. Within three years the Civil War was to break out. When it did, the government quickly sold all the supplies and equipment except ammunition; and this they piled in a lonesome spot on the desert and exploded, to keep it out of what might be called unfriendly hands. Mormons purchased many of the supplies of food and clothing at much less than the original cost to the government; and thus the people of Utah eventually profited from Johnston's army as they had earlier from the gold rush.

CHAPTER THIRTEEN

TROUBLE IN ZION

I

For a few months after the arrival of the army in Utah, Brigham Young curtailed the activities of the church. Suspicious of the army, he wished nothing to happen that could serve as an excuse for the government to apply its force. Notably he postponed the general conference at which he and his leaders were accustomed to stand up before the membership in the Bowery or the old Tabernacle. Social activities were reduced, and a few events were scheduled which would allow a mingling of church leaders and gentiles. General Johnston remained equally aloof, keeping to his headquarters at Camp Floyd and refusing even to visit the city. Governor Cumming was still friendly to the Mormons.

The federal judges who had accompanied the army were another matter. Still smarting under the indignity and the discomforts of their winter on the plains, they seemed bent on provoking a clash between the Mormons and the government.

"The speculators still seem determined to let no opportunity slip to create a 'muss,'" a Mormon wrote in a letter to the East. "There are strong rumors that Judge Sinclair is about to bring a large detachment of troops to this city to convince the inhabitants that he really is a much more important personage than they have any idea of."

The judge had threatened that when he opened his May term of court for 1859 he would have three-fourths of the army from Camp Floyd quartered within the city. Before this could happen another judge, sitting in Provo, called upon the army to protect his court, and a detachment of a thousand soldiers was sent to his aid. The citizens of Provo protested to the governor. Governor Cumming ordered Johnston to remove the troops. Johnston refused. Only after several months of negotiations and an appeal to the State Department in Washington was the governor able to enforce his order to have the troops withdrawn.

Throughout the course of these events Brigham remained in the background. He broke his self-imposed seclusion once, at the end of August 1858, to entertain the governor and a group of his leaders at a "Pic Nic" in Big Cottonwood Canyon. Colonel Alexander called upon him once at his home, and Brigham remarked afterward that if he and the colonel could have met a year earlier the army might have been spared its harrowing winter across the mountains. For the most part Brigham confined himself to affairs directly concerning the church, instructing missionaries, organizing his settlements, and, above all, pressing forward with the construction of the temple.

At the time when the army entered the territory the temple foundations alone had been constructed. Located at the eastern edge of the temple block, the basement structure appeared little more than a rectangular well measuring 193 by 105 feet. Beside it was a mound of earth scooped out of the excavation, a sawmill, and heaps of granite blocks hauled laboriously by ox-team from the nearby mountains. Nevertheless, it was said that the saints had already expended more than a million dollars on it. The granite had been cut high in the mountains and hauled by ox-team down to the city. A canal was begun to expedite the movement of the stone, but this proved a failure. The foundation walls were sixteen feet thick at the bottom, and the granite blocks were so large that a single one demanded a wagon for hauling. No such haste as had been shown in the construction at Kirtland or Nauvoo was being employed here, for Brigham believed he was building for eternity.

"We shall attempt to build a temple to the name of our God," he told his followers. "This has been attempted several times, but we have never yet had the privilege of completing and enjoying one. Perhaps we may in this place, but if, in the providence of God, we should not, it is all the same. It is for us to do those things which the Lord requires at our hands, and leave the result with him."

Earlier he had said, "I do know it is the duty of this people to commence to build a temple. Now, some will want to know what kind of building it will be. Wait patiently, brethren, until it is done, and put forth your hands willingly to finish it. I know what it will be. I scarcely ever say much about revelations, or visions, but suffice it to say, five years ago last July I was here, and saw in the spirit the temple not ten feet from where we have laid the chief corner- stone. I have not inquired what kind of a temple we should build. Why? Because it was represented before me. Wait until it is done. I will say, however, that it will have six towers, to begin with, instead of one. Now do not any of you apostatize because it will have six towers, and Joseph only built one. It is easier for us to build sixteen, than it was for him to build one."

After the war the walls of the temple began to rise. Haulers were called upon from the pulpit to leave other tasks and assist in bring- ing down the heavy stones from the mountains while the roads were good. Woodcutters and carpenters and stonemasons donated their labor or worked out their tithing. Brigham's vision was not the flash of illumination that had produced Joseph's temples at Kirtland and Nauvoo; it was undoubtedly influenced by what he had seen of Eu- ropean churches in England and by sketches brought back from the Continent by his brother-in-law Truman O. Angell. If the Kirtland temple was an enlarged Puritan meeting house, the Salt Lake tem- ple was to be a reduced cathedral, with the lower structure con- taining a rather commonplace hodgepodge of the nineteenth cen- tury and medieval baroque, surmounted by the spires of Brigham's vision, their thrust reflecting the impulse of the mountains which surround them and the hope of the builders—a hope which was eventually to be symbolized in the figure of the Angel Moroni, blowing the trump of the last judgment from the central spire on the east.

Brigham was not destined to see the finished building, for it was not completed in his lifetime. He was, however, the master builder, even though his brother-in-law Truman Angell was listed as the official architect and had been sent to Europe to obtain ideas for the construction.

Brigham Young's personal appearance at the time, and the clarity of his thinking as a religious leader, are reflected in the words of two widely read writers of the period.

In 1859 Brigham was interviewed by Horace Greeley, editor of the New York *Tribune*, who was traveling through Kansas and Utah to California. Greeley described Brigham as "very plainly dressed in thin summer clothing, and with no air of sanctimony or fanaticism. In appearance, he is portly, frank, goodnatured, a rather thick-set man . . . seeming to enjoy life, and to be in no particular hurry to get to heaven. His associates are plain men, evidently born and reared to a life of labor, and looking as little like crafty hypocrites or swindlers as any body of men I ever met. The absence of cant or snuffle from their manner was marked and general; yet I think I may freely say that their Mormonism has not impoverished them, that they were generally poor men when they embraced it, and are now in very comfortable circumstances."

Greeley was frank in the questions he put to Brigham, and the prophet seemed anxious to reply without equivocation.

Greeley asked, "Am I to regard Mormonism . . . as a new religion, or simply a new development of Christianity?"

Brigham replied, "We hold that there can be no Christian Church without a priesthood directly commissioned by, and in immediate communication with the Son of God and Savior of mankind. Such a church is that of the Latter-day Saints, called by their enemies Mormons; we know no other that even pretends to have present and direct revelations of God's will."

Greeley: "Then I am to understand that you regard all other churches professing to be Christian as the Church of Rome regards all churches not in communion with itself—as schismatic, heretical, and out of the way of salvation?"

Young: "Yes, substantially."

Greeley: "Apart from this, in what respect do your doctrines differ essentially from those of our Orthodox Protestant churches —the Baptist, or Methodist, for example?"

Young: "We hold the doctrines of Christianity, as revealed in the Old and New Testaments—also in the Book of Mormon, which teaches the same cardinal truths and those only."

Greeley: "Do you believe in the doctrine of the Trinity?"

Young: "We do; but not exactly as it is held by other churches. We believe in the Father, the Son, and the Holy Ghost, as equal but not identical—not as one person. We believe all the Bible teaches on this subject."

Greeley: "Do you believe in a personal devil—a distinct, conscious, spiritual being, whose nature and acts are essentially malignant and evil?"

Young: "We do."

Greeley: "Do you hold the doctrine of eternal punishment?"

Young: "We do; though perhaps not exactly as other churches do. We believe it as the Bible teaches it."

Greeley: "I understand that you regard baptism by immersion as essential?"

Young: "We do."

Greeley: "Do you practice infant baptism?"

Young: "No."

Greeley: "Do you make removal to these valleys obligatory on your converts?"

Young: "They would consider themselves greatly aggrieved if they were not invited hither. We hold to such a gathering together of God's people, as the Bible foretells, and that this is the place, and now is the time appointed for its consummation."

Greeley: "The predictions to which you refer, have usually, I think, been understood to indicate Jerusalem . . . as the place of such gathering."

Young: "Yes, for the Jews—not for others."

Greeley: "Let me now be enlightened with regard more especially to your church polity; I understand that you require each member to pay over one-tenth of all he produces or earns to the church."

Young: "That is a requirement of our faith. There is no compulsion as to payment. Each member acts in the premises according to his pleasure, under the dictates of his own conscience."

Greeley: "What is done with the proceeds of this tithing?"

Young: "Part of it is devoted to building temples, and other places of worship; part to helping the poor and needy converts on their way to this country; and the largest portion to the support of the poor among the saints."

Greeley: "Is none of it paid to bishops, and other dignitaries of the church?"

Young: "Not one penny. No bishop, elder, no deacon, nor other church officer, receives any compensation for his official services. A bishop is often required to put his hand into his own pocket, and provide therefrom for the poor of his charge; but he never receives anything for his services."

Greeley: "How, then, do your ministers live?"

Young: "By the labor of their own hands, like the first apostles. Every bishop, every elder, may be daily seen at work in the field, or the shop, like his neighbors; every minister of the church has his proper calling, by which he earns the bread of his family; he who cannot, or will not do the church's work for nothing is not wanted in her service."

Horace Greeley, deeply concerned by the question of slavery, was struck by the Mormons' preoccupation with the wrongs that had been practiced against them in Missouri and Illinois, while at the same time they were silent about this most pressing of national issues. Once, while meeting with Brigham's Council of the Twelve, he arose and protested.

"I have not heard tonight, and I think I have never heard, from the lips or the journals of any of your people, one word in reprehension of that gigantic national crime and scandal, American chattel slavery. You speak forcibly of the wrongs to which your feeble brethren have from time to time been subjected; but what are they all to the perpetual, the gigantic outrage involved in hold-

ing in abject bondage four millions of human beings? This obsti-
nate silence, this seeming indifference on your part, reflects no
credit on your faith and morals, and I trust they will not be persisted in."

Elder John Taylor, who was then president of the Twelve, replied.

"The subject of slavery," he answered, "is one on which Mr.
Greeley is known to be enthusiastic, as we are on the subject of
our religion. We cannot help speaking of our religion at every
opportunity, as he cannot help speaking of slavery. Those who do
not relish this or that topic must excuse its introduction."

The New York editor had forgotten that he had asked Brigham
Young about the church's position in regard to slavery. Brigham
had replied that the Mormons believed slavery would be abolished
only when God's curse upon Ham had been removed, for they
considered the Negroes to be descendants of Ham. When Greeley
asked if this meant that Utah, if admitted to the Union, would be a
slave state, Brigham replied, "No; she will be a free state. Slavery
here would prove useless and unprofitable. I regard it generally as
a curse to the masters. I myself hire many laborers, and pay them
fair wages; I could not afford to own them."

The next year another distinguished visitor arrived in Salt Lake
City. He was Richard F. Burton, who proposed to write a book
about the Mormons, second in a series to be written on the sacred
cities of the world. He had already written on the Mohammedan
culture. Governor Cumming introduced him to Brigham Young,
whom he described as "neither morose nor methodistic," and added,
"Where occasion requires, he can use all the weapons of ridicule to
direful effect, and 'speak a bit of his mind' in a style which no one
forgets."

Burton gave us the first description of Brigham's beard, familiar
in all official portraits, which he had apparently now only just begun to grow—a "fringe" beard, with the long upper lip and the
upper chin shaved, the hair growing down the cheeks and beneath
the chin. He also described Brigham speaking at one of the Sunday
services. Brigham entered late, after another speaker had begun his

sermon. He was dressed in a suit of gray homespun, and he wore a tall "steeple-crowned" hat with a black ribbon, which he did not immediately remove. On his hands he wore black kid gloves. As he took his seat on the platform he nodded to those near him and settled back for the conclusion of the address, seemingly aware that the eyes of the congregation were upon him. The speaker at the rostrum hurried to a conclusion. Another hymn was sung by the choir and the congregation. Then, Burton reported, a great silence came over the assembled saints, a silence which "told us that something was about to happen: *that* old man held his cough; *that* old lady awoke with a start; that child ceased to squall." Brigham removed his hat, advanced slowly to the pulpit, bent over and expectorated into a spittoon which was concealed by the drapery of the platform; he took a slow drink of water from a decanter at his elbow; then, gripping the pulpit with both hands, he leaned forward toward his audience.

The discourse, [Burton went on] began slowly; word crept titubantly after word, and the opening phrases were hardly audible; but as the orator warmed, his voice rose high and sonorous, and a fluency so remarkable succeeded falter and hesitation, that—although the phenomenon is not rare in strong speakers—the latter seemed almost to have been a work of art. The manner was pleasing and animated and the matter fluent, impromptu, and well turned, spoken rather than preached. . . . Of course, colloquialisms of all kinds were introduced, such as "he become," "for you and I," and so forth. The gestures were easy and rounded, not without a certain grace, though evidently untaught. . . . The address was long. God is a mechanic. Mormonism is a great fact. Religion has made him (the speaker) the happiest of men. He was ready to dance like a Shaker. At this sentence the Prophet, who is a good mimic, and has much of the old New English quaint humor, raised his right arm, and gave, to the amusement of the congregation, a droll imitation of Anne Lee's followers. . . . The saints have a glorious destiny before them, and their morality is remarkable as the beauty of the Promised Land: the soft breeze blowing over the Bowery, and the glorious sunshine outside make the allusion highly appropriate. The Lamanites, or Indians, are a religious people. All races know a God and may be saved. After a somewhat lengthy string of sentences concerning the great tribulations coming on earth—it has been coming for the last 1800 years—he concluded with good wishes to visitors and gentiles generally, with a solemn blessing upon the President of the United States, the territorial governor, and all such as be in authority over us, and, with an amen which was loudly re-echoed by all around, he restored his hat, and resumed his seat.

In Brigham's dealing with both distinguished visitors, he was conscious that his every word would eventually appear in print, and he seldom went into more detail about Mormon doctrine than was absolutely necessary. He did not deny Mormon differences from other Christian sects, but he strove to emphasize with Greeley the Mormons' dependence upon the Bible in order to offset the general belief outside Utah that for the Mormons the *Book of Mormon* had replaced the scriptures as the basic authority for their doctrine. What remained unsaid was that the Mormons saw the Old and the New Testament not as the final and absolute authority, except as they referred to what the Mormons considered the first two dispensations of time; they saw the *Book of Mormon* as a similar authority for this, the final, dispensation, and it stood in relation to the New Testament much as the New Testament stood in relation to the Old. Beyond this, however, they saw the total Scriptures as continuing so long as the Word of God was to be had. The fact that the New Testament ended when it did they understood as evidence of the Great Apostasy following the death of the apostles of Christ. The revelations of Joseph Smith, the sermons of Brigham and his fellow apostles were as much scripture and authority as was the *Book of Mormon*, so long as those revelations and sermons reflected the spirit of divine inspiration. Something of this was behind Brigham's reply to Horace Greeley, when he said that he knew of no other church that pretended to have present and direct revelations of God's will.

But the Mormons distinguished between divine inspiration and true authority. Others besides Mormons could become inspired of God for his ends—Martin Luther, John Calvin, John Wesley, even Columbus and the founding fathers of the American republic. Authority, on the other hand, had come with the restoration of the priesthood, as returned to earth by means of the visionary appearances of John the Baptist and of the apostles Peter, James, and John, and was thus in exclusive possession of the Mormon Church, to be shared with others only through the ceremonies which the Mormon Church administered.

The concept of the gathering, which Greeley hinted at in his question about compulsory immigration of Mormons to Utah, was based upon a particularly nineteenth-century American concept, that America was destined to be the favored of all nations, carried to its extreme emphasis in Mormonism through Joseph Smith's teaching that America—and specifically western Missouri—had been the site of the original Garden of Eden. From the mountains of Utah, the Mormons of Brigham Young's day believed—and Mormons today still believe—the church will spread until it has engulfed all of western America, perhaps the whole of the continent. This was manifest destiny with a theological justification. If the Jews were to gather in Jerusalem, it was to fulfill promises made to them as one of the tribes of Israel; but they were a lesser people, and their promise was less great than that made to the Mormons, because the descendants of Judah had refused to accept Christ and because the Mormons were descended of more faithful and more worthy ancestors—the tribes of Joseph and Benjamin, the most favored sons of Israel. To accept the Mormon Church has ever been a sign that the convert is a member of one of these two favored tribes; and to accept this fact has usually meant to yearn for reuniting with your brethren, as surely as the orthodox Jew yearns to join his brothers in Zion.

Perhaps it was Mormonism's pragmatic nature which, more than any other single aspect, made it a living religion for its converts. Although God was absolute, the working out of His plan of salvation depended less upon His will than it did upon the will of the individual, so that the Kingdom of God was not established by divine fiat, but only through a working-out by the community of saints in a day-by-day struggle against the powers of evil. Yet even God—whom the Mormons refer to as "the God of this world"— was seen as relative, absolute only in terms of His own sphere of existence; for He was to be seen in terms of other gods of other worlds in a universe of worlds upon worlds, in the galaxies which extend beyond man's abilities to visualize any limits to their existence. Our own world we are coming to know and understand with more and more exactness. In scientific terms, we are unfolding the mysteries of nature; in Mormon theological terms, we are preparing the day when man shall have brought God's plan to completion. When this day comes (and no Mormon pretends to know exactly when it will come), then certain individuals will have prepared themselves to become gods in their own right, perhaps to rule over some realm in outer space, much as the god of our own world rules over this.

This polytheistic element in the Mormon religion is one which the Mormons do not stress, having learned from experience how little the world in general appreciates novelty, particularly in theology; but it is available as speculation in much that has been written by Mormon theologians, and it is often a subject of discussion in Mormon study groups. Missionaries in particular are advised not to discuss the mysteries with strangers and investigators, but to confine themselves to "first principles," which are "faith, repentance, and baptism," after which all knowledge will be added as the convert shows himself worthy of it. Nevertheless, it is necessary to understand these elements of pragmatic and materialistic utopianism in order to understand many of the words which Mormons speak in public, as for instance this single passage from an address delivered by a Mormon before the Congress of Religious Philosophies held in San Francisco in 1915:

We hold it to be reasonable, scriptural and true, that man's period of earth-life is but one stage in the general plan of the soul's *progression;* and that birth is no more the beginning than is death the close of individual existence. God created all things spiritually before they were created temporally upon the earth; and the spirits of all men lived as intelligent beings, endowed with the capacity of choice and the rights of free agency, before they were born in flesh. They were the spirit-children of God. It was their Divine Father's purpose to provide a means by which they could be *trained and developed,* with opportunity to meet, combat, and overcome evil, and thus gain strength, power and will, as means of *yet further development through the eternities of the endless future.* For this purpose was the earth created, whereon, *as on other worlds,* spirits might take upon themselves bodies, living in probation as candidates for a *higher and more glorious future.*

The italics have been added to point out the progressivism represented, and the relativism hinted at, in the Mormon elder's address. None of these elements are new in Mormonism in the present century. All were available before the death of Joseph Smith in 1844.

Brigham Young made few attempts to influence the religious doctrines handed down to him by Joseph Smith, either by speculation or by alteration, and on the two occasions when he did so, the effects were bad. The first time was when he encouraged the reformation of 1856, with its extreme views of the doctrine of blood atonement. The second time was when he speculated publicly that Adam and Christ were the same person; that is, that the original sin had been committed by the same personage by whom it was later atoned for; and this led to such outcries and ridicule by gentiles and apostates that the subject was hastily dropped. What this amounted to, his opponents charged, was Adam-worship. The important thing here, however, is not the fact that such speculation may prove dangerous, but the fact that it could exist, for the Mormon meetings such as Greeley and Burton attended were not formal and highly ritualized functions. The speaker stood up with little preparation and spoke as the "inner voice" directed. His words were more often than not conditioned by just such speculation as he had engaged in while going about his regular labor during the week or by discussions he had engaged in with other Mormons; and what he said, regardless of how he said it, was often more exciting to the Mormon in the audience than to the uninitiated gentile. Not infrequently an idea would escape which, like an important piece in a puzzle, made other pieces somehow more recognizable and useful. Not only was the faith of the individual Mormon growing through the accumulation of what he considered wisdom, but even the wisdom itself seemed to develop, much like a growing organism;

and generally such development came during periods of stress in the community.

The presence of almost three thousand United States troops at Camp Floyd after 1858 increased the prosperity of the territory, but it made the Mormons restless. In July 1861 the troops were ordered out. Everything except military supplies was sold at auction.

The Civil War had broken out. The nation had other things more important than the Mormons to consider. Buchanan had been replaced by Abraham Lincoln. Soon after Lincoln's inauguration, T. B. H. Stenhouse, a Mormon representative in the East, paid him a call to determine what the new administration's policy toward the Mormons would be. After hearing the question, Lincoln remained silent a moment, then finally spoke. "Stenhouse," he said, "when I was a boy on the farm in Illinois there was a great deal of timber on the farm which we had to clear away. Occasionally we would come to a log which had fallen down. It was too hard to split, too wet to burn, and too heavy to move, so we plowed around it. That's what I intend to do with the Mormons. You go back and tell Brigham Young that if he will let me alone, I will let him alone."

If this remark reflected (as it may have) Lincoln's anxiety over the possibility that Utah might ally itself with the rebellious South, his fears were groundless. At a council meeting of March 4, 1861, Brigham said that he did not wish Utah mixed up with the secession movement. In October, when the transcontinental telegraph line from the East reached Utah, Brigham was invited to send the first message. He addressed it to President Lincoln. "Utah has not seceded," he flashed through the frail wire that stretched for the first time across mountains and plains, "but is firm for the Constitution and laws of our once happy country."

When he used the term "once happy country" he was probably thinking not only of the Civil War, but also of events which were of much more intimate concern to him.

2

The Mountain Meadow Massacre, as it became known, occurred shortly after word had come from the East that a federal army was approaching Utah. Brigham's knowledge of the event at the time was slight. During the visit of Captain Van Vliet, in the fall of 1857, Brigham received a courier from the settlements of Iron County, two hundred and fifty miles to the south, who carried a message stating that a company of emigrants on their way to California had arrived among them. Given less aid than they had expected from the Mormons, they had grown belligerent and threatening. A group of them, who called themselves the Missouri Wildcats, boasted that they had helped to murder Joseph Smith. Others threatened that when they got to California they would raise an army and return to assist the federal troops. The Mormons heard that they had poisoned a spring in central Utah, killing some cattle belonging to the Indians. The message to Brigham related these facts and rumors and asked the prophet's advice. Brigham sent back word that the emigrants should under no conditions be molested. They should be allowed to pass through the settlements as rapidly as possible. He did warn his followers that they should make every effort not to create trouble with the Indians.

"Go in haste, and do not spare horseflesh," the messenger quoted Brigham Young as saying. "The emigrants must be protected if it takes all the men in southern Utah."

But Brigham's message arrived too late. Although the messenger left Salt Lake City the same day he arrived, he did not get back to Cedar City before the entire company of approximately one hundred and twenty persons had been murdered by the Indians and the whites. Even then, Brigham did not learn the details of the killing. He was led by his followers to believe that it had been an Indian massacre. That he persisted in this belief for many years there can be no doubt. Like Governor Ford of Illinois, he did not believe his people capable of such cruelty. By 1859 his own investigations indicated that some Mormons had been involved. The full horror of the atrocity was not to become known until some time after 1863.

Briefly, what had happened was this: The party of emigrants bound for California arrived at Buttermilk Fort, now Holden, 175 miles south of Salt Lake at a time when the saints were apprehensive at the approach of a federal army and were prepared to resist invasion if it became necessary. Here the emigrants enraged the Mormons by telling them that their women were whores and by threatening that when they got to California they would recruit an army and return to Utah. They then went on to Cedar City and passed through it, with ill feeling and tension apparent on both sides.

As they arrived and camped at Mountain Meadow, thirty-five miles west and south of Cedar City, an indignation meeting was held in Cedar City after the regular church services. A resolution was passed to the effect that "we will deal with this situation now, so that our hands will be free to meet the army when it comes." Some Mormons felt that this was the chance to avenge the deaths of Joseph and Hyrum Smith (as members of the emigrant company had boasted they had participated in the murder), as well as Parley P. Pratt's murder (he had been killed that year in Arkansas, the state from which the bulk of the emigrants came). Other Mormons disagreed. It was at this point that a courier was sent to Brigham Young, asking his advice.

At Mountain Meadow, Indians, sensing the hostility of the Mormons, made the first attack on the company, and several Indians were killed. No attempt to restrain the Indians was made by the resident white men who were present, among whom was John Doyle Lee, the government Indian agent for the area, and a devout Mormon.

Following the first attack by the Indians, three members of the emigrant company left the camp in an attempt to get to Cedar City and enlist aid against what they thought was an Indian attack. One of these men was seen by one of the Mormons, who evidently became panicky at the thought that the presence of white men on the scene was about to be disclosed, and who shot and killed him. The other two emigrants escaped to the California road, but they were soon overtaken by Indians and also killed. The Mormons were now thoroughly frightened that their part in the ambush would be discovered, particularly if the remainder of the emigrants survived the Indian attack. They sent to their military commander in Parowan, Major William H. Dame, to ask what they should do.

Meanwhile the Indians threatened to turn against them, charging that the Mormons, who had advised them to fight the Amerikats, would not now come to their assistance. Ambiguous orders arrived from Major Dame in Parowan, suggesting that they allow the emigrants to leave, taking part of their stock and equipment to appease the Indians. But, Dame advised, "On no condition are you to precipitate a war with Indians while there is an army marching against our people."

By now there were approximately fifty-four Mormons on the scene, and between two and three hundred Indians, who were showing increasing anger at the indecision of the Mormons. Several of their braves had been killed, and they hinted that if they could not avenge themselves against the emigrants they might do so against the Mormons.

A council was held, in which it was decided that all the emigrants except the smallest children should die. John D. Lee, in explaining this meeting, wrote later: "We knew that the original plan was for the Indians to do all the work and the whites to do nothing, only to stay back and plan for them, and encourage them to do the work. Now we knew the Indians could not do the work, and we were in a sad fix."

According to prearranged plan, Lee, under a flag of truce, carried a message to the emigrants telling them that the Indians were angry at the killing of their braves and that the only way they could be satisfied was for the emigrants to surrender their arms and property and march under the protection of the whites to Cedar City. The young children were placed in wagons and taken from the camp. The adults followed on foot, each accompanied by a Mormon. The plan was for each Mormon, upon a prearranged signal, to shoot the man he accompanied. However, since many of the Mormons objected to killing, they were told merely to fire their guns into the air, after which the Indians would come in and complete the slaughter. All the emigrants were killed within a few minutes.

No sooner was the killing complete than disagreement broke out among the Mormon leaders as to who had been responsible. In the light of Brigham's message, which arrived nearly twenty-four hours too late, and undoubtedly also in the light of horror at the deed itself, a recognition of bad judgment and a sense of guilt came over them.

Despite the disagreement, it was decided that word should be given out that only the Indians were responsible; and this account was at first accepted. In a report to Brigham Young made eighteen days after the event, Lee presented the matter as an Indian massacre.

Brigham conducted an investigation under George A. Smith two years later, in 1859, but not until the federal judges had begun to take an interest and the principal Mormons involved had gone into hiding to avoid arrest and interrogation. There is no absolute proof to show that Brigham either did or did not know the full extent of the tragic mistake made at Mountain Meadow in 1857 until many years later. Although the gentile charges usually portrayed it as an official massacre ordered by Brigham Young, he made no attempt to clear himself by denial until he was called upon to make a statement in a federal court in 1876.

In 1875 John D. Lee was arrested for his part, and he was convicted two years later. He died before a firing squad at the site of the massacre, March 23, 1877—almost twenty years after the event —in a sense the scapegoat in an affair in which he considered himself as acting upon orders from his superiors. There is no doubt that the act was one of mob violence, caused in part by an unfortunate combination of attitudes and events; and in such cases it is difficult to fix individual responsibility.

The Mormons have ever since suffered a sense of guilt over the Mountain Meadow massacre, and it seems reasonable to conclude that Brigham Young shared this feeling. His advice had been good, but the warlike spirit he had engendered, both in his own people and in the Indians, had been at least partially responsible for the fact that the massacre took place before his messenger reached the scene.

On the spot where it occurred now stands a monument, erected by the Utah Pioneer Trails and Landmarks Association, in a valley almost as empty of inhabitants as it was in 1857.

3

With the removal of the federal troops from the territory and the beginning of the Civil War in the East, Brigham's position had become strengthened. There were still gentiles and federal officials in Utah, but the nation's attention was absorbed elsewhere. Abraham Lincoln made good his pledge to leave the Mormons alone, concentrating his energy on winning battles. Brigham was left free to consolidate his own power and influence.

Early in 1862 Indians threatened the overland mail route and the newly completed telegraph lines. Federal officials in Utah and Washington considered stationing United States troops in the West to keep these important routes of communication open. Brigham offered the Mormon militia. He believed that the Indian scare had been precipitated by gentiles, anxious for the return of federal soldiers to the territory. He telegraphed his delegate in Washington that "the militia of Utah are ready and able, as they ever have been, to take care of the Indians, and are able and willing to protect the mail line, if called upon to do so." His offer was endorsed by the territorial governor, and Abraham Lincoln authorized the calling up of ninety mounted men for three months' service between Laramie and Fort Bridger.

From both the Mormon and the non-Mormon point of view, such an arrangement would appear the utmost in cooperation. In Utah, however, the political situation was explosive. Gentile merchants who had remained on after the departure of Johnston's army sought every possible excuse for stirring up trouble. The situation was such that any incident, great or small, would have served as an

excuse to direct frantic appeals to Washington, in an attempt to revive the old animosity.

Such an excuse was not slow in coming. Between 1859 and 1862
a Mormon convert by the name of Joseph Morris had claimed to
receive a series of revelations telling him that Brigham Young was
no true prophet of God. Brigham had more or less ignored Morris's
claims, for it was known that the convert, who was of Welsh
descent, had suffered an injury before his arrival in Utah that,
the Mormons believed, had mentally deranged him. The church
had twice excommunicated Morris for adultery before he began
making his claims of prophecy, then out of pity for his condition
had readmitted him. After the receipt of his "revelations" he was
finally excommunicated for heresy, but he was not prevented from
proselyting in the territory, even though his presence must have
been an irritation to the church.

Morris preached the oft-heard claim that the appearance of
Christ on earth was imminent, and he succeeded in attracting to
himself several hundred followers. These he convinced that, since
they were soon to enjoy the blessings of the millennium, they
should consecrate all earthly property and goods into his keeping.
When the announced time for the "appearance" came and passed,
most of his followers became disillusioned and they demanded the
return of their property. Morris refused to give it up, so the claimants turned to the federal courts for assistance. Morris disregarded a
writ of habeas corpus, served upon him by the territorial marshal,
so Chief Justice Kinney appealed to the governor to call up a company of the militia to serve as a *posse comitatus* to enforce his order.
Acting Governor Frank Fuller issued the requisition, and a troop of
Mormon militiamen, under General Robert T. Burton, was ordered
to serve.

In all this Brigham Young played no observable part. He undoubtedly believed that it was a matter between the federal officials
and the small band of Morrisites. However, the troops were Mormons; the opposition were Mormon apostates. Morris and his followers had established themselves in a community that was a virtual

fort, on the Weber River a few miles above Ogden. Burton marched his soldiers there and asked that the wanted men surrender themselves into the hands of the marshal. When his order was not complied with he fired a cannon into the compound (Burton maintained that he first fired two empty shots as a warning, but this was denied by the Morrisites); two women were killed by the first shot. Morris and his followers resisted, and firing back and forth continued for three days. In the end the Morrisites surrendered; but when the troops entered the compound they found that Morris had been killed. In the whole affair two members of the posse were killed and six of the Morrisites.

According to another version, told in an affidavit made by one of the Morrisites and denied by the Mormons and Burton, Morris was still alive when the troops entered the compound, but was shot down in cold blood by Burton after a brief colloquy.

The affair had results far beyond the question of whether an arresting officer had or had not exceeded his authority. To the gentiles and the world at large it became another illustration of the Mormons' willingness to slaughter erring apostates. The blame was laid at Brigham's door, and a regiment of troops was ordered from California to replace the Mormon Legionnaires. Their commander was Colonel P. E. Connor, a veteran of the Mexican War and a convinced anti-Mormon. He entered the territory firm in the belief that the Mormons were disloyal, and he lent his influence to every gentile and apostate who stood in opposition to Brigham Young. He refused to station his troops at Camp Floyd, but marched them through the city and encamped on the mountain slopes to the east, within firing distance of Brigham Young's house.

It was not long before Connor let it be known that he would entertain any charges anyone wished to make against the Mormons, as well as protect any informer who carried information to him. "My policy in this territory," he wrote once to a fellow officer, "has been to invite hither a large gentile and loyal population, sufficient by peaceful means, and through the ballot box, to overwhelm the Mormons by mere force of numbers, and thus wrest from the church—disloyal and traitorous to the core—the absolute and tyrannical control of temporal and civic affairs, or at least a population numerous enough to put a check on the Mormon authorities and give countenance to those who are striving to loosen the bonds with which they have been so long oppressed."

Aware of Connor's attitude, Brigham asked his people what this tyranny was of which the Mormons were accused. "We call upon the people to live that their sick may be healed by the virtue and power of their holy religion, and this is called oppression. The 'Mormons' all listen to the advice of one man, and this is called despotism. We teach our females to be virtuous and industrious, and this is called bondage."

Brigham did not refer often to Connor's presence on the outskirts of the city, but the presence of the troops was a constant irritation to him. Emigration from the East to California increased during the war years, so that there was a steady stream of people entering the city during the summer months, families escaping the horror and privation of the war, some men running away from service in the conflicting armies. Many of these Connor attempted to retain in the territory, telling them the country belonged as much to them as it did to the Mormons. When a minor gold strike was made by some of his soldiers at Bingham Mountain, he spread the word, hoping by this means to attract more gentiles to Utah. He outfitted his men with equipment for prospecting, and encouraged them to search for the wealth he was sure existed and which, when it was discovered, would cause the Mormons to be swamped with an influx of outsiders as California had been overrun in 1849.

Connor's enmity to the Mormons can be understood mainly in the light of the general prejudice which he had brought with him, and which was increased by the accounts of gentiles and apostates after his arrival. Brigham's speeches of this period concerning the war in the East were frequent, but they were, on the whole, temperate, mostly lamenting what he considered unnecessary bloodshed.

"According to accounts," he said in 1863, "in all probability not less than one million men, from twenty to forty years of age, have gone to the silent grave in this useless war, in a little over two

years, and all to gratify the caprice of a few— I do not think I
have a suitable name for them, shall we call them abolitionists, slaveholders, religious bigots, or political aspirants? Call them what you
will, they are wasting away each other, and it seems as though they
will not be satisfied until they have brought universal destruction
and desolation upon the whole country. It appears as though they
would destroy every person."

It may be that such words sounded traitorous to Colonel Connor
in the midst of war. Brigham's attitude did come close at times to
representing "a plague on both your houses." He accused the
North of political chicanery; the evils of the South he blamed on
greed in their treatment of their slaves, as well as miscegenation,
which he considered a violation of the laws of God. He did not,
however, approve of secession, and he believed firmly in the constitution.

The apostates and dissident Mormons who visited Connor's Camp
Douglas on the eastern foothills of the city complained that Brigham controlled, or had the power to control, every action of their
lives. What this meant was that Brigham could "counsel them" to
move to one of the outlying settlements, and if they did not do it
they could be threatened with disfellowship. He could call them to
go upon a mission, and they dared not refuse. He would even tell
them where, and in what manner, they were to conduct their businesses; and if they did not their fellow Mormons were advised not
to do business with them. Politically, they claimed, Mormon society
was a theocracy, with Brigham Young at its head; freedom and
individual rights were dead under this system.

The fact of Mormon theocracy, Brigham did not deny. "What
do I understand by a theocratic government?" he asked his saints.
"One in which all laws are enacted and executed in righteousness,
and whose officers possess that power which proceedeth from the
Almighty. That is the kind of government I allude to when I speak
of a theocratic government, or the Kingdom of God upon the
earth. It is, in short, the eternal powers of the gods."

For the most part the Mormon community approved the counsel

of Brigham and his leaders, for they had learned by long experience that what was good for the kingdom was also good for them. When some of them had wanted to leave for the goldfields in 1849, Brigham predicted that those who remained would, within a few years, be able to buy and sell those who deserted. Some had rebelled at being sent to colonize isolated settlements, but now most of them were prospering as they never had before. A few had thought that his opposition to the federal troops was a futile gesture. Brigham had proved them wrong. His actions, they believed, were dictated not by self-interest but by his judgment of what would be best for all of them, whether Mormon or gentile.

Such views were intolerable to Colonel Connor, as they had been to gentiles before him. Occasionally, too, Brigham's advice ran counter to the desires, even the convictions, of some individual Mormons. When this happened, the Mormon was forced to choose between acceptance or excommunication. If he persisted "in error" and either apostatized or was cut off from the church, he was welcomed with open arms by the gentile party in the territory, which, between 1862 and 1868, was centered at Camp Douglas. Because so much damage had been done by apostates, who carried their differences with them into the camp of the enemy, Brigham came to look upon Colonel Connor's headquarters as the center of vice and dissension in the kingdom. Even apparently loyal Mormons who were attracted there, he began to look upon with suspicion.

In 1868, after the ending of hostilities between the North and the South, Connor's troops were withdrawn, and a financial crisis occurred in the East which slowed down the emigration to the West. Now both the Mormons and the "large gentile and loyal population" which Connor had urged to remain in the territory (most of whom had become businessmen or unsuccessful prospectors) were left without sufficient trade. Brigham's solution to the problem of depression in the area was quick and decisive. He called his own Mormon businessmen together and proposed that they combine their stock and talents into one large, cooperative enterprise, to be known as Zion's Cooperative Mercantile Institution. It would be an organization to serve the needs not only of Salt Lake City but of every settlement of the territory, with branches scattered from St. George on the south to Cache Valley in the north.

Brigham's proposal was agreed to by most Mormon businessmen, who were already threatened by failure, but it caught the gentile merchants by surprise. The Z. C. M. I., as it became known, they maintained would monopolize the trade of the whole area. Perhaps it would, Brigham agreed. He had always urged the saints to deal with their own people, who were laboring to build up the kingdom. What were the gentiles doing? At the same time that they were appealing to the Mormons for trade, they were attempting to destroy Mormon society. When the gentile merchants offered to sell out to him, to dispose of their stock at a twenty-five per cent reduction on its assessed valuation, Brigham scorned the offer. Under such conditions, he told the merchants, they would still make a greater profit than anyone else doing business in the territory at the present time.

Brigham's proposal was a shrewd means of saving the business of the territory for the Mormons themselves, and it was a step in the direction of the Order of Enoch, which he always believed must be established before the Kingdom of God could become a thoroughly selfless society; but it appealed to certain individual Mormon businessmen (particularly those who had conducted a flourishing trade with Connor's troops) as little as it did to the gentiles.

Chief among the dissenters was an English convert by the name of W. S. Godbe, who had come to Utah first in 1851 and had prospered as a merchant first by hauling supplies across the plains by wagon, then by doing business with Johnston's army at Camp Floyd and Connor's troops at Camp Douglas. Godbe, justifying his opposition to Brigham in terms of the principle of individual rights, attracted the support of a small group of individual Mormons who had come to believe that Brigham, as a person, had abrogated to himself an unhealthy degree of influence and power over his followers. To them, the foundation of the Z. C. M. I. was less a cooperative venture than it was a monopoly, less a threat to their personal prosperity than a symbol of Brigham's unbridled authority in secular as well as ecclesiastical matters.

The New Movement, as the efforts of this group became known to themselves and their sympathizers, or the Godbeites, as they became known to the Mormons, included such influential members as T. B. H. Stenhouse, a Scotsman and a journalist who had been president of the Swiss and Italian mission and had briefly served as Mormon spokesman in Washington; Amasa Lyman, a former member of the Council of the Twelve, who had been excommunicated for repeated deviation in doctrine; Edward W. Tullidge, an editor and writer, who was later to recant and become an official historian of the church; E. L. T. Harrison, an architect and writer; and Eli B. Kelsey, a leading elder and businessman. This group of dissenters was well above the average of Mormon society in education and intellect. They were not apostates in the usual sense; they were reformers and excommunicants.

Brigham's conflict with the Godbeites has seemed to most historians the result of his inflexible desire to maintain an autocratic control over his people, and so it must have seemed to Godbe, Stenhouse, Harrison, and their fellows; but it was, in fact, dictated by the necessities of Mormon settlement as Brigham saw them. The very life of the Mormon colony depended upon cooperation. Their move from Illinois had been a vast cooperative enterprise; their survival in the early years had been the result of cooperation —protection in the wilderness, the development of irrigation, the extending of their settlements, the building of public works, and, above all, the maintenance of their peculiar religious traditions. In other Western settlements, particularly the mining camps, where growth had been more haphazard and individualized, there had been a much greater amount of violence and confusion than in the Mormon settlements; and eventually an even stronger show of authority became necessary than among the Mormons in order to achieve a peaceful society.

It may be true that Brigham had by 1868 become so firmly entrenched in his position as the almost infallible head of a society

numbering more than 70,000 persons in Utah alone that his manner
had become too rigid and assured to brook disagreement. He had,
after all, been at the head of the church in Utah for more
than twenty years; he had seen his kingdom grow and progress.
From the beginning, he had ignored or swept aside men who opposed him, and he did the same to the Godbeites now. All were
excommunicated and thus driven into the camp of the gentiles,
where they were capable of doing the Mormons irreparable harm.

Godbe became the founder of the Salt Lake *Tribune*, a newspaper which remained a critic of Brigham and his policy for many
years; Stenhouse moved from the territory, and, despite the fact
that his daughter had married one of Brigham's sons and remained
true to the church, he and his wife wrote and printed in the East
two of the most damning books ever to appear against the Mormons
—doubly damning in that they gave the appearance of fairness and
knowledge of the Mormon community.

The case of Edward Tullidge is significantly different. His ran-
cor against Brigham probably dated from 1857, the year following
the handcart emigration, for he had been in England the year before
as a missionary, and he was shocked by the blame Brigham leveled
upon Franklin D. Richards and Daniel Spencer for the tragedy
which overcame the late companies. He was convinced that
Richards had been made the scapegoat for the failure of the emigration and that the blame should, more rightly, have been placed
upon Apostle John Taylor, who had been in charge of outfitting
the companies in America, or upon Brigham himself, who had encouraged Richards and Spencer to predict the safe transport of the
saints across the plains. Consequently, when Tullidge became editor of the *Utah Magazine* with Godbe and Harrison at Camp
Douglas, he devoted an issue to absolving Richards and Spencer
and to placing the blame upon Taylor and Brigham Young.

Brigham received word of the "exposé" before publication, and
he acted with typical dispatch and energy. He ordered the entire
issue destroyed. There was no question of the rightness or wrong-
ness of Brigham's action in his own mind, even though his action
aroused a howl of protest from the camp of the gentiles and the

apostates. Brigham conceived, rightly, of the whole New Movement as an attack aimed at his authority. He considered his office, as he had considered the office of Joseph Smith before him, as the rock upon which the whole structure of the church was built. He had pondered the question of whether or not Joseph had been justified in destroying the press of the Nauvoo *Expositor* in 1844, and he had convinced himself that Joseph had acted correctly and could have been defended legally. His authority was Blackstone, who limited the freedom of the press to statements of criticism that did not threaten the government of a state. To the devout Mormon, who considered himself a subject of the Kingdom of God, to speak against the "chosen mouthpiece of heaven" was an act of treason, and so it seemed to Brigham Young.

The question of the limits of freedom and responsibility of the press in a democratic society has never been an easy one. Neither has been the question of the rights of the individual member of a church to oppose the policy of those in authority over him. Since Mormonism was both a church and a society, the problem was intensified and extended. Most cooperative religious societies in America failed because of the absence of firm authority, yet the price one paid for such authority was often independence of thought on the part of individual members. There is no doubt that, during the last days of Brigham Young's leadership, the Mormon church did pay such a price.

Edward Tullidge's strength, like the strength of the apostle he attempted to defend, was the sincere disinterestedness of his motives; and it was this quality which led him back into the church. Godbe and Stenhouse were probably as sincere in their positions as Tullidge; they were stronger and more independent thinkers; but they were by no means lacking in self-interest, as their careers in opposition to the church continued to testify. Still, one cannot help feeling that, in the case of the Godbeites, Brigham missed an opportunity to establish a policy less rigorous than that of forceful exclusion, which might have allowed such genuine talents as those of Godbe, Harrison, and Stenhouse to be utilized for the continued benefit of the community of saints; which would at least have prevented them from becoming the strong enemies of Mormonism they did become.

In the establishment of Zion's Cooperative Mercantile Institution, on the other hand, one can see the revival of a hope in Brigham's mind that had been allowed to slumber since the days of Far West—the hope that, economically, the saints could become a community as free from individual greed as that city which Joseph maintained he had seen in a vision, the City of Enoch, so pure of self-interest that it had been taken bodily into the heavens; for such was the Kingdom of God on this earth, the ultimate end of the community that in 1868 was Utah Territory. Such a hope was to revive periodically, again and again, both in Brigham's mind and in the minds of Mormon leaders who followed him. And even today, despite the present make-up of Mormon society, little different from society elsewhere in the United States, the hope still slumbers; even today, when Z. C. M. I. has become a modern department store (the first of its kind in the country, the Mormons say) and the usual Mormon leader is a member of the Republican party, social machinery in the form of a "welfare plan" has been set in motion in anticipation of that time when God will announce, or the forces of nature will compel, Mormon society to provide equal opportunities for all, economically as well as socially and theologically.

CHAPTER FOURTEEN

BRIGHAM YOUNG'S
LAST DAYS

I

By 1870 the population of Brigham's territory numbered 90,000. The settlements stretched north past Ogden and into Box Elder and Cache counties in Utah, then on into Idaho and Wyoming. To the south, they extended beyond the populous settlements of Utah County to Nephi, Fillmore, Beaver, Parowan, Cedar City, and St. George. They reached eastward from Nephi into Sanpete County and south and west of St. George into Arizona and southeastern Nevada. By now the pattern of development was almost complete. Although the population increased, it did not spread. Wherever there was water the Mormons had settled. Sometimes there turned out to be not enough, and then the settlers would move to a new location. For some of them who had been in the church as long as Brigham, their present homes represented the sixth, seventh, or eighth attempt to locate permanently. Most of them were now settled, and their names would mark the land for a century to come; but for a few the wandering was not yet over, as the arid land stirred and shuffled, shook them from place to place in search of sustenance.

At first Brigham made annual trips into the new communities, investigating their conditions, advising them on the most minute matters of settlement, preaching that this was Zion and that the Lord would look out and care for them. In the beginning these trips were arduous. He and his company would travel in a string of carriages and wagons, averaging twenty-five to thirty miles a day. Often they had to camp between villages, and they could travel only when the weather allowed. Later, as the settlements increased, he came more and more to depend upon the hospitality of his people. Toward the end of his life he could scarcely pass through the smallest community without some local official's importuning him to stop.

During the Civil War years Brigham's health began to deteriorate. He established a home in St. George, where the desert climate remained mild as California during the winter months, and each autumn he would make the three-hundred-mile journey for his health. Yet even here he was not free of worry and labor, and his visits to the settlements were frequent.

When he returned to Salt Lake City from an absence, his reception was no less cordial—and more impressive—than it had been in the settlements. Word of his coming would be announced beforehand, and flags and bunting would suddenly appear on stores, homes, and public buildings. The number of carriages in the streets would multiply. Brass bands, cavalry, and artillery groups would assemble. Schools would be dismissed, and the children, in their Sunday best, would appear in groups, carrying banners reading, "Welcome Brother Brigham," "Long Live the Lion of the Lord," which they would prepare to wave when his carriage approached, coming up State Street from the south.

Men on horseback and in carriages would drive down the highway to meet Brigham's party. The road to the south was visible for a distance of almost twelve miles, to the point of the mountain, so many in the city could see the two processions when they met. They would see Brigham's procession pause and receive the greetings of those who had gone out from Salt Lake; then they would watch as the long procession of both parties moved slowly toward them. Soon they would hear the music of the bands, then cheers as Brigham's party moved past the first of those waiting beside the roadway on the outskirts of the city, then more cheers as the carriage with Brigham in it, leading the procession, came upon more and more of the saints waiting to greet him.

The parade would end and disband when Brigham entered the Eagle Gate, which was the entrance to his property, at the north end of State Street. The crowd, by this time numbering between ten and twenty thousand, would press toward the entrance of the Beehive House, which was Brigham's principal residence. The bands would continue to play, but their music would often be drowned out by the shouts from the crowd, asking to have another look at their leader. The last of the shots of a twelve-gun salute would echo above their heads from the eastern hillside.

Brigham was sixty-five when the Civil War ended. Despite the Morrisites and the Godbeites, despite the opposition of Colonel Connor and the gentile community, despite the difficulties of the post-war economic disorder, despite the failure of Congress to grant statehood to Utah, he had never been held more warmly in the minds of his people, and he had never exercised more power and influence than he did now during the last decade of his life. It was during this period that a gentile visitor to Salt Lake warned the East that they were making a mistake by underestimating Brigham Young's abilities and his influence. Brigham had, he said, "the great American talent of *un-cornerableness*. . . . I believe," he said, "that Brigham Young was brought out by Mormonism; but I believe that if any other cause with which he might have identified himself had taken as strong possession of his nature, it would have developed him as fully, and that with the usual Christian creed and training, he would have made another Beecher in the pulpit, another Webster in the Senate, and a Sherman in the Army unsurpassed by Tecumseh."

Though Brigham Young became in his lifetime almost a god to his people, nevertheless he was a man among them. He was a businessman and a family man as well as a prophet. He was the proprietor of many businesses, including a hotel, sawmills in Cottonwood Canyon, and a shipping company on the waters of Great Salt Lake; and he owned more property throughout the city than anyone knew about for sure. He had the largest family in the territory, numbering twenty-four wives and a great many children, the exact number of whom was unknown. (Brigham himself is quoted as having said about this time that he had forty-seven.) These he educated in his own separate schoolhouse on his property. He owned three houses in the center of Salt Lake City, known respectively as the White House, the Beehive House, and the Lion House; and here he lived with most of his wives. He had farms near the city and a few cottages scattered throughout it; he had his winter house in St. George. In each of these a wife was installed. The minor details of the management of such property he usually left to the wife, seeing only that she got regular deliveries from his own family bakery and from his own gardens, orchards, and mills. One wife complained that he was niggardly and neglectful, but all the others testified that he was merely cautious and thrifty—a careful manager with very definite ideas about extravagance in dress and the dangers of a too-rich diet.

Most of Brigham's wives lived in the Lion House, which had been built with identical apartments and where all meals were taken in common. Mary Ann Angell occupied the White House, which had been the first to be constructed in the valley, while Clara Decker was the mistress of the large, impressive Beehive House, which was Brigham's official residence. There was no discernible pattern of living for Mormon polygamous families. Where there were few wives, each was likely to have her own residence, perhaps even in a different settlement from the others, but such an arrangement demanded a certain economic well-being. In the poorer families (and there were relatively few of the poorer members who practiced polygamy in the earliest days) or in the establishments with many wives, families would live together, sharing the household tasks, as they did in the Lion House. Such community living was considered a trial by many members who shared it, but it was also welcomed by those who believed firmly that trials of faith were a necessary initiation into the kingdom.

Despite Brigham's church and family duties and his business obligations, his interest in an active social life never diminished. He had encouraged dancing and theatricals in Nauvoo after the death of Joseph, he encouraged them on the plains en route to Utah, and he continued for the rest of his life to take pleasure in them.

The first theatricals had been performed in the Bowery, but they later occupied a building constructed just south of Brigham's estate and called the Social Hall. In 1861 Brigham conceived of a theater, which, after it was finished in 1862, remained for many years the marvel of acting companies between Chicago and San Francisco. Modeled in part after the Niblo Theatre in New York, it became known as the Salt Lake Theater and housed performances by many important actors during the second half of the century.

Although such prominent entertainers as Mr. and Mrs. Sedden Irwin, Lawrence Barrett, E. A. Sothern, Adelaide Nelson, E. L. Davenport, Julia Dean Hayne, and the Tony Pastor Company played there during Brigham's lifetime, the theater belonged to a Mormon theatrical company known as the Deseret Dramatic Association, and Brigham had Thomas A. Lynne, a popular tragedian, brought from New York to train his actors and direct their productions. In addition to theatrical troups, such well-known lecturers as Mark Twain, Henry Ward Beecher, Thomas Nast, Artemus Ward, Sir Henry M. Stanley, Anna Dickinson, Susan B. Anthony, and Anna Howard Shaw made appearances on the stage, as did such popular musicians as Ole Bull, the violinist, and Parepa Rosa, the singer.

In the early days produce and merchandise were acceptable at the box office in lieu of cash. Artemus Ward, in his humorous lecture on the Mormons, listed some of the receipts taken in the night he performed in Salt Lake City:

20 bushels of wheat
5 " " corn
4 " " potatoes
2 " " oats
4 " " salt
2 hams
1 live pig (Dr. Hingston chained him in the box-office)
1 wolf-skin
5 pounds of honey in the comb
16 strings of sausages—2 pounds to the string

1 cat skin
1 churn (two families went in on this; it is an ingenious churn, and fetches butter in five minutes by rapid grinding)
1 set of children's undergarments, embroidered
1 keg of apple-sauce
  One man undertook to pass a dog (a cross between a Scotch terrier and a Welsh rabbit) at the box-office, but the doctor very justly repulsed them both.

When Brigham attended the theater he sat in a rocking chair in the center of a box reserved for him, usually surrounded by several of his wives and some of his children. Occasionally one of his daughters would perform. At least once Brigham called a performance off when the action became too violent and bloody. He preferred comedy to tragedy. "There is enough tragedy in everyday life," he explained, "and we ought to have amusement when we come here."

In 1863 Brigham began the construction of a new tabernacle on the Temple Block. Since the tabernacle was the general meeting house for the Salt Lake Stake of Zion, as opposed to the temple, in which only the rituals were performed, and the ward churches, which housed the individual congregations, the old one had long since been outgrown. It had seated three thousand persons. The new one, when completed, would hold between eight and ten thousand. It was to be 250 feet long, 150 feet wide, and 80 feet high, with no interior pillars. Brigham adapted a principle of bridge-building to its construction. Its roof was formed of wooden arches, the arches resting upon forty-four buttresses of trimmed sandstone masonry, thus eliminating the necessity of inside supports and providing an uninterrupted view of the pulpit from any seat in the auditorium. The peculiar shape of the building, like a great inverted bowl, proved upon completion to provide remarkable acoustics, so that speakers could be heard in a whisper from the pulpit to the rear of the building. Equipped later with an organ constructed by a Mormon convert in Australia and shipped across the Pacific Ocean, the building has become the most familiar tourist attraction in Salt Lake City, where visitors today are entertained by demonstrations of its acoustics and by concerts on the organ and by the tabernacle choir. The building was completed for use at the general conference of the church held in October 1867.

In 1865 Brigham began plans to connect the settlements north and south with the main telegraph line, using poles cut by the Mormons in the mountains and wire and insulators purchased by Mormon missionaries in Europe.

The line was completed from Salt Lake City to Ogden by 1866, and in a message to President Lorin Farr and Bishop Chauncey West, Brigham dedicated the new system "to the Lord God of Israel, Whom we serve for the building up of His Kingdom; praying that this and all other improvements may contribute to our benefit, and the glory of God."

In May 1868, Brigham took a contract for the grading and masonry construction of the Union Pacific Railroad from the head of Echo Canyon to its junction with the Central Pacific in the vicinity of Ogden. There had been speculation in the East concerning Brigham's attitude toward the railroad. Gentiles had seen in the improved transportation into the West the gradual destruction of the Mormon empire; and they had expected Brigham to look with disfavor upon the entrance of the railroad into Utah. On May 24 the Omaha *Herald* reported the unexpected event:

Habitual haters of the sagacious rule of the Mormons in Utah predicted, not more than two years ago, that the leaders of that people would do all in their power to hinder and obstruct the building of the national highway to Salt Lake. What must have been the surprise of those people when they read yesterday's special telegram to the *Herald*, which announced that the far-seeing Brigham, instead of impeding the great work, had actually taken the entire contract to build it from Echo Canyon to the City of the Saints.

The two railroad lines, the Union Pacific and the Central Pacific, approached Utah from the east and the west. In 1869 the western line sweated across the Nevada desert and the Utah salt flats, rushing to outdistance the eastern, which was making laborious progress down the rocky course of the Weber River above Ogden. That winter Brigham went to Ogden to meet with Leland Stanford and Thomas C. Durant, representing the competing roads, to pick a site for the depot. After the meeting, Leland Stanford is said to have remarked "that it was a wonderful thing that Brigham Young should have been able to build up such a community, and to govern and control it as he did. 'But,' he said, 'as soon as Brigham Young with his master mind passes away, that will be the end of Mormonism.'"

Such remarks had been heard before. Now, with the coming of the railroad, many confidently believed, as Colonel Connor had just a few years before, that the Mormons would become "assimilated" and destroyed by the influx of gentiles.

In 1863, during Connor's stay, a logger in Bingham Canyon picked up a piece of ore which he sent to Camp Douglas to be assayed. It was found to contain gold and silver. That autumn, spurred on by the colonel, a minor gold rush began, with the soldiers and a few Mormons and gentiles from Salt Lake City staking out claims and digging feverishly for the wealth they were certain awaited only a single stroke of the pick.

Colonel Connor saw the gold strike as a means of accomplishing his cherished aim. "I have bent every energy and means of which I am possessed, both personal and official," he wrote, "towards the discovery and development of the mining resources of the Territory, using without stint the soldiers at my command, whenever and wherever it could be done, without detriment to the public service." By contrast, Brigham Young told his followers on the twenty-fifth of October following the gold discovery:

It is a fearful deception which all the world labors under, and many of the people too, who profess to be not of the world, that gold is wealth. On the bare report that gold was discovered in these west mountains, men left their threshing machines, and their horses at large, to eat up and trample down and destroy the precious bounties of the earth. They at once sacrificed all at the glittering shrine of the popular idol, declaring they were now going to be rich, and would raise wheat no more. Should this feeling become universal on the discovery of gold mines in our immediate vicinity, nakedness, starvation, utter destitution and annihilation would be the inevitable lot of this people. Instead of its bringing to us wealth and independence it would weld upon our necks chains of slavery.

Precious metals were not then discovered in sufficient amounts to attract the "large gentile and loyal population" Colonel Connor desired for Utah; but the very mountain the prospectors were raking for gold turned out later to contain the richest open deposit of copper known to the world. The open-pit mines of Bingham Canyon, where a whole mountain is being eaten away by steam shovels, have since become one of the wonders of the West, and the basis for the giant corporation known as the Kennecott Copper Company.

With the completion of the overland railroad and the driving of the "golden spike" on the north shore of the Great Salt Lake on May 10, 1869, Brigham set to work, with his usual enterprise, to construct a connecting north-south line within the area of the Mormon settlements. By January the next year, Salt Lake City was connected by rail with Ogden through the Mormon-built Utah Central Railroad. Eventually the line pushed north to Cache Valley and south to Sevier, with a connecting branch extending into Sanpete County to the southeast.

Not all Brigham's industrial developments were successful. The growing of cotton and tobacco in the southern colonies failed, as did his early attempts to grow sugar beets and refine the sugar with machinery hauled laboriously across the plains. His iron works at Cedar City were unable properly to refine the ore which existed there. Even with his energy, the shortage of water and difficulties of transportation were deficiencies which could not be overcome; and Utah Territory refused to become as wholly self-sufficient as he desired. The Mormons had greater success with small local manufacturing, such as flour mills, tanneries, lumber mills, knitting and weaving mills, and salt works, than they did with the more ambitious projects. Besides, much of the Mormons' energies during these years were given over to the construction of public works: the theater, the tabernacle, and the temples.

The first Mormon temple in Utah to be completed was the St. George Temple, begun in 1871 and rushed to completion in 1877. Brigham Young in his frequent visits to the southern communities had become aware of a problem he had previously overlooked. Young couples desiring to marry were forced to make a three-hundred-mile journey to the Endowment House in Salt Lake City. Often they had to make the trip alone, camping out together for nights at a stretch on the lonesome prairies between settlements. Brigham understood the temptations of the flesh, and he had reason to suspect that not all these young couples arrived in Salt Lake in a state of chastity, regardless of their status when they had begun their journey. The St. George Temple was built of native red sandstone, its lower floor a smaller replica of the unfinished temple in Salt Lake, its single tower much like the one the Mormons had built in Nauvoo. At the same time another temple was constructed at Manti in central eastern Utah; while a third was begun at Logan, in Cache County, to serve the northern settlements. Work continued on the Salt Lake temple, but its completion did not now seem as urgent as that of the temples in outlying areas.

Important additions were also made at about this time to the Mormons' educational facilities. Brigham Young had never possessed the scholarly temperament of Joseph Smith, but Joseph had convinced him of the necessity of improvement, spiritually as well as in material things. "The glory of God is intelligence," Joseph had proclaimed in one of his revelations. Intelligence he defined as "light and truth." Truth he said was a knowledge of things as they have been, as they now are, and as they shall be. Brigham's response to this principle was reflected in both words and deeds.

"It is very desirable that all the saints should improve every opportunity of securing at least a copy of every valuable treatise on education," he told a group of missionaries departing for Europe in 1848, "every book, map, chart, or diagram that may contain interesting, useful, and attractive matter, to gain the attention of all children and cause them to love to learn to read."

At another time he told the whole body of his followers, "The first great principle that ought to occupy the attention of mankind, that should be understood by the child and the adult, and which is the mainspring of all action, whether people understand it or not, is the principle of improvement."

During the first winter the Mormons were in Salt Lake Valley two schools had been opened, one for the instruction of children, another for adults. At the meeting of the first territorial legislature in 1850, a law was passed authorizing the creation of a university, to be known as the University of Deseret. The university opened in a private house in 1850, then moved to the Council House. In 1855 Congress granted it 56,080 acres of land to provide funds. In 1854 the Union Academy was established under the direction of Orson Pratt, for the study of algebra, surveying, astronomy, chemistry, mineralogy, geology, and modern languages. In the same year the Hall of Science was opened to serve as the center for a lecture series, debates, and instruction in the sciences. In 1867 the University of Deseret was formally organized, with John R. Park, a graduate of Wesleyan University, as its first president.

And now, between 1871 and 1873, Brigham sent Dr. Park on a "mission" to the East and Europe to visit schools and obtain the best possible advice on administration and instruction. In 1875 Brigham established the Brigham Young Academy (later Brigham Young University) at Provo, and, two years later, Brigham Young College, at Logan. Eventually a system of Mormon academies stretched from the Snake River in Idaho to below the Rio Grande in Mexico.

Education in Utah was not, however, confined to the schools. Mormon meetings often resembled educational forums. The nature of the religion Joseph had bequeathed to Brigham stressed the principle of constant improvement in practical as well as intellectual matters. As an indication of the practical nature of many of Brigham's sermons, consider this homely advice to Mormon women:

Some women will set emptyings [yeast] in the morning, and let them stand until they sour, and mix up the flour with them, and sweeten with saleratus [baking soda] and then knead it ready for baking; and then as Sister Somebody comes in they will sit down and begin to talk over old times, and the first thing they know is, the bread is sour: "Dear me, I forgot all about that bread," and into the oven she puts it, and builds up a large fire, and again sits down to visit with her neighbor, and before she thinks of the loaf, there is a crust burnt on it from a quarter- to a half-inch thickness. So much of the bread is spoiled; there goes one-quarter of the flour;

it is wasted and the bread is sour and disagreeable to eat; and the husband comes home and looks sour, and is sour, as well as the bread. He finds fault and that makes the wife grieve, and there are feelings and unhappiness and unsatisfaction in the family.

Such sermons often puzzled gentile visitors, for they seemed foreign to both the evangelicism and the elegance of the religious preaching with which they were familiar. They illustrated, as well as anything could, the practical side of the religion of Joseph Smith and Brigham Young, in which everday reality and mysticism were inextricably interwoven.

Because of his actual achievements in colonization and the legends of his tyranny, Brigham had become by 1870 a national figure—as familiar a name to the country as that of the president himself. When Phineas T. Barnum visited Salt Lake City that year, following the completion of the railroad, he told Brigham that if he could exhibit him in New York he could guarantee him earnings of two hundred thousand dollars a year; "for," he said, "I consider you the best show in America."

2

The year 1870 was not the most promising in Mormon history, despite the departure of Connor's troops and the building of the transcontinental railroad. Depression in the East and drought in the West combined to cause suffering among the Mormons, particularly those in the outlying settlements. Business conditions east of the Mississippi affected the Mormons by slowing down the migration to California, upon which the Mormons had come to depend as the basis of trade with the outside world; drought at home dried up some of the streams upon which the Mormons depended for irrigation water, dangerously lowered even the best of them, so that where productivity didn't cease altogether it struck a frightening low.

In Salt Lake City, Brigham had seen the establishment of Zion's Cooperative Mercantile Institution as the answer to a problem facing the businessmen of the territory. For the outlying settlements, he recalled a similar cooperative venture—Joseph Smith's Order of Enoch. Now he suggested to his leaders that their only hope for survival lay in a more complete system of economic cooperation than they had heretofore achieved. He suggested that in marginal areas, or wherever the saints were willing, they pool their equipment, their property, and their energies and work in complete cooperation; for only by so doing could they build adequate reservoirs and canals to allow them to till the acres necessary to their survival. Thus, he said, they would not only increase their own comforts, but they would also take a great step toward the completely selfless society which Joseph had envisioned as the Kingdom of God. He sent his leaders out into the communities to preach the principles of cooperation and equality, and before long organizations known as the United Order were established in most of the outlying settlements.

In the settlements Brigham did not run into the degree or kind of opposition he had encountered in establishing the Z. C. M. I.; but neither did he obtain full cooperation. Human nature being what it is, many members who were themselves self-sufficient did not join the order, so that those who did were generally those who were in the greatest need. It worked best in the poorer communities, where most of the saints were in effect already equal. The most successful case was that of a community made up of saints who, on Brigham's advice, had left their hopeless situation on the Muddy River in Nevada in 1870 and resettled in Long Valley, in Kane County. By 1873, when the financial panic set in in the Eastern states, the two small communities of Mt. Carmel and Glendale in Long Valley had attempted to set up the United Order as Brigham had suggested. There was opposition among them, however, and in 1875 about one-third of the two hundred original families sold their homes and their property and moved a few miles up the valley, where they established a third village, to be entirely devoted to the cooperative system and which was at first known as Order City—later, Orderville.

The property involved in the founding of Orderville in July 1875 included every piece of personal or real property (valued at a total of $21,500 at 1875 prices) possessed by the settlers. It included 335 acres of land, 18 houses, 19 oxen, 103 head of cattle, 43 horses and mules, 500 sheep, 30 hogs, 400 chickens, a threshing machine, a reaper, a mower, a cane mill, 30,000 feet of lumber, and a variety of provisions and supplies. None of the property was indebted, and the settlers seemed convinced that the establishment of their order was the will of God as transmitted to them through Brigham Young.

The central building of the community was put up at once. It was a combined meeting house, dining hall, and social hall. It contained a kitchen and a bakery. The members followed by constructing a large apartment house, a United Order office and storehouse, a shoe shop, blacksmith shop, carpenter shop, cooper shop, tannery, and a schoolhouse. A garden house, a dairy barn, and sheep sheds were added, as was a woolen factory and a telegraph office. As the community grew and prospered it eventually obtained other land outside the general area, including a farm for early fruits and vegetables at Leeds, near St. George; as well as grazing rights in the Kaibab Plateau country, which they negotiated with the Indians.

The men of the community were elected to their jobs according to their training and ability. The wives were divided into groups, and each group took its turn in the dining hall and kitchen. It was an entirely communal system. Living space was granted according to the size of the family (many of the men had several wives), and all took their meals in the central building. During the first two years no wages were paid, each family drawing supplies according to need. Later, upon the advice of Brigham Young, credit was given according to work performed at a certain standard scale. Each day began with the blowing of a bugle, calling the members to prayers; then there were chores, and then breakfast. The call to work, the call to dinner, the call to evening prayers, the call to church services and socials, were all announced by the bugler from a position near the flagpole in the central square.

During the day, while the men worked in the shops or the fields, the mothers and daughters operated spinning wheels and handlooms. The younger children attended school. The community contributed to general Mormon church projects outside by furnishing materials and labor for the construction of the St. George Temple. They appointed two members to work on the temple at Manti and were credited with having done more work on that building than any other ward in their district.

Despite what would seem to have been a rather drab and regimented life, the community prospered for several years, and individual members were better off than they had been at any time since their settlement in the territory. According to one historian,

The group attained almost complete self-sufficiency. Changing price levels had little effect on the citizens of Orderville. Members of the Order raised broom corn and made their own brooms; they made their own soap and lye of local materials; a nearby coal mine furnished fuel and energy; they obtained red cedar from the canyons and made their own wooden buckets, tubs, kegs, barrels, firkins, and churns; they conducted a silk enterprise, produced silk threads, and wove handkerchiefs and other articles; they obtained leather from a Salt Lake tannery and fashioned their own leather products. Later they erected their own tannery and, using cowhides tanned with local barks, produced their own boots, shoes, harness, and saddles. A United Order cabinet shop made their furniture, spinning wheels, and shingles. Assigned workers cut and sawed timber for the community with a United Order steam sawmill. They produced an excess of wool and freighted it to . . . Provo and Salt Lake City . . . and with the "store pay" received for the wool and some few other items they purchased the supplies which they could not produce or do without.

The history of the community, and some of the stories in connection with it, are, in their revelations of universal human nature, probably typical of community life anywhere, and prophetic here, as elsewhere, of eventual failure.

The growing young men of Orderville had been children when they entered the community, so had contributed no property to the order and owned no legal shares in the corporation. So long as they were satisfied to work for a dollar and a half a day, which was the highest wage scale ever attained, the fact that they owned nothing in the corporation did not matter; but when jobs opened up at nearby Silver Reef, paying twice that amount for unskilled labor, they became dissatisfied. At the beginning Orderville had been the most prosperous of the surrounding communities, so much so that its members were the envy of their neighbors despite the sameness of their clothing and the apparent drabness of their living conditions.

As conditions became better, however, young men of the other settlements began to appear at Orderville socials dressed in bright new denim trousers, fancy shirts, and broad-brimmed Stetson hats. One young man of the Orderville group felt the need of new trousers. His own were not worn out, but as he grew they seemed to shrink, so he applied to the clothing committee for a new pair. As there were no holes and no patches in his trousers, he was turned down. With typical pioneer ingenuity, he set to work to discover a means of getting a new pair by himself. After the herders had docked the particularly large crop of lambs of that year, he went to the sheep sheds and gathered up the tails, which he secretly sheared. When he was later assigned to take a load of wool to Nephi, he took his own bag along and exchanged it for a pair of store pants.

His return to Orderville in the new clothing caused a sensation. The president of the order demanded an explanation: "You are requested to appear before the Board of Management tomorrow evening at half-past eight and to bring the store pants with you." When the young man explained, he was commended for his enterprise, but he was told that all members should wear trousers of the same cut and material. The store pants he had bought would be unseamed and used as a pattern for all the trousers made for the community in the future, and he would be given the first pair.

In the next few weeks the tailoring department was swamped with orders for new pants. The elders investigated. They found that the young men went to work as usual, but they often appeared to be loafing on the job. Then it was discovered that most of the old clothing was worn out, not in the knees and cuffs, which was usual, but in the seat. When the elders noticed groups of boys going to a shed where the grindstone was housed, they found their answer. The boys were wearing out the seats of their pants on the grindstone. In this case the elders saw the humor of the situation. Immediately a load of wool was shipped off to a nearby mill and traded for cloth, and all the young men in the community were supplied with new trousers. The incident was known for many years in Orderville as "The Pants Rebellion."

Another incident involved the wife of a man who was sent to Leeds to oversee the order fruit farm there. The wife took advantage of her husband's absence to wash and iron clothes for miners at nearby Silver Reef. The income she derived she spent on better clothing for her children. When the family returned to Orderville complaint was made that she had spent order money on her own children. She was investigated, but, "as she had always been a faithful worker, she was forgiven and told to 'Go (to work) and sin no more.'"

The Orderville community was always a little set apart from even its neighboring Mormon communities, and suffered eventually (and ironically) from the same defects that had destroyed the Mormon communities in Missouri—the antagonism of its neighbors. With the increase of prosperity outside Orderville, envy turned to ridicule. The saints of Orderville were looked upon as fanatics by their brethren in the remainder of the territory, and they were persecuted by laughter.

After the passing of the federal anti-polygamy law in 1881 the territory swarmed with federal agents attempting to spy out evidence of polygamous marriages. The plural wives of Orderville, like Mormon wives elsewhere, had to take off their wedding rings and preserve the knowledge of their marriages in private. Some of the most competent leaders, who were known polygamists, had to go into hiding. Even the routine of the usual Mormon community was disrupted. Orderville, which depended upon routine, was doomed, though the order continued in existence until 1885, and some of its corporate enterprises were in operation until 1900.

Brigham Young knew only the days of success in Orderville, for he died before the period of decline had set in. He did live long enough to recognize the difficulties of such a communal system, and he provided advice and assistance to the experiment before his death. He saw Orderville not only as support for the poorer families in the most depressed areas, but as an experiment which he fully believed all the saints would eventually come to, for it was the economic pattern of heaven—a life which they could live only when the Mormons were prepared to become, in fact as well as name, true saints, not only selfless in their demands, but selfless also in their desire to work at the top of their abilities for the good of the whole community.

3

The last days of Brigham Young were marked by two struggles, neither of which was to end until after his death—the attempt to achieve statehood for Utah and the attempt to preserve Mormon marriages. The two were intimately linked, for much of the outside opposition to the Mormons came as a result of polygamy, and it was this opposition which prevented the national government from granting statehood to Utah.

The first petition for statehood in 1849, which was denied, was followed by another in 1861, submitted over the protests of the territorial governor, John W. Dawson, who had succeeded Cumming. At this time a constitution was adopted and a slate of officers elected. In a convention held at the beginning of 1862, the constitution and the slate of officers were accepted, and a resolution asking its acceptance by the federal government was forwarded to Washington. When the Mormon delegate arrived he was met not by sympathy toward statehood, but by the first of a series of federal bills to be aimed at the Mormons' practice of plural marriage. The bill was passed and signed in July 1862.

A new slate of federal appointees arrived in Utah at about the same time. They included Stephen S. Harding as governor. In his first message to the legislature the governor called attention to the anti-polygamy bill, declaring that "no community can happily exist with an institution so important as that of marriage wanting in all those qualities that make it homogenial with institutions and laws of neighboring civilized countries having the same spirit." Harding ended his speech by advising individual Mormons to rebel against their leaders if they advised a disregard of federal law.

The territorial legislature was made up of Mormons. To indicate their displeasure with Harding's advice, they refused to vote an appropriation to carry on the business of the governor's office, then adjourned with little accomplished. The next day the previously elected "state officials" met in Salt Lake and invited Brigham, as the prospective governor, to deliver his own message. In a meeting in the tabernacle he told his followers, "I can tell the world that we mean to sustain the Constitution of the United States and all righteous laws. We are not by any means treasoners, secessionists, or abolitionists. We are neither Negro-drivers nor Negro-worshipers. We belong to the family of heaven, and we intend to walk over every unrighteous and unholy principle, and view everybody and everything as it is before God, and put everything in its place."

Brigham based his hopes on Abraham Lincoln's promise to leave the Mormons alone and in his belief that the anti-polygamy bill was unconstitutional. He knew that the president himself believed it was. Governor Harding, however, had no choice but to attempt enforcement of it. The governor and the federal judges showed unusual zeal. They fought back by seeking to undermine the source of Mormon secular authority—the local courts. Judge Charles B. Waite sent to Washington a bill which would forbid the Mormon-controlled courts to act in criminal cases and would strengthen the federal courts by empowering the United States marshal to select all juries. Such an act would have left the Mormons without a guarantee of representation in all criminal actions and would have put them at the mercy of the gentiles, for the United States marshal would certainly select only gentiles or dissatisfied Mormons for the juries.

When Brigham learned of this he summoned a mass meeting for March 3, 1863, which appointed a committee to request the resignation of the governor and two of the judges, including Judge Waite. In a speech in the tabernacle Brigham commented on the anti-polygamy bill and the federal officials' zeal in seeking its enforcement. "Find fault with me because I have wives!" he exclaimed. "They would corrupt every wife I had if they had the power." He took note of accusations made against the Mormons for lawlessness. "As for offering refutation to charges made against us," he said, "it would be impossible to keep pace with the thousands of freshly invented falsehoods that the powers spiritual and the powers temporal would produce to feed the credulity of the ignorant masses."

Brigham Young's influence had been increased by the fact that the powerful companies in the East who operated the mail and the telegraph lines depended upon peace with the Mormons to keep their routes open. Partly, no doubt, as a result of their influence, Governor Harding, his secretary, and Judge Waite were removed. Abraham Lincoln did not come to the aid of his appointees, for neither he nor his officials wanted trouble in the West while they were in the midst of war, and Lincoln himself had not been in favor of the anti-polygamy measure. J. D. Doty, who had been secretary of Indian Affairs for the territory, became the new governor. He died in office in 1865, and Charles Durkee succeeded him.

In 1869, when Ulysses S. Grant became president, conditions took a turn for the worse. Grant was advised by his Secretary of War, who had visited Utah and listened to the complaints of the gentile community, that what was needed to impress the Mormons was a strong federal authority. Grant was also spurred on by reformers who turned their attention from slavery to polygamy. In his message to congress he attacked Mormon marriages by referring to them as "licensed prostitution." He appointed as governor J. Wilson Shaffer of Illinois, and named James B. McKean of New York as Chief Justice. He instructed his appointees to use every effort to compel loyalty from the Mormons and to seek the abolishment of polygamy.

Governor Shaffer was ill when he was appointed, and he lived only a few months. That was long enough to accomplish his first aim, the disbanding of the Nauvoo Legion. In regard to polygamy he may have altered his view somewhat, for by 1869 the New Movement had added support to the gentile community, and such men as Godbe and Stenhouse were polygamists and could not be expected to oppose what they themselves practiced in all devotion. W. S. Godbe told the governor, "I married my wives in good faith. We have lived together for years, believing it was the will of God. The same is true of the Mormon people generally. Before I will abandon my wives as concubines, and cast off my children as bastards, I will fight the United States Government down to my boots. What would you do, Governor, in the like case?" To which Governor Shaffer is said to have replied, "By God, I would do the same."

Judge McKean, whom the Mormons called "the missionary jurist" because he had been a Methodist preacher, came determined to effect a reformation in the courts and in Mormon society. His first act was to declare the federal courts not subject to territorial law. This meant he need not depend upon either the territorial marshal, who had been responsible for supplying the venire from which juries were drawn, or the attorney general for the territory, who had been responsible for prosecution. Judge McKean's manner of eliminating the Mormons from participation in the legal affairs of the territory came to a test in a case in which a gentile saloon-keeper named Englebrecht had preferred charges against the territorial marshal for raiding his saloon and confiscating a supply of whisky. The judge drew up a jury in defiance of the territorial law, and this jury awarded the saloon-keeper damages of $59,063.25 against the Mormon officers.

The Mormon legislature struck back by deciding that if the courts of the territory were indeed all-federal courts, as McKean maintained, the territory need appropriate no money for their support. No appropriation was voted; and when the jurors for the spring term were called in 1871 the judge had to dismiss them.

"I shall stay here as long as I choose, or as long as the government at Washington shall choose to have me here," he told the jurors, "and I venture the prediction that the day is not far in the future when the disloyal high priesthood of the so-called Church of Jesus Christ of Latter-day Saints shall bow to and obey the laws that are elsewhere respected, or else those laws will grind them to powder."

Judge McKean eventually solved the problem of money by drawing upon the appropriations of the United States marshal's office to prosecute such cases as he considered most important. In the September term of court all except a handful of the jurymen were non-Mormons. The Mormons who were on the lists were excused when they testified that they could not be impartial in any case involving polygamy. An all-gentile jury was selected, and among the first to be indicted was Brigham Young. The charge was "lewd and lascivious cohabitation."

The law under which Brigham was ordered to stand trial was one which he had himself sponsored in the territorial legislature—an act designed to punish adultery. When Brigham's lawyer moved to quash the indictment by arguing that it had been issued in defiance of the law, Judge McKean denied the motion with one of the most ingenious arguments recorded in the annals of American law:

> Let the counsel on both sides, and the court also keep constantly in mind the uncommon character of this case. The supreme court of California has well said: "Courts are bound to take notice of the political and social conditions of the country which they judicially rule." It is therefore proper to say that while the case at bar is called "The People *versus* Brigham Young," its other and real title is "Federal Authority *versus* Polygamic Theocracy." The government of the United States, founded upon a written constitution, finds within its jurisdiction another government claiming to come from God— *imperium in imperio*—whose policies and practices are, in grave particulars, at variance with its own. The one government arrests the other, in the person of its chief, and arraigns it at this bar. A system is on trial in the person of Brigham Young. Let all concerned keep this fact constantly in view; and let that government rule without a rival which shall prove to be in the right.

As one reporter pointed out, what Judge McKean was trying to say was that "Brigham was indicted for lewd cohabitation that he might be tried for polygamy and punished for treason."

When the writ was issued for Brigham's arrest he was in Provo, on his way to the southern settlements. He returned to Salt Lake and submitted to arrest, posted bail for five thousand dollars, and continued to St. George, where he was to dedicate the site for the temple. The dedication took place in November, and Brigham had every reason to believe that he would be left unmolested at his winter home until the spring term. Judge McKean had other ideas. Under the supposition that Brigham had fled to the south to avoid the trial, he called the case for January 9, 1872.

Many of Brigham's friends urged him not to return. He was in his seventy-second year, and Salt Lake City was three hundred miles away. January weather north of St. George was uncertain. Travel at that time of year would have been dangerous even for a young man. Brigham maintained, however, that "the voice of the Spirit" bade him return, and he left St. George on December 17 and arrived at Draper, after a difficult, storm-harassed trip in an open buggy, on the twenty-sixth. Draper was then the terminus of the Utah Southern Railroad, and from here a special train carried Brigham into Salt Lake that evening.

When he arrived in the city he was met by another warrant issued by McKean, this one on the charge of inciting to murder. Despite Brigham's show of willingness to stand trial, the judge refused to admit him to bail. When Brigham's attorney pleaded ill health, Judge McKean allowed Brigham to remain under house arrest. He was not brought to trial, and it is said that he spent the next five months sitting in a rocker before his window, a shawl spread over his shoulders, contemplating this new threat to the kingdom.

In April the United States Supreme Court handed down a decision in the Englebrecht case. McKean's whole system of impaneling juries was held to be unconstitutional. The decision automatically released Brigham from all of his indictments. On April 28 the prophet again stood before his followers at spring conference in the tabernacle. A murmur of appreciation flowed over the congregation as he remained silent a moment before speaking. He was smiling broadly.

"A word to the Latter-day Saints," he said finally. "Good morning!"

The congregation responded, "Good morning!"

"How do you do?" Brigham asked.

"Very well!" answered the congregation.

"How's your faith in the Lord?" he inquired.

"Strong!" they replied.

"How do you think I look after my long confinement?"

"First rate!" the congregation answered.

He told them he had never felt better in his life. He thanked the government for forcing him to take a good rest. He had enjoyed the Spirit of the Lord, he said, and he looked forward to serving them for a long time yet.

Even then Brigham must have known that the battle for statehood had been set back. Communications from the East resembled those he had received before the days of the Utah War, relating tales of attacks in the press and in the halls of Congress. Foremost among the attackers were clergymen and female agitators for women's rights. Characteristic of the attacks from the pulpit were the words of the well-known Reverend De Witt Talmage, who told his listeners in the East "that polygamy will never be driven out of Utah except at the point of the bayonet." The Reverend Dr. Crosby, a fashionable Chicago minister, announced that "Mormonism ought to be dynamited." Kate Field, one of the leaders of the suffragette movement, wrote to Mark Twain, an author recently turned publisher, to inquire if he would be interested in printing a book attacking Mormon polygamy. Twain replied cautiously:

Your notion and mine about polygamy is without doubt exactly the same; but you probably think we have some cause to quarrel with those people for putting it into their religion, whereas I think the opposite. Considering our complacent cant about this country of ours being the home of liberty of conscience, it seems to me that the attitude of our Congress and people toward the Mormon Church is matter for limitless laughter and derision. The Mormon religion *is* a religion; the negative vote of all the rest of the globe could not break down that fact; and so I shall probably always go on thinking that the attitude of our Congress and nation toward it is merely good trivial stuff to make fun of.

Twain added that he would like to see Mormonism extirpated, "but," he said, "always by fair means, not these Congressional rascalities."

The first anti-polygamy bill, passed in 1862, had made marriage to more than one woman a crime in the territories, not in the states. The Mormons evaded this law by maintaining that they did not *legally* marry their wives, according to the laws of the United States. This was an appeal to a technicality, but the Mormons knew that the law had passed Congress only when it had been so amended as to be aimed directly at them, carefully worded so that it would not endanger the extramarital relations of citizens elsewhere in the country.

In 1869, under pressure from President Grant, two bills were introduced into Congress, one aimed directly, the other indirectly, at Mormon polygamy. The indirect attack was made in a bill which would have given the vote to women in all the territories. The bill was introduced on the assumption that Mormon women, if allowed to vote, would rise in rebellion and overthrow a system which held them in bondage. This measure was called "A Bill to Discourage Polygamy in Utah." Its sponsors were amazed when the Utah delegate arose to speak in its favor, and they were dumfounded when *The Deseret News* published editorials supporting their proposed legislation. It was withdrawn hastily.

The Mormons, in turn, gleeful at the bewilderment of the legislators in Washington, passed an almost identical bill at the next session of their territorial congress; and Utah thus became the first section of the country to pass a bill giving the vote to women.

The direct attack on polygamy came in another bill, known as the Cullom Act, which passed the House in March 1870; but this bill was the one which aroused the antagonism of W. S. Godbe and his fellow members of the New Movement, which fact moved Governor Shaffer to oppose it, for it would have made it necessary for any person married under polygamy to disavow all wives except the first. Godbe himself traveled to Washington to argue against it, and he made such a strong case for the apostates with plural wives that the Senate finally defeated it.

By the 1870s there was not a doubt in Brigham's mind that the principle of plural marriage was of God, and that it would work if given enough time, though he had himself orginally accepted it with misgivings. How well it actually did work is a question upon which even Mormons today can take extreme poles of opposition. Many are still living who remember life in a polygamous household, and even here there is little agreement. Some recall bitter feuds between the families of surviving wives over rights and inheritances. They recall that "It was the blackest day of Mother's life when Father married Aunt Sue." (It was the custom for children to refer to their father's "other" wives as "Aunt.") Or they report that, all the years they lived in a plural household, they never heard one cross word spoken between one wife and another. "I remember Aunt Sue," they may say; "she was almost as much a mother to me as my own mother was."

The most serious study of Mormon polygamous marriages was recently conducted by a grandson of Brigham Young who has become a well-known sociologist; and Kimball Young in his book *Isn't One Wife Enough?* indicates that on the whole they worked surprisingly well. They worked best where the ideals of romantic love had been supplanted by the other ideal of "celestial marriage." The usual hazards of monogamous marriage—jealousy, avarice, and the domination of the husband—were intensified under polygamy; but the Mormons maintained, and many of the marriages cited by Kimball Young show it to be a fact, that faith in the ideal of the kingdom could overcome most of the conventional prejudices. The early Mormons were inured to hardship, and where they accepted the difficulties of plural marriage as just another of the necessary burdens of human existence they succeeded best.

There was always something a little humorous about the relationship. Outsiders who visited Utah relished stories such as the one that portrayed Brigham in competition with his son, Brigham, Junior, for the hand of Lizzie Fenton—a contest which, if it ever occurred, was won by son over father, for Brigham, Junior, married the lady.

It was probably a gentile who originated the story of Brigham's manner of dealing with his wives when the time came to go to bed, but among Mormons as well as gentiles it is probably the best known among many apocryphal accounts of Brigham's polygamous relations. It was said that Brigham would indicate his choice of sleeping partner for the night by placing a chalk mark upon her door, so that the lady could be prepared to enjoy his embraces. Quite often, the story goes on, some jealous wife would note the mark, erase it, and place it upon the door of her own room.

Nothing is known authoritatively of Brigham's intimate family life, for he himself showed great reserve in discussing it, and he was impatient with visitors when they attempted to pry. Nevertheless, we do know that Brigham Young married in his lifetime twenty-seven women. One of these, his first wife, Miriam, died before polygamy was practiced. Six were widows of Joseph Smith. One of his wives was married, at her request, after she had served as a servant in his home for seven years—in emulation of Jacob's servitude in the Old Testament. A few of Brigham's wives remained childless, although one gave him ten children and two others seven apiece. He had a total of fifty-four children, not counting adopted children or the previous children of widows whom he married. The greatest number of marriages in a single year was eight. These occurred in 1846, the year the Mormons departed from Nauvoo. This fact suggests that at least one of the motives for marriage was the sense of responsibility toward single women—to provide protection during the dangerous exodus from Illinois.

In Salt Lake City, "Mother Young," as Mary Ann Angell came to be known, occupied the original White House. The large Beehive House, which served as Brigham's official residence, was presided over by Clara Decker, the wife with whom he made the pioneer journey to Utah. In 1856 he built the Lion House, so called because of the sculptured stone lion decorating the entrance. At one time the Lion House held as many as twenty wives and their children. It was constructed with a large central dining hall on the bottom floor and apartments above. Many visitors to Salt Lake attempted to determine the number of Brigham's wives by counting the gabled windows that lined the upper story.

Susan Young Gates, the first of Brigham's children to be born in the Lion House, has given the most comprehensive description of life in this communal household. It began at eight o'clock in the morning, when breakfast was served, and ended at seven in the evening with family prayers. In detail, it seems to have been characteristic of most Mormon households, with a necessary insistence upon economy and regularity. Brigham ate with his family only in the evening. Then he would sit at the head table with two of his wives, usually with Eliza R. Snow (the most publicly prominent of his wives) on his right and "Aunt Twiss"—so called because she had formerly been married to a man named Twiss—on his left. After the family prayer, on evenings when Brigham did not have business elsewhere, he would sit in the large parlor in the Beehive House with his wives and older children. Sometimes there would be music by the children, as the wives knitted or darned; occasionally his sons and daughters would be leaving for an evening elsewhere, and they were expected to show themselves before their father, who would examine and comment upon their dress. Susan Gates makes life in the Young household seem orderly and monotonous, which it probably was most of the time.

Because of the number of Brigham's marriages, the usual image of him is of a man continuously taking to himself new wives, As a matter of fact, most of his marriages were made before his arrival in Utah. Between 1847 and 1863 he took only two wives, Eliza Snow, the poetess, who had been one of Joseph Smith's wives, and Eliza Burgess, the English girl who had served as a domestic in his house for seven years. Beginning in 1863, he made the first of his three final marital ventures, two of which attracted more attention in Utah and outside than all the others combined. The first was to Harriet Amelia Folsom, the last to Ann Eliza Webb in 1868.

Amelia did not arrive in Salt Lake until 1862, although her family had been in the church for many years. She was a tall, accomplished young woman of twenty-five. Apparently Brigham fell violently in love with her, and it was said that his carriage could be seen at all hours of the day, parked before her parents' house. It was said, too, that Brigham's manner changed at this time. He took a greater interest in his personal appearance—his beard became trimmer and his dress more stylish. The spectacle of their prophet, at the age of sixty-two, in love with a young girl amused the Mormons; it aroused a malicious glee in the gentiles, who believed that they had now found that crack in the Mormon prophet's armor.

Brigham's marriage to Amelia took place in 1863, just a year following the passage of the first anti-polygamy measure in Washington, and doubtless represented a rebellion against the attempt on the part of the federal government to suppress polygamy. After the marriage Amelia became the reigning favorite, accompanying him more frequently than his other wives to the theater, to social engagements, and on his trips to the settlements. She became the possessor of an elaborate mansion which soon became known throughout Utah and the nation as "Amelia's Palace."

If it is true, as has been said, that Brigham won his young bride only by promises of a fine house and special privilege, such promises did not prevent him from making other ties with other women, and those soon, for within two years he married again, Mary Van Cott, a widow of twenty-one, and he became a father by her in his seventieth year.

Brigham's final marriage to Ann Eliza Webb in 1868 was his only real marital disaster. Brigham was sixty-six, while Ann Eliza was a handsome divorcée of twenty-four, the mother of three children. She refused to live in the Lion House and resented the quarters with which Brigham supplied her. By her own accounts, she was jealous of the attention Brigham paid to Amelia, and she did her best to arouse resentment in Brigham's other wives. She accused him of stinginess when he refused to support her mother as well as herself. Contrary to her own report, it was said that Brigham married her only at her parents' request, to provide a home and care for her children, and to bring honor to the family.

Ann Eliza was the source of many of the stories later told about Brigham's relationships with his various wives, and particularly with Amelia. She told of the time Brigham had taken Mary Van Cott to the store to select furnishings for her cottage. They had just finished making their selection and were about to enter Brigham's carriage when Amelia came hurrying down the street. She saw Brigham's carriage and paused, then saw Brigham and his bride. With no acknowledgment, she picked up her skirts, stepped in front of them, and entered the carriage, slamming the door after her as she did so. She told the coachman to drive her home. The coachman looked at Brigham, hesitating. Brigham was too dumfounded to say anything, and Mary was furious with anger. "Home, I say," Amelia repeated. The coachman flicked the horses with his whip, and the carriage pulled away, leaving Brigham and Mary standing together in the roadway.

Ann Eliza also reported the time that she was walking toward Brigham's house a few steps behind Amelia. Amelia entered the gate first, then slammed it shut, saying, "There, madam! I'd like to see you get in now."

When Ann Eliza did succeed in getting the gate opened, she saw Amelia on the path ahead of her, scolding Brigham's gardener. When Amelia had left, she asked the gardener what the trouble was. "Oh," he replied, "it is Mrs. Amelia. Did you hear her scolding me just now? Wasn't she awful? She's that mad because you came in, that she had to let out on somebody, and I suppose I came in the handiest. But ain't she a master hand to scold, though? Why you'd ought to hear her give it to me sometimes. I'm pretty well used to it, and don't mind very much. It's some consolation to think that Brother Brigham gets it worse than I do, and when he's round, I'm safe."

Eventually Ann Eliza decided to run a boarding house and asked Brigham's permission, which he granted. Here she gained a reputation among the gentiles, many of whom she put up at her house, as a Mormon wife (and a wife of the prophet at that) who was willing to talk freely and frankly on the subject of Mormonism and polygamy. Soon her gentile boarders and friends began to hint that she could gain much consolation from leaving Brigham and suing him for the support she deserved. They told her that she could count on their support, on the support of Judge McKean, and on most of the outside world. After seven years of marriage to Brigham, she left him and moved in with her gentile friends.

Her defection came just at the time when Judge McKean's anti-polygamy crusade had reached its peak. When she sued Brigham for divorce, alleging "neglect, cruelty, and desertion," she stated that her husband was worth $8,000,000 and had an income of $40,000 monthly. She asked for $1000 a month during the period of the trial, and $6000 for counsel fees, $14,000 at the granting of the decree, and $200,000 maintenance. Brigham's attorney replied that the president's fortune was not in excess of $600,000, and that his income did not exceed $6000 a month. "The purpose of Ann Eliza Young was extortion," as one historian put it, so Brigham resorted to the old technicality. In the eyes of the law, he said, he had only one wife, Mary Ann Angell, and he charged furthermore that Ann Eliza had never been legally divorced from her first husband. He considered his obligation to Ann Eliza sacred but not legal, and he offered to settle upon her $100 a month to fulfill that obligation. When Judge McKean ordered him to pay $3000 counsel fees and $500 a month alimony before the trial, Brigham refused. He was found guilty of contempt of court, fined twenty-five dollars, and sentenced to spend one day in jail.

Such action by the judge presented a nice dilemma to those battling along with him against Mormon polygamy. They had themselves always maintained that Mormon marriages were illegal. By ordering Brigham to pay alimony to Ann Eliza, Judge McKean appeared to have recognized the legality of her marriage. Five days after Brigham's sentence the judge was removed from office. His successor, David B. Lowe, ruled that there had been no legal marriage; therefore, there could be no divorce and no alimony. This was to be the final decision, although the case was to come up in later sessions of court under Judge Lowe's successors, with judgment given and reversed several times. It dragged on until 1877, just a few months before Brigham's death, when it was finally decided in his favor.

Ann Eliza joined the gentile crusade against her people. She lectured for several years in the East and the South upon the evils of Mormonism and polygamy. In the year before her suit was finally disallowed, she published a book titled *Wife No. 19*. Why she chose nineteen as her number remains a mystery; she was, in fact, Wife Number Twenty-seven.

For a subject of the stature of Brigham Young, it would be simpler for the biographer if he had some final defeat to record—if he could show his character going down finally before some inexorable force which he had by his own mistakes brought into play. Some historians have seen him that way, pointing to the final defeat of polygamy as the beginning of the dissolution of his dream. Toward the end of Brigham's life, to be sure, polygamy was under attack, but little more so than it had been since the days when it was first publicly announced. There seemed no signs that Mormon society would not continue to grow and prosper. Even Brigham's experiment with the Order of Enoch was prospering during his last days. Mormons have often speculated on how the fight for polygamy might have fared, had Brigham lived a few years longer and been able to direct it.

The fact is, the hope for the survival of polygamy lay not with Brigham but with the United States Supreme Court, and Brigham knew this and pinned all his hopes on the guarantee of Mormon rights under the Constitution. Once the Supreme Court declared polygamy illegal, neither Brigham nor anyone else could have saved it, and Brigham would have known this too. His attitude would have been, as it was with the Order of Enoch when it was tried in Missouri, that the world was not yet prepared to accept so advanced a principle, and it would have been put aside until the time was right—as, indeed, it eventually was by the leaders who followed him.

Brigham spent the last years of his life "building up the kingdom," as he had so consistently done from the beginning. He was concerned with missionary activity—perfecting the system by which his elders were sent abroad to proselyte—and with improving the organization of the stakes and wards at home. He presided at the dedication of the temple at St. George, where he became so wrought up at the sins of the world that he pounded the newly constructed rostrum with his cane and left marks that are still to be seen. He dedicated sites for the temples at Logan and Manti, and he pushed the construction of the yet unfinished building on Temple Square in Salt Lake City.

On Thursday, August 23, 1877, Brigham was working in his office attached to the Beehive House. He did not feel well, and he complained of nausea and "an inclination to vomit." The next day he was in pain, but still laughing and joking with those about him who seemed more troubled than he about his illness. By Wednesday it was obvious to all his friends that he was in serious danger. He lay for long periods apparently lifeless. Once he roused a little and spoke. Those by his bedside heard the words, which were, "Joseph, Joseph, Joseph." At one minute past four in the afternoon, he died.

His burial ceremony was conducted from the tabernacle on September 2, in accordance with his written instructions:

When I breathe my last I wish my friends to put my body in as clean and wholesome a state as can conveniently be done, and preserve the same for one, two, three or four days, or as long as my body can be preserved in a good condition. I want my coffin made of plump one and one-quarter inch boards, not scrimped in length, but two inches longer than I would measure, and from two to three inches wider than is commonly made for a person of my breadth and size, and deep enough to place me on a little comfortable cotton bed, with a good suitable pillow for size and quality; my body dressed in my temple clothing, and laid nicely into my coffin, and the coffin to have the appearance that if I wanted to turn a little to the right or to the left, I should have plenty of room to do so. The lid can be made crowning.

At my interment I wish all of my family present that can be conveniently, and the male members to wear no crepe on their hats or on their coats; the females to buy no black bonnets, nor black dresses, nor black veils, but if they have them they are at liberty to wear them. The services may be permitted, as singing and a prayer offered, and if any of my friends wish to say a few words, and really desire, to do so; and when they have closed their services, take my remains on a bier, and repair to the little burying ground, which I have reserved on my lot east of the White House on the hill, and in the southwest corner of this lot, have a vault built of mason work large enough to receive my coffin, and that may be placed in a box, if they choose, made of the same material as the coffin—redwood. Then place flat rocks over the vault sufficiently large to cover it, that the earth may be placed over it—nice, fine, dry earth—to cover it until the walls of the little cemetery are reared, which will leave me in the southeast corner. This vault ought to be roofed over with some kind of temporary roof. There let my earthly house or tabernacle rest in peace, and have a good sleep, until the morning of the first resurrection; no crying or mourning with anyone as I have done my work faithfully and in good faith.

Twenty-five thousand people visited the tabernacle for the last view of Brigham's body on the day of his funeral. Many of them had known him since the days in Nauvoo—a few had known him even in Kirtland. With him they had labored across the wastes of three future states to found and make their home in a fourth—in a mountain valley, more than a thousand miles beyond civilization.

Pioneer. Trailblazer. Empire-builder. These are good American words, somewhat tarnished now through careless usage. In the case of Brigham Young they not only retain their luster, they have gained in luster since his death. When he set off to traverse a continent he was neither an adventurer nor an explorer; yet his life was an adventure from the moment he accepted Joseph Smith's religion; he explored an area comprising the uninhabited one-fifth of a continent. When he scratched his messages on slabs of pine or on bleached buffalo skulls and scattered them across the Western plains, he marked the trail of national expansion for more than a century to come. The least likely area of the West he colonized, protected, and built up. From his religious zeal (which was not wholly religious in the way we must often think of it) he fashioned a unique society—a society both American and not American, both traditional and beyond tradition. He may not have fashioned the Kingdom of God, as he hoped he had, but if he didn't, what did he fashion? That question has perplexed many to the present day.

〚〛

CHAPTER FIFTEEN

THE KINGDOM OF GOD

I

At Brigham's death hope revived among the enemies of the Mormons. He had been at the head of the church almost thirty-five years, and many of the ablest Mormon leaders had preceded him to the grave. Willard Richards had died of palsy in 1854; Parley P. Pratt had been murdered in 1857; Heber C. Kimball, who had stood beside Brigham since their conversion in New York, had died as the result of an accident in 1868; and George A. Smith had died two years before Brigham in 1875. With Brigham himself gone, the gentiles were divided between those who believed that the church was about to wither away and those who felt that now was the time to strike a final blow.

The Mormons themselves, although they mourned the loss of their leader, had no doubt either about the identity of his successor or about the ability of the kingdom to survive. Brigham was now in paradise with Brother Joseph and Brother Willard and Brother Parley and Brother Heber and Brother George A., but their own responsibilities continued. He had made it clear to them that their new leader would come, as he had come, from the quorum of the Twelve Apostles.

The man at the head of the Twelve in 1877 was John Taylor, the last of those who had stood by Joseph Smith in Carthage jail. An Englishman by birth, he had been converted by Parley Pratt in

Canada in 1836. He had begun his career in the church as a missionary to his native land in 1839. In 1840 he had represented the Mormons before the United States Congress in an attempt to obtain redress following the Missouri persecutions. After 1849 he made a reputation in France by meeting in public debate both the followers of Fourier and members of the French clergy. In 1877 he was in his seventieth year. He possessed neither Joseph's imagination nor Brigham's personality and statesmanship, but he was in appearance impressive—tall, bearded, showing few signs of debility—and he enjoyed the full confidence of his followers.

By the time John Taylor became "Prophet, Seer, and Revelator" of the Mormon Church, only one significant battle remained to be fought—the battle to preserve polygamy—which no Mormon leader, in all probability, could have won. The anti-polygamy law of 1862 had proved impossible to enforce because of the judicial system of the territory and because of the unified stand of the Mormons against it. In 1881 Senator George F. Edmunds introduced a bill designed to correct some of the deficiencies. His bill defined polygamy as "unlawful cohabitation," and it provided that both this charge and a charge of unlawful marriage could be joined in the same indictment. It provided also that persons guilty of such acts be excluded from voting or holding public office or serving on juries connected with polygamy.

The bill was aimed directly at the Mormons. Its intention was to disenfranchise the principal Mormons and keep them off the juries where their fellows were being tried. The Mormons objected to it not only on these grounds but also because it condemned men without trial and because it was an *ex post facto* law. Also it placed the Mormons, who practiced their marriage out of a sense of religious conviction, in the same class with all adulterers, pimps, and prostitutes in the nation. The Mormons' attitude toward the bill was one of resignation, as expressed by Wilford Woodruff, who wrote during its discussion: "If the nation can stand it, we can."

In the East in 1882 mass meetings conducted by clergymen were held in most of the principal cities in favor of the bill. At one such, a former Vice President of the United States, Schuyler Colfax, was present when a Chicago bishop declared that "if the measures then pending in Congress were not sufficient to heal the 'political cancer,' there were three hundred swords ready to cut it out."

In Utah the Mormons held their own meetings, at which four separate memorials were addressed to Congress, signed by a total of more than sixty-five thousand men and women. Mormon men said that "whatever of polygamy exists among the Mormons, rests solely upon their religious convictions." The women stated, "We your petitioners hereby testify that we are happy in our homes, and satisfied with our marriage relations and desire no change." A body of young men testified, "We deny that the religious institution of plural marriage, as practiced by our parents, and to which many of us owe our existence, debases, pollutes, or in any way degrades those who enter into it"; and the young women declared, "We have been taught and conscientiously believe that plural marriage is as much a part of our religion as faith, repentance and baptism. . . . We solemnly and truthfully declare that neither we nor our mothers are held in bondage, but that we enjoy the greatest possible free-dom, socially and religiously."

When the Edmunds Bill was signed by the President on March 22, 1882, John Taylor had just completed and moved into a large and impressive new house on South Temple Street in Salt Lake City. The building had been designed to house himself, his remain-ing six wives, and twenty-seven surviving children. Under the new law, he feared that the enemies of the church would attempt to make him a test case. After a solemn family council, it was decided that all his wives except his first should leave the new house for the present and return to their former homes.

In the spring conference of the church in April, Taylor spoke out forcefully against what he considered discriminatory legislation, and he predicted that the Mormons would outlive their enemies. "We do not wish to place ourselves in a state of antagonism," he an-nounced to the country; "we will fulfill the letter, so far as practi-cable, of that unjust, inhuman, oppressive, and unconstitutional law, so far as we can without violating principle; but we cannot violate every principle of human right at the behest of corrupt, unreasoning, and unprincipled men."

Prosecution under the Edmunds Act created heroes among the Mormons. The first two were women who refused to reveal information concerning their marriages when ordered to do so by the court. One of the women was far along in pregnancy when she was called in, questioned, and committed to jail. After one day's imprisonment she was released to bear her child. The second woman, although she had not had a happy marriage and was preparing to divorce her husband for non-support, refused to testify against him on the grounds that she believed the principle of plural marriage to be "of God" and not subject to an earthly tribunal.

The most famous case was that of Rudgar Clawson, later to become an apostle, but then a young man of twenty-seven. Clawson was already a Mormon hero, for just a few years earlier, as a missionary in the Southern states, he had seen a companion killed by an anti-Mormon mob. He had stood up to the leaders of the mob, rescued his companion's body, and returned it to Utah. When he was tried by the courts under the Edmunds Act, convicted of both polygamy and unlawful cohabitation, sentenced to four years' imprisonment, and fined eight hundred dollars, the Mormons maintained that the act was shown up in its true colors. If Rudgar Clawson, a temperate and admirable young man, had chosen, as John Taylor remarked in a speech following his trial, to walk in the ways of the present world, he might have been free today. As it was, he had taken a plural wife openly and hallowed the association by a sacred ceremony. "Why," Taylor asked, had not Clawson and his plural wife done "as tens of thousands of others do, live in the conditions of illicit love? And then if any child should be feared from this unsanctified union, why not still follow our Christian exemplars, remove the fetal encumbrance, call in some copyist of Madame Restell, the abortionist, male or female that pollute our land? That would have been, *sub rosa*, genteel, fashionable, respectable, Christian-like, as Christianity goes in this generation."

The stated aim of the Edmunds Act was "purification of the

American home," but no one had any doubt that it was the Mormon home that was under attack. Mormons and Mormons alone were prosecuted under it. Senator Edmunds introduced more specific legislation in 1884—an act known as the Utah Bill. Reintroduced as the Edmunds-Tucker Act in 1885, this bill was ostensibly aimed at polygamy, but in effect was designed to destroy the Mormon Church. It dissolved the church as a corporation, confiscated the funds of its various organizations, and abolished Utah's women's suffrage legislation. It provided that a wife or husband could testify against the other and that complaints concerning sexual offenses could be registered by persons other than the injured party. It also made all facts concerning Mormon marriages part of the public record. This bill was passed in February 1887.

With the passage of the Edmunds-Tucker Act, not only were the traditional legal safeguards of liberty removed from the Mormons, but their very existence as a corporate body was denied. The Mormons' attitude was that the Constitution guaranteed these rights, that the bill had been passed by corrupt legislators, and that if they held out long enough the Supreme Court would come to their aid. In the meantime, with each case that reached the courts, broadened interpretations of the law were handed down by the federal judges. In a famous ruling by Judge Charles S. Zane in May 1885, "unlawful cohabitation" was defined as a relationship not necessarily involving sexual relations. This meant that it was enough merely to show that a marriage ceremony had been performed, whether or not "cohabitation" could be proved. Equally objectionable to the Mormons was the ruling that "unlawful cohabitation" was not a completed single act, but a continuing offense, so that the charge could be broken up into individual offenses, thus multiplying the terms of punishment almost indefinitely.

The Mormons attempted to get around the first ruling by keeping their marrying officers secret even from those who were being wed. A couple would appear before a screen or veil, where they could hear only the voice and see only the hands of the priest who joined them. In that way they were in a position honestly to swear that they could not identify the person who had performed the ceremony. Likewise, the elder who participated could swear that he did not recognize the persons whom he had married. Such evasions were not particularly successful, and they only intensified the fury of the prosecution. With each passing day, more and more enforcing officers entered the territory. The second ruling resulted in fantastically long prison terms for offenders, increased the suffering of widows and children left unprotected, and made more determined the Mormons' resistance to arresting officers.

Members of the Mormon communities still think of the decade 1880-90 as a period of persecution, the hardships of which equaled those suffered in Missouri and Illinois. Male members of the church went into "the underground," so that the efforts of federal officers to serve them with warrants became a game of continuous hide-and-seek, played out on the foothills and in the mountain valleys of the sparsely-settled areas of Utah, Idaho, Arizona, and Nevada. Women and children were left at the mercy of imported officers of the law, known to them as "Feds," whose persistent snooping and spying it became their chief occupation to frustrate.

In a memorial to Congress in 1886 the women of Utah catalogued and described innumerable indignities practiced upon them by the federal officers, probably in the hope of winning sympathy from an age proud of its gallantry to women. They reported instances of officers' breaking into homes and rushing into bedrooms while the women were still undressed or in the act of dressing. If a woman was still in bed the officer would strip the bedding from it, remarking that he had found more than one Mormon "cohab" hiding beneath the bedclothes of his wife's bed and he wasn't going to miss the chance to get another. Rugs were torn up, chests and closets emptied. Even the chimneys were probed and outhouses torn open.

In Parowan, Edward M. Dalton was killed by a deputy, who claimed that Dalton was trying to escape. Near Eagle Rock, Idaho, according to the memorial, two deputy marshals visited the house of Solomon Edwards at eleven o'clock one night.

[They] arrested Mrs. Edwards, his legal wife, after she had retired to bed, and required her to accompany them immediately [seven miles] to Eagle Rock. Knowing something of the character of one of the deputies, from his having visited the house before, when he indulged in a great deal of drinking, profanity, and abuse, [Mrs. Edwards] feared to accompany them without some protection, and requested a neighbor to go along on horseback while she rode in the buggy with the two deputies. On the way the buggy broke down and she, with an infant in her arms, was compelled to walk the rest of the distance—between two and three miles. They could have no reason for subpoenaing her in the night and compelling her to accompany them at such an untimely hour, except a fiendish malice or a determination to heap all the indignities possible upon her, because she was a Mormon woman, for she never attempted to evade the serving of the warrant, and was perfectly willing to report herself at Eagle Rock the next day. She was taken to Salt Lake City to testify against her husband.

An officer in Idaho, who later wrote a book recounting his experiences as a federal marshal, once joined up with a traveling circus in order to enter the city of Montpelier without being detected by the men he wished to accost. Such ruses were necessary because the whole territory had been made suspicious of strangers. Anyone not readily identified seemed likely to be one of the hated officers, and children were instructed not to talk with anyone they met on the roads or in the villages and to report to their parents the presence of any unknown person in the area. Not a few Mormon men constructed secret rooms in their homes, where they hid out during the entire period, leaving them only occasionally at night to do the necessary work on their farms. Many houses constructed at that time, and still existing in Utah, contain extra doors leading to the outside, so that the husbands could not be surprised and cornered. Conditions were particularly hazardous for Mormons living in the outlying settlements of Idaho and Arizona, where they were not in the majority. In 1885 John Taylor traveled into Arizona to investigate conditions and to prepare, if necessary, for the removal of the Arizona Mormons into Mexico. It was while Taylor was in California on the return journey that the Edmunds-Tucker Bill became law. Members of the church urged Taylor to remain away from Utah, but he came back, issued a final epistle to his followers, then himself went into hiding.

During the next few years the central organization of the church almost ceased to function. Its property was attached and its buildings closed. Most of the leaders were in the "underground," and they could communicate with their members only through an occasional letter smuggled out of hiding. On November 1, 1886, John Taylor turned seventy-eight, and his family met in the new house to celebrate his birthday. He was not with them. He had sent them a long letter, but few of those present knew where it had been written. There were rumors that Taylor had begun to show the effects of his close confinement, and in July 1887 two of his wives were summoned to his hiding place in Kaysville, a few miles north of Salt Lake City. His two counselors, Joseph F. Smith and George Q. Cannon, were also called to his bedside. He died on July 25, a little less than ten years after the death of the man who had preceded him.

From the beginning, the Mormons had based their hopes for relief upon their belief that the Edmunds-Tucker Act would be declared unconstitutional. Persecution continued for almost three years following the burial of John Taylor. Then, in May 1890, the Supreme Court handed down its decision—the act was declared constitutional. The Mormons had no further recourse, and even if they had, they were probably too weary to have pursued it. They had kept up their resistance as long as they had hope, but now all hope was gone. In addition, Congress began talking of even more stringent measures to take against the Mormons.

Since Taylor's death no successor to him as president of the church had been announced. An announcement would have served to make the new president the object of an even more vigorous search than that conducted for Taylor. All Mormons, however, understood the order of appointment. They knew their new head would be the president of the Twelve Apostles, Wilford Woodruff. No sooner was the issue of constitutionality of the anti-polygamy laws decided by the court than a meeting was called in Salt Lake City. Woodruff's name was proposed in the usual manner, and he was sustained by the membership through a show of hands.

Woodruff's first act was to send emissaries to Washington to consult with Congress. He did not hope for much sympathy for the Mormons, but he thought he could forestall the impending action against them. He did not instruct his delegates to announce that the Mormons were prepared to abolish the practice of polygamy, but he told them to feel out the attitudes of the various members of Congress toward such an action. What could the Mormons expect in return? Would the members of Congress, for instance, consider statehood for Utah if polygamy were abolished?

Woodruff's word from Washington must have been encouraging. On September 25, 1890, he issued a document which has ever since been known to the Mormons as "the Manifesto." The president's message was not given out to his people as a revelation; it did not retract the Mormons' belief in the divine sanction of the principle of plural marriage. In his announcement Woodruff stated, "Inasmuch as laws have been enacted by Congress forbidding plural marriages, which laws have been pronounced constitutional by the court of last resort, I hereby declare my intention to submit to those laws, and to use my influence with the members of the Church over which I preside to have them do likewise."

For those in Washington who had opposed the Mormons on political grounds, such an announcement was sufficient. Not all the reformers were pleased, and a few Mormons continued to resist both the law and the manifesto. However, no serious measures were again taken by Congress, and on January 4, 1896, Utah was admitted to statehood.

Officially, but quietly, the Mormon church continues to affirm the principle of polygamy, but its leaders explain that the persecution of the 1880s indicated that the world is not yet ready for so enlightened a practice—that polygamy is another example that God's law is too heavy a burden for man in his present state of imperfection.

The Mormons of the present show little inclination either to practice polygamy or to preach the principle. Despite the fact that in the years following the Manifesto polygamous families continued to exist in Utah (particularly the families of those young men who had entered into the practice in defiance of the Edmunds-

Tucker Act), no such marriages have been contracted with the approval of the church since 1890.

A few families in disagreement with Woodruff's Manifesto did move into Mexico and into Canada and continue the practice, but where their actions came to the attention of the authorities of the church (including instances of two members of the Council of the Twelve), such members were excommunicated. More recently a small group who call themselves the Fundamentalists have been discovered practicing polygamy in the Short Creek area of northern Arizona, and they have been both prosecuted by the civil authorities and excommunicated by the Mormons. No attempt has ever been made by the church to re-establish the practice, and what seems most likely is that any attempt to revive it officially today would meet with stronger opposition inside the church than outside it.

2

Wilford Woodruff died in 1898. He was succeeded by Lorenzo Snow, a brother of the Mormon poetess and "plural" wife of both Joseph Smith and Brigham Young, Eliza R. Snow. He was born in Ohio in 1814 and baptized into the church in Kirtland in 1836. Snow's most serious problem was the precarious financial condition of Mormondom. The general prosperity which had existed at the time of Brigham Young's death had been wiped out by the years of persecution. Not only had the church's property been impounded, but conditions had been such that little normal business could be conducted. The cooperative societies had all but disappeared. The general membership was poor. The church itself was deeply in debt and threatened with bankruptcy.

Snow met this problem by calling some of the leading Mormon businessmen together and seeking their advice. Among them were such men as Jesse Knight and David Eccles, who had begun the accumulation of personal fortunes in the mining and lumber industries. They proposed that the church bond itself to its own members, pay off the current debts, and be prepared to meet continuing obligations. Bonds were issued to the sum of one million dollars, they were subscribed to in varying amounts by members of the church (mostly by such men as Snow had called together), and financial stability was restored. At the same time the principle of tithing was reaffirmed by the sending of home missionaries into all the wards, emphasizing the importance of the payment of a full tithe of ten per cent of each member's gross income, thus guaranteeing the steady retirement of the bonds as business improved.

Lorenzo Snow died in the fall of 1901, the last of what might be called the first generation of church leadership. His successor was Joseph F. Smith, a son of Hyrum Smith, who had been born in Far West, Missouri, at the time his father was in jail. Joseph F. Smith was a mild-mannered man, with much the same temperament as his father. His term was one of consolidation and reconstruction, carried on quietly and efficiently. At the beginning of his administration much anti-Mormon feeling still existed. In 1898 Brigham H. Roberts, a prominent Mormon, had been elected to Congress, then denied his seat because he was a polygamist. In 1906 a similar test occurred. Reed Smoot had been elected to the Senate in 1902, and his seat was challenged on the same grounds by much the same kind of opposition as the Mormons had known earlier: the non-Mormons of Salt Lake and gentiles of the East who had access to such popular periodicals as *Everybody's*, *Pearsons*, *McClure's*, and the *Cosmopolitan*. Joseph F. Smith's defense of Smoot won the sympathy of Theodore Roosevelt and much of the nation, so that Smoot was eventually seated, and he served one of the longest terms in the Senate, being defeated finally in the Franklin D. Roosevelt landslide of 1932 by a Mormon New Dealer, Elbert Thomas.

Although the early years of Smith's presidency were those in which the gentiles were confidently predicting the end of Mormonism, the fortunes of the church gradually improved. Direct opposition to the church diminished in the East; in Utah, gentiles and Mormons established a workable, but uneasy, peace. Smith worked to improve the Mormon educational system, which included a university, a college, and a number of academies, in addition to a state university and a state college, both divorced from the church but patronized mostly by Mormons. He constructed meeting houses and public buildings. He rebuilt and expanded the missionary system. He constructed new temples at Cardston in Alberta, Canada, and at Laie, Hawaii, the first to be built outside the boundaries of the United States. With his death in Salt Lake City in November 1918, just a week after the conclusion of World War I, an era both in the history of the nation and in the history of the Mormon Church came to an end.

Smith was succeeded by Heber J. Grant, the son of Jedediah Grant, Brigham Young's reform preacher of the 1850s, who became the first of the Mormon presidents to have been born and reared in Utah. Like his father's career before him, Heber J. Grant's term was marked by controversy within the church. At the time of his appointment Grant was a vigorous businessman of sixty-three. Politically he was an arch-conservative; theologically he was a strong fundamentalist. His administration during the 1920s saw and directed the greatest growth in material prosperity the Mormon Church has ever known. The 1930s found both Grant and the church more firmly entrenched, more at peace with neighbors, than ever before in the Mormons' one-hundred-year history; but these years also found Grant and his leaders not only out of step with the national movement toward depression-reform measures, but out of step too with a large liberal element within their own ranks.

In a sense, Grant was defeated when Reed Smoot was retired from the senate in 1932, even though Smoot's successor was a devout Mormon. He was further defeated in 1934, when Utah became the thirty-sixth and decisive state to ratify repeal of the Eighteenth (prohibition) Amendment to the Constitution—a particularly damaging blow to the prestige of Mormon leadership, since the Grant administration had carried its opposition not only to drinking but to smoking and to the consumption of such beverages as tea and coffee (Joseph Smith's so-called "Word of Wisdom") far beyond the demands of the earlier leadership of the church. More important than these overt actions, however, was the disquieting sense among many members that so much of Heber J. Grant's energy had gone into building up the temporal structure of the church that it was difficult for them to believe that he was not more interested in worldly goods than in heavenly expectations. He was a member of, or chairman of, so many boards of directors that skeptical members of the church often asked themselves how much time President Grant had for spiritual affairs.

Not all the charges made against Heber J. Grant were just, coming as they did during a period of national desperation as the result of economic collapse, but there was enough truth in them to make the last years of Grant's life a period of greater uncertainty for a large and intelligent portion of the Mormon membership than any time since the New Movement in the 1870s. Grant died in 1945, following the close of World War II, just short of his ninetieth birthday.

His successor was a man almost of his own generation, George Albert Smith, who was seventy-five years of age when he took office and who served only a little more than five years. A grandson of Brigham Young's popular councilor, George A. Smith, he was a gentler person than Grant, but too old and in too poor health to provide vigorous leadership. He officiated at the celebration of the one-hundredth anniversary of the arrival of the Utah pioneers, in the summer of 1947, and he did nothing to alter the conservative policies of his predecessor. His administration gave rise to fears that the church had become an organization destined to be administered by aged patriarchs of an ultra-conservative cast—men whose judgments were too likely to be affected by the least lively minds among their subordinates.

Such fears were not dispelled when Smith died in 1951 and was succeeded by David O. McKay. McKay was seventy-seven, two years older than Smith had been; but he had served as a member of the Council of the Twelve since the age of thirty-two and as a councilor to both the preceding presidents. His interests had been centered less in business and politics than in educational and ecclesiastical matters. His first actions showed him to be a more vigorous and strong-minded administrator than most of his followers had anticipated. He curbed the authority of some of Grant's most conservative leaders, whose business interests and political bias had had much to do with determining church policy during the thirties and forties. He showed an increased interest in the church's educational system. He put new life into the missionary activity, and he pushed forward with all speed the construction of several new temples, including one larger even than the Salt Lake Temple, at Los Angeles, and the first temple to be constucted in Europe, at Bern, Switzerland. His administration was more tolerant than former administrations had been of individual differences of opinion, political and personal, among his followers. In short, at a time when many observers, both Mormon and non-Mormon, had come to fear that the church was developing into a too rigid corporate structure, losing contact with its people and with the times, David O. McKay seems to have brought a warmth of personality and a liberality of temperament into the office of president. Although his policy remained orthodox and essentially conservative, it seems to have allowed the church a greater chance of remaining what it had been predominantly under Joseph Smith and Brigham Young, a social organism capable of anticipating the needs of the times.

3

Writers on Mormonism have persisted almost to the present in their insistence upon the gradual disappearance of Mormonism as a religion and as a society. The earliest predictions were based upon the importance of such leaders as Joseph Smith and Brigham Young, whose personalities so dominated the Mormon community that observers lost sight of the solid structure Joseph established before his death in Illinois in 1844 and Brigham fortified and strengthened after the removal of the Mormons to Utah in 1847. The next resulted from the development of the West, when it was assumed and believed that the discovery of mineral resources followed by the onrush of a large gentile population would so engulf the Mormons that their society, which would remain static, would be overwhelmed and assimilated by outsiders. The final prediction was one current during the ascendancy of religious "modernism" during the twenties and thirties, when it was assumed that the interest of Mormonism had become more and more secularized, that its energies had degenerated into a struggle for financial supremacy, and that whatever vestiges of spiritual influence remained were doomed by the spread of enlightenment and reform.

None of these charges was wholly without merit, but the two last predictions were based upon fallacious attitudes current in America at the times they were made, first, as to the nature of Western settlement, and, second, an undue optimism on the part of reformers that an "age of religious superstition" was about to be superseded by an "age of reason." The first attitude, which saw the West as a vast reservoir of hidden wealth and golden opportunity, was wrong more in degree than in actual fact, for recent shifts in population have indeed demonstrated that even in our own age great numbers of people still see the West as a "land of promise"—an adequate fulfillment of Horace Greeley's enjoinder to "go West, young man!"; but it is to be doubted that the specific intention of Greeley's remark was fulfilled either by the "Okies" who flooded California and the Pacific Northwest during the 1930s or by the deluge of industrial workers who have settled there since World War II. In any case, the Mormon country of Utah, western Colorado and Wyoming, southern Idaho, northern Arizona, and eastern Nevada has been less affected than other portions of the West, for the simple reason that the Mormons had already filled it to its relatively meager capacity, considering the available water supply and the amount of arable land. Although the Mormon Church may have seemed at the end of the last century to have been undergoing a kind of crisis, with its own weakness following the persecutions, it came back in the years afterward and came to dominate the area culturally as well as financially. Likewise in the 1930s, when the rigid fundamentalism of Heber J. Grant appeared to have alienated the liberal element of Mormonism almost to a point of apostasy, a similar crisis seemed to have developed. However, with the accomplishment of limited economic reforms, disillusionment with modernism in religion, and the nationwide revival of religious belief (accomplished both inside and outside the Mormon Church), the

Mormons seem to have regained much of the vigor which marked their early history.

What most outsiders (and many Mormons themselves) fail to recognize is that the Mormon Church, while it has existed now for more than a century and a quarter, is still a youthful religion, as religions go, and that its history is the story of crisis after crisis, each resulting in a certain loss—a certain sloughing-off of irrepressible elements—but also in a period of increased growth and influence with its members. As a religion, it is unique in its particular combination of traditional Christianity, with a strong emphasis upon Hebraic elements, and native American qualities and aspirations. With its priesthood and its temple ritual, it is more formalistic than Unitarianism; in its modified materialism, it is less transcendent and mystical than Christian Science; in its utopianism and its belief that it is participating in events of the last dispensation of time, it is Adventist, but its adventism is less rigid than that of most reform churches that preach the advent of Millennium, nearer to the pragmatism of William James and the relativism of much modern science. The Mormons do not deny an ultimate ideal of perfectibility, but they lay stress upon the proper conjunction of events in time and the ideal, believing that the achievement of a limited objective is all that is possible at any given moment and is to be preferred above the grand failure. In fact, they see such limited advance as the order of the universe, including the gods, who are but men, existing not in perfection but in a state more nearly approaching perfection than man.

As a result of these qualities, Mormonism startled America in the nineteenth century, which was, although liberal in its general views, conservative in its attitude toward religion. The gradual disappearance of anti-Mormon feeling has resulted less from the fact that the Mormons as a group have changed than from changes that have been wrought outside the Mormon community. The Mormons are no longer thought of by those who know them at all as "a peculiar people." It is a recognition of this fact which surprises most visitors to Utah today. Evidence there is of Mormon history, in the temple and the tabernacle on Temple Square, the monuments to Joseph

THE KINGDOM OF GOD

and Hyrum Smith; in the Brigham Young monument on the principal intersection of Salt Lake City, the Pioneer Monument at the entrance to Emigration Canyon; there is even a monument to the seagulls that saved the crops in 1847 (produced by a grandson of Brigham Young); there are Brigham's three houses near the corner of State Street and South Temple Street; there is the Eagle Gate, which originally formed the entrance to Brigham's estate, through which now pass automobiles and omnibuses up State Street toward the capitol; there is a museum, constructed by the Daughters of the Utah Pioneers, which repeats the very shape of the old Salt Lake Theater, torn down in the 1930s to construct a modern telephone building.

But where are the signs of quaintness in the inhabitants? Brought up on the anti-Mormon accounts of the last century, the tourist in Salt Lake City today expects to see bearded patriarchs, perhaps with a last lecherous gleam in their eyes; subdued women, still suffering the domination of an all-male priesthood; and fanatical young men and women, burning to spread the light of the gospel in foreign parts. What the tourist finds is a kind of magnified image of himself: smooth-shaven and carefully tailored businessmen, fashionably dressed and extremely independent women, and an energetic and ambitious youth.

Where the Mormons differ from the national average, according to statistics, is in the unusual length of time they devote to education, their low rate of illiteracy, their high birth rate and low death rate, the size of their families, their frequent church attendance, their activity in public affairs, and their relative abstinence from tobacco and alcohol. The effectiveness of Mormon education is indicated by the fact that, according to statistics of the National Education Association, Utah stood first in the nation in the number of years of schooling completed by its citizens (12 as compared with a national median of 9.3 and a low of 7.6); it stood second in the percentage of its young men who passed the United States Armed Forces Qualification Test (1.9 failures among all who registered with Selective Service, as against a national median of 16.4 and a high of 56), third in the nation in the low percentage of the population with less than five years of schooling, and third in the percentage of its population with four or more years of college. According to the *Statistical Abstract of the United States* for 1955, Utah's death rate was the lowest in the country at 7.2 per thousand of population; its birth rate was exceeded by only one other state (New Mexico had 34.7 live births per thousand of population, compared with Utah's 32.6). In a recent study of the birth rate among women graduates of American universities made by the Population Research Bureau, it was discovered that Utah's Brigham Young University was "the most prolific campus, as usual." E. L. Thorndike's study of "the Origin of Superior Men" showed that Utah ranked first of all the states in the proportion of its citizens represented in *American Men of Science*. In *Leaders in Education*, Utahans were tied for second place. In *Who's Who*, Utah stood fourth in the nation.

Unfortunately there are no statistics to indicate the degree of Mormon temperance. The fact that Utah cast the deciding vote to repeal the prohibition amendment suggests that the Mormons are not as fanatically opposed to the sale of alcohol as they are sometimes made to seem. Joseph Smith advised against the use of alcohol, tobacco, tea, and coffee in what has become known as "The Word of Wisdom," in 1833. Since then abstinence has become one of the chief measures of the Mormon's devotion to his religion and a means of testing a member's worthiness to participate in the temple ceremonies or to hold responsible office in the church. Frank S. Mead, in his *Handbook of Denominations in the United States* goes so far as to use Mormon temperance to account for the high birth rate and low death rate. "It is," he says, "the direct result of Mormon abstinence from liquor, tobacco, and so forth."

In none of the qualities indicated by the statistics, however, is the Mormon so different from other Americans that he calls attention to himself. In most society outside Utah his religious practices go unnoticed. Yet he is likely himself to call attention to them, for in his own mind Mormonism remains a singular community, different as a religion from those he comes in contact with and different as a society because his religion plays so large a part in it. Even when he is not devoutly religious, he is never unconscious of his origins; and Mormonism stands as an object against which he can rebel as well as one that can be wholeheartedly embraced. The "Jack-Mormon," as lukewarm members have become known, may retain his identification with Mormon society, even when he has lost his faith in the religion.

But relatively few Mormons apostatize, and fewer still are converted to other faiths, for Mormon youth education is too thorough. Almost from birth to the end of college, religious activities occupy much of their time. In the beginning there are Sunday-school classes and a week-day instruction period known as Primary. At the age of twelve boys and girls become members of the Young Men's and Young Women's Mutual Improvement Association, which provides instruction as well as such activities as the Boy Scouts, the Beehive Girls, dances, theatricals, and athletic competition in leagues organized church-wide. At twelve the boys, too, become eligible for ordination into the lowest order of the priesthood, the Deacon's Quorum, from which they can progress, step by step, up the hierarchy of leadership. By the age of eighteen young men and women may be called to perform missionary service, either in the United States or elsewhere in the world, for a period of approximately two years.

From the beginning of adulthood on, all Mormons are expected to perform some service in the administration of the church. In addition, they are expected to devote a certain amount of time to welfare work, either support of the poor through the Ladies' Relief Society, or general welfare work designed to keeping the many church storehouses stocked. They are expected, as well, to perform the various ceremonies for the dead by regular visits to the Mormon temple. When a Mormon attends high school in a Mormon community, he also attends one or more classes of religious instruction a day, conducted in a "seminary" located adjacent to his school. If he goes to college, he is provided similar instruction at an "institute of religion" located near the campus. A Mormon who moves from Utah to another state usually makes his first social contacts at a Mormon ward or branch located in the city where he settles.

Such prolonged preoccupation with Mormonism is nothing new, and the Mormon, who is particularly well read in his own history, knows it to be the pattern of Mormon society since the days of Brigham Young. What it produces is an uncommon sense in the young Mormon that Mormon history is part of himself. The Mormon becomes conscious of belonging to a well-defined cultural group, set apart from the outside world by traditions of group activity. He has an uncommon attraction to place—the place being the mountains and valleys of the West (United States statistics show that Utah has the least mobility of population of all the states in the nation). He carries with him a firm belief that success comes as a blessing of heaven, but that it is earned by faith and works. In the qualities that include a sense of his being "chosen" and a memory of persecution, the Mormon is a little like the American Jew, but with fewer physical characteristics to distinguish him and with a shorter history. In his sense of history and tradition, he is most like many Southerners, but without the Southerner's nostalgia for an aristocratic social structure and without the Southerner's sense of loss. In his qualities of industry and frugality, he resembles the New Englander of the old type, whose soil, like that of Utah, could be made to yield a living only after back-breaking labor, and whose roots were in the Puritan tradition, much as the roots of Mormonism are. The Mormons are not typical Westerners, in that their communities have a look of permanence, as though here were settlers who came intending to make a home, not merely with the hope of accumulating wealth and then moving on. Even those Mormon communities which have been affected by the shift of population toward the West in recent years still do not have the look of newness or the transient atmosphere found in so many cities of the West. Salt Lake City, which now has more non-Mormons in it than Mormons, remains predominantly Mormon, since it is the center of an empire dominated by Mormons, reflecting Mormon traditions and history. As in all such societies, however, the least change from the past may be seen in the villages and small towns that dot the Mormon country, where tractors and automobiles have replaced horses and oxen, but where the worship is carried on much as it was in

Brigham Young's day, in churches and temples built in the last century.

Perhaps the key to an understanding of the modern Mormon lies just here—in an understanding of the past of Mormonism which he has inherited. No Mormon can be wholly unconscious of the historical background, and no one who wishes to understand Mormonism can afford to be. From the time he enters the world the Mormon child begins to hear, in his family and in his religion classes, the tales of heroism and fortitude displayed by his ancestors—not only the stories of public events such as the building of communities at Kirtland and Nauvoo, the raising of temples, the migration to Utah and the development of irrigation, but also the personal tales of persecution and suffering within his own family which have been handed down by word of mouth. Few Mormon families do not have at least one personal martyr who died at Haun's Mill, in the march across Iowa in the dead of winter, in the emigration from Europe, or in the long trek across the Western plains. The path of Mormon migration, from New York to Ohio to Missouri to Illinois to Utah, is dotted with Mormon shrines, which each year attract thousands of Mormon visitors, for whom such places as the Hill Cumorah, where Joseph Smith claimed to have uncovered the golden plates, the Kirtland temple (still standing), the green slopes of Nauvoo, or the old Mormon cemetery at the site of Winter Quarters (now a suburb of Omaha) serve to bring the past again to life.

But it is not only in places and events that the past continues to exist, but in the activities of the Mormons themselves. Present-day Mormonism continues to exist without a paid clergy, which means that every Mormon is still required to devote much time and energy to conducting affairs of the church, in addition to whatever secular employment he may have. Visitors who marvel at Mormon prosperity (as non-Mormons earlier marveled at Mormon industry and fortitude) must remember that a system of social cooperation exists in the church today, less spectacular than that which existed in earlier times, but not dissimilar. Where the early Mormon labored with his hands to construct a temple or a city, the modern Mormon is called upon to donate time, energy, and money to an extent unequaled in any other modern religious society for the same ends, and the affluence of the church testifies to the degree in which he complies. It is reasonable to suppose that in the event of national or local catastrophe, the only possible contingency which could make the present in any way comparable to the past, the close-knit theological organization conceived by Joseph Smith and perfected under Brigham Young could again be employed, quickly and efficiently, for the survival of Mormon society.

The growth in membership among the Mormons is less noticeable than in many other religions, because of the concentration of members in the Intermountain West. Nevertheless, the church has grown from 150,000 members at the time of Brigham's death to 1,300,000 in 1956, not counting the 130,000 Mormons belonging to schismatic branches. The most important reason for this phenomenal growth may be the missionary system, in which several thousand young Mormons are continuously active, proselyting in all parts of the world as they did in the early days of the church. Traveling in pairs, they preach, teach, and convert new members without financial assistance from the church, except as it is occasionally donated by the missionary's home congregation. In order to become a missionary a young man or woman either must be self-supporting or must have financial support from members of his family. The appeal now, as it was in the past, is the appeal of an active faith in which doctrine is related to contemporary problems and contemporary needs. Although a newly converted member, before he is baptized, must acknowledge his belief in the divine nature of Joseph Smith's mission, the most important feature of his religion is the work he himself does by participating as a member of the lay priesthood in one of the many church organizations. To use a Mormon expression, he "works out his salvation."

The Mormon emphasis upon movement and change, inherent in Joseph Smith's teaching that salvation is a continuing process not a sudden transformation, exists as a kind of safety valve to enable Mormon theology to keep pace with social change. In its early history Mormonism survived when many of the more extreme sects that were contemporary with it perished, because Joseph Smith's foresight provided safeguards against bad errors in policy. During Brigham Young's rule principles which he considered true could be applied or deferred, depending upon his estimate of the condition of the Mormons to accept them. The Mormons failed in their practice of a socialized economic order, and they failed in their attempt to practice polygamy. In the present society such ideals persist, even when a majority of the members would be opposed to their immediate practice.

An interesting example of this is provided by the present Mormon Church Welfare Program set up in 1936 by Heber J. Grant. Its aim, as Grant expressed it, was "to set up, insofar as possible, a system in which the curse of idleness will be done away with, the evils of the dole abolished, and individual thrift and self-respect once more established among the people." Grant had become concerned at the number of Mormons who were on federal relief at the height of the depression. Although his plan was in opposition to the measures taken by the New Deal of Franklin D. Roosevelt, Grant's program went far beyond anything Roosevelt would have dared enact on a national level. Following the lead of Brigham Young in the 1870s, when Mormon businessmen had been incorporated into Zion's Cooperative Mercantile Institute and when such cooperative societies as Orderville had been established, Grant called upon the Mormon membership to come to the relief of its indigent brothers by assisting them to obtain what was necessary for their own support. A central storehouse was established in Salt Lake, with auxiliary storehouses in each stake. Bishops were instructed to rent or buy land which was not then in use, to raise animals and produce, to preserve and can fruits and vegetables, and to enlist the services of every ablebodied member of the congregation, wealthy or poor, to assist in filling the storehouses. Unemployed members in need of relief were given employment on such projects, while members not on relief donated what time they could.

With the approach of World War II, as the need of the Mormons was relieved by full employment in the 1940s, the Welfare Program had little opportunity to show what it could do in forestalling suffering in a period of economic depression. But the machinery had been set in motion. "Welfare work" became another established obligation of the practicing Mormon, and, interestingly enough, it has become an added means of unifying the widespread branches of the church. Welfare Square in Salt Lake contains the Bishop's Central Storehouse. It is composed of warehouses, a grain elevator, a dairy, a coal yard, and shops for the renovation and repair of clothing and furniture. It maintains a fleet of trucks which travel to all points of the West where there are Mormon-owned industries that have produced an excess of what is needed for their immediate area. They bring citrus fruits from the Salt River Valley in Arizona, sugar from a northern Utah refinery, salmon from an Oregon cannery, tuna and oranges from Southern California, potatoes from Idaho, and cloth from New York. The church program operates a cheese factory and a coal mine; it has numerous farms and dairies; it even provides such services as barbering, tailoring, butchering, and all forms of distribution in the larger areas. The aims of the plan were stated in a somewhat broader manner than in Grant's statement by David O. McKay when he addressed a group of welfare workers just before the beginning of World War II:

Brothers and Sisters, you are in the front trenches tonight ready to go over the top and I trust you have in your hearts and your hands the ammunition necessary to wage a successful battle. Some of you may not like my comparing the Welfare Plan to a war but we are in a war against idleness, against depression, a war against social enmity and to establish brotherhood and fraternalism among the membership of the church.

Most Mormons would be startled if it were pointed out to them that the aims of the Welfare Plan as suggested by McKay's remarks resemble closely the aims of socialism: community ownership of the means of production in order to "war against social enmity and to establish brotherhood and fraternalism"; but they do not fail to see in it the aims of Joseph Smith's Order of Enoch, or Brigham Young's United Order.

National prosperity has kept the need for the services of the Welfare Plan at a minimum since its founding in 1936. However, it has continued to expand from what was at the beginning a mere skeleton outline to a working organization which could, conceivably, take over the whole Mormon economy in case of a disaster or a depression great enough to make such extreme measures necessary. In the meantime, it serves as the Mormon version of the ever-normal granary, and at the end of the Second World War, when the Mormon storehouses were bulging and there was relatively little need at home, thousands of pounds of clothing and foodstuffs were sent to the needy of Europe, first to the Mormons themselves (for there had been large congregations of Mormons in Europe before the war, particularly in Germany, Belgium, Holland, and Scandinavia), then to general European relief.

As in its social customs, so also in its theology Mormonism represents what appears to many outsiders as a paradox. Claiming to be a highly spiritual religion, with its roots in a belief in divine revelation, it nevertheless engages in a form of worship of a highly practical nature. The Mormon has never lost his faith in inspiration—what Brigham Young called "the still, small voice"—but inspiration, the Mormon believes, is designed to assist him as much to solve immediate problems as to settle complex doctrinal matters. On the level of the local ward practical problems exist and must be dealt with in meetings if they are to be solved at all: the labors of ward teachers, who visit monthly each Mormon family in its home; the calling of missionaries; the assignment of work on the local welfare projects; the carrying on of temple work. No one of these activities can be said to be devoid of spirituality, for they are services rendered according to a religious ideal, but they do involve a great deal of practical planning and organization which can be accomplished only in the regular meetings.

Modern Mormonism still sees itself as a form of schooling. The Mormon believes that man learns by doing, so that children and the youth of the church play a much greater part in the worship than in other modern religions. A non-Mormon is sometimes astonished to attend a Mormon service and find that he is expected to sit and listen to a succession of "two-minute" sermons delivered by children between the ages of six and sixteen. He may be startled to hear a report of the success of the ward basketball team at a recent allchurch tournament or to hear that a young couple from the ward have won the dance contest at a recent church-sponsored "Gold and Green Ball." He will soon learn that each Mormon must be prepared at all times to get up before a congregation and offer a prayer, make a report, or even deliver a brief sermon. To this end he has been schooled since he was a child. The only way a Mormon can avoid participating directly in the active worship of his ward or stake is to remain away from all meetings; and even this is difficult to do, because he will receive monthly visits from the "ward teachers," who will wonder if there is not some reason why the brother has not been attending services—illness, for instance. He will find it easier in the long run to attend and accept the responsibility than to avoid it.

It was customary for writers during the 1920s and 1930s to point out that the Mormon dream was fading, that the Mormons were no longer a separate people, that, more and more, Mormon worship had come to resemble that of any other religious group, and that the average Mormon was little different from any other average American. The argument for such a case was based upon the belief that, as one writer put it, America had assimilated the Mormon culture. Dale L. Morgan, a writer who prepared the *Utah Guide* and who probably knows more Utah history than any other single person today, expressed such an attitude when he prepared an article on Salt Lake City for a book published in 1947:

> The instinct of the Saints was to be sufficient unto themselves in all things, and Brigham Young's herculean thirty-year labor on the American frontier was above all a struggle to achieve this dream. The dream was nullified by the industrial revolution which transformed America during his lifetime, but it was a dream impossible in any circumstances, by reason of the fundamental contradictions at work in Mormon society itself. Since their own sense of destiny prevented their withdrawal from the world, the Mormons finally had to come to terms with the world.

Such a view was easy to hold at the end of the last century, when historians were predicting that the flood of gentiles into Utah to develop the mineral resources of the area would inundate Mormon culture and wrest political power from the hands of the Mormon leadership. It was still easy to believe as late as the 1930s, during the administration of Heber J. Grant, when the temporal power and the wealth of the church as an organization stood in unpleasant contrast to the condition of most of the members then suffering the results of the stock-market crash of 1929.

What such an argument fails to take into account are the changes which have taken place in American life. The industrial revolution, to which Mr. Morgan refers, did indeed transform America; but no more than the social revolution that followed it and culminated, perhaps, in the New Deal and Fair Deal administrations of Franklin D. Roosevelt and Harry S. Truman. One need not be so optimistic as Massimo Salvadori, whom *Life* magazine calls "President Eisenhower's favorite European student of America," to be astonished that an American Republican president can approve of an economic appraisal of American life that celebrates reforms accomplished during twenty years of Democratic administration. The fact is that the ideal of limited reform advocated by most American politicians today is nearer to the ideal of Brigham Young's cooperative enterprises than it is to the rugged individualism of the last century. This would appear to mean that American life in general has moved nearer the ideal of Brigham's society of equals, not the contrary.

Dale Morgan, in his article on Salt Lake City, writes:

The Mormon Church, of course, is the master condition of Salt Lake City's differentness. The church was the instrument of its creation, and church and city have lived in the most intimate of symbiotic relationships. Through nearly a century Salt Lake City has been the best evidential proof that Mormonism has had, the pragmatic proof that Mormonism "works." And throughout that century the life of the city has been profoundly tempered by the creative energies of the church, and by the ebb and flow of its fortunes. It is to the Mormon Church that Salt Lake City even now owes its status as a world capital, with roots implanted deeply in nearly every country. It is equally to the Mormon Church that Salt Lake City owes the singular internal tensions which still shape its life.

Perhaps this is all we need insist upon—that the Mormon Church remains a force within the life of the country which it built. Even the existence of "internal tensions" testifies to a vitality inherent in it. That there are tensions, no thoughtful Mormon would deny. One can hear more serious criticism of the church today in Utah than outside it; although most Mormon critics would band together to defend the church, today as in the past, if the attacks did come from outside.

A common complaint is that the structure of the church has become so large that what once represented an easy line of communication between the ordinary Mormon and the highest authority in the church has now broken down. Communication from top to bottom still works efficiently, but the member who once had a voice in advising his superiors through the priesthood quorums now finds his way barred by men in the lower ranks of authority who are too afraid of the men above them to risk carrying criticism up the ladder of leadership. Some Mormons also complain at the increasing financial demands made upon them by the church. They do not object so much to the system of tithing, by which each member is expected to contribute annually one-tenth of his gross income, but to special assessments for ward maintenance, for new church buildings, for missionary support, and for the various activity programs. A good many Mormons object to what they consider an undue emphasis put upon conforming to the Word of Wisdom. Such conformance, they say, was not demanded in the early days, when Brigham Young saw the ideal of temperance as something to be striven for, not as an absolute sign of worthiness.

Perhaps the chief tension exists now, as it did in the past, between the rights of the individual Mormon and the tremendous power concentrated in the church leadership. Even while admitting the need for a strong central leadership in a community which still holds a belief in divine guidance, the ordinary Mormon—like the individual elsewhere—has his own ideas about his rights to express himself in opposition to the president and the apostles of the church.

The Mormon farmer may have thoughts different from Apostle Ezra Taft Benson, the Secretary of Agriculture in the Eisenhower

administration, and he will often be frank in expressing that disagreement while at the same time taking pride in the selection of
Benson for so important a national office. A Mormon professor at
Brigham Young University may be highly critical of the policies
of his president, Ernest Wilkinson, whose reputation was made as
a successful attorney, not as an educator, and the chances are that
he will defend his academic freedom as jealously as will his col-
league who teaches at the state university.

Perhaps the most serious and unrelieved tension exists between
the leadership of the church and Mormon scholars and writers who
deal in church history. The problem has been suggested by Dale
Morgan, who wrote: ". . . it is hopeful that voices are lifting up
within the church to cry the necessity for new and more liberal
attitudes, to ask the church to deal with its history honestly, with
no sentimental prettifying of the pioneers or too hidebound an interpretation of its doctrines."

The real problem was expressed by Juanita Brooks, a devoted
practicing Mormon, who took upon herself the task of making a
final evaluation of the guilt and innocence of those Mormons who
participated in the Mountain Meadow Massacre. Although her
book remains the most thorough study of that event in Mormon
history, Miss Brooks charged that authorities of the church withheld from her vital and necessary information which it had in its
possession.

Such objections are not, of course, limited to Mormon society. In
a certain alarming manner they may be said to mirror many features
of modern American life. But to say this is not to answer the accusations of the liberal Mormons. Mormon society, they say, has
shown itself in advance in many tendencies of American life during
the course of its history, partly as a result of the vision of Joseph's
leadership, partly because of Brigham Young's executive talent. If
it is to continue to prosper, spiritually as well as materially, it must
continue to draw upon the boldest members of its society, if not
without the usual safeguards against novelty and error, at least
without timidity and fear.

Despite such criticism, it is likely that Brigham Young, if

he could see his Mormon empire today, would be less startled than most nineteenth-century pioneer leaders. His kingdom has grown beyond imagination, but it still lies foursquare, on the western slope of the Wasatch mountains. It is an empire which comprises not one city alone, but also smaller cities and villages, as he envisioned it, scattered like oases wherever water could be found and crops grown, spreading like fingers into valleys of the mountains from Arizona to Canada, from the peaks of the Rockies into the western desert. Brigham's old lines of communication from Zion to the outside world have not been altered, they have only multiplied and been improved and extended. The flood of converts which brought the saints to the West has not ebbed, it has reached a point of saturation and has begun to flow backward into a world which was once a world of enemies. Mormon temples, once the unique possession of the central Mormon community, now pierce the sky from Hawaii in the west to Switzerland in the east, from Arizona to Canada.

Perhaps the greatest testimony to the genius of Joseph Smith and Brigham Young is that so much of Mormonism is merely expansion and growth; so little, alteration. The wide highways of Salt Lake City, which existed half a century before the automobile, have not yet become outdated, providing as they do room for diagonal parking with space remaining for four lanes of automobile traffic. Many generations of Mormon missionaries preceded the builders of temples in foreign parts. Mormon reclamation and conservation came before nationally sponsored public works. The flowering of Zion represents a kind of miracle, but one in which no one except the Mormon, with his belief in his own particular miracles, really believes. Whether we see it as a kind of happy accident, or as an unconscious creation, or as what Brigham Young said it was, the establishment of the Kingdom of God, there is an element of the miraculous about it—an element of the unexplainable and the inexplicable.

Joseph Smith and Brigham Young told their followers not to be satisfied until the "kingdom" had spread to cover the earth. It is a long way from achieving such a goal, but in the mind of the devout Mormon there is no doubt that it will eventually. Yet even this does not mark the boundary of the ambition of the saints, for to them the kingdom extends from earth into eternity, combining what is transient with what is everlasting. If the medieval Christian saw the natural world as the counterpart of heaven, the Mormon finds heaven in the cosmos. Like the constellations of space, the Mormon says, the kingdom is endless and boundless; or, at least, if it is bounded, its boundaries are forever beyond the sight and beyond the comprehension of men. Whatever its bounds, such is the limit of the possibility of the individual Mormon for improvement in all the virtues of Christian living.

BIBLIOGRAPHY

INDEX

A SELECTED BIBLIOGRAPHY

*of works dealing with Brigham Young and the Mormons for the
convenience of those who wish to do additional reading.*

Alter, J. Cecil. *Utah the Storied Domain.* Chicago and New York, 1932 (3 vols.).

——. *James Bridger.* Salt Lake City, 1925.

Anderson, Mary A. *Ancestry and Posterity of Joseph Smith and Emma Hale.* Independence, Mo., 1929.

Anderson, Nels. *Desert Saints; The Mormon Frontier in Utah.* Chicago, 1942.

Arbaugh, George B. *Revelation in Mormonism.* Chicago, 1932.

Arrington, Leonard J. *Orderville, Utah: A Pioneer Mormon Experiment in Economic Organization.* Logan, Utah, 1954.

Bailey, Paul D. *Sam Brannan and the California Mormons.* Los Angeles, 1943.

Bancroft, H. H. *History of Utah.* San Francisco, 1891. See also *History of California.*

Beadle, J. H. *Life in Utah.* Philadelphia, 1870. The account of a federal officer in Utah.

Bennett, John C. *The History of the Saints.* Boston, 1842. One of the most remarkable of the anti-Mormon books, by the man who joined the Mormons in Illinois and became an assistant to Joseph Smith before apostatizing and writing this exposé.

Birney, Hoffman. *Zealots of Zion.* Philadelphia, 1931.

Bishop, W. W. *Mormonism Unveiled: The Life and Confessions of John D. Lee.* St. Louis, 1882.

Brodie, Fawn M. *No Man Knows My History: The Life of Joseph Smith.* New York, 1945. The most complete biography of Joseph Smith.

Brooks, Juanita. *The Mountain Meadow Massacre.* Stanford University, 1950. The most complete and scholarly examination yet made of this historic event in early Utah history.

Brown, Charles Farrar. *Artemus Ward's Lecture on the Mormons.* London, 1882.

Brown, J. S. *Life of a Pioneer.* Salt Lake City, 1900. The remarkable account of one of the Mormons' most active scouts and colonizers.

Burton, Richard. *The City of the Saints.* New York, 1862. An outstanding work, representing the personal observations by the author of Mormon society in Utah in the middle of the nineteenth century, along with an interesting analysis of Mormon theology.

Campbell, Alexander. *Delusions: An Analysis of the Book of Mormon.* New York, 1832. An interesting consideration of Mormon scripture by the founder of the "Campbellite" or Christian Church.

Cannon, Frank J., and Knapp, G. L. *Brigham Young and His Mormon Empire.* New York, 1913.

Carleton, J. H. *Mountain Meadow Massacre.* Washington, D. C. (Government Printing Office), 1912.

Caswell, Henry. *The City of the Mormons; or, Three Days at Nauvoo.* London, 1842. A missionary bishop from England visits Nauvoo.

Clayton, William. *Journal: A Daily Record of the Journey of the Original Company of "Mormon" Pioneers from Nauvoo, Illinois, to the Valley of the Great Salt Lake.* Salt Lake City, 1921.

Clemens, Samuel L. *Roughing It.* New York, 1903.

Cowley, Matthias. *Wilford Woodruff: History of His Life and Labors.* Salt Lake City, 1909.

Cradlebaugh, John. *Utah and the Mormons.* Privately printed, 1863.

Creer, Leland H. *Utah and the Nation, 1846-1869.* Seattle, 1929.

Crocheron, Augusta J. *Representative Women of Deseret.* Salt Lake City, 1883.

Daniels, William M. *A Correct Account of the Murder of Generals Joseph and Hyrum Smith.* Nauvoo, Ill., 1845.

Egan, Howard. *Pioneering the West.* Richmond, Utah, 1917.

Ferris, Benjamin C. *Utah and the Mormons.* New York, 1854.

Ford, Thomas. *A History of Illinois.* Chicago, 1854. A valuable account of the Mormon trouble in Illinois from the point of view of the state administration.

Fuller, Metta Victoria. *Mormon Wives.* New York, 1856.

Gates, Susan Young. *The Life Story of Brigham Young.* New York, 1930. Memories of a daughter of Brigham Young.

Goodwin, S. H. *Mormonism and Masonry.* Salt Lake City, 1938.

Gove, Jesse A. *The Utah Expedition, 1857-1858.* Concord, N. H., 1928.

Greeley, Horace. *An Overland Journey.* New York, 1860.

Gregg, Thomas. *The Prophet of Palmyra.* New York, 1890.

Gunnison, J. W. *The Mormons.* (No place listed), 1856.

Hamblin, Jacob. *A Narrative of His Personal Experience.* Salt Lake City, 1909.

Hickman, William A. *Brigham's Destroying Angel.* New York, 1872 (Salt Lake City, 1904).

Howe, Eber D. *Mormonism Unveiled.* Painesville, Ohio, 1834. The first notable anti-Mormon book, utilizing the affidavits obtained by the Mormon apostate Philastus Hurlbut in 1833.

Ivins, Anthony W. *The Relationship of Mormonism and Freemasonry.* Salt Lake City, 1934.

Jarman, W. *Uncle Sam's Abscess*. Exeter, England, 1884.

Jensen, Andrew. *Latter-Day Saints Biographical Encyclopedia*. Salt Lake City, 1901 (4 vols.). A useful biographical guide to leading figures in the Mormon church by the former church historian.

Journal of Discourses, 1854-1886. Liverpool (there are approximately 24 vols.). Transcripts of major speeches delivered by leading Mormons. A primary source of information concerning the beliefs of such Mormon leaders as Brigham Young, Heber C. Kimball, Wilford Woodruff, John Taylor, and George A. Smith.

Kane, Mrs. Eliza D. *Twelve Mormon Homes Visited in Succession on a Journey through Utah to Arizona*. Philadelphia, 1874.

Kane, Thomas L. *The Mormons*. Philadelphia, 1850.

——. *The Private Papers and Diary of*. San Francisco, 1937.

Kelly, Charles, and Birney, Hoffman. *Holy Murder*. New York, 1934.

Kennedy, James H. *Early Days of Mormonism; Palmyra, Kirtland, and Nauvoo*. New York, 1888.

Kimball, Heber C. *Journal*. Salt Lake City, 1882.

Larson, Gustive O. *Prelude to the Kingdom*. Francestown, N. H., 1947. Contains a complete account of the social-welfare program.

Lee, John Doyle. *A Mormon Chronicle: the Diaries of John D. Lee*. Pasadena, 1955.

——. *Life and Confessions*. Philadelphia, 1877.

Linn, W. A. *The Story of the Mormons*. New York, 1923.

Little, James A. *From Kirtland to Salt Lake City*. Salt Lake City, 1890.

Ludlow, Fitz Hugh. *The Heart of the Continent*. New York, 1870.

Lyfford, C. P. *The Mormon Problem*. New York, 1886.

McNiff, William J. *Heaven on Earth; A Planned Mormon Society*. Oxford, Ohio, 1940.

Morgan, Dale. *The Humboldt*. New York, 1943.

——. *Jedediah Smith and the Opening of the West*. Indianapolis, 1953.

Nibley, Preston. *Brigham Young, the Man and His Work*. Independence, Mo., 1936. Contains excellent quotations from Brigham Young's journals not elsewhere available.

Paden, William. *Temple Mormonism, Its Evolution, Ritual, and Meaning*. New York, 1931.

Piercy, Frederick. *Route from Liverpool to Great Salt Lake Valley*. Liverpool, 1855. Contains an account of Mormon emigration from England, along with excellent drawings of the route.

Pratt, Orson. *Absurdities of Immaterialism*. Liverpool, 1849.

Quaife, Milo M. *The Kingdom of St. James*. New Haven, 1930. The most complete account of James J. Strang, leader of a Mormon schismatic group.

Quincy, Josiah. *Figures of the Past*. Boston, 1883. An early meeting with Joseph Smith in Nauvoo.

Rémy, Jules. *A Journey to Great Salt Lake City*. London, 1861. An account of early Mormon society in Utah by a French traveler.

Riley, Isaac W. *The Founder of Mormonism; A Psychological Study of Joseph Smith, Jr.* New York, 1902.

Roberts, B. H. *Life of John Taylor.* Salt Lake City, 1892.

———. *The Rise and Fall of Nauvoo.* Salt Lake City, 1900.

———. *History of the Church.* Salt Lake City, 1901-1906. The official history of the Mormon Church.

Shook, Charles A. *The True Origin of the Book of Mormon.* Cincinnati, 1914. An example of the use of "the Spaulding Theory" to account for the origin of the *Book of Mormon.*

Smith, Eliza R. Snow. *Biography and Family Records of Lorenzo Snow.* Salt Lake City, 1884.

Smith, Joseph (and Heman C. Smith). *History of the Church of Jesus Christ of Latter-Day Saints.* Lamoni, Iowa, 1897-1908 (2 vols.). Church history from the point of view of the Reorganized Church.

Smith, Joseph. *History of the Church of Jesus Christ of Latter-Day Saints; Period I.* Salt Lake City, 1902 (6 vols.). Joseph Smith's account of events during his lifetime.

Smith, Joseph F., Jr. *Blood Atonement and the Origin of Plural Marriages.* Independence, Mo., 1905. A Mormon explanation of the doctrines of blood atonement and plural marriage, by a descendant of Hyrum Smith and a president of the Mormon Church.

Smith, Lucy Mack. *Biographical Sketches of Joseph Smith the Prophet and His Progenitors for Many Generations.* Liverpool, 1853. An imaginative work by Joseph Smith's mother.

Spaulding, Solomon. *The Manuscript Found.* Lamoni, Iowa, 1885. The manuscript which gave rise to the so-called Spaulding theory of the origin of the *Book of Mormon.*

Stansbury, Howard. *An Expedition to the Valley of the Great Salt Lake.* Philadelphia, 1855.

Stegner, Wallace. *Mormon Country.* New York, 1942.

Stenhouse, Fanny. *Tell It All.* Hartford, Conn., 1874. The wife of a former Mormon leader writes about her experiences as a Mormon.

Stenhouse, T. B. H. *The Rocky Mountain Saints.* New York, 1873. A Mormon apostate recounts his experiences and his reconsidered views of the church.

Tracy, Albert. "The Utah War—Journal of Captain Albert Tracy." *Utah Historical Quarterly* (vol. 13). Salt Lake City, 1945.

Tullidge, Edward. *History of Salt Lake City.* Salt Lake City, 1866.

———. *Life of Brigham Young.* New York, 1876.

———. *The Women of Mormondom.* New York, 1877.

Waite, Catherine V. *The Mormon Prophet and His Harem.* Cambridge, Mass., 1866.

Webb, Robert C. *The Real Mormonism.* New York, 1916.

Werner, M. R. *Brigham Young.* New York, 1925. The most complete biography of Brigham Young from the point of view of a non-Mormon.

West, Franklin L. *Franklin D. Richards.* Salt Lake City, 1924.

Whitney, Orson F. *History of Utah.* Salt Lake City, 1892 (4 vols.).

———. *Life of Heber C. Kimball.* Salt Lake City, 1888.

Widtsoe, John A., ed. *Discourses of Brigham Young.* Salt Lake City, 1925. Selections from Young's public speeches arranged according to theological, social, and political topic-headings.

Wyl, Wilhelm. *Mormon Portraits, Joseph Smith the Prophet, His Family and His Friends.* Salt Lake City, 1886.

Young, Ann Eliza Webb. *Wife No. 19.* (No place of publication), 1876.

Young, Brigham. *Discourses.* (See under Widtsoe.)

Young, Brigham. *Life of Brigham Young.* (*Millennial Star,* Liverpool, 1863-1864.) Salt Lake City, 1893. Events of church history under Brigham Young's leadership.

Young, Kimball. *Isn't One Wife Enough?* New York, 1954.

Young, Levi Edgar. *The Founding of Utah.* New York, 1923.

Young, Lorenzo. "Biography and Diary of Lorenzo Dow Young." *Utah Historical Quarterly* (vol. 14). Salt Lake City, 1946.

INDEX

The abbreviations JS and BY refer to Joseph Smith and Brigham Young.

WASH.
Columbia R.
Missouri R.
MONTANA
N. DAKOT
Salmon R.
OREGON
IDAHO
Snake
S. DAKOT
Missouri River
WYOMING
Hall
South Pass
Ft. Laramie
PIONEERS
Sutter's Mill
NEVADA
Carson
Bridger
NEBRASKA
North Platte R.
San Francisco
COLORADO
Ft. Leavenwort
Pueblo
CALIF.
St.
KANSAS
INDIAN
TERRITORY
Los Angele
San B
San Die
OKLA
TEXAS